# SAFEGUARDING
# DEMOCRATIC
# CAPITALISM

# Safeguarding Democratic Capitalism

## U.S. Foreign Policy and National Security, 1920–2015

Melvyn P. Leffler

**PRINCETON UNIVERSITY PRESS**

PRINCETON AND OXFORD

Published by Princeton University Press,
41 William Street, Princeton, New Jersey 08540

In the United Kingdom: Princeton University Press,
6 Oxford Street, Woodstock, Oxfordshire OX20 1TR

press.princeton.edu

*Jacket photographs*: (*top*) courtesy of Shutterstock; (*bottom*) FEMA / Alamy Stock Photo

ISBN 978-0-691-17258-3

British Library Cataloging-in-Publication Data is available

This book has been composed in Adobe Text and Gotham

Printed on acid-free paper. ∞

Printed in the United States of America

10  9  8  7  6  5  4  3  2  1

*For*
*Sarah and Jake*
*Elliot and Naomi*
*and for*
*Audrey, Carol, and Nava*

מדור לדור
*From Generation to Generation*

# CONTENTS

Woodrow Wilson declared war in 1917 hoping that the United States would make the world safe for democracy and capitalism. He wanted to defeat the Central Powers and thwart the rise of Bolshevism. But after the U.S. Senate repudiated the Treaty of Versailles and the League of Nations, and after the Democrats were defeated in the elections of 1920, Republican policymakers embarked upon a sequence of policies that affronted Wilson's supporters and subsequently garnered much criticism from historians. After World War II, claiming to have learned the lessons of the past, U.S. officials assumed the role of hegemon in the world capitalist economy and projected American power around the globe. For more than forty years they waged a tenacious Cold War against the Soviet Union and world communism. Stunned by the fall of the Berlin Wall in 1989 and the disintegration of the Soviet Union in the early 1990s, Republican and Democratic policymakers sought to consolidate and institutionalize the global ascendancy of democratic capitalism. But fearing isolationist impulses and eschewing the role of global policeman, they pursued inconsistent policies that aroused criticism and perplexed contemporaries. The tragic attacks on 9/11 ended Washington's ambivalence. President George W. Bush launched a global war on terror with the goal of creating a balance of power in favor of freedom—free people and free markets.

In this volume, I have assembled essays that seek to address questions of enduring importance about the course of American foreign relations and the making of U.S. national security policy from the end of World War I to the global war on terror. If Republican officials in the 1920s embraced Wilson's goal of liberal capitalism, as they did, why did they reject the role of hegemon in the international political economy and why did they refrain from playing a more constructive role in European financial affairs? Why, in particular, did the United States not cancel or reduce the war debts of European allies when so many contemporaries recognized their importance to the resolution of other European political and economic controversies? Likewise, why did the United States fail to guarantee the security of France, and why did it not incur strategic commitments and assume responsibilities commensurate with its power?

In contrast, after World War II the United States changed direction. I seek to illuminate the factors that impelled the United States to reconceive its vital security interests and project its power around the globe. Why, I ask, did U.S. officials wage the Cold War with such an expansive conception of national security and why did they incorporate countries like Turkey into an American-led alliance system? More importantly, why did the United States win the Cold War, and how did the lessons extrapolated from its so-called triumph affect subsequent U.S. diplomacy? And if there was tension between the means and ends of American foreign policy during the 1990s, as there was, in what sense did the 9/11 attack transform American national security policy? Subsequently, when the global war on terror led to intractable wars in Iraq and Afghanistan and when it intensified partisan conflict at home, how worrisome was the budgetary retrenchment for the future of American security?

While addressing these important questions, I also seek to interrogate the evolution of my own thinking about the making of American national security policy. As a graduate student in the late 1960s I was agitated by the war in Indochina and inspired by the writings of William A. Williams and his students. But as I studied the evidence I was pulled in different directions. I came to believe that the domestic sources and domestic structures emphasized by the Wisconsin revisionists were only part of the foreign policy equation—an important part, but only a part. Studying national security policy also required an understanding of the configuration of power in the international arena and the perceptions of threat it did (or did not) engender. Perceptions, of course, raised the question of human agency and individual cognition. My interpretive lens, therefore, evolved yet again as I tried to grasp the relationships between the needs of the domestic political economy, external configurations of power, and the values, assumptions, and actions of our national leaders. This volume, then, is also a book about my own intellectual journey.

I am very grateful to Eric Crahan, my editor at Princeton University Press, for affording me this opportunity to assemble some of my essays and articles and to reflect on them. Several people have read the contents of this volume, commented on a draft of my introductory essay, and offered sage advice. I am indebted to Jeff Engel, Richard Immerman, Frank Costigliola, Will Hitchcock, Brian Balogh, and Phyllis Leffler. They have made this book better than it otherwise would have been.

# Introduction

## EMBRACING COMPLEXITY

"It can't go on much longer!"

I meant the Vietnam War. I remember uttering words along these lines in 1966. I was in my last year as an undergraduate at Cornell University. I was not a leader of any antiwar groups; I was a quiet, lonely follower. I was appalled by the fighting in Indochina and remember marching sullenly down the streets of Ithaca on a demonstration or two. I did not think the carnage could last much longer. I was wrong.

In that year, 1966, I was preoccupied with what I would do after graduation. I had no idea that I would become an historian of U.S. foreign relations. I had no notion of how my views would evolve from a focus on the domestic ideological and economic roots of policy to a preoccupation with threat perception. Even less could I have imagined that I would spend so much time wrestling with the possibilities of reconciling "revisionism" and "realism" and analyzing how perceptions of configurations of power abroad affected thinking about the preservation of core values and democratic capitalism at home. And since I would be trained in traditional approaches to diplomacy, I had not a clue about how the explosion of scholarship on culture, memory, and emotion would influence my growing fascination with the complicated interactions between human agents on the one hand and fundamental structures of political economy and international politics on the other hand.

When I finished college, my future was murky. I applied to law schools, graduate schools in history, and one or two programs dealing with international relations. I had choices, but when Ohio State University's History

Department offered me funding—the chance to experiment with graduate school without going into debt—the issue was resolved.

My intent was to study labor history. As an undergraduate in Cornell's School of Industrial and Labor Relations, I fashioned an eclectic program around history and economic development. Although I did not take any courses with Walter LaFeber, the gifted young assistant professor of American diplomatic history who had recently joined the Cornell faculty and who would subsequently have a major impact on my thinking, I did study American labor history with Gerd Korman. I wrote a substantial paper for him on the impact of the Bolshevik Revolution on the American labor movement. Working with Korman made me attentive to primary sources, reading carefully, and extrapolating meaningful generalizations from factual detail. He nurtured my interest in graduate study. He told me about a young labor historian who had joined the faculty at Ohio State: David Brody. He predicted, correctly, that Brody would become one of the leaders in the field. When I got to Ohio State, Brody was on leave. He never returned.

I was adrift. I gravitated to courses in U.S. diplomatic history and modern American history. I had little idea of what I would focus on, but my aversion to the Vietnam War clearly animated my interest in studying U.S. foreign relations. I enrolled in courses taught by a young professor, Marvin Zahniser. His expertise was in early American diplomacy, and he had written a book on C. C. Pinckney. He was then exploring the possibility of a big project regarding U.S. diplomatic missions that failed. Soon, he would turn his attention to writing a general history of Franco-American relations. Wearing a white shirt and a tie, often a bow tie, he presented learned but very traditional lectures. I found him distant, meticulous, rather inscrutable. His dispassionate aura perplexed me when my own emotions were pulsating. I had little idea of how he would influence my intellectual journey, but he did. He nurtured my love for research, encouraged me to interrogate my own predilections, and imparted a quest for "objectivity," however elusive, that would shape so much of my scholarship.

During my first years at Ohio State I also enrolled in courses with John Burnham, Mary Young, and Andreas Dorpalen, an imposing, eminent historian of German history. In Burnham's course, we read Gar Alperovitz's recently published *Atomic Diplomacy*.[1] Though Burnham seemed to take no position on the book, his probing queries aroused passionate discussion. The atomic bomb, Alperovitz claimed, was dropped not to defeat the Japanese and save American lives, but to intimidate the Soviets and shape the course of post–World War II diplomacy. The broad implications were clear: the United States was responsible for the origins of the Cold War.

1. Gar Alperovitz, *Atomic Diplomacy: Hiroshima and Potsdam* (New York: Vintage, 1965).

At the same time, in which course I do not recall, I read William A. Williams's *The Tragedy of American Diplomacy*, one of the era's most influential books critiquing the long trajectory of American foreign policy.[2] Perhaps David Green assigned it in his course. David Green had just come to Ohio State, as the second "diplomatic" historian, to be Zahniser's colleague, focused on modern U.S. foreign relations. Two young men could hardly have been more dissimilar. Green was a recently minted PhD student from Cornell, where he had studied with Walter LaFeber. Green was passionate, an ardent opponent of the Vietnam war, a fierce critic of U.S. foreign relations, a charismatic lecturer, and an enthusiastic revisionist who reinforced the themes of Williams's critique of American diplomacy. Not simply the Cold War, but also the wars in Indochina and the virulent anti-Americanism in Latin America were the result of America's open door imperialism, its lust for markets to solve the problems of overproduction, and its exceptionalist, self-deceiving ideology of innocence.

Green was a doer as well as a talker. He challenged us. One day in his lecture course—I think it was the day after Martin Luther King Jr.'s assassination—he boldly asked the students to hand in their draft cards; as I recall, he was going to take them out to the "Oval"—the vortex of Ohio State's campus—and burn them during one of the ongoing demonstrations. I sat there nervously; no, I was not yet ready to burn my draft card. Yes, I was ready to take over the administration building, which a few of us briefly did around that time. Although I ruminated endlessly about the war and was appalled by the daily body counts, the scenes of guerilla warfare, the use of napalm, the conflagration of villages, and the suffering of ordinary women, children, and soldiers, I was unprepared for Green's bold assault on my conscience. He paid a heavy price, forced (I think) to resign.

I turned my attention to studying U.S. foreign relations history. I was now wrestling more deeply with the sources of American power and the harm it was inflicting. How could this war in Indochina be explained? How long could it last? Could it happen again?

The answers to my questions were emerging in the ballooning revisionist literature on the history of American foreign policy. Around this time, I read LaFeber's *New Empire*, a reinterpretation of late-nineteenth-century American expansion.[3] I was writing a paper for Zahniser on the mission by Stuart Woodford to Madrid in 1898 to head off the coming of war with Spain. LaFeber's book seemed powerful and nuanced. He emphasized the domestic roots of policy and stressed the importance of markets abroad for the preservation of

2. William A. Williams, *The Tragedy of American Diplomacy* (Cleveland, Ohio: World Publishing Company, 1959).

3. Walter LaFeber, *The New Empire: An Interpretation of American Expansion, 1860–1898* (Ithaca, N.Y.: Cornell University Press, 1963).

democratic capitalism at home. Highlighting purposeful decision-making, he forced readers to think carefully about the connections between politicians and key business factions. Zahniser advised that I examine the role of Congress and take cognizance of the weaknesses of the presidency. By then, I thought the revisionists were right: U.S. foreign policy stemmed from domestic economic needs and anxieties about social stability. But Zahniser, Burnham, Dorpalen, and Young—all in their different ways—seemed to want to rein me in. They impelled me to read carefully, immerse myself in the evidence, consider divergent interpretations, and wrestle with historiographical debates.

I had to pick a dissertation topic. I had written a seminar paper on Franco-American relations in the mid-1930s. It seemed that many scholars already had written about U.S.-European relations during that decade. I was not likely to say anything new about the diplomacy of Franklin D. Roosevelt, the alleged isolationism of the era, and the gradual American embroilment in World War II. In contrast, the decade of the 1920s was enticing. New manuscript collections were becoming available, and historians had paid rather little attention to the course of American foreign policy between Woodrow Wilson and Roosevelt. Moreover, I had a terrific guide to the era—Williams's compelling chapter "The Legend of Isolationism in the 1920s" in *The Tragedy of American Diplomacy*.[4] By using new materials like the Warren Harding Papers at the Ohio Historical Society and the Myron Herrick Papers at the Western Reserve Historical Society, I could turn attention away from the old fashioned questions of America's rejection of the Treaty of Versailles, nonparticipation in the League of Nations, and foolish embrace of the Kellogg-Briand Pact. I could focus instead on what really mattered to the men making policy in the 1920s: war debts, reparations, private loans, and trade—the economic and business questions that I assumed were the core of U.S. foreign relations, the very questions that diplomatic historians had mostly ignored or treated simplistically. Moreover, the revisionist historians were teaching me what sources to use— business journals, trade convention proceedings (like those of the National Foreign Trade Council), banking periodicals, the manuscript collections of key financiers and industrialists, and the records of the Treasury and Commerce departments. The State Department was not alone in making U.S. foreign policy.

I moved to Washington. Because I had a grant from the Mershon Foundation, I had the rare opportunity to spend many months researching in the National Archives. First, I learned how to use the decimal file system, a master key to researching the exhaustive papers of the Department of State. I realized that the documents compiled in the *Foreign Relations of the United States* (*FRUS*) series, the official guide to the history of American diplomacy, could

4. Williams, *Tragedy*, chapter 4.

be deceptive.[5] Compilers in the late 1930s and 1940s had not been especially interested in economic and financial questions, and they certainly did not integrate materials from other government agencies into their volumes. Consequently, the amount of material on debts, reparations, and trade was rather meager compared to the voluminous corpus of diplomatic and political correspondence saved lovingly in those rectangular, gray archival boxes that were rolled out to me on one dolly after another for month after month, many of them from Record Group 39, Records of the Bureau of Accounts in the Treasury Department, and from RG 151, Records of the Bureau of Foreign and Domestic Commerce. As for the records in RG 59 of the Department of State, I remember mastering the key decimal file numbers that, after forty years, I still vividly recall: 851.51, 811.51, 851.00, 851.62, 462.00R296, etc. At the same time I grew increasingly aware that the organization of the *FRUS* volumes by country, while understandable, could be misleading: you could not study Franco-American relations without also examining U.S.-German relations and U.S.–United Kingdom relations.

I found that isolationism was a myth. The United States was hugely embroiled in European affairs in the 1920s. After all, European diplomacy during that decade was all about these very matters: reparations, war debts, private loans, tariffs, trade, currency stability—and arms limitation and France's quest for security. The general thrust of my argument became clear: after Versailles, the United States jettisoned collective security and political commitments as a means to nurture European stability. But the quest persisted: the overall goal of U.S. foreign policy toward France and toward Europe was to promote stability along liberal and capitalist lines and to avert radical revolution. U.S. officials—like President Warren G. Harding, Secretary of Commerce Herbert C. Hoover, Secretary of the Treasury Andrew Mellon, and Secretary of State Charles Evans Hughes—recognized that the restoration of stability in Europe was important to the vitality of the American economy at home, the promotion of exports, the maintenance of full employment, and the health of the farm sector of the American economy, which was floundering from insufficient demand and low prices.

While the broad outlines of my dissertation formed in my head, the organization and presentation of my dissertation were not yet resolved when I decided to turn my attention to a more immediate goal. I realized I needed to publish an article to help position myself to compete in what seemed a terrible job market. I selected a narrow topic: the origins of Republican war debt policy, 1921–1923. This matter had received little attention in the scholarly literature, and the prevailing view was that insistence on war debt repayment

---

5. Department of State, *Papers Relating to the Foreign Relations of the United States, 1920–1933* (Washington, D.C.: Government Printing Office, 1935–1949).

revealed the ignorance and indifference of U.S. officials about the requirements of European stability. I already had uncovered a lot of material demonstrating beyond any doubt that businessmen and financiers as well as experts
in the Treasury, Commerce, and State departments recognized clearly that
war debts burdened the key debtors—Britain, France, and Italy. War debt re-
payments complicated the settlement of the reparations controversy, they
retarded efforts to restore currency stability, and they constricted the promotion of world trade and American exports. Just as the open door revisionists
were arguing, American businessmen and officials in Washington were not
stupid. They knew these payments had to be scaled down if they were to stabilize the international economy along liberal and capitalist lines.

But as I labored on this article I expanded my research and examined the
proceedings and periodicals of business groups and trade associations that
were not quite so dependent on markets abroad. I looked at the legislative
debates and analyzed the views of congressmen and senators. I saw countervailing evidence: a lot of Americans were less concerned about markets
abroad and more concerned with the level of taxation at home. Relief to European governments meant higher taxes for Americans because revenue to
the U.S. treasury would be reduced while the U.S. government still had to pay
interest and principal to owners of U.S. war bonds. Consequently, proposals
to lower the war debt payments of European governments—while Americans
were suffering from the postwar economic slump in 1921 and 1922—sparked
xenophobic sentiment, aroused racist predilections and ethnic prejudices,
and reinforced the postwar disillusionment. Officials did want to reduce debts
and promote U.S. exports, but they also wanted to lower taxes, encourage
domestic investment, preserve the sanctity of contracts, and win elections.
Priorities clashed; trade-offs were unavoidable. Policymakers had to balance
conflicting imperatives.

I presented all of this in my article "The Origins of Republican War Debt
Policy, 1921–1923: A Case Study in the Applicability of the Open Door Interpretation." (See chapter 1.) I was thrilled when *The Journal of American History*
accepted it for publication. The article underscored the salience of the open
door interpretation yet questioned some of its conclusions. In the course of
writing it, I began grappling with issues that would confound me for many
years. I uncovered considerable evidence affirming the significance of exports
to businessmen and officials; yet such concerns did not always translate into
coherent policy. Policymakers and business elites did seek to fashion a stable,
liberal, and capitalist international order, but other goals were also important:
lowering taxes, controlling inflation, and protecting the home market. The
foreign policy history of the United States government was more complex
than I imagined. Even while the fighting in Indochina escalated and my op-

position to the war there became more passionate, my understanding of the sources of U.S. policy became more uncertain.

Resolving all these issues was less important in the short run than finishing my dissertation. I defended it in the spring of 1972 and landed a job at Vanderbilt University. I was one of five hires that year; Vanderbilt was rapidly changing, starting to highlight scholarly achievement, and scaling up the demands for tenure, a goal that was on my mind from my first day there. And the expectations were pretty clear: no book, no tenure. I decided to send out my dissertation for publication, thinking that my article in the *JAH* and the enthusiastic support of my mentors at Ohio State boded well for my future.

Then came some dramatic disappointments. One of the worst days of my professional career was at the American Historical Association convention, I think in December 1972 (or perhaps 1973). I was strolling through the book exhibits, and suddenly I saw a volume on one of the shelves, *American Business and Foreign Policy, 1921–1933*, by Joan Hoff Wilson.[6] At the time I never had heard of her and knew nothing about the prospective publication of this book. But I opened it up and my heart sank. It was organized precisely as I had organized my dissertation, with chapters on war debts, trade, etc. She examined business opinion almost precisely as I had. I knew this because I sat down on a chair adjoining the book booth and skimmed through page after page after page. Did I have anything new to say that Wilson had not said? With a pronounced tendency toward seeing the darker side of my future, with ingrained thinking that I never really was suited to be a successful academic, with my parents' reservations pulsating through my mind, I was distraught.

And perhaps for good reason. Not long thereafter, I received a referee report from the University of North Carolina Press. The reader praised my dissertation manuscript, but voiced strong reservations. He said my topical organization obscured the interaction of issues and obfuscated causal analysis. He also encouraged me to write a chapter on Woodrow Wilson to establish a context for studying Republican diplomacy and for analyzing continuities and discontinuities over time.

My dismay was extreme. But the advice was good. It reinforced my view that I had to differentiate my book from Joan Hoff Wilson's account. I would shift my attention from business attitudes to decision-making in the American government and give more nuanced attention to causal factors and to means and ends. Organizing my evidence chronologically, rather than topically, would help illuminate the policy process because officials grappled every day with the intersection of war debts, reparations, loans, currency stabilization,

---

6. Joan Hoff Wilson, *American Business and Foreign Policy, 1920–1933* (Lexington, Ky.: University Press of Kentucky, 1971).

tariffs, and trade. Writing an opening chapter on Woodrow Wilson, moreover, would allow me to highlight continuities in goals (the quest for a stable capitalist international order) and disparities in tactics (the Republicans' repudiation of collective security and embrace of economic diplomacy). But to do these things, I had to reorganize my entire dissertation and start anew. I would rewrite from page one.

This required yet more research. The Herbert Hoover Presidential Library had now opened and friends were telling me it contained mountains of essential documents. At the same time, new books and articles were illuminating the workings of the Federal Reserve Bank of New York and the critical role of central bankers, including Benjamin Strong, the governor of the Federal Reserve Bank of New York, in orchestrating the restoration of currency stability and the gold exchange standard in the mid-1920s. I needed to look at the papers of the Federal Reserve Bank of New York and gain an appreciation of its interactions with the investment banking community of New York, the Treasury Department, and European central bankers. Figuring out how the American government operated in the 1920s, how it interacted with functional elites in the business, banking, and agricultural communities, and how it balanced conflicting imperatives and clashing priorities were now my central tasks.

As I was despairing over my academic future and pondering my capacity to reconceptualize my dissertation manuscript, Ellis Hawley asked me to contribute a chapter on foreign policy to a book he was editing on Herbert Hoover as secretary of commerce. Hawley had come to Ohio State while I was writing my dissertation. Graduate student friends of mine sang his praises and told me I had to audit one of his courses. He had just written a brilliant book on the New Deal and the problem of monopoly.[7] Now, he was turning his attention to Herbert Hoover and the evolution of what he called the associational state. This framework would shape the writing of American domestic history for decades to come. It riveted attention on the formal and informal connections between government and functional elites in the American political economy. Hawley was developing and extrapolating from new interpretations of the Progressive Era that highlighted the importance of experts, the development of professional associations, the quest for efficiency, and the desire to find mechanisms that would mitigate political conflict, thwart radical movements, nurture productivity, and create a consumer paradise. For Hawley, Herbert Hoover was the central figure in the evolution of these developments.[8] But Hawley stayed at Ohio State only briefly. He moved to the University of Iowa,

7. Ellis Hawley, *The New Deal and the Problem of Monopoly, 1933–1939* (Princeton, N.J.: Princeton University Press, 1965).

8. Ellis W. Hawley, "Herbert Hoover, the Commerce Secretariat, and the Vision of an 'Associative State,' 1921–1928," *Journal of American History*, 61 (June 1974): 16–40; Hawley, *The Great*

where he could easily exploit the materials at the Hoover Library and train generations of students, the most important of whom (for my purposes) was Michael Hogan, who became a lifetime friend, intellectual comrade, and occasional probing critic.

I put aside the revision of my dissertation to work on this essay for Hawley's book. (See chapter 2.) The exercise was critical to my intellectual development. By focusing on Hoover, I saw how domestic developments shaped approaches to foreign policy questions. As secretary of commerce during most of the 1920s, Hoover reorganized that department to position the United States to benefit from and exercise a constructive role in the world political economy. Hoover interjected himself into all matters of foreign relations, and he put his subordinates to work acquiring new data on natural resources and markets around the globe. Like other scholars at the time, including Mike Hogan, Frank Costigliola, Joan Hoff Wilson, Carl Parrini, Robert Van Meter, Emily Rosenberg, and Joseph Brandes, to name just a few, I recognized how carefully Hoover labored to take issues out of politics, gather statistical data, hire experts, and find solutions that would reconcile divergent priorities.[9] He championed innovative thinking about the role of invisible items (for example, overseas loans and tourist expenditures) in redressing trade imbalances and smoothing the functioning of the global political economy. By studying Hoover, one could see why Republican officials relied on private financiers, central bankers, tariff commissioners, and an agent general for reparations to grapple with the explosive financial and commercial questions of the 1920s. Allegedly, these "experts" would take such issues out of politics and resolve them objectively in ways that would palliate the sensibilities of clashing interest groups and competing nation-states. They would thereby help stabilize the international economy along liberal and capitalist lines.

While working on this essay on Hoover, I grappled with his worldview. He epitomized the economic approach to international diplomacy in the 1920s. Arms limitation was integral to this approach—a necessary means to cut government expenditures, balance budgets, stabilize currencies, and encourage

---

*War and the Search for a Modern Order: A History of the American People and their Institutions, 1917–1933* (New York: St. Martin's Press, 1979).

9. Joan Hoff Wilson, *Herbert Hoover: Forgotten Progressive* (Boston: Little Brown, & Co., 1975); Carl P. Parrini, *Heir to Empire: United States Economic Diplomacy, 1916–1923* (Pittsburgh: University of Pittsburgh Press, 1969); Michael J. Hogan, *Informal Entente: The Private Structure of Cooperation in Anglo-American Economic Diplomacy, 1918–1928* (Columbia, Mo.: University of Missouri Press, 1977); Robert H. Van Meter, "The United States and European Recovery, 1918–1923: A Study of Public Policy and Private Finance," PhD diss., University of Wisconsin, 1971; Joseph Brandes, *Herbert Hoover and Economic Diplomacy: Department of Commerce Policy, 1921–1928* (Pittsburgh: University of Pittsburgh Press, 1962); Frank Costigliola: *Awkward Dominion: American Political, Economic, and Cultural Relations with Europe, 1919–1933* (Ithaca, N.Y.: Cornell University Press, 1984).

world trade. Hoover thought prosperity would heal the wounds of World War I, reconfigure the aspirations of governments, mitigate class conflict, stifle revolutionary impulses, and nurture individual opportunity. He was interested in world order and focused on fashioning a new era of perpetual prosperity, yet was unwilling to incur strategic obligations abroad. I appreciated the mechanisms and processes that were being designed to settle contentious international financial and economic issues, but did this make American foreign policy realistic in the era following Versailles? Was it sensible to brush aside France's requests for security guarantees, repudiate collective security, and disdain strategic obligations if Washington officials wanted to fashion a stable, liberal, and capitalist international order? Had Hoover, Hughes, Mellon, and their subordinates found an appropriate balance between domestic priorities and external demands? Were they employing and deploying American power in effective ways to achieve their goals? Few historians had thought so.[10]

These questions prompted me to look much more carefully at the political issues I previously had downplayed in my dissertation. (See chapter 3.) For a generation of "realist" scholars writing after World War II, it seemed incontrovertible that, after the Versailles Conference and the domestic fight over the League of Nations, Republican officials had irresponsibly rebuffed France's demands for security and ignored the responsibilities commensurate with the power that the United States had achieved. These "realist" analysts believed that American aloofness from the political affairs of Europe contributed significantly to the dynamics that led to the Second World War.[11] Yet my reading of the evidence suggested that these Republican officials were not quite so naive, ignorant, or irresponsible. They believed that France's definition of security would alienate the Germans, weaken the fragile Weimar Republic, and make another war inevitable. Republican officials did not want to incur commitments to a vision of security that they thought was inherently incompatible with the requirements of long-term European stability. Nor did they think that American promises could reshape French attitudes about France's security needs.

In other words, Republican officials, like Hughes and Hoover, possessed a sense of the limits of American power in the emotionally and politically vola-

10. For critical views, see, for example, Robert H. Ferrell, *Peace in Their Time: The Origins of the Kellogg-Briand Pact* (New Haven, Conn.: Yale University Press, 1952); William Leuchtenburg, *The Perils of Prosperity, 1914–1932* (Chicago: University of Chicago Press, 1958); Selig Adler, *The Uncertain Giant, 1921–1941: American Foreign Policy between the Wars* (New York: Macmillan, 1965); Alexander De Conde, ed., *Isolation and Security: Ideas and Interests in Twentieth Century American Foreign Policy* (Durham, N.C.: Duke University Press, 1957).

11. For an illustrative work, see Robert E. Osgood, *Ideals and Self-Interest in America's Foreign Relations* (Chicago: University of Chicago Press, 1953).

tile years after Versailles. They wanted to act within the constraints imposed by an American electorate disillusioned by the results of the war and alienated by what Americans regarded as the self-serving actions of Paris, Berlin, and London. Policymakers in Washington wanted to find limited ways to promote European stability and reassure France without assuming responsibilities that exceeded their assessment of American interests. They did this through a variety of instruments that focused on modulating, if not solving, the contentious economic and financial problems afflicting Europe.

I started to think that Republican officials were neither especially isolationist nor singularly expansionist, but pragmatic and opportunistic. Neither the revisionists nor the realists seemed to have accurately synthesized the complexity of U.S. foreign policies in the era of the Republican ascendancy. In fact, my new research suggested that their approach to arms limitation and neutrality constituted a measured way to play a constructive role in European affairs without guaranteeing a status quo that could not last, given the inevitable German desire to be treated more equally and generously. I showed how the Kellogg-Briand Pact—a war-renouncing agreement that generations of historians had mocked as an international kiss—served as a starting point for Republican officials to rethink their neutrality position, should a European power embark on aggressive war. They never carried through on this modest way to meet France's demands for security. But this seemed like a tempered and reasoned response to conditions that then existed: there was no threat to U.S. security; the French seemed predominant; the demands of Weimar leaders appeared reasonable; the need to nurture gradual change seemed prudent; the assumption that prosperity could slowly change attitudes and bring about more reasonable compromises did not appear unfounded. Of course, all of this turned out to be wrong. But could this have been foreseen in the 1920s and early 1930s?

The broad outlines of my book were now clear to me, but this article had an interesting history. Two or three journals rejected it, not because of its substance, but because of its length. I felt frustrated because I had a sense that the article was a real breakthrough, an ambitious attempt to transcend the binaries about "isolationism" and "open door expansionism" and at the same time interrogate the meaning of "realism" in historical context. A colleague told me about *Perspectives in American History*, the annual publication of Harvard University's Charles Warren Center. It published long essays on a variety of topics. I submitted my essay, and it garnered an enthusiastic response from Ernest May, Harvard's renowned diplomatic historian, who refereed the article. Although *Perspectives* was not widely read and my article never received a lot of attention, I still consider it one of the most important of my career. And the very fact that it did wind up in a prestigious outlet nurtured a conviction that I often repeat to my graduate students: if you have something good, you should stick with it and not get dissuaded by a sequence of rejections. Article publication is a crapshoot, but often it takes just one enthusiastic reader to make publication a reality.

After completing this article, I turned my attention for two or three years to fashioning a real book. I remember it as a time of great anxiety, not knowing if I would beat the tenure clock and not certain about the book's prospective reception. I knew it was not as profound as some of the great new volumes then appearing on European diplomacy by Charles Maier, Stephen Schuker, and Jon Jacobson.[12] Nonetheless, *The Elusive Quest: America's Pursuit of European Stability and French Security, 1919–1933*, along with other major volumes on U.S. foreign relations in the 1920s by Michael Hogan, Frank Costigliola, and Joan Hoff Wilson, helped reshape our understanding of the interwar years and influenced an evolving neo-revisionist trend in the interpretation of U.S. diplomatic history known as corporatism.[13] U.S. policy toward Europe in the 1920s was not isolationist.

Rejecting the Treaty of Versailles and the League of Nations did not mean that the United States was abandoning Wilson's pursuit of a stable liberal and capitalist world order.[14] It did not mean that the United States was eschewing its responsibilities. In fact, officials spent considerable effort seeking to balance interests and commitments, reconciling divergent pressures, and working with businessmen and bankers to design ingenious, apolitical mechanisms to conduct an effective foreign policy.

But the bottom line was that U.S. foreign policy did not create the stable, open door, liberal capitalist world order that supposedly was its goal: it failed; it was an elusive quest. I was still perplexed by the essential question: if U.S. officials regarded an open door international order as vital to the nation's health and security, why did they not do more to offset the imbalances in the international political economy and thwart the rise of totalitarian aggression? The last chapter of my book demonstrated that Roosevelt, as he assumed the presidency in 1933, cared even less than Hoover about stabilizing Europe. Al-

12. Charles S. Maier, *Recasting Bourgeois Europe: Stabilization in France, Germany, and Italy in the Decade After World War I* (Princeton, N.J.: Princeton University Press, 1975); Stephen A. Schuker, *The End of French Predominance: The Financial Crisis of 1924 and the Adoption of the Dawes Plan* (Chapel Hill, N.C.: University of North Carolina Press, 1976); Jon Jacobson, *Locarno Diplomacy: Germany and the West, 1925–1929* (Princeton, N.J.: Princeton University Press, 1972).

13. Melvyn P. Leffler, *The Elusive Quest: America's Pursuit of European Stability and French Security, 1919–1933* (Chapel Hill, N.C.: University of North Carolina Press, 1979); Hogan, *Informal Entente*; Wilson, *American Business and Foreign Policy*; Costigliola, *Awkward Dominion*. For "corporatism," see Hogan's essay in Michael J. Hogan and Thomas G. Paterson, eds., *Explaining the History of American Foreign Relations* (New York: Cambridge University Press, 1991), 226–37.

14. A key book that influenced the thinking of many "corporatist" scholars mentioned in note 13 above was N. Gordon Levin's *Woodrow Wilson and World Politics* (New York: Oxford University Press, 1968).

though Roosevelt eventually would transform American foreign policy, initially he did even less than his Republican predecessors to satisfy France's demands—even as Adolf Hitler consolidated power in Germany and the world depression persisted.[15]

In an essay for the volume *Economics and World Power* edited by Sam Wells and William Becker, I tried again to address these perplexing issues. I dug more deeply into the perceived salience of exports to American economic well-being in the late 1920s and early 1930s. I examined statistical data more closely than ever before to assess the importance of markets abroad to the health of different sectors of the American economy. I could not ignore the conclusion of U.S. Commerce Department officials: "The significant fact is not that our foreign markets are unimportant, but rather that the domestic market predominates."[16] Hoover believed this; so did Roosevelt.

But did not U.S. military leaders realize that looming threats were emerging beyond the oceans? Were they not aware that bolder action was imperative before the international capitalist order collapsed and democratic nations were engulfed by totalitarian aggressors? I examined military records that I had not previously perused, an undertaking that would hugely shape the rest of my academic research. I started to examine threat perception. I found that army and naval officials were not alarmed by developments in the early 1930s. Even after the Manchurian Incident of 1931 and subsequent Japanese military action around Shanghai in 1932, the president of the General Board of the Navy insisted that the United States had to "put its own house in order without worrying about other nations." France and America, concluded U.S. Army intelligence in 1932, represented "the essence of capitalism and have the great common interest of saving this system from anarchy." But it was not deemed prudent to guarantee French security, lest such guarantees "perpetuate French hegemony over the Continent." American commitments might embroil the United States without engendering a real change in French policy.[17]

As I grappled with these interpretive issues concerning the gap between U.S. diplomatic objectives and U.S. commitments, I started thinking about my next book. I knew I wanted to write about the origins of the Cold War. In the late 1970s, détente was collapsing and Soviet-American relations were dramatically deteriorating. Oil prices soared, the American economy staggered, our European allies floundered, and U.S. power seemed to wane. Unrest in the Third World seethed, Islamic radicals seized power in Iran, regional strife engulfed the Horn of Africa, and the Sandinistas took power in Nicaragua. As

15. Leffler, *Elusive Quest*, 316–61.

16. Melvyn P. Leffler, "1921–1932: Expansionist Impulses and Domestic Constraints," in William H. Becker and Samuel F. Wells, Jr., *Economics and World Power: An Assessment of American Power since 1789* (New York: Columbia University Press, 1984), 225–75, quotation on 259.

17. Ibid., 261–64.

American economists and journalists wondered whether capitalism could survive, Soviet leaders seemed intent on exploiting Western weaknesses and gaining influence at American expense.[18] A new group of neoconservatives arose. They exaggerated the Kremlin's strength and talked aloud about fighting and waging nuclear war.[19] They also launched a long campaign to emasculate "state" capacity and narrow the government's role in the domestic political economy.[20]

In this context, no topic seemed more important than the history of Soviet- American relations. Big new books were appearing reinterpreting the onset of the Cold War and demonstrating American responsibility for it. If the open door interpretation did not serve as a conclusive guide to explaining American foreign relations before World War II, revisionists like Gabriel Kolko and Lloyd Gardner were showing that the Great Depression and World War II had exercised a decisive influence on the perceptions of U.S. officials about the world they needed to remake after Germany and Japan were defeated. Policymakers in Washington had learned that the United States economy could not recover from depression without markets abroad, and they were now determined to fashion a world order along liberal and capitalist lines.[21]

From these powerful revisionist writings I sensed that the Great Depression and World War II solidified American thinking about America's role in the world. Policymakers now used the term "national security" to describe what they needed to do to safeguard America's vital interests. But what did that term mean and how did vital interests become associated with the preservation of markets abroad, if my own research had demonstrated that this had not been the case before the late 1930s? I decided that I could explore these questions by taking advantage of a unique research opportunity: the government had just opened a huge collection of the records of the Joint Chiefs of Staff ( JCS), the U.S. military leaders who had helped forge the strategy that defeated the Axis powers.[22] These documents transcended the wartime experience and shed light on the opening years of the Cold War. I could interrogate how the concept of national security had evolved and probe its

18. "Can Capitalism Survive?," *Time*, 106 (14 July 1975): 52–63. This was the front page story.

19. Anne Hessing Cahn, *Killing Détente: The Right Attacks the CIA* (University Park, Pa.: Pennsylvania State University Press, 1998); Robert Scheer, *With Enough Shovels: Reagan, Bush, and Nuclear War* (New York: Vintage Books, 1983).

20. Justin Vaïsse, *Neoconservatism: The Biography of a Movement* (Cambridge, Mass.: Harvard University Press, 2010).

21. See, for example, Gabriel Kolko and Joyce Kolko, *The Limits of Power: The World and United States Foreign Policy, 1945–1954* (New York: Harper & Row, 1972); Lloyd Gardner, *Architects of Illusion: Men and Ideas in American Foreign Policy, 1941–1949* (Chicago, Ill.: Quadrangle, 1970).

22. Record Group 218, Records of the Joint Chiefs of Staff, U.S. National Archives.

fundamental ingredients through the prism of military leaders and defense officials. In this manner, I thought I might make my own unique contribution to illuminating the origins of the Cold War.

The task was daunting. Although I had done a little research in military records of the 1920s and 1930s, I had no clue what awaited me. In those days military history and diplomatic history were distinct fields, and few historians of American foreign relations made extensive use of military records. I went back to the National Archives to talk to the archivists dealing with military documents. They provided me with the indexes to the JCS files. They were intimidating. I decided to start with JCS requirements for overseas bases.[23] The number of boxes must have been in the hundreds. I knew I would never exhaust them, but I learned after a few weeks that JCS papers went through many iterations, sometimes with only the slightest revisions. They would not consume as much time as I had initially feared, but they alerted me to the difficult enterprise I had embarked upon. It would take me years to examine the many topics that I deemed most important, among which were assessments of the intentions and capabilities of the Soviet Union, threat perception, the role of atomic weapons, and the occupations of Germany and Japan. My research gradually expanded into archival records of the Army and Navy, the office of the secretary of defense, and many officials, including James Forrestal, the first secretary of defense.

I presented my views in "The American Conception of National Security and the Origins of the Cold War, 1945–1948." It was the most important article of my career, and it appeared in the profession's flagship journal, *The American Historical Review*. (See chapter 4.) I argued that U.S. defense officials and military leaders conceptualized the basic requirements of postwar security before World War II concluded. They wanted an extensive system of overseas bases, air transit rights, a strategic realm of influence in the Western Hemisphere, and, most of all, a balance of power in Eurasia. More than anything else, defense officials and military leaders had learned that an adversary, or coalition of adversaries, that dominated Europe and Asia could integrate the resources, industrial infrastructure, and skilled labor of those continents into a war machine that could challenge the United States, wage protracted war, and endanger its security.

More boldly, I argued that when the war ended, Soviet actions did not threaten U.S. security requirements; instead, these requirements were endangered by the social turmoil, political chaos, and economic paralysis that engulfed Europe and Asia. Postwar conditions provided opportunities for leftist and communist parties to win elections or seize power and for the Kremlin to spread its influence. At the same time, ferment in the periphery of Southeast

23. CCS 360 (12-9-43), RG 218, USNA.

Asia, the Middle East, and Africa bred revolutionary nationalist movements that challenged democratic allies in Western Europe, further weakened their economic and financial prospects, and opened opportunities for Soviet inroads. Soviet actions did not catalyze the sequence of events that led to the Cold War, and U.S. military leaders and intelligence analysts did not expect the Soviet Union to engage in premeditated military aggression. Their own very expansive definition of security requirements impelled U.S. officials to shore up weaknesses and vulnerabilities; these initiatives, a product of fear and power, aroused suspicions in Moscow. They triggered a sequence of actions and reactions, culminating in a protracted Cold War.

In a related article, I also showed how strategic thinking and military requirements shaped the diplomacy of the early postwar years. Looking closely at American relations with Turkey, I reconfigured understanding of the Truman Doctrine. (See chapter 5.) Soviet actions toward Turkey were not nearly as ominous as Washington portrayed them. U.S. interest in Turkey was sparked by American war planners. As early as 1946, they realized that if a major war with the Soviet Union erupted, British bases in the Cairo-Suez region would be critical to implementing American war plans and striking the Soviet Union. Turkey was essential to slow down any Soviet effort to overrun the entire Middle East. From bases in Turkey, the United States could attack vital oil fields and industrial infrastructure in Romania and Ukraine. U.S. officials wanted to provide military aid to Turkey to insure that Ankara would be amenable to U.S. strategic needs. Fear that Turkey might assume a neutral posture in wartime impelled U.S. officials to incorporate Greece and Turkey into NATO, after the North Atlantic Treaty was signed in 1949. Military leaders and civilian officials knew these decisions would arouse legitimate security concerns inside the Kremlin. Soviet leaders regarded these actions in their vulnerable southern underbelly as potentially threatening. But fear and power shaped U.S. diplomacy, and security requirements were the animating force.

At the same time, I wrote another article examining the diplomacy of the early Cold War. (See chapter 6.) Looking closely at the Yalta and Potsdam accords, I analyzed how the ambiguities embedded in their provisions engendered bitter recriminations. In his first meeting with V. M. Molotov, the Soviet foreign minister, President Harry S. Truman assailed the Kremlin for its failure to adhere to its Yalta promises. Molotov and Joseph Stalin rebutted these claims, insisting that British and American officials violated their own commitment to allow the Lublin communists to constitute the core of a reconstituted Polish provisional government. Soviet leaders also believed that the Americans were reneging on their Yalta promises regarding the payments of German reparations from the western zones of occupation. Domestic politics and the imperatives of Western European reconstruction drove these decisions in Washington and London as much as, or even more than, portentous

Soviet behavior. Whatever the motivations, Western claims and Western actions did not seem defensive to the men making policy in the Kremlin.

My close scrutiny of strategic planning and diplomatic developments in
the years immediately following World War II reinforced the revisionist critique of the Cold War. My *AHR* article in particular triggered angry reactions
and biting critiques from more traditional historians. In a "Forum" in *The
American Historical Review*, John Lewis Gaddis and Bruce Kuniholm ridiculed my interpretation and mocked my efforts. My argument that military
planners were pragmatic and not idealistic, Gaddis concluded, was about as
innovative as "discovering sex" at the age of 42. More trenchantly, my critics
claimed that my focus on defense officials obfuscated who was really making
policy—not military planners—and elided the difficult budgetary battles in
Washington that precluded any significant increase in defense expenditures in
the early postwar years despite the preferences of Pentagon officials. Basically,
my critics said that I was guilty of "archive-itis—the tendency of historians to
become so immersed in particular archives that they lose sight of the larger
context into which all archival revelations must eventually be set."[24] In their
view, the larger context and explanatory factors for why the wartime alliance disintegrated and the Cold War arose were Stalin's barbarity and Soviet
aggression.

I reacted sharply to these criticisms, but they exerted a tremendous impact
on my subsequent research.[25] I realized that to make my analysis about the
origins of the Cold War more persuasive, I had to show that military planners
alone did not possess these ideas about national security; I had to rebut claims
that U.S. actions were primarily defensive, and I had to demonstrate that the
absence of a major buildup in defense expenditures did not mean that policymakers were indifferent to U.S. strategic imperatives. I also had to explain why
American officials subsequently pivoted quickly to seek a preponderance of
U.S. military power. Most importantly, I had to think more carefully about
whether U.S. policies were as provocative and countereffective as I had
claimed in my *AHR* article, or whether they were justified by Stalin's personality and Soviet aggressiveness, as my critics insisted.

Rather than succumb to archivitis, I opened myself to its possibilities. I
spent four or five years doing additional research in the records of the
Department of State and in scores of manuscript collections at the Truman
Library and elsewhere. As I reexamined the dynamics of U.S. decision-
making, my analysis started to disappoint my friends on the left. Initially,
they had welcomed my thesis because my evidence from new sources vividly

24. "Comments," by John Lewis Gaddis, in *AHR* Forum: "The American Conception of National Security and the Origins of the Cold War, 1945–1948," *The American Historical Review* 89
(April 1984): 382–85.

25. For my reply, see ibid., 391–400.

demonstrated the expansionist conception of security and powerfully explained how fears about postwar ferment and anxieties about vacuums of power led to provocative U.S. actions. In other words, revisionists liked the way I outlined a classic "security dilemma"—a concept I embraced from the literature on international relations—emanating from an expansive definition of national security.[26] In their view, and in my view, some of the new documents opening up in Soviet archives in the late 1980s and early 1990s actually reinforced the basic contours of this argument.[27]

But revisionist scholars were disappointed that they did not see a greater emphasis on the economic and ideological wellsprings of U.S. policy. They were even more disappointed when I concluded my book with a rather balanced assessment of U.S. policies. In *A Preponderance of Power* I argued that, in view of uncertainties about Soviet intentions and the explosive conditions that existed after fifteen years of depression, war, and genocide, U.S. actions were partly wise, partly foolish, and mostly prudent. Revisionists welcomed the stress on foolishness when I highlighted the exaggerated fears of Soviet inroads into the Third World and when I portrayed how U.S. officials conflated fears about the appeal of Marxism-Leninism with the behavior and actions of Soviet officials. But revisionists resented my empathetic portrayal of the agonizing decisions U.S. officials faced and the wisdom and prudence they often displayed when confronted with a tyrannical regime led by a brutal dictator whose intentions were ultimately unknowable. William Walker, Bruce Cumings, Michael Hogan, and Michael Hunt rightly noted that I did not claim that a quest for export markets, or worries about another depression, or concerns with the world capitalist system, or ideological hubris shaped U.S. policies. To them, my focus on fear and power as central motivating factors sounded more like a return to realism than an endorsement of revisionism.[28]

26. For the concept "security dilemma," see, for example, Robert Jervis, "Cooperation Under the Security Dilemma," *World Politics*, 30 ( January 1978): 167–214; Charles L. Glaser, "The Security Dilemma Revisited," *World Politics*, 50 (October 1997): 171–201.

27. Melvyn P. Leffler, "Inside Enemy Archives: The Cold War Reopened," *Foreign Affairs*, 75 ( July/August 1996): 120–135. Gaddis disagreed. See John Lewis Gaddis, *We Now Know: Rethinking Cold War History* (New York: Oxford University Press, 1997). For my rebuttal, see Melvyn P. Leffler, "The Cold War: What 'Do We Now Know'?" *The American Historical Review*, 104 (April 1999): 501–524.

28. Melvyn P. Leffler, *A Preponderance of Power: National Security, the Truman Administration, and the Cold War* (Stanford, Calif.: Stanford University Press, 1992); see also, Leffler, *The Specter of Communism: The United States and the Origins of the Cold War, 1917–1953* (New York: Hill & Wang, 1995). For critiques, see Michael J. Hogan, "State of the Art: An Introduction," in Michael J. Hogan, ed., *America in the World: The Historiography of American Foreign Relations since 1941* (New York: Cambridge University Press, 1995), 12–15; Bruce Cumings, " 'Revising Postrevisionism,' or The Poverty of Theory in Diplomatic History," in ibid., 20–62, 127–39; Michael Hunt, "The Three Realms Revisited," ibid., 148–155; William O. Walker, "Melvyn P. Leffler, Ideology, and American Foreign Policy," *Diplomatic History*, 20 (Fall 1996): 663–73.

Their criticisms stung. Many of them emanated from friends with whom I had shared ideas for decades. Bill Walker had sat in the same classroom at Ohio State decades before when David Green had asked us for our draft cards. I did not think they were right when they claimed that I had jettisoned Williams's open door interpretation and embraced John Gaddis's postrevisionism.[29] I knew that I had followed the evidence as best I could, and I recognized that I did not fit easily into any of the prevailing categories. As I reassessed where I positioned myself in the interpretive wars about the origins of the Cold War, I realized that, unknowingly, I was marrying revisionism and realism. As I rethought and reread parts of *Preponderance of Power*, I saw that the most important passages were those where I claimed that democratic capitalism at home was endangered by ominous trends in the configuration of power abroad. U.S. officials were not primarily seeking to promote democracy or penetrate foreign markets. They were driven by their "ideological conviction that their own political economy of freedom would be jeopardized if a totalitarian foe became too powerful," or if the world divided into autarchic units. In 1940–41, Roosevelt warned that events abroad would lead to regimentation at home. Truman's advisers felt similarly in 1946–48. They realized that socioeconomic ferment and political turmoil in Europe could lead to geopolitical reconfigurations with dire implications for a free political economy at home. President Truman stated it succinctly: Such developments "would require us to become a garrison state, and impose upon ourselves a system of centralized regimentation unlike anything we have ever known."[30]

By the time I grasped the full implications of my own interpretive argument about the meaning of national security as a driving force behind U.S. foreign policy, the Cold War was over. It had ended, suddenly, and pundits, academics, and scholars heralded "the end of history," the termination of ideological conflict, and the dawn of a permanent, new era of liberal peace based on free markets, democratic governance, and human rights.[31] U.S. officials rejoiced over the dramatic turn in world events: "We know what works," exclaimed President George H. W. Bush. "Freedom works. . . . We know how to secure a more just and prosperous life for man on earth: through free markets, free elections, and the exercise of free will—unhampered by the state."[32]

29. John L. Gaddis, "The Emerging Post-Revisionist Thesis on the Origins of the Cold War," *Diplomatic History* 7 (Summer 1983): 171–90.

30. Leffler, *Preponderance of Power*, especially 12–15, 21–24, 159–164, 488–98; for the quotation by Truman, see *Public Papers of the Presidents of the United States: Harry S. Truman, 1952–1953* (Washington, D.C.: Government Printing Office, 1966), 189.

31. Francis Fukuyama's essay on the triumph of liberal democracy was an instant sensation. See Francis Fukuyama, "The End of History," *The National Interest*, Summer 1989. The article quickly became a best-selling book, *The End of History and the Last Man* (New York: Free Press, 1992).

32. George H. W. Bush, January 20, 1989, http://www.presidency.ucsb.edu/ws/?pid=16610.

I believed that such triumphalist interpretations dramatically misread the end of the Cold War, obfuscated its details, and misconstrued the lessons that could be extrapolated. As I increasingly collaborated with Odd Arne Westad, my friend and co-editor of the *Cambridge History of the Cold War*, and as I talked with Chen Jian, my colleague at the University of Virginia, I became convinced that the Cold War was a struggle about alternative ways of life—alternative ways of organizing modern political economies.[33] For the first part of the twentieth century, democratic capitalism had faltered—beleaguered by imperial struggles, colonial conquests, two world wars, a great depression, genocide, and forced migrations. Disillusioned peoples around the globe looked for new models: communism, fascism, and Nazism. After World War II, faced with the challenge of communism, democratic statesmen revived faith in their system, not by discarding the "state," but by refashioning state capacity to serve the needs of their people. This was what the New Deal was all about, and Roosevelt grasped its global implications as he carved out his vision for the postwar world. He was not alone. Democratic statesmen in postwar Europe and Asia reengineered state capacity to serve the needs of their people: with different permutations in different countries, the state promised full employment, provided medical care, ameliorated housing conditions, assisted the aged, made education accessible to the young, and supported research and innovation. Free markets required state capacity. "The state," I wrote, "complemented markets, structured markets, liberated markets, and helped allay the hardship caused by markets." (See chapter 7.) The West won the Cold War precisely because statesmen realized that national security meant proving the superiority of a way of life; that was done not so much by diplomacy or strategy, but by making democratic capitalism and social democracy serve the needs of their people.

My own thinking about the Cold War clashed with popular discourse in the 1990s. In the neoliberal decade that followed the toppling of the Berlin Wall, Republican and Democratic officials in the United States circumscribed and eroded state capacity as they labored to shape popular memory and sustain America's hegemonic position in the international arena. Without dangerous enemies abroad, they feared an isolationist backlash. The safety, security, and prosperity of Americans, they endlessly proclaimed, was the result of America's calculated effort to use its military power to nurture a democratic peace. In the mid-1990s, President Bill Clinton embraced the "Regional Defense Strategy," initially designed by Dick Cheney's Pentagon in 1992, and went even further to champion a military posture of "full spectrum superiority." Although Clinton thought force should be used prudently and sparingly,

33. Odd Arne Westad, *The Global Cold War: Third World Interventions and the Making of Our Times* (Cambridge, Eng.: Cambridge University Press, 2005).

he, like Bush, believed that dangers, if not yet apparent, nonetheless lurked over the horizon. (See chapter 8.)

While a sense of triumphalism pulsated through the country, I was convinced that the Cold War endgame had less to do with the defense buildup and moral clarity of Ronald Reagan than with the thinking, initiatives, and improvisation of Mikhail Gorbachev. But whoever was more responsible for the sudden and dramatic end of the Cold War, the role of individual agency could not be ignored. Baffled by developments I never had imagined would occur—the peaceful end of the Cold War—I decided to reexamine its trajectory. Why had it started? Why had it lasted so long? And why had it ended? Much of my intellectual energy had been spent thinking and writing about structures, interests, and processes; now, I was enticed to think more systematically about human agency and contingency. The outpouring of new documents from former communist countries allowed scholars to assess more carefully the perceptions and misperceptions of officials in different capitals.

I thought I could write an overall history of the Cold War by focusing on critical moments in time when key policymakers, like Eisenhower and Malenkov, Kennedy and Khrushchev, and Carter and Brezhnev glimpsed the possibility of change, but could not quite seize the opportunity to end the cycle of distrust and strife. Why had they failed, and why had Reagan, Gorbachev, and Bush succeeded? How important were structures? How important was strategy? How important were human agents?[34] In short, having spent almost a decade wondering how American policy shaped or failed to shape the post–World War I era, and after pondering for more than a dozen years why the Cold War occurred, I now turned my attention to understanding why it persisted, how it evolved, and why its winners prevailed.

As often happens over the course of an academic career, I was then sidetracked by administrative duties. I put aside this project for four years (1997–2001) while I served as dean of the College and Graduate School of Arts and Sciences at the University of Virginia. This experience was revelatory. I learned how hard it was for administrators to set priorities. I saw how difficult it was to manage time and make bureaucracies function smoothly. I witnessed organizational rivalries and participated in nasty budget fights. I entered into personal battles in which emotion and passion often dwarfed reason and calculation. I grappled with unaccustomed responsibilities: do you evacuate buildings when there are bomb threats, even when you know the threats are not likely to be credible? In short, I learned a lot about policymaking. I thought my background as a policy historian would enhance my administrative skills; at the end of four years

---

34. Melvyn P. Leffler, *For the Soul of Mankind: The United States, the Soviet Union, and the Cold War* (New York: Hill & Wang, 2007).

I concluded that my administrative experience would make me a better policy historian. I learned empathy.

I ended my job as dean in the summer of 2001 and went to Washington as a visiting scholar at the Woodrow Wilson International Center to resume work on my new Cold War book. The events of September 11, 2001, altered my direction. When I went to Oxford as Harmsworth Professor the following year, I was engulfed by the emotions and passions aroused by President George W. Bush's declaration of a global war on terrorism. Daily, I was asked to explain or justify American policy. I sometimes felt as if I were the State Department's personal emissary to Oxford. Perplexing and provocative was the Bush administration's National Security Strategy Statement of 2002.[35] Its ideological hubris, emphasis on military preeminence, and justification of preemptive or preventative action incensed most friends and colleagues at Oxford. Rather than give my Harmsworth lecture on my new thinking about structure, turning points, and human agency in the Cold War, I decided to put the Bush administration's reactions to 9/11 in historical perspective.[36]

Most observers judged the new national security strategy to be provocative and revolutionary. I did not see such a radical transformation. To me, the focus on unilateralism, ideological fervor, military superiority, and open door trade harked back to familiar tropes in American history. Even the emphasis on anticipatory action was not as novel as most commentators thought. I had learned that in the making of national security policy, fear, power, interests, and ideals always interacted in complicated and unpredictable ways, but the overriding goal of safeguarding democratic capitalism remained constant. During times of great peril, U.S. officials mobilized and employed America's extraordinary power. To catalyze support, they dwelled on the nobility of America's ideals and downplayed interests. Fear and power, often thought of as being apposite, were an explosive brew, capable of producing great good and great harm. What resulted often depended on the quality of the process and the quality of the judgment. Outcomes were contingent; human agents were critical. (See chapter 9.) The tendency of academic scholars (like myself)—historians and international relations specialists alike—to downplay the role of leaders was problematic.[37]

This focus on agency and contingency came into view as I worked on my book *For the Soul of Mankind: The United States, the Soviet Union, and the*

35. "The National Security Strategy of the United States of America," September 2002, http://www.state.gov/documents/organization/63562.pdf.

36. Melvyn P. Leffler, "9/11 and the Past and Future of American Foreign Relations," *International Affairs*, 79 (October 2003): 1045–63.

37. For writings about the role of leaders, see, for example, Daniel Byman and Kenneth M. Pollack, "Let Us Now Praise Great Men: Bringing the Statesmen Back In," *International Security*, 25 (Spring 2001): 107–46; Robert Jervis, "Leadership, Post–Cold War Politics and Psychology," *Political Psychology*, 15 (1994).

*Cold War.* The animating questions were: why did the Cold War last as long as it did, and why did it end when it did? My research demonstrated that external structures—the configuration of power in the international arena and the dynamics of the world political economy—repeatedly generated turning points when the Cold War might have been modulated or reconfigured, as it eventually was in the late 1980s. But policymakers made choices, and those choices often were driven by perceptions of threat and opportunity. The perceptions themselves, however, were shaped by emotions, beliefs, values, and memory. The ballooning literatures on cognition, perception, beliefs, and emotions helped me think anew about causation in national security decision-making, as did the theoretical work on constructivism. But, for me, most important was the evidence itself and the thoughts, comments, and writings of friends like Frank Costigliola (who was then doing pioneering research on the role of emotions in the making of U.S. foreign policy) and those of Bob Jervis and Richard Immerman (who had long been analyzing the psychology of decision-making).[38]

If outcomes were contingent, could any lessons be drawn? Since the late 1970s I had been interested in using my historical investigations to extrapolate lessons.[39] Ernest May and Richard Neustadt were pioneers in showing how policymakers always drew upon their own version of the lessons of the past to deal with prevailing challenges. May and Neustadt demonstrated how the extrapolations often were ill-advised, simplistic, and oblivious to historical context.[40] Historians, I believed, had a key role to play both in showing how extrapolations were made and how they should have been made. If memory—personal memory and collective memory—shaped policy, historians had an obligation to clarify the past and inform "memory" based on their research.

In the aftermath of the war in Iraq (2003) and the global war on terror—when threats from nonstate actors abounded and the hopes of the Arab Spring faded, when the U.S. military buildup peaked and American dreams of a democratic peace vanished, when congressional constraints and partisan battles deadlocked budgetmaking, and when voices proclaimed that diminishing resources might expose new vulnerabilities—the Aspen Strategy Group asked

38. See, for example, Frank Costigliola, "Emotions," in Frank Costigliola and Michael J. Hogan, *Explaining the History of American Foreign Relations*, 3rd edition (New York: Cambridge University Press, 2016), 356–73; Richard H. Immerman and Lori Helene Gronich, "Psychology," ibid., 334–55; and, among his voluminous works and articles, Robert Jervis, *Perception and Misperception in International Politics* (Princeton, N.J.: Princeton University Press, 1974).

39. See, for example, Melvyn P. Leffler, "From the Truman to the Carter Doctrine: Lessons and Dilemmas of the Cold War," *Diplomatic History* 7 (Fall 1983): 245–67.

40. Richard E. Neustadt and Ernest R. May, *Thinking in Time: The Uses of History for Decision Makers* (New York: The Free Press, 1986); also see Ernest R. May, *"Lessons" of the Past: The Use and Misuse of History in American Foreign Policy* (New York: Oxford University Press, 1973).

me to give a talk about the implications of budgetary austerity for the making of national security policy. Going against the grain, I argued that generous defense spending often tempted too much intervention and nurtured a sense of overweening power. The worst errors of the era following World War II—the march to the Yalu during the Korean War, the imbroglio in Indochina during the 1960s, the travail in Iraq after the attacks on 9/11—did not arise from a shortage of resources. In contrast, austerity often catalyzed imaginative thinking and systematic planning. Invited to present the essence of this talk to a meeting of the Joint Chiefs of Staff and combatant commanders, I emphasized that policymakers and commentators should avoid drawing simplistic conclusions between the levels of defense spending and the efficacy of national security policy. In closing, I suggested that the key to American security was making democratic capitalism work at home. (See chapter 10.)

What I had learned was that national security itself was an amorphous notion shaped by external realities, domestic circumstances, and personal perceptions. It meant different things to different people at different times. It was a dynamic concept, always changing, always contentious. Since the early 1990s I had been writing essays on the utility of the concept of "national security" as a guide to explaining American foreign relations. Citing the works of scholars writing about international relations, I noted that national security involved the delineation of external threats to core values—to the "American way of life," to democratic capitalism. Properly understood, "national security" was a capacious concept. My own thinking about it grew more refined over the decades as I read the many new books on "grand strategy" and as I pondered the implications of the new literatures on religion, human rights, development, race, and emotions. These writings helped to illuminate the many meanings of "core values."[41]

I grafted the new onto the old. My early embrace of open door revisionism and my ongoing conversations with friends like David Painter, Marty Sherwin, and Bob McMahon still shaped my conviction that one had to wrestle with the ideological and domestic economic roots of American foreign policy. But my quest to understand why strategic commitments were rejected after one world war, but embraced after another, made me forever cognizant about the degrees of importance assigned to foreign policy goals. Foreign policy became national security policy when officials believed (for whatever reasons) that developments abroad might endanger the preservation of core values at home—meaning private property, free enterprise, personal freedom, open markets, and the rule of law as well as the safety of American lives, national

41. The first version of this essay on national security appeared in Michael J. Hogan and Thomas G. Paterson, *Explaining the History of American Foreign Relations* (New York: Cambridge University Press, 1991).

sovereignty, and territorial integrity. Although the term "national security" was rarely used before World War II, it nevertheless had considerable explanatory power for the entire trajectory of U.S. history. (See chapter 11.)

In my evolving thinking, revisionism and realism were not alternative interpretive frames, but complementary. Structures—whether they be interest groups at home, the nature of the world political economy, or the distribution of power abroad—framed perceptions of threat or opportunity based on the memories, experiences, beliefs, values, and emotional predilections of individual officials, ethnic groups, racial minorities, and classes. In this respect, the new theoretical literature on "constructivism" helped me to understand how changing cultural norms and sensibilities shaped personal, group, and collective understandings of the core values that they wanted to preserve at home.[42] Most policymakers wrestled incessantly with conflicting pressures, clashing impulses, and competing priorities. They reacted to and tried to mold the views of key constituencies as they debated the meaning of events abroad for the preservation of their own most precious values at home.

My study of American foreign policy over the decades had gravitated toward an analysis of the meaning of national security. This was not intentional. It resulted from my long struggle to wrestle with evidence, often conflicting evidence, that led me to try to synthesize the three levels of analysis that scholars of international relations often talk about: the individual, the domestic/state, and the international.[43] By using the concept of national security, I was able to analyze the motives shaping U.S. policymakers, examine their perception of threat and opportunity, assess their willingness to incur commitments and responsibilities abroad, study their readiness to employ military power, and gain an appreciation of how they saw the links between external configurations of power and the preservation of democratic capitalism at home. As I embraced complexity, studied the evolving literature on grand strategy, and grappled with contingency, my empathy for the policymakers grew.

This attitude was reinforced after I joined the Miller Center at the University of Virginia in 2005. This nonpartisan institute focused on the study of the presidency and encouraged multi-disciplinary collaboration. I had the good fortune to work with Jeff Legro, a political scientist and scholar of international relations. Together, we orchestrated two conferences that focused on

42. Peter J. Katzenstein, ed., *The Culture of National Security: Norms and Identity in World Politics* (New York: Columbia University Press, 1996); Robert Jervis, "Identity and the Cold War," in *Cambridge History of the Cold War*, ed. by Melvyn P. Leffler and Odd Arne Westad (3 vols., New York: Cambridge University Press, 2010), 2: 22–43.

43. See the way Robert Jervis grapples with these issues: Robert Jervis, "Do Leaders Matter and How Would We Know?" *Security Studies*, 22 (April 2013): 153–79.

strategic thinking and contemporary policymaking.[44] We brought together former officials, leading scholars, and public intellectuals with strikingly divergent ideological predilections. Their discussions and papers, along with my ongoing interviews of former officials in the George W. Bush administration, further highlighted my appreciation of the complexity of national security decision-making. Talking to former officials about the global war on terror and the conflicts in Afghanistan and Iraq illuminated just how hard it is to design goals, set priorities, estimate threats, reconcile values and interests, link means and ends, mobilize public opinion, and calculate outcomes.

Interviews nurtured my empathy for the agonizing decisions policymakers make, but they also reinforced my conviction that there is no substitute for the written record. Seeking to spin history as they see it, and relying on friendly journalists to assist them, officials with predilections for specific policy options seek to shape our collective memory. The only check on their efforts is access to official documents. Yet growing secrecy, poor recordkeeping, and proliferating e-mail correspondence make preservation of the historical record more difficult than ever before. Hence we scholars have a vital role to play: demanding declassification, recording history as objectively as possible, informing public discourse, and creating a credible understanding of the past that future officials can reference when they face the challenges ahead. As we do so, we must challenge ourselves as well: using theoretical approaches in neighboring fields to interrogate our own assumptions; wrestling honestly with evidence that challenges our own ideological predilections; and staying focused on explaining causation.[45]

I hope my writings on national security and foreign policy infuse empathy and complexity, yet hold officials accountable for the decisions they make and suggest lessons that can be extrapolated. When fear, power, and hubris can lead officials astray with portentous consequences, prudence and balance remain the defining qualities of good statesmanship. Ideological zealotry, inchoate fears, global economic competition, and overweening power may tempt officials to do too much, yet they must not be indifferent to real threats and do too little. Nor can they ignore the domestic sources of national security, the ones that made "victory" possible in the long Cold War. If national security is about preserving the core values of democratic capitalism at home, as it is,

44. The results of these conferences appeared in two volumes: Melvyn P. Leffler and Jeffrey W. Legro, *To Lead the World: American Strategy after the Bush Doctrine* (New York: Oxford University Press, 2008); *In Uncertain Times: American Foreign Policy After the Berlin Wall and 9/11* (Ithaca, N.Y.: Cornell University Press, 2011).

45. Some of my thoughts on these matters can be found in my presidential address to the Society of Historians of American Foreign Relations. See Melvyn P. Leffler, "New Approaches, Old Interpretations, and Prospective Reconfigurations," *Diplomatic History*, 19 (Spring 1995): 173–96.

officials must recognize that full employment, income fairness, educational opportunity, health insurance, and security in old age are the prerequisites for a satisfied citizenry. Credibility of the system at home over the long run is as important as the credibility of commitments abroad.

Fifty years have passed since I walked those Ithaca streets wondering how long the tragic conflict in Indochina could persist. Nowadays, protracted wars have become a way of life. I somehow feel less angry, less passionate, and perhaps wiser and a lot sadder. Wiser because I do think I understand the confluence of factors—personal, domestic, and international—that lead to such wars; sadder because I also think I understand the human dimension— the fear and hubris, the zealotry and idealism, the greed and power, the ambition and sense of responsibility—that makes it so difficult for policymakers to mitigate conflict and ameliorate the human condition.

But sadness is not despair. Personally, my life as an historian has been challenging and fulfilling. My goals—seeking truth, questing for objectivity—always engender condescending smiles from my colleagues and friends who know so well how elusive such goals are and who think that after a lifetime of effort I should know better. But these values, however self-deceiving, have brought rich rewards as I have tried to understand the past and gained an appreciation of the complexity of human affairs and international relations. They still shape what I try to do; they inspire me to tackle what I continue to believe are the fundamental questions of international relations and political economy: making war and peace, assuming commitments and deploying force, shaping the role of government in relation to the market, and protecting human dignity.

# 1

# The Origins of Republican War Debt Policy, 1921–1923

## A CASE STUDY IN THE APPLICABILITY OF THE OPEN DOOR INTERPRETATION

Like most graduate students studying diplomatic history in the 1960s, I was enormously influenced by the writings of the "Wisconsin school" led by William A. Williams. Following the research agenda of many of Williams's students—like Walter LaFeber, Tom McCormick, Lloyd Gardner, and Carl Parrini—I turned my attention to the views of businessmen, especially those interested in international trade. I looked at the proceedings of elite business, banking, and farm organizations like the National Foreign Trade Council, the National Association of Manufacturers, the Chamber of Commerce of the United States, the American Farm Bureau Federation, and the Investment Bankers Association. I found that the Wisconsin school was remarkably prescient in illuminating the interest of American businessmen and agricultural spokesmen in foreign markets. Far from ignorant about the needs of European reconstruction after World War I, elite factions of the American business, banking, and farm sectors grasped that war debt payments were intimately related to the controversies over German reparations, the restoration of European currency stability, the promotion of American exports, the alleviation of unemployment, and the revival of agricultural prosperity.

Yet translating these views into constructive policy was hard. Bankers, manufacturers, traders, and farmers cared greatly about levels of postwar taxation that would be affected by cancellation of the war debts or even the reduction of interest rates. Nor could officials in the executive branch make policy on their own. Secretary of the Treasury Andrew Mellon asked Congress for the flexibility to renegotiate war debt settlements but was rebuffed. Legislators—responding to their constituents—assigned priority to tax relief and veterans' bonuses. Legislators also wanted to rein in presidential power after feeling infuriated and belittled by Woodrow Wilson's use of executive authority. Enhancing the power of the legislative branch was sufficient motivation for congressmen and senators to circumscribe Mellon's initial request for flexibility.

Studying the origins of war debt legislation in a microscopic way helped me to see the complexity of the policymaking process and to understand the diversity of motives bearing on decision-makers. My fascination with the role of business and economics in the making of U.S. foreign policy grew, but I also saw the pluralism within the business community, the messiness of the legislative process, and the salience of organizational pressures within executive branch departments. I was still impressed with the insights offered by the Wisconsin school, yet was wrestling with the conflicting evidence I was uncovering within business journals, trade associations, and archival collections.

This article was originally published in the *Journal of American History* 59 (December 1972), 585–601.

———

The open door interpretation of American diplomatic history, now widely disseminated by reputable scholars and articulate spokesmen, demands rigorous analysis. The appeal of the interpretation rests in its simplicity. According to this thesis, American diplomacy is a function of domestic policy. Unable to find internal solutions to the chronic problems of overproduction and unemployment, American policymakers have looked abroad to reconcile the dilemmas of the American capitalist system. This externalization of internal difficulties has compelled the American establishment to search for foreign markets to absorb the unparalleled quantity of goods produced in American factories and on American farms.[1]

This article will examine the origins of Republican war debt policy and will evaluate the utility of the open door thesis as a guide to this analysis. It will contend that American debt policy was the result of uneasy compromises between hostile branches of government, which themselves were wracked by

1. William A. Williams, *The Tragedy of American Diplomacy* (New York, 1959). See also Walter LaFeber, *The New Empire: An Interpretation of American Expansion 1860–1898* (New York, 1963); Walter LaFeber, *America, Russia, and the Cold War, 1945–1966* (New York, 1967); Lloyd C. Gardner, *Economic Aspects of New Deal Diplomacy* (Madison, 1964); Thomas J. McCormick, *China Market: America's Quest for Informal Empire, 1893–1901* (Chicago, 1967).

a multitude of conflicting pressures and irreconcilable goals. In this complex and changing situation the search for markets was an important consideration. Nevertheless, among economic interest groups and government officials, the quest for foreign outlets was counterbalanced by fiscal and political considerations.

At first thought, American war debt policy hardly seems susceptible to the open door interpretation. The standard work on the subject denounces the economic ignorance of American policymakers.[2] Historians generally have castigated American debt policy as economically unwise and illustrative of American insularity and provincialism in the early post–World War I era.[3] Until recently, they have agreed that American insistence on debt repayment reflected a widespread ignorance of the unity of international economic and financial processes.[4] They have claimed that the public's antipathy to debt cancellation as well as its obsession with the sanctity of contracts compelled American policymakers to disregard economic criteria.[5]

In the years immediately following the Versailles conference, however, a wide and representative spectrum of the American banking, business, and agricultural community did recognize the interdependence of European and American prosperity. These groups—the Chamber of Commerce of the United States (CCUS), the National Association of Manufacturers (NAM), the National Foreign Trade Council (NFTC), the American Bankers Association (ABA), and the American Farm Bureau Federation (AFBF)—realized that European economic reconstruction and European political tranquility were prerequisites for the healthy functioning of the American economy. These perceptions intensified as the postwar boom collapsed in 1920, as the American economy moved swiftly from recession to depression in 1921, and as the European reparations crisis culminated in the occupation of the Ruhr

2. Harold G. Moulton and Leo Pasvolsky, *War Debts and World Prosperity* (New York, 1932), 378.

3. Benjamin Rhodes summarizes the economic criticisms of American debt policy. Benjamin D. Rhodes, "Reassessing 'Uncle Shylock': The United States and the French War Debt, 1917–1929," *Journal of American History*, 55 (March 1969), 787–88. See also Dexter Perkins, "The State Department and Public Opinion," *The Diplomats, 1919–1939*, Gordon Craig and Felix Gilbert, eds. (2 vols., New York, 1965), 1: 282–303.

4. Rhodes, "Reassessing 'Uncle Shylock,' " 787–88. Recently, however, several authors, including Rhodes, have contested the notion of American inflexibility and intransigence on the debt issue. See Carl P. Parrini, *Heir to Empire, United States Economic Diplomacy, 1916–1923* (Pittsburgh, 1969), 249–59; Robert K. Murray, *The Harding Era* (Minneapolis, 1969), 360–65. See also Joan Hoff Wilson, *American Business and Foreign Policy, 1920–1933* (Lexington, Ky., 1971), 123–56.

5. Perkins, "State Department and Public Opinion," 301–03; L. Ethan Ellis, *Republican Foreign Policy, 1921–1933* (New Brunswick, 1968), 210–11; John Hicks, *Republican Ascendancy, 1921–1933* (New York, 1960), 136; Betty Glad, *Charles Evans Hughes and the Illusions of Innocence* (Urbana, 1966), 219.

in 1922–1923. Businessmen and bankers increasingly agreed that "the great outstanding problem of the world today is the restoration of the normal producing and consuming power of Europe and whether she wishes it or not, America is intimately and profoundly concerned in the solution of that problem."[6] Since Europe was virtually the exclusive market for American farm products, agricultural leaders were equally aware of the need to resuscitate the European market as a means of solving the problems of overproduction and low prices.[7]

Those elements of the European economic crisis that most affected American exports and that most worried American businessmen were the depreciation of foreign currencies and the fluctuation of foreign exchanges. Depreciation of foreign currencies and the corresponding appreciation of the American dollar contributed to increased competition from European producers throughout the world. The appreciation of the dollar also meant increased difficulty in marketing American goods in European markets. Even greater concern was aroused by the harrowing phenomenon of fluctuating exchange rates. Fluctuation of exchanges eliminated the elements of predictability and stability that were so important to business transactions. Exchange fluctuations made Europeans hesitant to borrow because they were unable to estimate the amount of foreign exchange that would be needed to repay loans. Little wonder that American business leaders believed the stabilization of European currencies and the concomitant increase in European purchasing power would bring a long era of prosperity to the United States.[8]

6. J. T. Holdsworth, "A Foreign Loan Policy that Will Enable our Factories to Get to Work," *Official Report of the Ninth National Foreign Trade Convention* [National Foreign Trade Council (NFTC)] (New York, 1922), 7–11. For a few illustrative comments on American interest in European reconstruction, see American Economic Association, "Report of the Committee on Foreign Trade," Jan. 9, 1920, box 721(A), Records of the Bureau of Foreign and Domestic Commerce, RG 151 (National Archives); "Committee on Banking and Currency Report," *Proceedings of the Twenty-Fifth Annual Convention* [of the National Association of Manufacturers (NAM)] (New York, 1920), 5–7; "Final Declaration," *Official Report of the Eighth National Foreign Trade Convention* [NFTC] (New York, 1921), viii; Special Committee of the Chamber of Commerce, "European Problems Affecting American Business," *Nation's Business* [Extra Edition], 9 (Oct. 5, 1921), 1–7. See also the proceedings of the 1922 convention of the Chamber of Commerce of the United States, *Nation's Business*, 10 (June 5, 1922).

7. Report of the Executive Secretary [American Farm Bureau Federation (AFBF)], *The Federation's Third Year* (Chicago, 1922), 15–20; J. S. Wannamaker to Warren Harding, Dec. 3, 1921, Folder 1, File 227, box 197, Presidential Case File (PCF), Warren Harding Papers (Ohio Historical Society); Richard Edmonds to Harding, Dec. 9, 1921, ibid.; James R. Howard, "Europe, the Farmers' Market," *Nation's Business*, 10 (June 5, 1922), 24–26.

8. F. C. Schwedtmann, "Address," *Proceedings of the Twenty-Seventh Annual Convention* [NAM] (New York, 1922), 340, 350; A. C. Bedford to William Borah, Dec. 20, 1921, box 215 (Europe), William Borah Papers (Manuscript Division, Library of Congress); Special Committee of the Chamber of Commerce, "European Problems Affecting American Business," 3; John Ross

American economic interest groups generally recognized the interrelationships of American and European prosperity and were well aware of the unity of international financial and economic processes. The real dilemma was the transformation of this understanding into constructive action with regard to the war debts. In fact, many of the nation's economic leaders and business organizations did realize that one of the connecting links between European and American prosperity was the war debt.[9] As a result, they made many important suggestions on how to deal with the debts most effectively in order to cushion their harmful effect on international financial and commercial movements.

American economic leaders and economic interest groups most frequently proposed that the United States defer interest payments or cancel part of the debt.[10] These recommendations indicated widespread apprehension over the dual impact of debts on foreign exchanges and on American exports. Numerous American economists and business leaders realized that "everything . . . that makes an unusually great demand for credits to send to America tends to raise the exchange and to decrease our foreign trade."[11] Consequently, debt payments had to be regulated and moderated in order to increase American exports and to mitigate commercial competition, dumping, and unemployment.[12]

---

Delafield, "Those Difficult War Debts," *Nation's Business*, 10 (April 1922), 34, 36, 38; "Final Declaration," *Official Report . . . Ninth . . . Convention* [NFTC], vii.

9. John F. Dulles, "Allied Indebtedness to the United States," *Annals of the American Academy of Political and Social Science*, 96 (July 1921), 173–74; John H. Williams, "What Should We Do With the Allied Debt?" *Journal of the American Bankers Association*, 14 (Feb. 1922), 541–42; R. C. Leffingwell, "War Debts," *Yale Review*, 12 (October 1922), 25–28; "A Summary of Views on Cancellation of the Inter-allied Debts," *Congressional Digest*, 2 (1922–1923), 77–82; "Committee on Banking and Currency Report," *Proceedings . . . Twenty-Fifth . . . Convention* [NAM], 10; "Report on European Conditions," *Official Report of the Tenth National Foreign Trade Convention* [NFTC] (New York, 1923), 23; Otto H. Kahn to Harding, Aug. 31, 1921, Folder 2, File 172, box 170, PCF, Harding Papers.

10. American Economic Association, "Report of the Committee on Foreign Trade"; "Platform for American Industry," *Proceedings . . . Twenty-Fifth . . . Convention* [NAM], 224–28, 237; *Commercial and Financial Chronicle*, 113 (July 9, 1921), 120–21.

11. Delafield, "Those Difficult War Debts," 34. Recognition of the interrelationship between debts and trade and between debts and exchange rates was quite widespread. See E. M. Patterson, "Cancellation of European War Debts to the United States," *Annals of the American Academy of Political and Social Science*, 96 (July 1921), 180–81; John F. Dulles, "The Allied Debts," *Foreign Affairs*, I (Sept. 15, 1922), 130–31; Leffingwell, "War Debts," 37–38; Williams, "What Should We Do With the Allied Debt?" 542; "Resolutions Adopted at the Twenty-Seventh Annual National Live Stock Association," Jan. 17, 1924, File 800.51/485, General Records of the Department of State, RG 59 (National Archives); E. J. Gittins to Borah, March 17, 1926, box 264 (Foreign Debts), Borah Papers.

12. Frank A. Vanderlip, "The Allied Debt to the United States: An Effective Plan for Its Payment," *Consensus*, 7 (February 1922), 3–39; Wannamaker to Harding, Dec. 5, 1921, Folder 2, File

In return for the proposed postponement or partial cancellation of the debt, American proponents of these measures expected that the European debtor nations would agree to undertake action to reduce reparation payments, to balance their budgets, to stabilize their currencies, to liberalize their trade restrictions, and to limit their expenditures on armaments.[13] Fred Kent, vice president of Bankers Trust Company, became the leading advocate of such a settlement.[14] He believed that "if a portion of the Allied debts [could] be cancelled in exchange for agreements which will promptly place European countries on a sound financial basis, the restoration of the buying power of Europe [would] be greatly accelerated, and the total national income of America [would] be increased."[15] To drum up domestic support for the plan, Kent discussed the proposal with other prominent bankers, farm leaders, and government officials who were worried about the destruction of European purchasing power.[16]

There were numerous other recommendations urging further postponement of debt payments, greater flexibility in the negotiation of debt agreements, and a more comprehensive approach to the settlement of both debts and reparations.[17] One of the more striking characteristics of all these proposals, however, was the lack of a sustained effort to secure unilateral and complete cancellation. Though full cancellation would have contributed to the restoration of European purchasing power and to the stabilization of European

57, box 88, PCF, Harding Papers; "A Summary of Views on Cancellation of the Inter-allied Debts," 79–80.

13. Williams, "What Should We Do With the Allied Debt?" 543; Dulles, "Allied Indebtedness to the United States," 175–77; Patterson, "Cancellation of European War Debts to the United States," 180; Leffingwell, "War Debts," 40; *Commercial and Financial Chronicle*, 115 (Dec. 30, 1922), 2343–44; "Report on European Conditions," *Official Report . . . Tenth . . . Convention* [NFTC], 9–10, 22.

14. Fred I. Kent, "Factors that Will Help the Exchange Situation," *Official Report . . . Ninth . . . Convention* [NFTC], 409–11; "Our Finance and Europe's," *Nation's Business* [Extra Edition], 10 (June 5, 1922), 35–36; Kent to Herbert Hoover, Dec. 2, 1923, box 3 (Japan), Fred I. Kent Papers (Princeton University library); Kent to Charles Evans Hughes, Jan. 24, Feb. 9, 1923, box 3 (J), ibid.

15. Chamber of Commerce, "Proceedings of the Second Congress," Brochure No. 32 (Paris, 1923), 138–45.

16. Kent to Hughes, Feb. 20, 1923, box 3 (Japan), Kent Papers; Kent to Hoover, Dec. 2, 1923, ibid. For Kent's discussion with officials of European governments, see Kent to Seward Prosser, March 27, May 23, 1923, box 4 (Seward Prosser), ibid.

17. Clarence J. Owens to Hughes, Oct. 31, 1922, File 800.51/433, General Records of the Department of State; Resolution of the Board of Directors of the Chamber of Commerce of the United States (CCUS), Sept. 29, 1922, File 800.51/428, ibid.; "Resolutions of the American Bankers Association," *Journal of the American Bankers Association*, 15 (November 1922), 322; *Proceedings of the Twenty-Eighth Annual Convention* [NAM] (New York, 1923), 311; *Consensus*, 8 (April 1923), end-paper; "The Balance Sheet of Europe: Reparations and International Debts," *Consensus*, 8 (March 1923), 17–31.

currencies, American business leaders and economic interest groups rejected it as a viable policy alternative. This was not the result of their ignorance of the impact of the war debts on the international economy, but because of their preoccupation with high domestic taxation, their concern with reparations, and their fear of a hostile public reaction. Even those who advocated partial cancellation, explicitly or implicitly, excluded the British debt from such treatment.[18] This illustrates the difficulty, even among business groups, of translating open door aspirations into logical and concrete action.

The crushing burden of taxation that manufacturers, export-oriented businessmen, and international bankers felt they were experiencing prompted them to limit their proposals to partial cancellation, usually of the pre-Armistice loans. They understood that, if European governments did not honor their wartime obligations, the burden of paying off the war debt of the United States government would fall upon the American taxpayer.[19] While businessmen might extol the commercial advantages that would flow from a reconstructed Europe, they were equally certain that there was no possibility of economic prosperity "if every business activity continues to be oppressed by a multiplication of taxes."[20] The *Commercial and Financial Chronicle* put the matter bluntly: "The war has left the country with tax burdens which, unless speedily lightened, must prove crushing. In these circumstances we cannot become an almoner of the world of nations, even if we would." Though postponement of interest for a few years might be permissible, cancellation and repudiation were unthinkable.[21]

Thus, while acknowledging the intimate link between European economic recovery and American prosperity, many business and farm leaders refrained from advocating outright cancellation of the debt. They were too concerned with the impact of taxation upon the American economy and upon their profit margins.[22] Some were apprehensive that cancellation would benefit British

18. See Dulles, "Allied Debts," 127–28; Patterson, "Cancellation of European War Debts to the United Sates," 180–81; Leffingwell, "War Debts," 38–39; *Commercial and Financial Chronicle*, 115 (Dec. 30, 1922), 2843–44.

19. A substantial percentage of the proceeds of the Liberty and Victory bond issues was re-loaned by the United States government to the European Allies. Interest, maturity, and other terms of these loans were similar to the terms on which the American government had borrowed from the American people. The United States treasury hoped to repay American bondholders with funds obtained from the Allied debtors. If the latter failed to pay, the government would have to obtain the necessary revenue from the American taxpayers.

20. "Final Declaration," *Official Report . . . Eighth . . . Convention* [NFTC], x.

21. *Commercial and Financial Chronicle*, 113 (July 9, 1921), 121.

22. The part of the press that opposed any cancellation frequently justified its position on the basis of the unparalleled tax burden then being endured by the American people. "What about that $10,000,000,000?" *Literary Digest*, 70 (Aug. 13, 1921), 11–12; "Our 'Moral Obligation' to Our European Debtors," ibid., 74 (Aug. 19, 1922), 13–15.

industry and commerce at the expense of American business.[23] Most American economic interest groups, although eager to reap the benefits of a reconstructed European market, were not ready to bear the tax burden that would make this possible.[24]

A few of the nation's leading bankers may have considered virtual cancellation an unsavory but necessary solution to the unsettling international financial situation, but in the early 1920s they steadfastly refrained from publicly advocating this alternative. Cognizant of the public's antipathy to cancellation and sensitive to charges of conflict of interest, the bankers generally limited themselves to the advocacy of partial cancellation. Thomas Lamont of J. P. Morgan and Company was particularly sensitive to congressional accusations that financiers sought cancellation only because it would enable European governments to pay their debts to private bankers.[25]

In addition, there was a widespread belief in the early 1920s that the enormous reparation payments were the crux of the international financial dilemma. All the evils of the European economic environment—inflation, unbalanced budgets, exchange depreciation—could easily be traced to the extent of the reparations burden imposed upon Germany. These observations often diverted attention from the debt issue. They fostered the belief that the United States might contribute most effectively to a European settlement by facilitating a reparations agreement and by lubricating the European economy with loans and credits.[26] American business leaders and economic interest groups considered these solutions to the European economic crisis to be far more expedient than the full cancellation of the debt. To advocate full cancellation and to acknowledge the possibility of higher taxes was to risk economic hardship and political oblivion. Even those who recommended partial cancellation carefully balanced the advantages to flow from increased trade with the disadvantages to ensue from a heavier tax burden.

The Harding administration was aware of the business community's desire for a reconstructed and stable European market. In early June 1921, Paul Warburg, chairman of the board of the International Acceptance Bank, informed both the president and the undersecretary of state that "it is of infinitely

23. F. H. Rawson to Myron Herrick, Dec. 17, 1921, Folder 4, box 12, Myron Herrick Papers (Western Reserve Historical Society).

24. They were also unwilling to risk the possible demoralizing impact that cancellation might have on all credit arrangements.

25. Holdsworth, "Foreign Loan Policy that Will Enable our Factories to Get to Work," 9; *Commercial and Financial Chronicle*, 115 (Dec. 30, 1922), 2843–44; "Bankers Not Urging Cancellation of Allied Debts," *Bankers Magazine*, 104 (April 1922), 631–32.

26. Howard, "Europe, the Farmers' Market," 24–26; Special Committee of the Chamber of Commerce, "European Problems Affecting American Business," 1–7; "Report on European Conditions," 10–15, 25.

greater value to the United States to reconstruct a world in which we can trade in peace and security than to have on our books obligations of our comrades at arms which they cannot pay."[27] In subsequent meetings the bankers told Harding and leading members of his cabinet about the impact of the exchange problem on American trade. These discussions must have impressed the president, who had already indicated his desire to enlarge the nation's foreign commerce.[28]

As a result, in late June 1921, Secretary of the Treasury Andrew Mellon decided to ask Congress to pass legislation that would provide him with virtually unlimited authority to determine interest rates and maturity dates, to defer interest payments, and to accept the obligations of one nation for those of another. He desired this extensive discretionary power in order to devise a comprehensive plan that would take account of the financial plight of the debtors. In fact, Mellon wanted increased flexibility in order to mitigate the impact of debt settlements on exchange rates and on American exports.[29]

This is not to say that Mellon was considering even partial cancellation. In fact, his request for broad authority indicated the absence of any definite plan for carrying out refunding and revealed his desire to be able to negotiate unhampered by legislative restrictions. His testimony before the Senate Finance Committee and the House Committee on Ways and Means was vague, often contradictory, and reflected his own ambivalence. No doubt he wanted to reconcile the conflicting demands of trade and fiscal policy while remaining politically discreet.[30]

Congressional reaction to the proposed legislation was crucial for the determination of all subsequent American policy on the debt issue. Congress refused to abdicate control over debt refunding. By providing for the creation of a five-man commission under the chairmanship of the secretary of the treasury to negotiate debt settlements and by circumscribing the field of negotiation, Congress effectively tied the hands of the executive. In October 1921, the House prohibited the exchange of bonds of any foreign government for those of another and forbade the cancellation of any part of such indebtedness except through payment. In late January and early February 1922, the Senate

27. Paul Warburg to Henry P. Fletcher, June 13, 1921, File 800.51/285, General Records of the Department of State.

28. "Western Bankers' Dinner and Conference at the White House," June 23, 1921, Folder 1, File 57, box 88, PCF, Harding Papers; Harding to Hoover, May 17, 1921, Folder 1, File 3, box 5, ibid.

29. United States Senate, Committee on Finance, *Refunding of Obligations of Foreign Governments* (Washington, 1921), 3–5, 57–58. See also House of Representatives, Committee on Ways and Means, *Refunding Foreign Obligations* (Washington, 1921), 15–16.

30. Committee on Finance, *Refunding of Obligations*, 4–5, 17, 29–30, 56–63, 79–86; Committee on Ways and Means, *Refunding Foreign Obligations*, 9–16. Mellon was intensely concerned with the fiscal plight of the nation, and he believed the depression of 1921 was the result of high taxes. William Larimer Mellon, *Judge Mellon's Sons* ([Pittsburgh?], 1948), 408–09.

went even further and stipulated that the loans be repaid within twenty-five years and that the rate of interest not be less than 4.25 percent. The more stringent Senate version became law. Indeed, Senate Republicans had to close ranks to ensure that the freedom of the commission to defer interest payments was not also proscribed.[31]

This determination of Congress to restrict the flexibility of the executive and to demand full payment of the debt was the result of a diversity of motivations. Congressmen and senators were influenced by their interpretation of the Constitution, by their distrust of the executive branch of the government, by their political affiliation, and by their local constituencies. Both Republicans and Democrats desired to maintain legislative control over debt refunding. They insisted that Congress should not abdicate its constitutional privilege to control governmental financial affairs. They claimed that debt refunding was an integral part of the congressional responsibility to tax and to appropriate.[32] Most Democrats insisted that the treasury department negotiate settlements under existing legislation and then submit them to Congress for approval.[33] They could never muster sufficient Republican support to pass such a measure, but they were able to join with Republican dissidents to circumscribe executive action with regard to interest and maturity.

This movement to restrict the authority of the treasury was not only the result of constitutional scruples but also, in large part, the consequence of many legislators' distrust of the motives and actions of the executive branch. Much of this distrust stemmed from events occurring during the Wilson administration. Congressmen recalled with considerable resentment that their wishes had been repeatedly and purposely ignored by Wilson's treasury department.[34] Mellon rekindled this distrust and further exacerbated legislative-executive relations when he supported the former administration's decision to defer interest payments for two to three years and when he appealed for even broader authority.[35] An aroused Congress then forced the Harding administration to accept the creation of the World War Foreign Debt Commission to negotiate debt settlements.

31. Harold G. Moulton and Leo Pasvolsky, *World War Debt Settlements* (New York, 1929), 221–23. It should be recalled that the proposed legislation was to replace those provisions of the Liberty and Victory loan acts relating to the conversion and refunding of the demand obligations received from the Allies. *Cong. Record*, 67 Cong., 1 Sess., 3021–23 (June 24, 1921).

32. Refunding of Obligations of Foreign Governments," *Senate Report*, 67 Cong., 1 Sess., No. 264 (Serial 7918), Part II, 4–5; *Cong. Record*, 67 Cong., 1 Sess., 6615–18 (Oct. 21, 1921).

33. "Refunding of Obligations of Foreign Governments," 2–4; "Refunding Foreign Obligations," *House Report*, 67 Cong., 1 Sess., No. 421 (Serial 7921), Part II, 8–10.

34. Senate, Committee on the Judiciary, *Loans to Foreign Governments* (Washington, 1921), 5–10.

35. Committee on Finance, *Refunding of Obligations*, 173; "Refunding of Obligations of Foreign Governments," 1–5.

Restricting the authority of the treasury and the entire executive branch as a matter both of principle and of pique was only a prelude to examining the explicit terms of the refunding legislation. From the outset, Congress made clear its intention to forbid exchanging the obligations of one country for those of another. They were shocked by the thought of exchanging valuable British or French obligations for those of Germany, which were considered to be practically worthless. Members of both parties on the Senate Finance Committee and the House Ways and Means Committee expressed apprehension that the United States would be saddled with the worst securities and that England would emerge free of her debt to the United States. Consequently, they objected vociferously to any transaction involving the substitution of the debts of one nation for those of another.[36]

The passion with which the principle of "substitution" was opposed was a clear illustration of the congressional desire to prevent any action that might incur a heavier burden of taxation upon the American people. In fact, the tax issue immediately became one of the crucial themes of the entire debate. The Democrats, in an intensely partisan spirit, made every effort to use the debate on debt refunding to demonstrate their concern for the American taxpayer. They insisted that Republican leniency on the debt issue was a clear illustration of that party's callousness toward the fiscal predicament of the American people. To Democrats, such as Senator Kenneth McKellar of Tennessee, the issue was perfectly clear: "We are taxing the American people as they have never been taxed before in the history of the Republic. The burdens of taxation are greater to-day than ever in its history. If we collect but the interest upon these loans, we will of necessity reduce the taxation upon our own people by one-seventh."[37] The public's preoccupation with taxation made Republican lawmakers very sensitive to the impact of such Democratic rhetoric.

In a similar manner, the Democrats exploited the debt issue to demonstrate their support for American veterans who were trying to obtain passage of a bonus law. On several occasions, Democrats amended bills so as to earmark war debt interest payments and part of the principal for a veterans' bonus. Democrats decried American charity toward Europe while domestic needs were disregarded. They argued that it was now time for the former Allies to show their gratitude to American veterans by providing them with a bonus. In a typically partisan spirit, Democratic Senator James Heflin of Ala-

36. *Cong. Record*, 67 Cong., 1 Sess., 3022–25, 3243 (June 24, 30, 1921); Committee on Finance, *Refunding of Obligations*, 24–31, 167, 179–80; Committee on Ways and Means, *Refunding Foreign Obligations*, 13–15.

37. *Cong. Record*, 67 Cong., 1 Sess., 6858 (Oct. 27, 1921). For other references to the tax issue, see ibid., 3025, 3751, 6618 (June 24, July 14, Oct. 21, 1921); *Cong. Record*, 67 Cong., Sess., 1631–32, 1771–72 (Jan. 24, 26, 1922); "Refunding of Obligations of Foreign Governments," 5.

bama inquired of the Republican opposition, "How do you expect the American people to believe that you are the friend of the American soldier?"[38]

Opponents of the administration found other ways to use Mellon's debt proposal to attack the administration for its indifference to the pressing ills of American society and for its subservience to Wall Street. Several senators charged that the administration's bill was designed to serve the interests of bankers at the expense of the American farmer and the American soldier. Senator James Reed of Missouri declared that the original legislative request was "the most impudent proposal ever put before a legislative body." In general, the critics claimed that full interest on the debt had to begin immediately in order to provide credits for the farmers, bonuses for the soldiers, and tax relief for the public.[39]

These expressions were not merely reflections of negative partisanship. If they were, the large Republican majorities in both houses of Congress would have secured swift passage of the administration's bill. In reality, legislators were responding to widespread public pressure for tax relief, for agricultural credits, for veterans' compensation, and for unemployment relief. By compelling European debtors to repay the debt in full, congressmen gave the appearance of responding to the needs of their constituencies.[40]

Thus, the factors most decisively influencing the passage of debt legislation in Congress in 1921 and 1922 were electoral considerations, partisan politics, and intra-governmental rivalries. While debating the debt proposal, Congress demonstrated relatively little concern with the expansion of American trade. Only occasionally did Republicans justify their desire to be lenient on the basis of the needs of American commerce.[41] Several senators, while opposing the delegation of power to the executive on constitutional grounds, did recognize the travail of Europe. They stated that if the administration required additional flexibility with regard to the debts in order to exert a salutary influence in Europe, then the president should demonstrate such a need and Congress would respond constructively. Meanwhile, they could not be indifferent

38. *Cong. Record*, 67 Cong., 1 Sess., 7477 (Nov. 7, 1921). For references to the partisan nature of the debate, see ibid. , 3754–55, 7400 ff., 7475–77 (July 14, Nov. 5, 7, 1921); *Cong. Record*, 67 Cong., 2 Sess., 1579–80, 1627–28, 1638 ff., 1967–75 (Jan. 23, 24, 31, 1922).

39. *Cong. Record*, 67 Cong., 2 Sess., 1812, 1882, 1888, 1906, 1967, 1970–71 (Jan. 27, 30, 31, 1922). The opponents of the administration also claimed to be protecting the interests of the general public against Republican high tariff advocates who were said to be prepared to countenance cancellation in order to make the creation of high tariff barriers economically justifiable. *Cong. Record*, 67 Cong., 1 Sess., 6601, 6606–07 (Oct. 21, 1921).

40. For many letters from constituents and varied pressure groups to Boies Penrose, see Records of the United States Senate, 67 Cong., 1 Sess., Allied Debts, RG 46 (National Archives); boxes 204 and 215 (Foreign Debts), Borah Papers.

41. *Cong. Record*, 67 Cong., 1 Sess., 3022–23 (June 24, 1921); *Commercial and Financial Chronicle,* 113 (July 2, 1921), 18.

to the more pressing domestic issues of taxation, deflation, and unemployment—issues they did not specifically attribute to the current decline in foreign trade.

The Harding administration was not indifferent to the changes Congress was making in the proposed legislation. By initially soliciting wide discretionary powers, it misjudged the temper of the Congress. Thereafter, it was on the defensive. Yet, Mellon persisted in his efforts to obtain broad authority. Considerable pressure was exerted on Republican members of the Senate Finance Committee and of the House Ways and Means Committee to report out bills acceptable to the administration.[42]

The Republican administration, however, was unable to impose its will upon the sixty-seventh Congress despite a Republican majority of twenty-four in the Senate and 170 in the House. Effective Republican leadership in the Senate virtually had disappeared. The situation was well described by Mark Sullivan in a letter to George Harvey:

> All in all things in the Senate are very much in a mess. Harding and his Cabinet are deeply concerned about it. Harding is repeatedly urged to assert leadership himself; but both by temperament and principle is disinclined to do so.

Eventually, Mellon and Harding counseled the House Ways and Means Committee to accept the Senate amendments despite their confining restrictions. Rather than risk an open struggle and endless delay, the administration apparently was satisfied to have emerged solely with the power to defer interest payments.[43]

Harding's reluctance to engage in a bitter struggle with the Senate was influenced by both fiscal and political considerations. In July he had appealed to the Senate to reject a veterans' compensation bill. He warned that it would be fiscally irresponsible to pass it.[44] The Senate acquiesced. Given the popularity of the bonus bill, however, it was politically inexpedient for the leader of the Republican Party to insist on generous treatment of European debtors while disregarding the needs of American veterans. If the fiscal predicament of the nation was as ominous as he indicated, he could only be consistent by demanding payment from the former Allies. In addition, the president perceived the economic recession in terms of the tax burden and not in terms of

42. *Cong. Record*, 67 Cong., 1 Sess., 6620 (Oct. 12, 1921); ibid. , 67 Cong., 2 Sess., 1576–77, 1627–32, 1886, 1900, 1958–59, 1966–67, 1971, 1976 ( Jan. 23, 24, 30, 31, 1922).

43. Mark Sullivan to George Harvey, Sept. 24, 1921, Presidential Personal File (PPF) 60, Harding Papers; Frank W. Mondeli to Harding, Feb. 3, 1922, Folder 3, File 57, box 88, PCF, ibid.

44. "Soldiers' Adjusted Compensation Bill," *Senate Executive Docs.*, 67 Cong., 1 Sess., No. 48 (Serial 7932), 3–8.

the nation's foreign trade. "It is unthinkable," he insisted, "to expect a business revival and the resumption of the normal ways of peace while maintaining the excessive taxes of war."[45]

The administration's decision to accept the Senate amendments and, thus, to assume an inflexible stance vis-à-vis the nation's debtors reflected an indifference to European conditions that was in no sense a true portrayal of the government's real attitude. In 1922 and 1923, the United States government sought ways to reconcile the conflicting domestic and international pressures bearing on the debt issue. These efforts intensified as the European situation deteriorated in the summer and autumn of 1922 and as pressure multiplied within the American business and diplomatic community for the United States to undertake some constructive action to alleviate the European crisis. Mellon's reluctant acceptance of the congressional legislation indicated not so much the administration's indifference to the European dilemma, as its belief that the solution of Europe's economic and political crisis depended upon a reconciliation of German-French questions over which the administration could exert little influence.[46]

Despite appearances to the contrary, within the Harding administration there was always an awareness of the impact of debts on the European imbroglio. As early as October 1921, Hughes could "fully appreciate" the efficacy of a plan calling for British and American debt cancellation as well as Allied reduction of reparations. Shortly thereafter, several of Hughes's subordinates in the state department declared that the restrictive amendments passed by the Senate were "most unfortunate."[47] The recognition of the complex web of interrelationships between debts, reparations, exchange fluctuations, and trade eventually compelled the administration to give lengthy and serious consideration to a comprehensive plan for European reconstruction submitted by S. R. Bertron, prominent banker and former member of the Root diplomatic mission to Russia in 1917. Bertron recommended that the United States accept German bonds in payment of the Allied debts, guaranteed by each of the Allies to the extent of their own individual indebtedness. According to the Bertron formula, the British would then be obligated to cancel the French debt to England and the French would be obligated to reduce German reparations by the same amount. Germany would issue a well-secured five billion dollar loan, the proceeds of which would go to France over a five-year

45. Ibid., 4.
46. Hoover to Harding, Jan. 4, 1922, Folder 2, File 3, box 5, PCF, Harding Papers; Julius Klein to Walter S. Tower, Jan. 4, 1922, box 600.2, Records of the Bureau of Foreign and Domestic Commerce; Department of State, *Papers Relating to the Foreign Relations of the United States 1922* (2 vols.; Washington, 1938), II, 168–70, 181–82.
47. Hughes to Louis Marshall, Oct. 22, 1921, File 811.51/3023, General Records of the Department of State; Arthur N. Young to Dearing, Feb. 8, 1922, ibid., 800.51/280.

period. This would release Germany from all further obligations. Subsequently, all the Allies would cooperate in the economic rehabilitation of Russia.[48]

Harding was intrigued with this plan. He hoped that "it might offer a means of settling the whole European debt problem." He instructed Mellon, Hughes, and Hoover to examine it carefully and to discuss it with him. Mellon was said to be favorably impressed by the proposals. Assistant Secretary of State Leland Harrison considered them likely to constitute the substance of an eventual solution.[49]

After careful appraisals of the Bertron proposals in both June and December, the administration ultimately rejected them. In a letter to Bertron, Harding revealed the crux of the problem. Nothing "of this tremendous importance," he wrote, "could be accomplished without the sanction of Congress. Those in Executive responsibility have really very little authority."[50] In addition, Secretary of Commerce Hoover warned the president of the ominous international entanglements that might ensue from America's becoming, in essence, Germany's sole creditor. Hoover also cautioned that implementation of the plan might encourage the pro-German population in the United States to agitate for remission of the debt. He therefore advised Harding not to pursue a course that would throw the debt question into the political arena.[51] For the most part, the State Department echoed similar objections to the plan: it was politically inexpedient; Congress would object to it; the United States would assume the risks of becoming the sole creditor of Germany; the plan ignored the European sources of the reparations imbroglio and especially France's desire to weaken Germany.[52]

The administration, while rejecting Bertron's suggestion, continued to seek some means to alleviate the European crisis. In late summer and early autumn 1922, the State Department formulated plans to obtain Allied acceptance of a proposal to create an international committee of businessmen to determine Germany's capacity to pay reparations. Despite Hughes's energetic efforts to secure French adherence to the principle of capacity to pay, Premier

48. S. R. Bertron to Harding, May 26, 1922, Folder 3, File 57, box 88, PCF, Harding Papers; "Bertron Plan," May 17, 1922, File 800.51/341, General Records of the Department of State.

49. Harding to Bertron, June 2, 1922, Folder 3, File 57, box 88, PCF, Harding Papers; Harding to Hughes, Hoover, and Andrew Mellon, June 2, 1922, ibid.; Harding to Hughes, June 2, 1922; De Witt Clinton Poole to Hughes, May 16, 1922; Leland Harrison to William Phillips, May 24, 1922, File Nos. 800.51/450, 344, 343, General Records of the Department of State.

50. Harding to Bertron, June 2, 1922; Folder 3, File 57, box 88, PCF, Harding Papers.

51. Hoover to Harding, June 9, 1922, ibid.

52. Young to Harrison, May 23, 1922, File 800.51/343, General Records of the Department of State; Harrison to Phillips, May 24, 1922, File 800.51/344, ibid.; Memo by Young, June 9, 1922, File 800.51/450, ibid.; Young to Hughes, Dec. 13, 14, 1922, File 800.51/499, 451, ibid.

Raymond Poincaré resolutely opposed this proposal.[53] He would not consent to any reduction in reparation payments unless the French debt to Britain was proportionately diminished and the percentage of French reparation allotments increased. England, however, would not assume such sacrifices unless it was partially relieved of its debt to the United States.[54] Consequently, the American attempt in 1922 to solve the reparations crisis independently of the debt issue through the creation of a commission of experts failed.

During these months, American diplomats in Europe, as well as business groups at home, encouraged the Harding administration to reevaluate its stand on the debt question.[55] Yet Harding refused to countenance cancellation. In mid-October he had authorized Hoover to deliver an address strongly opposing cancellation. He could not reverse himself before the November elections. The Harding administration was caught in a vise: congressional restrictions, fiscal demands, and political expediency encouraged caution and placing responsibility for the reparations crisis upon France; diplomatic warnings, business pressures, and moral scruples compelled constructive action. Consequently, the administration tried to pursue a middle course by facilitating a European economic and financial settlement without sacrificing anything of importance to the American people. This was to be done by creating an "experts committee" to determine Germany's financial capacity.[56]

When France stymied this approach and when the elections were over, Harding stated that the War Debt Commission needed more flexibility if the United States were to exert a salutary influence in European affairs. Both Harding and Hughes felt that congressional insinuations that the administration had not done enough to improve conditions in Europe were spurious. They claimed that congressional restrictions on debt refunding as well as French intransigence on reparations prevented the United States from taking the initiative and effectively intervening in the European crisis.[57]

As a result of its concern with the European situation, the Harding administration undertook a significant step by negotiating a debt settlement with Britain that disregarded the restrictions enumerated by Congress. This accord provided for repayment of the debt over sixty-two years with interest

53. Department of State, *Papers Relating to the Foreign Relations . . . 1922*, 2, 165–203.

54. James Logan to Hughes, Dec. 8, 14, 22, 1922, box 9, Henry Fletcher Papers (Manuscript Division, Library of Congress).

55. Logan to Hughes, Sept. 22, 1922, ibid.; Department of State, *Papers Relating to the Foreign Relations . . . 1922*, 2, 171–75, 176.

56. *Commercial and Financial Chronicle*, 115 (Oct. 21, 1922), 1780–81. For Hughes's proposal to establish a committee of experts, see Charles E. Hughes, *The Pathway of Peace, Representative Addresses Delivered during His Term as Secretary of State (1921–1925)* (New York, 1925), 53–58.

57. *Cong. Record*, 61 Cong., 4 Sess., 982; Hughes to Henry Cabot Lodge, Feb. 1, 1923, box 31 (Lodge), Charles E. Hughes Papers (Manuscript Division, Library of Congress).

increasing from 3 to 3.5 percent. The very favorable response to this debt settlement in both houses of Congress and in the press indicated that the administration had struck a popular compromise between the imperatives of fiscal and commercial policy.[58] It had temporarily reconciled the conflicting demands of world stability and domestic politics. Businessmen and politicians alike supported the accord because they believed it would facilitate American exports without unduly burdening the American people with additional taxes. It was frequently emphasized that the reduction of interest to between 3 and 3.5 percent reflected the anticipated normal level of interest rates over a long period of time. It was therefore difficult for critics to claim that cancellation had been countenanced and the well-being of the American taxpayer jeopardized.[59]

The American debt settlement with Britain set definite precedents for all subsequent negotiations. Thereafter, the War Debt Commission was free to conclude accords on more realistic terms and to submit them to Congress for approval. Eventually, through interest reductions, the War Debt Commission cancelled substantial parts of the French, Italian, and Belgian debts. By the mid-1920s, circumstances had changed sufficiently to enable many congressmen to approve such accords without fear of political retaliation. The national debt was being retired more quickly than anticipated, taxes had been reduced, and business prosperity immunized many groups from the tax impact of debt cancellation. Congressional suspicion of executive authority had been placated by the preservation of the legislature's ultimate power to veto all refunding accords. As a result of all these factors, the War Debt Commission could focus greater attention upon the exigencies of European financial stability and expanded American exports without confronting inflexible congressional opposition.

The terms of the British debt settlement, however, also illustrated that the War Debt Commission would have great difficulty in fully accommodating the desires of American exporters and European governments, especially when their needs could not be reconciled with the imperatives of the American domestic economic and political situation. As already indicated, interest rates on the British debt were adjusted in relation to anticipated long-term rates

---

58. "How America Feels about the British War Debt," *Literary Digest*, 76 (Feb. 3, 1923), 14–15; "The First Step Toward World Solvency," ibid., 76 (Feb. 17, 1923), 9–12; *Consensus*, 8 (April 1923), endpaper.

59. Senate, Committee on Finance, *Refunding of Obligations of Foreign Governments* (Washington, 1923), 11–19; House, Committee on Ways and Means, *Refunding Foreign Obligations—British Debt* (Washington, 1923), 1–2; J. E. Edgerton to Harding, Folder 3, File 57, box 88, PCF, Harding Papers; Robert W. Bingham to Harding, Folder 3, File 227, box 198, ibid.; Gerrard Winston, "American War Debt Policy," 11, box 220, Records of the Bureau of Accounts (Treasury), RG 39 (National Archives).

rather than attuned to the performance of the British economy. This muted some criticism from the domestic opponents of cancellation, but it also imposed too heavy a burden upon the British economy and thus eventually led to other economic dislocations.[60]

After 1923 there was greater emphasis on framing the terms of the debt settlements in accordance with the debtors' capacity to pay.[61] This principle, however, remained vague and amorphous. In effect, the terms of subsequent debt settlements reflected the War Debt Commission's careful balancing of internal and external pressures.[62] President Calvin Coolidge and Mellon alternately defended the agreements from diametrically opposed criticisms. In response to critics who supported further cancellation, the administration emphasized the demands of American taxpayers and the extent of the generosity already demonstrated by the American government. In response to critics who questioned the wisdom of this generosity, the administration enumerated the requirements of American trade.[63]

While the American debt settlement with Britain set precedents for the future, it did not depart substantially from the experience of the past. Congressional influence in decision-making was modified, but not circumvented. Conflicting fiscal and commercial pressures were compromised, but not reconciled. The political intensity of the issue was cooled, but not quenched. As a result, Republican debt policy in the 1920s illustrated the difficulty of formulating foreign policy in an atmosphere of political partisanship and economic transformation. The indecisiveness of American policymakers in handling the debt issue did not result from their ignorance of economic factors. It stemmed from the conflict between commercial and fiscal requirements on a politically sensitive issue that was often discussed in moral platitudes. The same difficulty of setting priorities plagued the business community as well.

Examining the origins of American debt policy from the perspective of the open door interpretation not only reveals much about debt refunding but also a great deal about the open door thesis itself. By focusing attention on certain

60. Hoover felt that the terms of the British debt accord should have been more lenient. Herbert Hoover, *The Memoirs of Herbert Hoover* (3 vols.; New York, 1952), 2, 178; Winston, "American War Debt Policy," 11.

61. World War Foreign Debt Commission, Combined Annual Reports of the World War Foreign Debt Commission with Additional Information Regarding Foreign Debts Due the United States, Fiscal Years 1922, 1923, 1924, 1925, and 1926 (Washington, 1927), 36–38.

62. The War Debt Commission did not function in a scientifically objective way. Much economic data was accumulated, but the extent to which it was used is uncertain. The commission was always sensitive to the reactions of Congress. For an example of the economic data used in framing a debt settlement, see boxes 58 and 59, Records of the Bureau of Accounts (Treasury).

63. Howard H. Quint and Robert H. Ferrell, eds., *The Talkative President: The Off-the-Record Press Conferences of Calvin Coolidge* (Amherst, Mass., 1964), 193–94, 195, 196, 198; World War Foreign Debt Commission, *Combined Annual Reports . . .* , 300–11.

apparent economic imperatives of American diplomacy, exponents of the open door thesis have compelled all diplomatic historians to grapple with a complex set of criteria that heretofore had been frequently minimized. By failing to weigh and to balance the relative importance of commercial considerations vis-à-vis other economic, fiscal, strategic, and political factors, they have been able to emphasize a particular viewpoint of foreign policy development. To examine the commercial aspects of foreign policy, however, is to analyze only one phase of a complex process. Consequently, the full significance of the open door thesis will emerge only after its advocates—and its critics—judiciously weigh the relative importance of frequently conflicting pressures upon those responsible for shaping national policies.

# 2

# Herbert Hoover, the "New Era," and American Foreign Policy, 1921–1929

As a graduate student I read extensively in the burgeoning literature on the Progressive movement. New books and articles highlighted the diverse strands of progressivism and the complex motives of the so-called reformers. While Richard Hofstadter and George Mowry focused on the status revolution and the psychological adjustments necessitated by the economic transformation of the nation, Gabriel Kolko, Robert Wiebe, Alfred Chandler, and Samuel Hays illuminated the complexity of the business response and the importance of the managerial revolution under way. No student of the Progressive Era, however, could ignore the growing labor strife, the organization of working men and women, the challenge of assimilating millions of immigrants, and the spread of ideological radicalism. Robert Wiebe seemed most effectively to synthesize the divergent developments in his book *The Search for Order, 1877–1920* (New York: Hill and Wang, 1967).

In the quest for stability, professionals, managers, and enlightened businessmen loomed large. They appeared to possess the knowledge and the methods to study societal problems objectively, and to offer solutions that might reconcile clashing interests and serve the needs of the larger community without overextending the role of government.

Herbert C. Hoover was such a man. In the 1970s, his place in American history was being reconceived by historians like Joan Hoff Wilson and Ellis Hawley. In their view, Hoover was not the heartless and dogmatic conservative who waged relentless war against the New Deal; actually, he was a "forgotten progressive." (See Joan Hoff Wilson, *Herbert Hoover: Forgotten Progressive* [Boston: Little, Brown, and Company, 1975.]) Trained as an engineer, widely traveled, and committed to scientific management, Hoover wanted to use knowledge to transcend class divisions and national rivalries without overextending the reach of government. Serving as an adviser to President Woodrow Wilson during World War I and orchestrating the distribution of relief after the conflict, he believed that the system of democratic capitalism was beleaguered by mass politics and the ideological appeal of rival systems of political economy. He wanted to safeguard the American way of life, the defining quality of which was individual opportunity. He believed that to achieve this goal he had to encourage businessmen, workers, and farmers to see that their interests could be served through voluntary cooperation.

By the time I was doing my research on the 1920s, Hoover's influence inside the Harding administration was well understood. As secretary of commerce, he asked for and was granted permission to deal with all matters relating to the nation's business and prosperity. He injected himself into all the complicated issues of European reconstruction and international trade. His interests stretched from Latin America to Western Europe to Southeast Asia. There was no place on the globe that escaped the purview of the economists and experts who staffed the Bureau of Foreign and Domestic Commerce.

But how exactly did Hoover's "progressive" background, engineering training, and ideological beliefs influence his approach to the problems of European reconstruction? In this essay I tried to explore how the progressive search for apolitical solutions at home based on objective criteria and voluntary collaboration influenced the foreign policy of the postwar decade. I also wanted to explain why that approach failed.

Hoover was no isolationist. He was totally aware of the economic interdependence of the world. He wanted peace, arms limitation, and stability, yet was unwilling to incur U.S. strategic commitments. Carefully calculating America's responsibilities abroad in relation to its priorities at home, he championed incremental initiatives and apolitical solutions.

His approach seemed to work for a while, but then fell apart because of flawed assumptions, the exigencies of the financial collapse and Great Depression, and his own political aspirations. Involvement without commitment made sense but did not work. But rather than opt for additional commitments, Hoover slowly retrenched.

This essay appeared in a volume edited by Ellis W. Hawley, *Herbert Hoover as Secretary of Commerce: Studies in New Era Thought and Practice* (Iowa City: University of Iowa Press, 1974), 149–179.

———

In recent years there has been a continuing reappraisal of the career of Herbert Hoover placing him in the domestic progressive tradition from which he stemmed. No longer is Hoover portrayed as the reactionary and callous conservative reluctant to use governmental powers to alleviate distress and to cope with the problems of the depression. Instead, he increasingly appears as a twentieth-century enlightened manager and scientific reformer engrossed in the problems of stabilizing modern industrial society, involved in the effort to promote harmony between capital and labor, devoted to the task of fostering cooperative competition among businessmen, committed to the use of systematic approaches to solve national problems, and inclined to accept limited governmental responsibility in the struggle to manage the business cycle and eradicate poverty. Hoover, of course, carefully placed constraints on the functions of government. Moreover, he loathed the proliferation of bureaucracy, extolled the principles of self-help and voluntary cooperation, and glorified the virtues of equal opportunity and individual initiative. His significance, therefore, rests in his being a transitional figure in American history in his effort to adapt traditional American principles and values, such as individual opportunity and free enterprise, to a new era that he correctly recognized was under way.[1]

Hoover's emphasis on recognizing the interdependence of the modern world, on fostering the use of experts, on finding apolitical solutions, on encouraging private voluntary and cooperative action, and on enlarging but circumscribing the role of government characterized his approach to foreign policy no less than his attitudes toward domestic policy. Indeed, the transference of Hoover's assumptions and methods from the realm of domestic policy into the arena of international diplomacy was remarkable. And just as his domestic policies provided a bridge between the New Freedom and the New

1. See, for example, David Burner, *Herbert Hoover: A Public Life* (New York, 1979); Joan Hoff Wilson, *Herbert Hoover: Forgotten Progressive* (Boston, 1975); Craig Lloyd, *Aggressive Introvert: A Study of Herbert Hoover and Public Relations Management* (Columbus, Ohio, 1972); Martin L. Fausold and George T. Mazuzan, *The Hoover Presidency: A Reappraisal* (Albany, 1974); Robert H. Zieger, *Republicans and Labor, 1919–1929* (Lexington, 1969), especially pp. 61–70, 271ff.; Ellis W. Hawley, "Herbert Hoover, the Commerce Secretarial, and the Vision of an Associative State, 1921–1928," *Journal of American History*, 61 (June 1974), 116–40; Evan B. Metcalf, "Secretary Hoover and the Emergence of Macro-economic Management," *Business History Review*, 49 (Spring 1975), 60–80; Barry D. Karl, "Presidential Planning and Social Science Research: Mr. Hoover's Experts," *Perspectives in American History*, 3 (1969), 347–409; Carolyn Grin, "The Unemployment Conference of 1921: An Experiment in National Cooperative Planning," *Mid-America*, 55 (April 1973), 83–107; Albert U. Romasco, *The Poverty of Abundance: Hoover, the Nation, the Depression* (New York, 1965); Gary Dean Best, *The Politics of American Individualism: Herbert Hoover in Transition* (Westport, Conn., 1975); the essay by Ellis Hawley in J. Joseph Huthmacher and Warren I. Susman, eds., *Herbert Hoover and the Crisis of American Capitalism* (Cambridge, Mass., 1973), pp. 1–33; Robert H. Zieger, "Herbert Hoover: A Reinterpretation," *American Historical Review*, 81 (October 1976), 800–810.

Deal, so did his foreign policies constitute a critical link in the evolution of American foreign policy in the twentieth century. In other words, Hoover's "New Era" approach to foreign policy took notice of America's important place in world economic affairs, but did not make the functioning of the world economy the primary responsibility of the United States government; it acknowledged the interrelationships between the American economy and the international economy, but did not consider the survival of American liberal capitalistic institutions contingent upon overseas expansion; it accepted the fact that events elsewhere affected American interests, but did not call for political and military action to protect those interests; it took cognizance of the impact of World War I on international economic and social affairs, but did not call for the military suppression of revolutionary movements; it postulated the superiority of American institutions, but did not call for their forceful imposition upon others. This orientation toward international affairs distinguished Hoover from post–World War II globalists and identified him with those World War I functionalists inside and outside the peace movement who called for a managerial approach to world order and world peace.[2] Yet, despite the balance and perspicuity that characterized Hoover's approach to foreign policy, it ultimately failed because of its own inherent inconsistencies and because of Hoover's personal failure to live up to the high standards he set for himself. These themes can be elucidated by briefly examining Hoover's view of international relations and by more closely analyzing his managerial approach to European affairs.

I

Hoover realized that the advancement of science, the progress of technology, the revolution in transportation and communication, and the migration of capital had bred worldwide economic interdependence. The Great War had magnified the social consequences of this economic interdependence by unleashing new social philosophies and ideological movements that competed for the support of peoples everywhere. Referring to the chaos in Europe in

2. Internationalists during the era of the First World War recognized the interrelationships between American well-being and world stability, but unlike post–World War II globalists they wanted to carefully circumscribe the nation's political commitments. See Warren F. Kuehl, *Seeking World Order: The United States and International Organization to 1920* (Nashville, 1969); also see Charles de Benedetti, "Alternative Strategies in the American Peace Movement in the 1920s," *American Studies*, 13 (Spring 1972), 69–71. Two excellent studies shedding considerable light on Hoover's approach to foreign policy in the 1920s are: Joseph Brandes, *Herbert Hoover and Economic Diplomacy: Department of Commerce Policy 1921–1928* (Pittsburgh, 1962); Joan Hoff Wilson, *American Business and Foreign Policy, 1920–1933* (Lexington, Ky., 1971). For a brief discussion of globalism and its implications, see William Taubman, ed., *Globalism and Its Critics: The American Foreign Policy Debate of the 1960s* (Lexington, Mass., 1973).

1920, Hoover stated that "every wind that blows carries to our shores an infection of social disease from this great ferment; every convulsion there has an economic reaction upon our own people."[3] Indeed, the forces of technology had bound together the fate of all peoples and had knit together the economies of all nations. During his goodwill tour of Latin America in 1928, Hoover explained to his listeners in Rio de Janeiro:

> A century ago, our countries could and did live a more primitive life without the exchange of products of the Temperate Zone for coffee, rubber, and a score of other articles. Today, however, but for the products which we exchange, not a single automobile would run; not a dynamo would turn; not a telephone, telegraph, or radio would operate; a thousand daily necessities and luxuries would disappear. In fact, without these exchanges of commodities, huge masses of humanity who have now become dependent upon an intensive and highly attuned civilization could not be kept alive.[4]

Given his view of the unified structure of the modern world economy, Hoover often stressed the importance of maintaining international peace and world stability. He firmly believed "that the delicate machinery of social organization, of production and commerce upon which our civilization is founded [could] not stand such a shock [as the war] again."[5] Moreover, he assumed that if world peace and international stability could be maintained, world demand would tend normally to grow.[6] This assumption was of great importance because Hoover postulated a close interrelationship between world purchasing power, American exports, and the overall economic well-being of the United States. Economic recovery and financial stability abroad meant prosperity at home. In 1928 Hoover described the workings of the business cycle on an interdependent world economy in the following way:

> The forces of credit, communications, transportation, power, foreign relations, and whatnot must all be kept in tune if steady employment is to be

3. "Mr. Hoover's Inauguration Address to the American Institute of Mining and Metallurgical Engineers," February 17, 1920, copy in New York Public Library; also see Herbert C. Hoover, *Addresses Delivered during the Visit of Herbert Hoover to Central and South America, November-December, 1928* (Washington, 1929), pp. 33, 36, 47; Herbert Clark Hoover, *The New Day: Campaign Speeches of Herbert Hoover* (Stanford, 1928), p. 11.

4. Hoover, *Addresses*, p. 58.

5. Herbert Hoover, "America's Next Step," *World Peace Foundation Pamphlet Series*, 6 (1923), 67–68.

6. Department of Commerce, *Fourteenth Annual Report of the Secretary of Commerce* (Washington, 1926), p. 34 [hereinafter this source shall be cited as Department of Commerce, *Annual Report* (year), page]. Also see undated memorandum, "Hoover's Thoughts on Foreign Trade," [mid-1920s], Herbert Hoover Papers (Herbert Hoover Presidential Library, West Branch, Iowa), Commerce Section, Foreign Trade; Hoover, *New Day*, p. 98.

assured. A failure in any part imposes a penalty upon labor through unemployment. Break this chain of relationship at any point and the whole machine is thrown out of order. . . . Cease exporting automobiles to South America or Europe, and automobile workers are thrown out of work in Michigan. The suffering does not stop there. It only begins. The steel mills slacken in Pennsylvania and Indiana. The mines employ fewer workers at Lake Superior. And every farmer in the United States suffers from diminished purchasing power.[7]

Hoover, as an enlightened business manager in the progressive tradition, felt that it was entirely possible to cope with the problems of the worldwide business cycle through the application of human intelligence, the utilization of expertise, and the institution of cooperative action. In 1920, he called upon his fellow engineers to take a more active interest in solving national and international problems, and he urged all Americans to adopt "the attitude that marks the successes of America, the attitude of the business man, of the engineer, and of the scientist." The great problems of the day, he proclaimed, were susceptible to solution through quantitative analysis and cooperative action.[8] And subsequently, he repeatedly urged the accumulation of statistical information that would enable the United States to play a more intelligent role in world affairs. At the Geneva Economic Conference in 1927, for example, American representatives suggested that one means of coping with the world agricultural crisis was through the better collection of data pertaining to production, markets, prices, consumption patterns, and costs of production. This was the essential prerequisite for possible subsequent cooperative efforts to regulate agricultural production and land utilization on an international scale.[9] Through such methods of scientific investigation and voluntary cooperative action, Hoover believed much progress was possible.

In domestic affairs Hoover had little faith in the ability of political institutions or legislative enactments to settle complex modern problems. In 1924 he wrote, "Regulation and laws are of but minor effect on . . . fundamental things. But by well-directed economic forces, by cooperation in the community" sub-

7. Hoover, *New Day*, pp. 64–65; also see, for example, ibid., pp. 117–19; Herbert Hoover, "Backing up Business: The Larger Purpose of the Department of Commerce," *Review of Reviews*, 78 (July 1928), 278–79.

8. For the quotation, see Herbert Hoover, "Foreword," in Elisha M. Friedman, *America and the New Era* (New York, 1920), p. xxiv; also see "Mr. Hoover's Inauguration Address to the American Institute of Mining and Metallurgical Engineers," February 17, 1920, p. 8; Department of Commerce, *Annual Report*, 1922, pp. 30–32; Conference on Unemployment, *Report of the President's Conference on Unemployment* (Washington, 1921), pp. 28–30, 33–34, 158–59.

9. United States Interdepartmental Committee, "Agriculture," March 1927, Records of the Bureau of Foreign and Domestic Commerce (RG 151, National Archives), 600.2 (Geneva, Agriculture). For a good brief description of the work of the experts in the Department of Commerce, see Brandes, *Hoover and Economic Diplomacy*, pp. 3–22.

stantial progress was possible. Accordingly, he hoped to establish close ties between the administrative side of government and associational forces in the community.[10] Similarly, in foreign affairs he had little confidence in the efficacy of international political agreements and sought to avoid accords that were based on coercion. Instead he was willing to rely on "seasoned public opinion. . . . Its mobilization at home and the cooperation in its use with other nations abroad is our contribution to peace." Thus, Hoover could be satisfied with arms limitations and consultative agreements (for example, the Washington treaties and the Kellogg-Briand Pact) that did not provide for inspection and enforcement. This was the corollary of voluntarism on the domestic level. "[T]he essence of accomplishment in government," and in international relations Hoover might have added, "lies in that threadbare expression—cooperation," not compulsion.[11]

By advocating the application of business principles to international relations, Hoover desired to take international questions out of the hands of politicians where they often were treated on the basis of emotion and to put them into the hands of experts where they would be analyzed according to the dictates of fact. Domestic and international political factors, in his opinion, only confused and obscured what were admittedly complex but, nevertheless, soluble international questions. These questions, Hoover contended, were more predominantly economic than at any time in American history. For this reason, he considered them susceptible to the type of empirical investigation and systematic management that he so greatly cherished. Consequently, after World War I, Hoover sought to develop viable institutional mechanisms that would provide for the settlement of international issues in an impartial way and on an objective basis. And for those disputes that did not lend themselves to solution by economic experts and financial analysts, he advocated the use of legal formulae and juridic principles. These, too, supposedly had the advantage of underscoring the importance of apolitical considerations and impartial examination.[12]

Hoover maintained that the American government still had an important but circumscribed role to play in the resolution of great international

10. Department of Commerce, *Annual Report*, 1924, p. 10; Theodore Joslin, ed., *Hoover After Dinner: Addresses Delivered by Herbert Hoover* (New York, 1933), pp. 9–10; Conference on Unemployment, *Report*, p. 29; Herbert Hoover, *American Individualism* (Garden City, 1922), pp. 10–11.

11. For the quotations, see Joslin, *Hoover After Dinner*, pp. 10, 23; also see Hoover, *New Day*, p. 39; Hoover, "America's Next Step," 65–66.

12. For Hoover's attitudes, see, for example, Hoover, "America's Next Step," 64–65; "Mr. Hoover's Inauguration Address to the American Institute of Mining and Metallurgical Engineers," February 17, 1920, p. 8; Hoover to Benjamin Strong, August 30, 1921, Benjamin Strong Papers (Federal Reserve Bank of New York, New York City), 013.1 (Hoover); Hoover, *New Day*, pp. 39, 115.

questions. Its legitimate obligation was to sponsor empirical studies, to encourage private cooperative action, to cultivate apolitical institutions, and to promote a modified open door.[13] He warned, however, that it was economically unconstructive and politically destabilizing for the government to enter directly into international business transactions or to assume political commitments. Government credits and state monopoly controls politicized international business affairs, aroused national sentiments, and bred international animosity. In addition, such direct state economic intervention stifled constructive competition and generated inefficient production.[14] Thus, Hoover's conception of the New Era in American foreign policy was one in which the United States government played a continuous and constructive but carefully delimited role in helping to preserve world peace, prosperity, and stability.

## II

Since Hoover believed that modern civilization was complex, organic, and ever-changing, he disdained comprehensive solutions to international questions and advocated piecemeal and systematic efforts to cope with pressing world problems.[15] In 1923, he maintained that "wisdom [in international affairs] does not so much consist in knowledge of the ultimate; it consists in knowing what to do next." He praised the Harding administration, of which he was a leading member, for the success of the Washington Disarmament Conference and for the current recommendation to join the Permanent Court for International Justice. Emphasizing that these were only initial steps toward the ultimate goal of preserving world peace, he chided the critics of the administration. "Those who condemn the proposal [for joining the World Court] because it is merely one method are the ones who would have complained on the Wednesday night of Genesis, and would have gone to bed with a grouch because the Creator had not yet made a finished job of the sun and moon, and would have called a mass meeting on Thursday morning to de-

13. For discussions bearing on the nature of the open door policy during this period, see, for example, Wilson, *American Business and Foreign Policy*, especially pp. 157–219; Carl Parrini, *Heir to Empire: United States Economic Diplomacy, 1916–1923* (Pittsburgh, 1969); Joseph S. Tulchin, *The Aftermath of War: World War I and U.S. Policy toward Latin America* (New York, 1971); Michael J. Hogan, *Informal Entente: The Private Structure of Cooperation in Anglo-American Economic Diplomacy, 1918–1928* (Columbia, Mo., 1977).

14. See, for example, Hoover, "Backing up Business," 280; Herbert Hoover, *The Memoirs of Herbert Hoover*, 3 vols. (New York, 1951–52), 2:13–14; Herbert Hoover, "Momentous Conference," *Journal of the American Bankers Association*, 13 (January 1921), 462–63; also see Everett G. Holt, "Foreign Government Price Fixing of Our Import Raw Materials," in Department of Commerce, *Annual Report*, 1926, pp. 36–37.

15. Hoover, "Foreword," in Friedman, *America and the New Era*, p. 14; Joslin, *Hoover After Dinner*, p. 10.

mand more forward action." Such forward action, Hoover indicated, would be forthcoming. "[T]he rejection of one particular device [the League of Nations]," he stated, "does not mean that America has lost interest in finding a solution" to world peace and international cooperation.[16]

Indeed, Hoover had supported the League of Nations in 1919, not because he considered it an ultimate answer to the turmoil wrought by the war, but because it provided an institutional framework, that is, a World Council, where grievances could be raised, uncorrected wrongs discussed, cooperative action cultivated, and the "intelligence of the world" mobilized. He had not viewed the league as a mechanism for permanently embroiling the United States in the world's political and military affairs. Quite the contrary, he had hoped that the league would "forever relieve the United States of the necessity to again send a single soldier outside of our boundaries."[17] Precisely because he had considered the league a means to an end rather than an end in itself, he was prepared, when the Senate rejected the league, to seek other mechanisms and instruments that would enable the United States to contribute to world stability and prosperity without incurring political entanglements. But these means had to be based on the use of expertise, the promotion of voluntary action, and the subordination of political factors.

Before accepting the position of secretary of commerce in 1921, Hoover requested and was granted authority to deal with all aspects of the American economy.[18] He immediately set to work to cope with the severe economic slump that was then under way. Like most businessmen of the day, Hoover believed that the expansion of foreign trade would improve the domestic economic situation. But the revival of commerce itself depended upon constructive efforts to solve pressing international economic questions, especially those pertaining to European economic reconstruction.[19] Therefore, Hoover began examining solutions to such problems as unstable currencies, excessive armaments, unsettled war debts and reparations, unproductive foreign loans, and depressed foreign trade.

In 1921 the international issue causing most alarm among American businessmen was the instability of currencies. Hoover considered this to be virtually the greatest impediment to foreign trade. In the immediate postwar years,

16. Hoover, "America's Next Step," 61–67.
17. "Mr. Hoover's Address Before the Students of Stanford University," October 2, 1919, 3ff., copy in New York Public Library. As opposition to the league proliferated, Hoover qualified his view and supported the peace treaty with reservations. See Hoover, *Memoirs*, 2:10–13.
18. Ibid., p. 36.
19. Ibid., pp. 79ff.; also see, for example, Conference on Unemployment, *Report*, pp. 147–49, 158–59; for the primacy of European affairs, see Robert Neal Seidel, "Progressive Pan Americanism: Development and United States Policy Toward South America, 1906–1931," PhD diss. (Cornell University, 1973), 521, 600.

fluctuating exchange rates and depreciating foreign currencies generated uncertainty, retarded exports, and enhanced the competitive ability of foreign products in the American market.[20] Hoover immediately sought to find ways to stabilize currencies and restore the gold standard as a means of facilitating worldwide economic rehabilitation and of promoting American overseas sales. During the summer of 1921, he turned his attention to the commercial and financial problems besetting Central European nations. He asked Benjamin Strong, governor of the Federal Reserve Bank of New York, whether private banking institutions here and abroad could not take responsibility for formulating a plan of financial cooperation aimed at rehabilitating currencies. Claiming that constructive political measures were unlikely, the commerce secretary urged that recovery depended upon divorcing economic from political action. He contended that the central banks of Europe and the Federal Reserve Bank of New York could bring about the stabilization of currencies through the mobilization of private capital and thereby avoid the political pitfalls inherent in governmental action.[21]

In the short run, the stabilization of currencies and the restoration of the gold standard were not achieved through central bank cooperation. But in the mid-1920s cooperation between central banking institutions became a primary instrument for fostering international currency stability as the essential prerequisite for the expansion of international commerce. Central bankers crisscrossed the Atlantic in their continuous attempts to keep in touch with foreign developments, to reconcile monetary policies, and to cooperate voluntarily in restoring a modified gold standard. In 1925, the Federal Reserve Bank of New York began extending credits to England and other major European nations to facilitate their return to a gold exchange standard. Subsequently, the Federal Reserve Board managed discount rates and engaged in open market operations with a close eye on European monetary developments. Adolph Miller, a member of the Federal Reserve Board, later recalled that this was regarded "as a brilliant exploit in central bank policy and as a demonstration of the reasonableness of the belief, that through well-conceived and well-timed monetary policy[,] the terrors of the business cycle

20. For Hoover's view, see Herbert Hoover and Hugh Gibson, *The Problems of Lasting Peace* (New York, 1942), pp. 213–14; for concern over the issue of currency instability, also see, for example, "Western Bankers Dinner and Conference at the White House," June 23, 1921, Warren Harding Papers, Ohio Historical Society (Columbus, Ohio), box 88, File 57, Folder 1; Charles E. Mitchell, *Back to First Principles* (n.p., 1922), pp. 8, 16; Special Committee of the Chamber of Commerce, "European Problems Affecting American Business," *Nation's Business*, 9 (October 5, 1921), 2–3; House, Committee on Banking and Currency, *Exchange Stabilization* (Washington, 1921).

21. Hoover to Strong, August 30, 1921, Strong Papers, 013.1 (Hoover); Strong to Pierre Jay, August 29, 1921, ibid., 320.115 (Jay).

could be largely if not wholly removed and price stability and economic prosperity be insured. It will not be forgotten that by many the opening of the year
1928 was heralded as the beginning in these respects, as well as in many others, of a new era."[22]

Republican officials applauded these developments. Treasury officials, in
particular, kept in close contact with Strong and his associates at the Federal
Reserve Bank of New York. They encouraged, supported, and sometimes even
guided specific actions.[23] By delegating the task of restoring the gold standard
to the central bankers, government officials (in the United States and abroad)
hoped to remove this goal from political considerations. Indeed, Strong always insisted that in return for Federal Reserve credits, central bankers abroad
had to achieve full independence from their respective governments. It was
hoped that if central bank policy were insulated from the political process,
then national and international monetary policies could be molded intelli-
gently on the basis of economic and financial criteria.[24] This informal collaboration of assumedly disinterested experts was not accompanied by any binding commitments and simply resulted from the bankers' common appreciation
of their mutual interests.

Central bank cooperation conformed to Hoover's standards of enlightened
action. It utilized "expertise"; it called for voluntary action; it was "apolitical."
It proceeded with the approval of the administrative side of government, the
Treasury Department. Therefore, though the secretary of commerce had mis-
givings about the utilization of discount rates and open market operations to
accommodate European financial needs, in the mid-1920s he did appreciate
the importance of Federal Reserve efforts to maintain currency stability. His
criticisms of Federal Reserve policies stemmed from his belief that Strong
was overemphasizing the international basis of American prosperity and

---

22. A. C. Miller, "The Federal Reserve Policies, 1927–29," *American Economic Review*, 25
(September 1935), 447; for central bank cooperation, also see the excellent studies by L. V. Chandler, *Benjamin Strong: Central Banker* (Washington, 1958); Stephen V. O. Clarke, *Central Bank
Cooperation, 1924–1931* (New York, 1967); Richard H. Meyer, *Banker's Diplomacy* (New York,
1970).

23. Evidence of the close contact between the Treasury Department and the Federal Reserve
Bank of New York may be found in the letters and memoranda pertaining to Strong's European
trips, 1925–29, Strong Papers, 1000.5–1000.9 (Strong's Trips); Winston-Strong Correspondence,
Bureau of Accounts (RG 39, National Archives), box 220; for Republican officials' support of
Strong's efforts, also see United States Treasury Department, *Annual Report of the Secretary of the
Treasury, 1928* (Washington, 1929), pp. 348–49; Howard H. Quint and Robert Ferrell, *The Talk-
ative President: The Off-the-Record Press Conferences of Calvin Coolidge* (Amherst, Mass., 1964),
p. 142; Chandler, *Strong*, pp. 247–58.

24. See Meyer, *Bankers' Diplomacy*, p. 8; for Strong's negotiations with central bankers, see,
for example, the memoranda of his talks with the French in 1926, Strong Papers, 1000.7 (Strong's
Trips, 1926).

underestimating the importance of sound internal financial conditions. But, in general, he acquiesced to Federal Reserve policies because he believed that the ultimate goal, the reestablishment of the prewar gold standard, would institutionalize a process of automatic adjustments between national economies and thereby diminish the prospect that national or international political considerations might interfere with financial developments.[25]

During 1921, however, the secretary of commerce quickly realized that before much progress could be made toward stabilizing foreign currencies, matters such as armaments and reparations had to be handled constructively. In May 1921, he wrote President Warren G. Harding:

> There is nothing that would give such hope of recovery in life and living as to have this terrible burden and menace [arms expenditures] taken from the minds and backs of men. As Secretary of Commerce, if I were to review in order of importance those things of the world that would best restore commerce, I would inevitably arrive at the removal of this, the first and primary obstruction.[26]

Hoover, like many of his contemporaries, viewed armaments as an impediment to economic rehabilitation because arms expenditures weighed so heavily on government finances, thus contributing to budgetary deficits and to currency instability. Naturally, then, he was a strong supporter of the Washington Conference of 1921.[27] And insofar as that conference limited naval armaments, reaffirmed the open door, and provided for consultation in East Asia, all without imposing political commitments, the treaties accorded with Hoover's emphasis on dealing with international issues on their merits through voluntary and cooperative international action.[28]

To Hoover, the progressive organization of peace demanded military retrenchment not only in naval armaments but also in land armaments. He was particularly upset with the French because of their large military expenditures and substantial standing army. French armaments constituted an unbearable strain on French finances, affected France's capacity to meet her wartime obligations, and caused economic dislocations throughout Europe.[29] France, of

25. Hoover's bitter criticisms of Federal Reserve policy are well known. See Hoover, *Memoirs*, 3:6–14. But also notice his recognition of the importance of Federal Reserve attempts to restore the gold standard. See Department of Commerce, *Annual Report*, 1925, pp. 35–37; ibid., 1926, pp. 12–13, 50.

26. Robert H. Van Meter, "The United States and European Recovery, 1918–23: A Study of Public Policy and Private Finance," PhD diss. (University of Wisconsin, 1971), 299.

27. Ibid., 295–305; also see Hoover to Harding, January 4, 1922, Harding Papers, box 5, File 3, Folder 2.

28. Hoover, "America's Next Step," 62–63.

29. Hoover to Harding, January 4, 1922, Harding Papers, box 5, File 3, Folder 2; Julius Klein to Walter S. Tower, January 4, 1922, BFDC Records, 600.2 (Genoa Conference).

course, would not voluntarily agree to limit land armaments without firm guarantees of her security. In other words, she refused to cooperate in the settlement of what Hoover liked to consider economic issues without inter-jecting political and strategic factors. As a result, the secretary of commerce sought other means to influence French behavior. Within the cabinet, he be-came the leading advocate of using financial leverage to force other nations to curtail arms expenditures.[30] Such proposals reflected his continuing pre-occupation with organizing the forces of peace, as he defined them, when economic arguments were rejected and when appeals to international volun-tarism were ignored.

In the early 1920s, the secretary of commerce maintained that the repara-tions issue was the other great impediment to European currency stability, world prosperity, and American well-being. The enormous reparations bur-den imposed upon Germany contributed to the fluctuation of European ex-change rates, the depreciation of European currencies, and the consequent weakening of European purchasing power. In addition, Hoover, like many bankers and businessmen, feared that the precipitous depreciation of the mark might enable German exporters not only to flood the American market with German goods, but also to outstrip their competitors in the quest for world markets. Therefore, the commerce secretary carefully estimated what Germany was capable of paying without disrupting world commercial and financial conditions.[31] But in the view of American officials, even more impor-tant than specific figures was the creation of some mechanism that would enable the United States to cooperate unofficially in the resolution of this problem, that would divorce the issue from political considerations, and that would facilitate the voluntary mobilization of the beneficent forces in the pri-vate banking community.[32]

30. Financial leverage could be exerted by either restricting private American financial aid or refusing to reduce war debt payments. See, for example, Hoover to Harding, December 31, 1921, Harding Papers, box 88, File 57, Folder 3; Hoover to Andrew Mellon, January 6, 1923, Hoover Papers, Commerce Section, Foreign Debts; Hoover to Charles Evans Hughes, November 20, 1924, General Records of the Department of State (RG 59, National Archives), 851.51/499 (filed as 800.51/499).

31. Hoover to Harding, January 4, 1922, Harding Papers, box 5, File 3, Folder 2; Klein to Tower, January 4, 1922, BFDC Records, 600.2 (Genoa Conference). For widespread business concern regarding the impact of reparations, see, for example, Special Committee of the Cham-ber of Commerce, "European Problems Affecting American Business," 3; Special Committee of the National Foreign Trade Council, "Report on European Conditions," in *Official Report of the Tenth National Foreign Trade Convention* (New York, 1923), pp. 15ff.; Strong to James A. Logan, October 3, 1921, Federal Reserve Bank Papers (Federal Reserve Bank of New York), C797.

32. Hoover, *Memoirs*, 2:182; Alan G. Goldsmith, *Economic Problems of Western Europe* (n.p., 1923), pp. 1, 22; Charles Evans Hughes, *The Pathway of Peace* (New York, 1925), pp. 53–58, 108; undated memoranda (probably August 1922), by Roland Boyden, Leland Harrison Papers (Man-uscript Division, Library of Congress), box 2.

The creation of committees of businessmen and bankers to study the reorganization of Germany's finances and to determine Germany's ability to pay reparations served as an ideal means to cope with the reparations crisis. The appearance of so-called experts dealing with the problem on a "business" basis raised the possibility of removing the issue from domestic politics in all nations and of facilitating an accord that politicians might accept without certainty of political retribution. Moreover, policymakers in the United States anticipated that the American experts would remain in close contact with government officials. Therefore, Republican officials assumed that the American experts could be relied upon to present the American program for a settlement based on economic, not political, considerations. At the same time, the experts were expected to stifle all proposals linking the war debt issue to a reparations settlement. They could do this without impairing American bargaining power because any reparations accord depended upon the flotation of an international loan in the United States.[33]

The Dawes Plan, however, did not entirely satisfy the secretary of commerce or his subordinates. The Commerce Department officials who served behind the scenes as technical advisers to the American experts complained that the Dawes annuities were too high, that the controls were too cumbersome, and that political factors had not been sufficiently disregarded.[34] But Hoover decided to support the Dawes Plan, as agreed upon in London in August 1924, because there was no constructive alternative. In his *Annual Report* for 1924, Hoover wrote that the plan was "the first effort to solve the reparations question purely on a commercial and economic basis." Moreover, it had won the voluntary support of prominent banking institutions. And perhaps most significant to the secretary of commerce, the plan had "within itself machinery for correction or alteration of details as difficulties arise in its execution." By establishing the office of agent general with extensive powers to regulate transfers, to oversee the entire Dawes machinery, and to recommend eventual revisions, the plan created the most apolitical machinery

33. For the ties between the "experts," government officials, and American financiers, see the materials in R-6, 12, 14, 16, Owen D. Young Papers (Van Hornesville, New York); Alan Goldsmith—Christian Herter Correspondence, in Leonard P. Ayres Papers (Manuscript Division, Library of Congress), box 4; diary entries, October-December 1923, William Phillips Papers (Houghton Library, Harvard University), box 1A; Thomas W. Lamont Papers (Baker Library, Harvard University), boxes 176, 177; also see Hughes, *Pathway of Peace*, pp. 108, 57–58; Charles G. Dawes, *A Journal of Preparations* (New York, 1939). For a superb account of American influence on the 1924 reparations settlement, see Stephen Schuker, *The End of French Predominance in Europe: The Financial Crisis of 1924 and the Adoption of the Dawes Plan* (Chapel Hill, N.C., 1976).

34. See the Goldsmith-Herter Correspondence in Ayres Papers, box 4; also see Goldsmith and Herring to Hoover, April 12, 1924, BFDC Records, 3266 (Incoming Confidential Cables); Alanson Houghton to William Castle, April 6, 1924, William Castle Papers (Herbert Hoover Presidential Library, West Branch, Iowa), box 4.

that could be expected to deal with such an emotion-laden issue. It was hoped that with the return of currency stability and the free flow of private capital, salutary economic forces might eventually permit additional constructive action.[35]

Hoover recognized that the problem of war debts was unavoidably linked to the other questions of reparations, arms limitation, and currency rehabilitation. As in the case of these other issues, he avowedly sought to divorce the war debts question from political considerations, to resolve it according to economic criteria, and to use it as an instrument to manage the determinants of European stability. Like other members of the Harding cabinet, he would have preferred to tackle the war debts controversy through the administrative side of government. But when Congress refused to relinquish control over this matter, Hoover accepted the World War Foreign Debt Commission as an appropriate institutional means to handle the debt settlements.[36]

Hoover, however, rejected the harsh terms set by Congress. Instead he urged that the War Debt Commission, of which he was a leading member, demand the full payment of principal, but adjust interest payments according to the capacity-to-pay formula. Interest payments, the secretary of commerce rightly contended, were of much greater quantitative significance over the long run than the return of principal. By adjusting interest payments according to the capacity of nations, he hoped to secure the largest possible return to the American people without disrupting currency stability and international commerce. He recognized that nations could make international transfers only through the export of gold, commodities, or services. And he realized that since there were limits on the ability of nations to export, adjustments had to be made to meet individual circumstances.[37] The capacity formula provided a means to study particular cases on their merits and to dispense

35. For the attitudes of Hoover and the Department of Commerce, see Department of Commerce, *Annual Report*, 1924, p. 7; Goldsmith to Ayres, August 19, 1924, Ayres Papers, box 4; for Hoover's desire to cooperate with the Agent General for Reparations, see Hoover to S. Parker Gilbert, August 5, 1925, Hoover Papers, Commerce Section, Gilbert.

36. For Hoover's views on the war debts, see Hoover to Harding, January 4, 1922, Harding Papers, box 5, File 3, Folder 2; Hoover to Mellon, January 6, 1923, Hoover Papers, Commerce Section, Foreign Debts; Hoover to John S. Hamilton, December 31, 1921, ibid.; for Hoover's Toledo speech, see *The Commercial and Financial Chronicle*, 115 (October 21, 1922), 1781ff. For the Republicans' initial desire to treat the war debts through the administrative branch of government, see Melvyn Leffler, "The Origins of Republican War Debt Policy, 1921–1923: A Case Study in the Applicability of the Open Door Interpretation," *Journal of American History*, 59 (December 1972), 591–92; Message of Harding to Congress, December 6, 1921, in Department of State, *Papers Relating to the Foreign Relations of the United States*, 2 vols. (Washington, 1936), 1:xxiii.

37. Hoover, drafts of letter to Joseph H. DeFrees, January 1922, Hoover Papers, Commerce Section, Economic Recovery in Europe; Hoover to Mellon, January 6, 1923, Hoover Papers, Commerce Section, Foreign Debts; Hoover to L. D. Coffman, April 27, 1926, ibid.

with political criteria. "In other words," Hoover wrote, "we slowly get ideas established into a practical economic basis, more and more stripped of the purely emotional side."[38] Accordingly, the interest payments of Italy, Belgium, and France were substantially reduced. Hoover insisted that these accords took accurate account of foreign economic conditions. But if the facts warranted greater remissions, Hoover intimated that he might still be more conciliatory. He told Thomas Lamont of J. P. Morgan and Company that he was willing to examine periodically the interest component of the debt agreements in light of changing economic circumstances.[39] He thereby acknowledged the need for continuous review in the complex task of negotiating debt settlements on the basis of the capacity formula.

According to Hoover, the capacity formula could be used not only to secure financially viable debt settlements, but also to extract concessions in other areas that would have a salutary impact on the European economy. Since the capacity formula was flexible, Hoover was willing to use it to elicit foreign concessions on such matters as arms limitation and budgetary reform. Debtors that reduced military expenditures, curtailed deficits, and stabilized currencies, Hoover argued, should receive favored treatment. This approach contradicted the notion of the capacity formula serving as a statistical means of determining what debtors could pay. But it provided Hoover with leverage in world affairs so that he could progressively organize the forces of peace.[40]

Hoover wanted to manage American capital outflows, in the same way that he adjusted war debts, to promote European stability and American prosperity. He had little doubt that experts could distinguish between productive and unproductive uses of capital, and therefore he advocated foreign loans for "reproductive purposes." In fact, the "reproductive" criterion in foreign loans was the corollary of the "capacity" formula in war debts. It could be used systematically both to reconcile internal and external demands for capital and to apply pressure on foreign nations to make concessions on vital international issues. In general, Hoover insisted that the making of foreign loans was "an economic blessing to both sides of the transaction" and that therefore the government had a moral obligation to guide American capital outflows into productive channels. He wrote Secretary of State Charles Evans Hughes in April 1922:

38. Hoover to Adolph Ochs, May 31, 1926, ibid.

39. Lamont to Dwight Morrow, October 29, 1925, Dwight Morrow Papers (Amherst College Library, Amherst, Mass.), Lamont File; also see Grosvenor Jones to Harold Phelps Stokes, January 4, 1926, Hoover Papers, Commerce Section, Foreign Debts; Hoover to Young, September 18, 1925, Young Papers, 1–13.

40. Hoover to Harding, January 4, 1922, Harding Papers, box 5, File 3, Folder 2; Memorandum, February 4, 1923, Hoover Papers, Commerce Section, Hughes; Hoover, "The French Debt," September 30, 1925, Hoover Papers, Commerce Section, Debts—France.

We are morally and selfishly interested in the economic and political recovery of all the world. America is practically the final reservoir of international capital. Unless this capital is to be employed for reproductive
purposes there is little hope of economic recovery.[41]

The United States government could effectively channel American loans
into productive purposes, Hoover maintained, by securing the voluntary cooperation of the private banking community. He denounced proposals for
direct governmental extension of loans and credits, claiming that they would
be based upon political criteria rather than economic fact, that they would be
influenced by ethnic groups in the United States, that they would lead to undesirable international political entanglements, and that they would invite
congressional meddling.[42] The objective, Hoover insisted, was not only to
help mobilize private capital for reproductive purposes, but also to insulate
the government from responsibility to intervene abroad to protect private
lending. This could be accomplished if the private banking community agreed
voluntarily to set productive loan standards in consultation with the administrative side of government.[43]

Hoover worked diligently to secure this private voluntary cooperation,
while simultaneously trying to avoid government responsibility to protect
private loans. The bankers were asked to inform the State Department regarding all proposed foreign loans. Then State, Commerce, and Treasury department officials decided whether such loans conflicted with national policies. If
they did, the bankers were so informed and were in essence requested not to
partake in the loans. Hoover wanted to define national policies in a broad way
and to ask the bankers to cooperate in barring loans to nations with large military establishments, unbalanced budgets, and unsettled war debt obligations.
Such nations, he claimed, constituted a menace to international stability and
world commerce.[44] He also disapproved of loans to government-sponsored

41. For the quotations, see Hoover to Hughes, April 29, 1922, General Records of the Department of State, 800.51/316; Herbert Hoover, *The Future of our Foreign Trade* (Washington,
1925), p. 13; also see Hoover, *Memoirs*, 2:85–91. For the government's definition of a "productive"
loan, see Treasury Department, *Annual Report*, 1926, p. 5. Initially, Hoover also had hoped to tie
American loans to American exports, but the complaints of bankers compelled a reassessment of
this practice. See Gilbert to Strong, May 21, 1921, Strong Papers, 012, 5 (Gilbert); Eliot Wad-
sworth to Fred Dearing, September 24, 1921, General Records of the Department of State,
811.51/3016.

42. For Hoover's opposition to government loans, see Hoover, "Momentous Conference,"
462–63; Hoover, *Memoirs*, 2:13–14.

43. See Hoover to Hughes, December 13, 1921, December 30, 1921, April 29, 1922, General
Records of the Department of State, 811.51/3043, 811.51/3106, 800.51/316.

44. In addition to the references cited in footnotes 41 and 43, also see Investment Bankers
Association of America, *Proceedings of the Eleventh Annual Convention* (Chicago, 1922), p. 173;
Hoover to Harding, December 31, 1921, Hoover Papers, Commerce Section, Foreign Loans; Gold-

monopolies and cartels because he considered them inefficient, uneconomic, and unsafe.[45] Furthermore, he frowned upon any loan that did not generate sufficient capital for repayment, such as loans to foreign municipalities.[46] Loans of the above types, he maintained, would eventually lead to transfer difficulties, defaults, and political entanglements. In essence, Hoover hoped to secure the voluntary cooperation of the American banking community and to apply financial leverage in his struggle to bring about European economic and financial stability. Since his Cabinet colleagues often objected to such informal cooperation with private bankers lest it generate undesired political entanglements abroad, Hoover was able to utilize American financial power only in a few instances, for example, in behalf of war debt settlements.[47]

Hoover's concern with currency stability, arms limitation, reparations, war debts, and foreign loans reflected his broader interest in maintaining international economic equilibrium in general and European financial stability in particular. He realized that if American exports were to expand without disrupting this equilibrium, foreign nations had to have sufficient dollar exchange. In order to cope with the liquidity problem, Hoover and his colleagues began to analyze the workings of the international economy and to study the flow of international payments. Recognizing that the United States had become a creditor nation, they were especially interested in the meaning and importance of invisible items in the nation's foreign economic relations. Hoover maintained that "a full comprehension of the invisible items and their approximate value is not only a profound importance in assessing our international balance sheet, but no sound conclusion can be made concerning the effect of foreign trade movements upon our credit structure or upon the ability of foreign countries to purchase our commodities or to pay their debts, or upon exchange rates, or upon the movement of gold, or the ultimate trend of

---

smith to W. C. Huntington, March 22, 1922, BFDC Records, 640 (French Loans); Hoover to Hughes, November 20, 1924, General Records of the Department of State, 851.51/499 (filed as 800.51/499). For secondary accounts of Republican loan policy, see, for example, Herbert Feis, *The Diplomacy of the Dollar* (Baltimore, 1950); Wilson, *American Business*, pp. 101–23; Tulchin, *Aftermath of War*, pp. 175–205.

45. See the excellent account by Brandes, *Hoover and Economic Diplomacy*, pp. 63–147.

46. *Commercial and Financial Chronicle*, 124 (May 7, 1927), 2687–88; for Hoover's attitudes on loans to German municipalities in particular, see the materials in Hoover Papers, Commerce Section; Foreign Loans—Germany; BFDC Records, 640 (Germany—Foreign Loans).

47. For opposition to Hoover's efforts to apply financial leverage on an extensive scale, see, for example, Harrison to Frank Kellogg, January 28, 1927, General Records of the Department of State, 800.51/558; J. T. Marriner to Castle, June 21, 1927, ibid., 800.51/566; Castle to Houghton, January 7, 1926, Castle Papers, box 2; *Commercial and Financial Chronicle*, 124 (May 7, 1927), 2687–88; Morrow to Lamont and Dean Jay, July 8, 1927, Morrow Papers, Lamont File; Brandes, *Hoover and Economic Diplomacy*, pp. 151–213.

price levels . . . without some comprehensive balance sheet including the invisible items."[48]

"Scientific" studies both of the invisible items in the American balance sheet and of the triangular nature of American trade eventually convinced Hoover that the United States could both maintain the protective principle and collect the war debts without endangering European financial stability. Capital outflows, tourist expenditures, and immigrant remittances, Hoover argued, would enable European nations to continue to buy American goods while repaying old debts. Therefore, he discounted the importance of the very favorable merchandise balance that the United States had with major European nations. But he also pointed out that those nations could expand their exports and secure dollar exchange in the tropical areas of the world where the United States had an unfavorable merchandise balance. Moreover, many European nations could go on receiving enormous sums of dollars as a result of their direct or indirect ownership of the raw materials in many tropical areas. Given these facts, Hoover argued that anyone who contended that the protective principle was irreconcilable with world prosperity simply ignored the findings of modern science.[49]

These claims, however, did not mean that Hoover or his subordinates in the Commerce Department were unaware of or indifferent to the need to expand merchandise imports. Indeed, they recognized that a smaller favorable balance of merchandise exports provided a sounder basis to carry on foreign trade. They acknowledged the need to increase imports and they stressed that such increments, especially of noncompetitive raw materials, would inevitably accompany domestic industrial development and material advancement. Throughout the 1920s, they noted that imports were increasing more rapidly than exports. This increase was sufficiently impressive, especially if measured in quantitative terms, that prominent economists and commerce officials began to believe that the nation's economic growth and improving standard of living would generate a large enough demand for foreign raw materials and luxury items to constitute a viable international equilibrium

48. See Hoover's foreword to "The Balance of International Payments of the United States in 1922," *Trade Information Bulletin*, No. 144 (Washington, 1923), 2; also see the subsequent studies put out annually by the BFDC entitled, "The Balance of International Payments of the United States in 1923 (1924, 1925, . . .]," *Trade Information Bulletins*, Nos. 215, 340, 399, 503, 552, 625, 698 (Washington, 1923–29); also see the annual statistical presentation and examination of American foreign trade in Department of Commerce, *Commerce Yearbook* (Washington, 1921–29).

49. Hoover, *New Day*, pp. 129–40; Department of Commerce, *Annual Report*, 1922, pp. 17–20; Hoover to Kellogg, July 28, 1926, Hoover Papers, Commerce Section, Foreign Debts; Ray Hall, "The United States Balance of Payments for 1927 and 1928," *Annalist*, 34 (August 16, 1929), 302, 310; Ray Hall, "French-American Balance of Payments in 1928: Our 'Unfavorable' Position," ibid., 34 (November 1929), 908.

regardless of American tariff barriers.[50] In fact, Hoover and his colleagues took particular pains to demonstrate statistically that the tariff did not greatly influence foreign purchasing power. They mustered data revealing that most imports were duty free, that a significant percentage of imports were luxury goods unaffected by duties, that essential dutiable imports came in regardless of rates, and that American customs barriers were not appreciably higher than those of other comparable nations.[51]

Hoover, therefore, never ceased to support the protective principle. In his view, it insured American producers and workers against competition from low wage areas and enhanced American prosperity, thereby augmenting the nation's demand for foreign goods, increasing immigrant remittances, enlarging American overseas tourist expenditures, and contributing to international financial stability. But while vigorously supporting the protective principle, he nevertheless emphasized that the setting of tariff rates had to be taken out of the political process, where they were subject to congressional logrolling, and placed in the hands of experts, where they could be managed on a "scientific" basis, according to the principle of equalizing the costs of production. He supported the Tariff Commission as an appropriate apolitical institutional device to mold tariff policy, and he urged it to make more vigorous use of the flexible provisions of the Fordney-McCumber Act.[52] And he sympathized with William Culbertson's efforts within the commission to make it a more politically independent body capable of formulating tariff policy not only according to its impact upon American industry but also with regard to its influence on international trade and finance.[53]

50. See, for example, Hoover, *Future of Our Foreign Trade*, pp. 11–12; undated memorandum, "Hoover's Thoughts on Foreign Trade" [mid-1920s], Hoover Papers, Commerce Section, Foreign Trade; Department of Commerce, *Annual Report*, 1922, pp. 18–20; "Foreign Trade of the United States in 1929," *Trade Information Bulletin*, No. 684, 1–5; G. B. Roorbach, "Capacity of World Markets to Absorb Europe's Surplus Products and to Afford Employment to Expanding Population," *Proceedings of the Academy of Political Science* ( January 1928), 77–96; F. W. Taussig, "Tariff Bill and our Friends Abroad," *Foreign Affairs*, 8 (October 1929), 9–10.

51. Department of Commerce, *Annual Report*, 1922, pp. 17–20; Hoover, *New Day*, pp. 35–40; Hoover to Oswald Knauth, December 23, 1922, Hoover Papers, Commerce Section, Tariff—1923–1925; Memorandum on the Probable Effect of the New Tariff on Our Import Trade, unsigned, undated, ibid.; J. Honn to Louis Domeratzky, September 28, 1922, ibid.; Henry Chalmers to Hoover, December 29, 1925, ibid.

52. For Hoover's support of the protective principle, see, for example, Hoover, *New Day*, pp. 128ff.; for his views on the application of the protective principle and the setting of tariff rates, see Hoover, *Memoirs*, 2:292–99; "The Beginnings of the Flexible Provisions of the Tariff Law," p. 11, box 296, Hoover Papers, Presidential Subject Files, Tariff Commission—Flexible; Ogden Mills to Hoover, April 23, 1930, ibid.; Hoover to Harding, March 16, 1923, Hoover Papers, Commerce Section, Tariff; Memorandum, unsigned, undated [March 1923, by Hoover?], ibid.; Henry Stimson to Felix Frankfurter, February 5, 1930, Felix Frankfurter Papers (Manuscript Division, Library of Congress), box 103.

53. Culbertson to Hoover, April 5, 1923, October 11, 1924, box 294, "Tariff Commission—

In general, then, Hoover's approach to foreign policy in the New Era focused on the need to develop "scientific" and "apolitical" mechanisms and formulae capable of fostering world order, European stability, and mutual cooperation. The War Debt Commission's use of the capacity formula, the Tariff Commission's adoption of the "costs of production" principle, the Commerce Department's championing of the "reproductive" loan criteria, the central banks' commitment to the gold standard, and the reparation experts' emphasis on Germany's "ability to pay" all reflected an effort to organize progressively the forces of peace by mobilizing expertise, generating voluntary action, and minimizing political imperatives. Hoover hoped that such tactics would enable the United States to play a continuous and constructive role in world affairs, to restore the free flow of private capital, and to remain independent of political and military commitments. In theory, it was a grandiose vision. But practically it failed because of Hoover's own departure from its rules and because of flaws within its conception.

## III

Hoover prided himself on being the enlightened manager liberated from antiquated assumptions, committed to the empirical method, and indifferent to political factors. In 1928, he confidently exclaimed: "It has been no part of mine to build castles of the future but rather to measure the experiments, the actions, and the progress of men through the cold and uninspiring microscope of fact, statistics and performance."[54] Such rhetoric sounded reassuring, but was far from accurate during the latter part of the 1920s. By the middle of the decade, Hoover became complacent, overestimated the soundness of the American economy, exaggerated the extent of world progress, and began operating in political arenas where fact often succumbed to expediency.[55]

Though by 1925 initial efforts had been undertaken to deal with many of the major international economic questions, few of them had been permanently resolved. Many prominent businessmen, bankers, and government officials, whom Hoover would have been inclined to call "experts," had they not

---

Dennis, Alfred," OF, HHCD; Homer Hoch to Hoover, May 7, 1923; ibid.; also see Culbertson to Morrow, September 10, 1921, "Culbertson," Morrow Papers; J. Richard Snyder, "Coolidge, Costigan, and the Tariff Commission," *Mid-America*, 50 (April 1968), 131–48.

54. Hoover, *Addresses*, p. 32.

55. For Hoover's complacence, see Hoover to Charles Hebberd, November 24, 1925, Hoover Papers, Commerce Section, Economic Situation in Europe; for a fair-minded evaluation by a former associate, see Joseph S. Davis, "Herbert Hoover, 1874–1964: Another Appraisal," *South Atlantic Quarterly*, 68 (Summer 1969), 295–318. Even while Hoover's reputation was at its peak, the *New Republic* began questioning his expertise. See, for example, "The Role of the Expert," *New Republic*, 56 (November 14, 1928), 340–41; also see George Soule, "Herbert Hoover, the Practical Man," ibid., 53 (December 28, 1927), 160–62.

disagreed with him, realized that readjustments would have to be made continuously if permanent stability were to be achieved. Owen Young wrote Hoover in January 1926 that he was troubled by national policies that demanded large payments from debtor nations, and then not only excluded their goods from the American market but also broke up their raw material monopolies that were instrumental in securing foreign exchange. Young was certainly not alone in recognizing that American tariff barriers, war debts collections, and loan policies strained the entire international economic system, jeopardized the gold standard, and threatened European stability.[56]

As the enlightened manager and supporter of apolitical machinery to handle such problems, Hoover might have been expected to encourage progressive steps to ameliorate existing difficulties. But he tended to remain inflexible and to disregard arguments and statistical evidence that conflicted with his own basic assumptions. For example, he often acknowledged that a closer balance between American merchandise exports and imports constituted a sounder basis for world trade, but he belittled the significance of the growing disparity between exports and imports in the latter 1920s.[57] Though he emphasized the need to increase imports in order to provide the rest of the world with dollar exchange, he combatted government controlled raw material monopolies abroad that boosted prices and foreign exchange earnings. He justified this by claiming that monopolies undermined efficient production,[58] but he supported both the protective principle and the costs of production formula that, as applied, contradicted the whole concept of comparative advantage and efficient international specialization. He maintained that "invisible" imports and foreign loans would provide the basis for a continued equilibrium in the balance of international payments, but he never developed an effective means of systematizing the extension of reproductive foreign loans;[59] nor did he analyze the growing quantitative importance of American earnings from previous investments abroad.[60] He often claimed that the triangular pattern of world commerce (American exports to Europe, European exports to the tropics, tropical exports to the United States) was the solution to Europe's balance of payments difficulties. But he overlooked the fact that the American campaign to expand exports to South America and Asia was deranging the triangular nature of international commerce.[61]

56. Young to Hoover, January 25, 1926, Young Papers, I-73; Gilbert to Garrard Winston, October 16, 1925, Strong Papers, 1012.1 (Gilbert); Winston to Strong, July 16, 1926, ibid., 012.6 (Winston); Memorandum, by Strong, May 27, 1928, ibid., 1000.9 (Strong's Trips).

57. Department of Commerce, *Annual Report*, 1927, pp. xix–xx.

58. For Hoover's views and actions regarding raw materials monopolies, see "Backing up Business," 280; Brandes, *Hoover and Economic Diplomacy*, pp. 63–147.

59. See Section III below.

60. Department of Commerce, *Annual Report*, 1927, p. xx.

61. Walter T. Layton, "Europe's Role in World Trade," *Proceedings of the Academy of Political*

Despite mounting evidence that the protective principle could not be reconciled with the nation's commercial and financial position in the world economy, Hoover would not abandon his commitment to it. During the 1928 presidential campaign critics charged that both Hoover's support of the protective tariff and his willingness to accept upward revisions were politically inspired. Though his campaign rhetoric suggests that political factors were not inconsequential, his vigorous support of the protective principle was based on the assumption that protectionism was vital to American prosperity and compatible with international financial equilibrium. As already indicated, he marshaled considerable evidence to show that protective tariffs did not significantly affect imports, but he usually failed to take into consideration the international payment difficulties stemming from simultaneous policies of import protectionism and export expansionism in a period of declining raw material prices. Fundamentally, protectionism was an article of faith for Hoover, conceived in advance of the evidence, rationalized by selective use of the "facts," and illustrative of his primary preoccupation with the domestic economy and his unabashed pride in the American system. All in all, his approach to the tariff question and the international liquidity problem engendered legitimate questioning about Hoover's reputation as an apolitical manager and farsighted economist.[62]

The same might be said about Hoover's attitudes and actions on the war debts issue. He proclaimed his willingness to examine this question on the basis of fact, not emotion. But he usually suspected that the foreign debtors were trying to dupe the American war debt commissioners. Consequently, he almost always took a hard line approach and defined "capacity" in the most exacting way possible. Lenient members of the War Debt Commission often were exasperated by his opposition to more liberal concessions. Treasury officials, like Garrard Winston, who studied the debt problem most intensively, believed the "facts" warranted larger remissions than Hoover thought advisable.[63]

---

*Science*, 12 (January 1928), 161–62; Taussig, "Tariff Bill," 11–12; H. Hallam Hipwell, "Trade Rivalries in Argentina," *Foreign Affairs*, 8 (October 1929), 150–54.

62. For Hoover's discussion of the tariff during the 1928 campaign, see Hoover, *New Day*, pp. 24–25, 70, 101–02, 128ff.; for a defense of the tariff that reveals Hoover's parochial nationalism, see "Draft," no date [1925], no signature [Hoover], Hoover Papers, Commerce Section, Foreign Loans—Great Britain; for criticism of Hoover, see "The Menace of Tariff Revision," *New Republic*, 56 (September 5, 1928), 60–62; "Role of the Expert," 340–42; Davis, "Hoover," 64–65. For an interesting analysis of the impact of American protectionism, which substantiates some of Hoover's assumptions, see M. E. Falkus, "U.S. Economic Policy and the 'Dollar Gap' of the 1920s," *Economic History Review*, 24 (November 1971), 599–623.

63. Winston to Morrow, July 8, 1926, Morrow Papers, Winston File; Memorandum, by Martin Egan, October 5, 1925, ibid., Lamont File; Richard Olney to Winston, October 22, 1925, Records of the Bureau of Accounts, box 220 (unmarked folder); diary entry, November 7, 1925,

In isolation the debt issue was not of great significance, but it assumed larger importance because it was very closely related to efforts to revise the Dawes annuities and to maintain European currency stability. Throughout 1927 and 1928, central bankers, the agent general for reparations, and other prominent international figures gave considerable attention to European financial problems. They recognized that Germany's reparations burden had to be lightened and England's financial strain relieved. Yet it was difficult to attack these problems without interjecting the war debts issue.[64]

Hoover, however, manifested little inclination to be helpful. Though he had acknowledged the possibility of revising the war debt accords, he refused to support any such action during the late 1920s. In fact, he praised the financial viability of the debt settlements and claimed that they imposed no financial hardships on debtor nations. He gathered an impressive array of statistics demonstrating that annual war debt payments were only a small percentage of budgetary expenditures, that they were an insignificant item in the total foreign trade of any nation, that they constituted less of a financial burden than armaments expenditures, and that they were often exceeded by annual American tourist expenditures abroad.[65] Though these statements were for the most part true, they disregarded the additional burden that war debt transfers placed on an international monetary system that already was under considerable strain. The invisible import items in America's balance sheet may have greatly exceeded war debt payments, but they were not large enough, not constant enough, to provide debtors with easy and steady access to dollar exchange.[66] Therefore, war debt payments did exacerbate, if not cause, the liquidity problem. In failing to place the war debts issue in the context of the myriad problems afflicting the international monetary system, Hoover used factual information not to enlighten the American people about the realities of that situation, but to distort that reality. This was totally contrary to his previous emphasis on studying a problem objectively, on mobilizing the public for voluntary action, and on managing the issue according to the best advice of experts.

volume 11, Charles E. Hamlin Papers (Manuscript Division, Library of Congress); also see Hoover's personal account of his negotiations with the Caillaux Mission in Hoover Papers, Commerce Section, Debts—France.

64. See the materials in Strong Papers, 1000.9 (Strong's Trips, 1928); Strong to Gilbert, March 3, 27, 1928, ibid., 1012.2 (Gilbert); Gilbert to Morrow, May 16, 1927, Morrow Papers, Gilbert File; Russell Leffingwell to Lamont, July 20, 1927, Lamont Papers, 103–12; Young to Basil Miles, January 9, 1928, Young Papers, R-30.

65. See Memorandum on War Debt Settlement [1927], Hoover Papers, Commerce Section, Foreign Debts; Hoover, *New Day*, p. 138.

66. For example, with the coming of the depression American tourist expenditures overseas rapidly diminished. Yet this had been an invisible import that Hoover often had referred to as providing the debtors with the capacity to pay war debts.

Hoover's failure to abide by the tenets of the New Era was especially apparent during the reparation negotiations of 1929. Once again international "experts" (businessmen and financiers) convened to resolve the reparations dilemma. As part of a final settlement they hoped to establish an international bank, the Bank for International Settlements, that would facilitate international transfers and that would foster currency stability. During these negotiations, the Hoover administration bitterly denounced any linkage between the war debt and reparation issues, opposed any official American connection with the proposed international bank, and initially objected to any American financial sacrifices on behalf of army costs or mixed claims. This negative attitude complicated the work of the experts and threatened to retard a constructive step toward international monetary stability. Hoover justified his actions on the basis of past American precedent (of separating the war debt and reparation issues), on the grounds of saving taxpayers' dollars, and on the merits of remaining aloof from Europe's political problems.[67] These reasons had a traditional ring, but they defied the best advice of the "experts," reflected a cowardly attitude toward breaking precedent, and illustrated a sensitivity to domestic political rather than international economic factors. Hoover's reaction to the Young Plan negotiations was certainly not in the best tradition of innovative management and apolitical statesmanship. The experts accused him of playing politics, but other factors played a role as well, including his emotional antipathy to the Old World, especially France, and his minimizing of international financial problems.[68]

Hoover's inability to jettison political considerations, to reappraise fundamental assumptions, and to manage properly internal and external economic variables indicated his personal failure to live up to the rigorous tenets of the New Era. But there also were flaws within the New Era approach that made constructive action on the international scene difficult. Hoover's emphasis on mobilizing voluntary and cooperative forces within the private sector, rather than extending governmental powers, had many merits, but also suffered from conceptual weaknesses. He relied upon private bankers to cooperate with his policy of extending loans for reproductive purposes only. But in their struggle to utilize available capital and to reap large profits, bankers

67. For the Hoover administration's attitude toward the negotiations leading to the Young Plan, see Department of State, *Foreign Relations*, 1929, 2:1029–83; Memorandum of Conversation between Mills and George Harrison, May 8, 1929, George L. Harrison Papers (copies deposited at the Federal Reserve Bank of New York, New York City), 2013.1; diary entry, August 28, 1930, volume 10, Stimson Diaries, Henry L. Stimson Papers (Sterling Library, Yale University).

68. For the experts' disillusionment with Hoover, see especially diary entries, April 10, 17, 1929, May 17, 18, 1929, "Notes on the Young Plan," by Stuart Crocker, Young Papers. Hoover's antipathy to Old World power politics is evident throughout his official career. See, for example, the latter chapters of volume 1 of his *Memoirs* that were written during the 1920s. Hoover, *Memoirs*, 1:275–482; Davis, "Hoover," 299–301.

disregarded his advice to refrain from loans to German municipalities. Hoover's theory of voluntarism postulated that when private groups were informed of the "facts," they would concur with the government on what constituted appropriate action. When the bankers disregarded his warnings, Hoover's limited conception of what constituted legitimate government action precluded more forceful measures to prohibit these loans. As a result, American capital continued to flow into Germany and the American financial system became increasingly intertwined with European financial developments. Hoover and his assistants looked upon this with great dismay. They expected a crisis to arise during which the bankers would pressure the government to insist that loan service receive priority over reparation payments. This foreshadowed not only an uncertain financial future, but also political entanglements in Europe. Yet Hoover presented no effective means of dealing with the situation. The secretary of commerce did not advocate direct government prohibition of unproductive loans even to German municipalities, lest it be interpreted to mean that the government was assuming responsibility to safeguard all loans it did not bar.[69]

The bankers' refusal to accept the government's guidelines regarding the "reproductive" nature of German loans illustrated another flaw in Hoover's New Era approach to foreign policy. He maintained that all critical issues could be studied in an objective way, systematically quantified, and then expertly managed. But most foreign policy issues inescapably involved political, emotional, and psychological factors that made "rational" decision-making difficult, if not impossible. For example, not only was there much discord on what constituted a productive loan, but even when agreement could be reached among government officials, it was hard to implement policy and direct the outflow of American capital.[70] Likewise, the capacity formula, as the Treasury Department pointed out, was "not subject to mathematical determination," but was "largely a matter of opinion." Despite the enormous amount of statistical data that was collected by the War Debt Commission (and the reparations experts), subjective judgments had to be made in deter-

69. For Hoover's attitude regarding unproductive loans, see Hoover to secretary of commerce, January 9, 1932, Hoover Papers, Presidential Subject Files, Foreign Affairs—Financial Correspondence; Grosvenor Jones to Robert Lamont, July 13, 1929, ibid. For the vast amount of information on American loans to Germany, see materials in Hoover Papers, Commerce Section, Foreign Loans—Germany; BFDC Records, 640 (Germany); Bureau of Accounts Records, box 85; General Records of the Department of State, 800.51/507½, 509½, 520, 558, 560, 561.

70. The difficulty of regulating the outflow of American capital was most evident in the government's futile effort to prevent loans to France so long as the French refused to ratify the debt agreement. See Jones to Hoover, February 17, 1927, Hoover Papers, Commerce Section, Foreign Loans—France; "The State Department and Foreign Loans," *The Index* (February 1928), pp. 6–7. For the difficulty of determining what constituted a "productive" loan, see, for example, A. N. Young, "The Loan Policy of the Department of State," *Far Eastern Review*, 24 (March 1928), 102.

mining what comprised a decent standard of living and what a nation would be willing to pay.[71] Moreover, since such decisions ultimately had to secure legislative approval, political considerations were never absent. Similar political and emotional factors help to explain Hoover's commitment to the protective principle. He never analytically demonstrated that "scientific" protectionism was the best means to reconcile the needs of the domestic economy with those of the international economy. Protectionism, however, not only accorded with Hoover's personal predilections, it also was politically expedient in the 1920s.[72]

Hoover's personal commitment to objective analysis was less than he realized; his own ability to discard political considerations was less than he supposed; his faith in voluntarism was greater than the situation warranted; and his pursuit of economic solutions to complex international questions was more inadequate than he presumed. The great issues of the day could not be solved by experts dealing exclusively with international economic and financial variables. In the modern industrial world, international economic issues were so closely intertwined with strategic and political factors that the latter could not be dismissed in dealing with the former. Thus, Hoover's great desire to integrate Weimar Germany economically into his cooperative capitalist system foundered on French apprehensions of what a revitalized, even though disarmed, Germany might portend for French security. Hoover's view of human behavior and international motivation presupposed that an economically satisfied and republican nation would be a cooperative partner in world affairs. But the French remained skeptical, and Hoover was slow to placate their anxieties. In fact, French obstructionism infuriated him and bred a deep distrust. "During the whole period from 1918 to 1939," he subsequently wrote, "[France] was the stumbling block to every proposal for world advancement." Given this attitude (and the domestic political climate), he tried to keep the United States free of commitments to guarantee what he considered to be France's self-destructive concept of security.[73]

<hr />

71. Treasury Department, *Annual Report*, 1926, p. 213. For the balancing of "subjective" and "objective" factors bearing on the debt issue, see Leffler, "The Origins of Republican War Debt Policy," 599–601. For the balancing of similar factors bearing on the reparations question, see especially the Goldsmith-Herter Correspondence, Ayres Papers, box 4.

72. For attitudes toward protectionism in the 1920s, see Frank W. Fetter, "Congressional Tariff Policy," *American Economic Review*, 23 (September 1933), 413–27; also see William R. Allen, "Issues in Congressional Tariff Debate," *Southern Economic Journal*, 20 (April 1954), 340–55.

73. For Hoover's attitudes, see, for example, Hoover and Gibson, *Problems of Lasting Peace*, p. 143; Hoover, *Memoirs*, 2:181–82; Hoover to Harding, January 4, 1922, Harding Papers, box 5, File 3, Folder 2. The French contended that in defining the armed strength of a nation, the industrial capacity of that nation had to be considered as well as its human and financial resources. See, for example, Department of State, *Foreign Relations*, 1927, 1:164.

## IV

The refusal to incur strategic commitments lest they embroil the United States in unforeseen political and military problems highlighted a vital element of Hoover's New Era approach to foreign policy. The maintenance of European stability and the extension of international trade, though immensely important to American self-interest, were not so vital as to necessitate strategic involvements and military guarantees. The United States, Hoover believed, was sufficiently self-contained to withstand upheaval and even revolution abroad, though naturally this would entail some difficult readjustments for the American economy. In fact, he found comfort in America's relative economic self-containment and claimed that, if necessary, this condition would enable the United States to sustain itself economically regardless of events elsewhere. In other words, according to Hoover, the domestic economy and the internal market remained the basic determinants of American well-being. This did not mean that events abroad were unimportant; it simply meant that they were not critical unless the nation's security was endangered. And in the 1920s Hoover saw no such threat.[74]

Thus, during the era of the Republican ascendancy, Hoover sought to establish a balanced view of the interrelationships between domestic well-being and international stability. He desired to play a constructive role in European and world affairs without compromising domestic priorities as he defined them and without incurring dangerous commitments as he perceived them. Yet his efforts to establish a stable world order failed because of his overconfidence in the ability of business experts to deal with complex problems, because of his disregard of the political and strategic ramifications of international economic issues, because of his unfounded faith in the ability of the private sector to respond wisely and unselfishly to international questions, because of his oversensitivity to domestic political crosscurrents, because of his suspicion of foreign peoples and foreign systems, and because of his personal inability to reassess the wisdom of traditional Republican principles like protectionism.

But despite all these shortcomings, Hoover's "New Era" approach to foreign policy deserves careful scrutiny and is entitled to sympathetic criticism.

74. For Hoover's views on the relative economic self-containment of the United States and its advantages, see, for example, "Drafts," by Hoover, January 1922, Hoover Papers, Commerce Section; Herbert Hoover, "A Year of Cooperation," *Nation's Business*, 10 (June 5, 1922), 13; Herbert Hoover, "The Question of Stability is a Great Human Problem," *Journal of the American Bankers Association*, 23 (October 1930), 257; also see Department of Commerce, *Commerce Yearbook*, 1924, pp. 460, 514–16; ibid., 1928, 92ff.; John Richard Meredith Wilson, "Herbert Hoover and the Armed Forces: A Study of Presidential Attitudes and Policy," PhD diss. (Northwestern University, 1971), 7–10.

During the 1920s, Hoover did seek to pursue a middle course between the extremes of irresponsible isolationism and dangerous overcommitment, policies that beleaguered American foreign relations in subsequent decades. While endeavoring to influence events abroad and make them conform to American interests and ideals, he remained wary of overestimating America's dependence on the international economy and skeptical of the benefits of strategic commitments when the nation's vital interests were not threatened. His efforts, although flawed, remain noteworthy because they underscore how difficult it is to balance American foreign interests with American overseas commitments and to reconcile domestic needs with international imperatives.

# 3

# Political Isolationism, Economic Expansionism, or Diplomatic Realism

## AMERICAN POLICY TOWARD WESTERN EUROPE, 1921–1933

The debates about U.S. foreign policy in the interwar years perplexed me. As I did my research, I was increasingly aware of the diverse strands of American foreign relations and the need to synthesize them. Republican officials in the 1920s and early 1930s did not seem to me to be especially isolationist or expansionist; nor did they seem unrealistic.

Although they did not wish to incur strategic commitments abroad, get embroiled in European political controversies, or defend the open door with the use of military force or economic sanctions, they were nonetheless engaged in and concerned with international affairs. Although they did want to expand U.S. markets abroad, gain access to critical raw materials, and direct U.S. private loans into productive purposes, they did not want to compromise domestic priorities or overextend the role of government in the American political economy. Seeing no short-term or even intermediate-term threats to vital U.S. interests, they were inclined to take measured steps to promote world stability and international order. They had a sense of the limits of American power and American interests, and they were not inclined to exaggerate their ability to alter French or Japanese views of their own vital interests.

I would like to thank the Mershon Foundation and the American Council of Learned Societies for financial support that facilitated research on this subject.

Among scholars there had been a temptation to conflate the events of the late 1930s with those of the 1920s. Conflation distorted analysis and assessment. Observing that there was no totalitarian menace and no great depression during the 1920s, I was inclined to see Republican policies more empathetically, if not sympathetically. I saw these policymakers struggling to find the right balance between domestic and foreign priorities; I saw them calculating how much responsibility they should incur to settle disputes abroad and deter adventurism. The absence of threat made them wary of commitments and entanglements, but they were not indifferent to U.S. military requirements.

Shortly after I finished my book, other historians like John Braeman thoroughly outlined the relative advances in U.S. military capabilities during the 1920s, compared them to those of other countries, and warned scholars not to confuse the configuration of power in the 1920s with that of the late 1930s. (See John Braeman, "Power and Diplomacy: The 1920s Reappraised," *The Review of Politics*, 44 [July 1982]: 342–69). Thereafter, many historians retreated from labeling the years after World War I as isolationist or imperialist. Joan Hoff Wilson suggested the term "independent internationalism" to capture the discordant features of Republican diplomacy. In his overall account of American foreign relations, George Herring described this era as "involvement without commitment." (See Joan Hoff Wilson, *American Business and Foreign Policy, 1920–1933* [Lexington, Ky.: University Press of Kentucky, 1971]; George Herring, *From Colony to Superpower: U.S. Foreign Relations since 1776* [New York: Oxford University Press, 2008], 436–83.)

When threats abroad were nonexistent and international markets were deemed less important than the health of the domestic market, what was the proper role of the United States in the world economy and the international political arena? Questions like this still perplex, and the extrapolations we once made from the experiences of the late 1930s might be less salient than we once thought.

This essay appeared in *Perspectives in American History* 8 (Harvard University Press, 1974), 413–61.

———

After World War II, American historians and political scientists criticized the moralistic tone and legalistic orientation of American diplomacy between Versailles and Munich. Strongly influenced by the American repudiation of the League of Nations, by the failure of appeasement, by the brutality of Nazi aggression, and by the emergence of Soviet expansionism, these scholars often equated realism with security agreements, with political involvement, and with the readiness to use force. They characterized American foreign policy in the interwar period as isolationist, and they condemned American officials for failing to realize that security could be guaranteed through military preparedness and political commitments. The realists claimed that American policymakers had disregarded the imperatives of power politics and had been guided "by a politically ignorant and irresponsible moral impulsiveness, a utopian view of the problems of mitigating international conflict and a blind aversion to war and the instruments of war as absolute evils."[1]

While concentrating their attack on the nation's political isolationism in the interwar period, the realists also criticized the foreign economic policies of the United States. They especially denounced American debt, tariff, and loan policies. They assumed that few Americans understood the significance of the transition from debtor to creditor status and they argued that American policymakers simply responded to the provincial demands of the American people. Thus, according to Selig Adler, "The foreign economic policies of the United States proved to be the most perilous aspect of neo-isolationism."[2]

In contrast to the realists' preoccupation with the isolationist elements of American diplomacy, many scholars since the middle 1950s have been placing a growing emphasis on the economic aspects of American diplomacy in the interwar period. These writings are difficult to categorize because they differ so widely in scope, analysis, and sources. They suggest, however, that the major foreign policy goal of American officials after World War I was to create a stable international economic and financial environment in which American industry and commerce could grow and prosper. According to these authors, this objective was never accomplished because of several factors: an unre-

1. For the quotation, see Robert E. Osgood, *Ideals and Self-interest in America's Foreign Relations* (Chicago, 1953), p. 362. The realist critique of American foreign policy is most closely associated with Hans Morgenthau and George Kennan. See Hans Morgenthau, *In Defense of the National Interest* (New York, 1951); Hans Morgenthau, "The Mainsprings of American Foreign Policy: The National Interest vs. Moral Abstractions," *American Political Science Review*, 44 (1950), 833–854; George Kennan, *American Diplomacy* (Chicago, 1951). These works have influenced an entire era of historiography. See, for example, Robert Ferrell, *Peace in Their Time: The Origins of the Kellogg-Briand Pact* (New Haven, 1953); Robert Ferrell, *American Diplomacy in the Great Depression: Hoover-Stimson Foreign Policy, 1929–1933* (New Haven, 1957); William E. Leuchtenburg, *The Perils of Prosperity, 1914–1932* (Chicago, 1958); John D. Hicks, *Republican Ascendancy, 1921–1933* (New York, 1960); L. Ethan Ellis, *Frank B. Kellogg and American Foreign Relations* (New Brunswick, N.J., 1961); Foster Rhea Dulles, *America's Rise to World Power* (New York, 1954); Betty Glad, *Charles Evans Hughes and the Illusions of Innocence* (Urbana, 1966); Alexander DeConde, ed., *Isolation and Security* (Durham, N.C., 1957); Selig Adler, *The Uncertain Giant 1921–1941: American Foreign Policy between the Wars* (New York, 1966); John Chalmers Vinson, *William E. Borah and the Outlawry of War* (Athens, Ga., 1957).

2. Adler, *Uncertain Giant*, p. 70; also see L. Ethan Ellis, *Republican Foreign Policy, 1921–1933* (New Brunswick, N.J., 1968), p. 36. For the influence of public opinion on foreign policy, see Dexter Perkins, "The State Department and Public Opinion," in Gordon Craig and Felix Gilbert, eds., *The Diplomats, 1919–1939* (New York, 1965), I, 282–303.

solved conflict persisted between the search for a world economic community and the struggle for American financial and commercial hegemony; a chronic tension remained between economic expansionism and political isolationism; too many divisions existed between nationalists and internationalists within the American business community; foreign governments continued to be skeptical of the utility and viability of a world economic community. Nevertheless, many of these more recent scholarly works reveal that American officials, international bankers, and big businessmen made a concerted, though ultimately unsuccessful, effort to cope with such matters as reparations, war debts, foreign loans, and international currency problems.[3]

The contrasting themes of political isolationism and economic expansionism have provided two alternative frameworks for studying American foreign policy. The intent of this essay is to examine whether American policy toward Western Europe between 1921 and 1933 properly falls within either of these categories. An examination of the evidence suggests that both schools of interpretation have depicted certain important aspects of American diplomacy during this period, but have failed to provide a satisfactory synthesis.[4] Consequently, many of the existing studies raise important questions that still need to be answered. Why, for example, did the United States involve itself in European economic matters while remaining formally aloof from European political issues? Why, in particular, did the United States refuse to guarantee French security when such action might have induced French officials not only to pursue a more conciliatory policy toward Germany but also to agree to some land disarmament? Having rejected the efficacy of political and strategic commitments, how did American leaders expect to influence the course of European affairs?

3. See, for example, William A. Williams, "The Legend of Isolationism in the 1920's," *Science and Society*, 18 (Winter 1954), 1–20; Carl Parrini, *Heir to Empire: United States Economic Diplomacy, 1916–1923* (Pittsburgh, 1969); Lloyd C. Gardner, *Economic Aspects of New Deal Diplomacy* (Madison, 1964), pp. 3–24; Joseph Brandes, *Herbert Hoover and Economic Diplomacy: Department of Commerce Policy, 1921–1928* (Pittsburgh, 1962); Joan Hoff Wilson, *American Business and Foreign Policy, 1920–1933* (Lexington, Ky., 1971); Lester V. Chandler, *Benjamin Strong: Central Banker* (Washington, D.C., 1958); Stephen V. O. Clarke, *Central Bank Cooperation, 1924–1931* (New York, 1967); Richard Meyer, *Bankers' Diplomacy* (New York, 1970); Paul P. Abrahams, "American Bankers and the Economic Tactics of Peace, 1919," *Journal of American History*, 56 (1969), 572–583; Elmus R. Wicker, "Federal Reserve Monetary Policy, 1922–1933: A Reinterpretation," *Journal of Political Economy*, 73 (1965), 325–343; Frank Costigliola, "The Other Side of Isolationism: The Establishment of the First World Bank, 1929–1930," *Journal of American History*, 59 (1972), 602–621; Melvyn P. Leffler, "The Struggle for Stability: American Policy toward France, 1921–1933" (unpub. PhD diss., Ohio State University, 1972); Robert H. Van Meter, Jr., "The United States and European Recovery, 1918–1923: A Study of Public Policy and Private Finance" (unpub. PhD diss., University of Wisconsin, 1971).

4. For additional comments on the two schools of interpretation, see the concluding pages to this chapter, Section VI, below.

These questions call for an analysis of the economic assumptions, financial tactics, disarmament proposals, security orientation, and neutrality policies of American officials during the Republican ascendancy. Such an examination will reveal that in devising policy toward Western Europe, American policymakers were neither ignoring the realities of international politics nor laying out a blueprint for American economic predominance. Guided by pragmatic considerations, they sought to promote European stability and American self-interest. Their dilemma was to accomplish this foreign policy goal without sacrificing domestic economic and political objectives and without involving the United States in European political and territorial controversies that were considered unrelated to vital American interests.

## I. Economic Assumptions

After World War I, American policymakers viewed international relations from an economic perspective. Republican officials and their associates in the business and banking communities believed that peace depended upon economic growth, business cooperation, and material prosperity. Secretary of State Charles Evans Hughes put the matter bluntly when he asserted, "There will be no permanent peace unless economic satisfactions are enjoyed." International amity, he maintained, would result from the improvement in the standard of living of all the peoples of the world. Hughes's colleagues concurred. Charles G. Dawes, chairman of the international committee of experts to resolve the reparations enigma, vice president of the United States, and subsequently ambassador to Great Britain, referred to economic peace as "the best antidote for war." And not surprisingly, during the depths of the depression President Herbert C. Hoover explained that "the problem before the world today is . . . to secure economic peace. . . . And who can say but the greatest act in the prevention of war is to allay economic friction." Such expressions illustrated the frequently articulated belief that economic factors had assumed a position of primacy in national and international affairs. American military leaders shared the same attitudes as their civilian associates; they, too, maintained that economic variables were of prime importance in shaping international behavior and in influencing the course of world peace.[5]

5. For the quotations, see Charles E. Hughes, *The Pathway of Peace* (New York, 1925), pp. 55, 109; Charles G. Dawes, *A Journal of Reparations* (London, 1939), p. 123; William Starr Myers, ed., *The State Papers and Other Public Writings of Herbert Hoover* (New York, 1934), II, 594–595. In 1927, Henry M. Robinson, the chairman of the American delegation to the International Economic Conference, concluded his report with the statement: "We are convinced that improvement in the economic conditions in Europe will make for universal peace." See Department of State, *Papers Relating to the Foreign Relations of the United States, 1927* (Washington, D.C., 1942), I, 245 [hereafter this source will he cited as *FR*]; for the emphasis on economic factors see also,

American policymakers were prone to emphasize the importance of economic factors in international affairs because they recognized that the industrial, technological, and transportation revolutions had bred worldwide economic and social interdependence. In 1928, President-Elect Hoover told an audience in Rio de Janeiro that without

> the products which we exchange, not a single automobile would run; not a dynamo would turn; not a telephone, telegraph, or radio would operate; a thousand daily necessities and luxuries would disappear. In fact, without these exchanges of commodities, huge masses of humanity who have now become dependent upon an intensive and highly attuned civilization could not be kept alive.[6]

Since the progress of technology and the migration of capital had knit together the international economy and since economic variables had assumed such importance in national affairs, world peace was thought to depend upon the material prosperity and economic stability of each nation. Senator Joseph I. France observed in 1922 that "the civilized world is an economic unity, a living organism, of which each of the various countries is a vital and indispensable organ and there can be no general well-being throughout the whole unless there can be health and vigor in every part."[7]

The economic approach of American policymakers to world affairs was neither a matter of political expediency nor of ideological purity. Indeed, the events leading up to World War I—the growth of alliances, the buildup of armaments, the balance of power—impelled Americans to be legitimately distrustful of these political-military means of preserving the peace. Secretary of State Frank B. Kellogg declared that the United States "does not believe that the peace of the world or of Europe depends upon or can be assured by treaties of military alliance. The futility of such as guarantees of peace is repeatedly demonstrated in the pages of history." In a similar vein, Senator William

---

for example, "Mr. Hoover's Inauguration Address to the American Institute of Mining and Metallurgical Engineers," February 17, 1920, p. 8, copy in New York Public Library. For similar feelings permeating the peace movement, see Charles Chatfield, *For Peace and Justice: Pacifism in America. 1914–1941* (Knoxville, Tenn., 1970), pp. 168–169. With regard to the Far East, Akira Iriye has noted that after World War I American officials "tried to bring about a new era of 'economic foreign policy' as a basis of reconciling and promoting" the interests of the great powers. See Akira Iriye, *After Imperialism: The Search for a New Order in the Far East, 1921–1931* (Cambridge, 1965), pp. 2–3. For the military perspective, see Fred Greene, "The Military View of National Policy, 1904–1940," *American Historical Review*, 66 (1961), 367–368.

6. Herbert C. Hoover, *Addresses Delivered during the Visit of Herbert Hoover to Central and South America, November–December, 1928* (Washington, D.C., 1929), p. 58.

7. Statement by Joseph I. France, *Congressional Record*, 67 Cong., 2 Sess., 2883 (February 22, 1922).

E. Borah asserted that "neither leagues, nor pacts, nor international courts can maintain peace when economic justice is absent." Prominent bankers and businessmen agreed. Owen D. Young claimed that he distrusted political measures to guarantee peace and prosperity because "if they get in the way of great economic forces, they break down."[8]

As a result of these attitudes the United States became, in the words of Henry Stimson, the champion of a "commercial and non-military stabilization of the world."[9] American officials, bankers, and businessmen focused their attention on the economic and financial aspects of international problems and sought to resolve them through the use of "experts," the application of "business methods," the mobilization of private voluntary cooperation in the financial community, and the subordination of political factors. The "expert" committees and the "capacity to pay" formula were excellent illustrations of the American desire to solve complex questions like reparations and war debts by trying to divorce economic and financial issues from their political context. These efforts reflected the prevailing notion that appropriate solutions to international disputes would emerge from the "objective" and "scientific" analysis of their economic roots. Domestic and international political factors only confused and obscured what were admittedly complex, but nevertheless soluble, international economic questions. "The problems in the economic field," Hoover claimed, were more easily resolved because they "contain less of the imponderables and more of the concrete." Such thinking was reinforced in the 1920s by the contemporary faith in expertise, the prestige of the business community, and the development of the social sciences.[10]

American policymakers believed that international economic stability would contribute to world peace; they just as strongly maintained that peace was essential for economic progress. Peace, stability, and economic progress were part of an interlocking process. The world had become too economically interdependent to tolerate political upheaval and military turmoil. Not only war, but also international friction and political uncertainty were anathema

8. Frank B. Kellogg, "The War Prevention Policy of the United States," *Foreign Affairs*, Special Supplement to Volume 6 (March 15, 1928), xi; Statement by Senator William E. Borah, "Should America Cancel Her War Debts," *Congressional Digest*, 10 (October 1931), 243; [General Electric Company], *Addresses of Owen Young and Gerard Swope* (New York, 1930), pp. 163, 179, 239.

9. Henry L. Stimson, "Bases of American Foreign Policy during the Past Four Years," *Foreign Affairs*, 11 (April 1933), 385–386.

10. For Hoover's statement, see Myers, *State Papers*, II, 595; for the emphasis on apolitical approaches to European questions, see, for example, Alan G. Goldsmith [chief of the Western European Division of the Department of Commerce], *Economic Problems of Western Europe* (n.p., 1923), p. 1; for an analysis of the policymaking orientation of American officials, see Melvyn P. Leffler, "The United States and European Stability, 1921–1933" (unpub. paper delivered at the Sixty-Seventh Annual Convention of the Organization of American Historians, April 1974, in author's possession).

to the complex network of high finance and big business. Secretary of State Stimson told the House Committee on Foreign Affairs in 1932:

> The world has become very much dependent upon credit for the movement of its commerce, and credit is a very delicate matter. It simply will not live where there is an atmosphere of uncertainty, and this condition affects the United States in my judgment very greatly. We have a very, very deep interest in having the credit structure of the world maintained. That is the only way we can get rid of our surplus goods and meet the unemployment problem in this country.[11]

Stimson's statement revealed the widely held American conviction that, given conditions of world peace and international economic and financial stability, world demand would grow and American exports would increase proportionately. The members of the National Foreign Trade Council declared in 1928 that "we who are the producers and traders in the United States have very much in common with the other peoples of the world. We wish them all peace, stability, and prosperity. So will their trade grow and thrive. So will ours advance."[12] Peace and economic stability abroad bred business confidence, encouraged the movement of private capital, stimulated investment and production, and generated an increase in world purchasing power. In turn, these developments not only redounded to the benefit of the American economy but also reinvigorated the currents of peace and stability themselves. John Carter of the Department of State summed up American diplomatic thinking in this regard:

> Our world policy could be summarized as "prosperity and peace" were it not that this oversimplification disguises the perfectly solid self-interest involved in such a policy and suggests hypocrisy rather than national common sense. Prosperity abroad aids prosperity in America, and general international peace both prevents the economic waste of war and precludes the necessity for piling up economically wasteful armaments.[13]

11. Statement by Stimson, in House, Committee on Foreign Affairs, *General Disarmament Conference* (Washington, D.C., 1932), pp. 32–33; also see Norman H. Davis, "Peace and World Trade," *Proceedings of the Academy of Political Science*, 13 (January 1929), 107; Robert P. Lamont, "Prospects of United States Foreign Trade," in National Foreign Trade Council, *Official Report of the Sixteenth National Foreign Trade Convention* (New York, 1929), p. 17 [hereafter this source will be cited as NFTC, *Official Report*]; James T. Shotwell, *War as an Instrument of National Policy* (New York, 1929), pp. 27–28, 30–31.

12. "Final Declaration," in NFTC, *Official Report*, 1928, p. x; also see, for example, Department of Commerce, *Fourteenth Annual Report of the Secretary of Commerce* (Washington, D.C., 1926), p. 34.

13. John Carter, "America's Present Role in World Affairs," *Current History*, 35 (November 1931), 162.

In their efforts to implement a foreign policy based on "prosperity and peace," American policymakers recognized the overriding importance of reconciling Franco-German differences in particular and of restoring European economic stability in general. Hoover wrote President Warren G. Harding in January 1922 that a program aimed at accomplishing these objectives would contribute to international peace, would prevent social chaos, would improve world trade conditions, and would benefit American exports.[14] Indeed, the deterioration of European financial, political, and social conditions in the early 1920s alarmed many Americans and convinced them that the interests of the United States and Europe were "indissolubly united."[15] This view was reinforced by the specter of revolution in Germany and by the precipitous slump in the American economy in 1920 and 1921. In October 1922, Alanson Houghton, the American ambassador to Germany, wrote Hughes that unless the United States assumed the initiative, "the [Bolshevik] tide will sweep restlessly to the Atlantic. This is not mere rhetoric."[16] More significantly, such warnings coincided with the outpouring of sentiment from business and farm organizations that the European crisis had to be resolved if the American economy were to be protected and the plight of American agriculture relieved. The farm sector was especially vulnerable to European developments because very large percentages of American cotton and wheat were exported to the Old World. Senator Charles McNary warned that "unless something is done to stabilize economic conditions in Europe this country is going to suffer."[17]

Key policymakers agreed. In one of his first speeches in his new office, Secretary of State Hughes declared that "the prosperity of the United States largely depends upon the economic settlements which may be made in Eu-

14. Hoover to Harding, January 4, 1922, box 5, File 3, Folder 2, Presidential Case File (PCF), Warren G. Harding Papers (Ohio Historical Society, Columbus, Ohio).

15. See introductory remarks by George Wickersham to Frank A. Vanderlip, "The Allied Debt to the United States," *Consensus*, 7 (February 1922), 3.

16. Houghton to Hughes, October 23, 1922, General Records of the Department of State, File 800.51/431, Record Group (RG) 59 (National Archives).

17. For McNary's statement, see *Commercial and Financial Chronicle*, 115 (December 30, 1922), 2847. For a few examples of the interest of American business and farm organizations in restoring European stability, see Special Committee of the Chamber of Commerce of the United States (CCUS), "European Problems Affecting American Business," *Nation's Business*, 9 (October 5, 1921), 1–8; Special Committee of the NFTC, "Report on European Conditions," in NFTC, *Official Report*, 1923, pp. 7–25; National Association of Manufacturers, *Proceedings of the Twenty-Eighth Annual Convention* (New York, 1923), pp. 288–289, 311; "The Balance Sheet of Europe: Reparation and International Debts," *Consensus*, 8 (January and March 1923); Report of the Executive Secretary of the American Farm Bureau Federation, in *The Federation's Third Year* (Chicago, 1922), pp. 15–20; James R. Howard, "Europe, the Farmers' Market," *Nation's Business*, 10 (June 5, 1922), 24–26; J. S. Wanamaker to Harding, December 3, 1921, box 197, File 227, Folder 1, PCF, Harding Papers.

rope." The restoration of European stability and the rehabilitation of European purchasing power would not only directly benefit American exports, but also would facilitate the economic development of other parts of the world, for example, Latin America, where American businessmen hoped to expand their own markets. In addition, important bankers and businessmen sought to revive European capital markets because they believed that European capital had an important role to play in developing economically backward areas outside of the Western Hemisphere. In general, then, Republican officials assumed that the stabilization and economic rehabilitation of Europe would generate worldwide economic growth, would stimulate total world demand, would contribute to world peace and social order, and would benefit American commercial interests.[18]

## II. Financial Tactics

Recognizing the interrelationships among European stability, world recovery, and American well-being, policymakers in the United States hoped that European stability would be fostered through the implementation of enlightened economic policies. "Economic relief," Hoover stated in the midst of the Depression, "means the swinging of men's minds from fear to confidence, the swinging of nations from the apprehension of disorder and guaranteed collapse to hope and confidence of the future."[19] An environment of hope and confidence, Hoover and his colleagues maintained, would encourage European statesmen to settle their political differences among themselves and would foreclose demands for the United States to become permanently entangled in European political and military affairs.[20] Since the early 1920s, Republican officials had feared that such entanglements might generate an

18. For Hughes's statement, see Merlo Pusey, *Charles Evans Hughes* (New York, 1951), I, 580; for the relationships between Europe and the rest of the world economy see, for example, Julius Klein, "Foreign News and America's Business," *Journal of the American Bankers Association*, 21 (September 1928), 193–194, 256; also see Robert Seidel, "Progressive Pan Americanism: Development and United States Policy toward South America, 1906–1931" (unpub. PhD diss., Cornell University, 1973), pp. 213–218; for the restoration of European capital markets, see, for example, memoranda by Benjamin Strong, May 24, 27, 1928, 1000.9, Benjamin Strong Papers (Federal Reserve Bank of New York); for clear statements on the interdependence of the world economy, see, for example, Herbert Hoover, *The Future of Our Foreign Trade* (Washington, 1925), pp. 7–8; Robert P. Lamont, "Prospects of United States Foreign Trade," p. 18.

19. For Hoover's statement, see *FR*, 1931, I, 163. In retrospect, however, it is clear that what policymakers considered "enlightened economic policies" (for example, the return to the gold standard) were sometimes outdated responses to entirely new circumstances.

20. For the emphasis on Europeans' resolving their own political problems, see, for example, Memorandum of Conversation between Arthur Henderson and Stimson, July 15, 1931, General Records of the Department of State, File 462.00R296/4506$^1/_2$; also see *FR*, 1931, I, 275, 280.

abrasive political controversy in the United States without necessarily helping the European situation.[21]

Rather than incur strategic commitments, American policymakers desired to use financial leverage to stabilize Western European affairs. They could do this either by regulating and directing the flow of American loans or by negotiating debt settlements in a way that rewarded those nations that accepted American objectives. During the 1922–1923 reparations crisis, some officials in the State and Commerce departments wanted to use war debts as a lever to stabilize Europe economically and to pacify Europe politically.[22] When domestic politics and other policy considerations precluded the use of the war debts in this manner, American officials made a concerted and successful effort to use private American capital to facilitate a reparations settlement, to stabilize the mark, and to deter future French military action against Germany. Throughout the negotiations culminating in the Dawes Plan, American diplomats and especially American bankers warned European officials that unless an acceptable reparations accord were adopted, American loans would cease.[23] Myron Herrick, the American ambassador to France, noted in a letter to President Calvin Coolidge that "it is universally conceded that our participation [in the Experts' Report] has made a most profound impression on Europe. . . . The fact that America is the creditor nation and is trusted in all Europe, even where she is despised, is a tremendous factor in our favor and also gives us a potential power to straighten out affairs over here."[24]

Indeed, once the reparations crisis was resolved, Secretary Hoover and other officials in the Commerce Department, the State Department, and the Treasury Department wanted to continue to exercise financial pressure in order to compel European nations to sign debt agreements. Policymakers like Treasury Secretary Andrew Mellon maintained that moderate debt settlements based on the "capacity to pay" principle would not only serve the in-

21. See, for example, Hughes to Trumbull White, November 22, 1923, box 48, Charles Evans Hughes Papers (Manuscript Division, Library of Congress).

22. Houghton to Hughes, October 23, 1922, General Records of the Department of State, File 800.51/431, RG 59; William Castle to Hughes, October 24, 1922, ibid., 800.51/432; Hoover to Harding, January 4, 1922, box 5, File 3, Folder 2, PCF, Harding Papers; Hoover to Andrew Mellon, January 6, 1923, box 367, "Foreign Debts," Official File (OF), Herbert Hoover Commerce Department (HHCD) Papers (Herbert Hoover Presidential Library, West Branch, Iowa).

23. For an extraordinarily revealing picture of the role of American bankers during the reparation negotiations in London during the summer of 1924, see boxes 176, 177, Thomas W. Lamont Papers (Baker Library, Harvard University); also see Leffler, "Struggle for Stability," pp. 114–121; Royal J. Schmidt, *Versailles and the Ruhr: Seedbed of World War II* (The Hague, 1968), pp. 175–231; Frank Costigliola, "The Politics of Financial Stabilization: American Reconstruction Policy in Europe, 1924–1930" (unpub. PhD diss., Cornell University, 1972), pp. 87–182.

24. Herrick to Coolidge, April 3, 1924, box 16, Myron T. Herrick Papers (Western Reserve Historical Society, Cleveland, Ohio).

terests of American taxpayers, but also facilitate the stabilization of European currencies and the expansion of American commerce. In the spring of 1925, Mellon, Hoover, and Kellogg agreed on the desirability of imposing an informal embargo on private loans to France, Italy, and Belgium until those nations negotiated debt settlements with the United States.[25] Hoover, and to some extent Kellogg, also desired to use the loan embargo as a means of pressuring European nations to reduce their military expenditures and to balance their budgets.[26] In addition, the secretary of commerce sought to utilize the war debts lever to accomplish the same multiple purposes. He refused to accept French Finance Minister Joseph Caillaux's final offer for a debt settlement in September 1925 because he wanted an accord that would provide the United States with sufficient leverage so "that someday we could trade some portion of these debts for a reduction of armament."[27]

While the secretary of commerce and other government officials were endeavoring to mold financial tactics to serve diplomatic ends, Benjamin Strong, the governor of the Federal Reserve Bank of New York, was making American financial support for European stabilization plans contingent upon the termination of European inflationary practices and the balancing of European budgets. Strong was convinced that monetary disorder was the greatest impediment to world commerce. In his efforts to use the Federal Reserve's financial resources to guide European nations back to the gold standard and to maintain European currency stability, he had the constant support and direct encouragement of officials in the Treasury Department. In January 1928, Mellon explained why Strong's actions constituted wise policy:

> The nations of the world must be reestablished on a sound financial basis if our surplus products are to find an export market. Only in this way can business compute in advance the price it must pay for raw materials and figure more accurately on the price which can be secured for finished products. If this can be done, business can operate on a larger scale and increase its foreign purchases, which means a greater demand for our surplus products and an expansion in business here and in other countries as well.[28]

25. Mellon to Coolidge, February 10, 1926, 012.6 (Winston), Strong Papers; Garrard Winston, "American War Debt Policy," pp. 12–14, in Records of the Bureau of Accounts, box 220, RG 39 (National Archives).

26. See, for example, Memorandum of Conversation between Leland Harrison and Hoover, November 20, 1924, General Records of the Department of State, File 851.51/506, RG 59; Memorandum, by Harrison, April 1, 1925, box 46, Leland Harrison Papers (Manuscript Division, Library of Congress).

27. See Memorandum, by Hoover, September 23, 1925, box 20, "Debts, France," Personal File (PF), HHCD; also see Memorandum, by Hoover, September 30, 1925, ibid.

28. For Mellon's statement, see Treasury Department, *Annual Report of the Secretary of the Treasury*, 1928 (Washington, 1929), pp. 348–349; for Strong's efforts to maintain European

The American involvement in European affairs in the 1920s was primarily economic and financial. This, however, did not mean that the United States remained aloof from European political affairs. The financial power of the United States significantly affected European political settlements as well as European economic agreements. American capital, for example, was needed not only for the reconstruction of devastated areas and for the stabilization of currencies, but also for the commercialization of German reparation bonds. Since French policy in the Ruhr and especially in the Rhineland was linked to the commercialization of German reparation obligations, the availability of American capital affected the entire climate of European politics.[29]

The impact of American financial power on European political developments was especially evident during the negotiations for a security pact in 1925. American bankers and officials informed both the French and the Germans that the return of political stability was a prerequisite for the extension of additional credits and loans. Strong bluntly told German leaders that the American financial attitude "would be very much governed by the degree to which confidence was felt in political conditions." Not surprisingly, German Foreign Minister Gustav Stresemann feared that without a security pact American financial aid would no longer be forthcoming. This apprehension increased his determination to bring the security negotiations to a successful conclusion. Likewise, both the conviction that "the establishment of security was essential to economic and financial recovery" and the belief that a European security pact would have a salutary impact on the United States impelled British Foreign Secretary Austen Chamberlain to patiently mediate Franco-German differences. The result was Locarno.[30]

---

currency stability, see 1000.4–1000.9 (Strong's Trips), Strong Papers; Chandler, *Strong*, pp. 332–422.

29. In the early 1920s, French Premier Raymond Poincaré, for example, considered the possibility of dealing with both the reparations crisis and the French financial dilemma through the commercialization of reparation bonds in the United States. See the letters in May and July 1922, from James Logan to Harrison, in boxes 8 and 9, Henry Fletcher Papers (Manuscript Division, Library of Congress); also in box 7, Harrison Papers. Subsequently, in 1926, Poincaré reconsidered this idea and intimated that the evacuation of the Rhineland might proceed in unison with the total commercialization of reparation bonds. See, for example, S. Parker Gilbert to Dwight Morrow and Russell Leffingwell, October 8, 1926, Records of the Bureau of Accounts, box 220 (unmarked folder), RG 39; Emile Moreau, *Souvenirs d'un gouverneur de la banque de France* (Paris, 1954), pp. 11, 142.

30. For Strong's statement, see Memorandum of Discussion at Reichsbank, July 11, 1925, 1000.6 (Strong's Trips, 1925), Strong Papers; for the impact of American financial power and the views of Stresemann and Chamberlain, see Ministère des Affaires Étrangères, *Documents diplomatiques belges, 1920–1940* (Brussels, 1964), II, 234 [hereafter this source will be cited as DDB]; Jacques Seydoux, *De Versailles au plan Young* (Paris, 1932), pp. 313–314; Eric Sutton, ed., *Gustav Stresemann: His Diaries, Letters, and Papers* (London, 1937), II, 137, 142, 148; W. N. Medlicott,

The Dawes Plan, the debt agreements, the currency stabilization programs, the Locarno treaty, and the related political accords that provided for the withdrawal of French troops from the Ruhr and eventually from the first occupied zone of the Rhineland altered the economic and political environment of Europe. These developments resulted, at least in part, from the judicious use of American financial power. Even when pressure was not directly exerted, European statesmen always had to consider how American capital would react to their initiatives and actions. Stresemann realized that "the whole question of the reconstruction of Europe cannot be settled without America." And Viscount D'Abernon, the British ambassador to Germany from 1920 to 1926, noted:

> In all the more important developments in Germany during post-war years, American influence has been decisive. Eliminate action taken on American advice, or in assumed agreement with American opinion, or in anticipation of American approval, and the whole course of policy would be altered.[31]

Thus, to explain the role of American capital in European affairs in the mid-1920s is to demonstrate that the United States greatly influenced the course of European political and economic affairs even without agreeing to political commitments.

American financial and economic policies, however, did not always contribute to the stabilization of Western European conditions. Not infrequently, Republican efforts to reduce taxes, to combat inflation, to raise tariffs, and to win elections undermined their attempts to effect European stability through the utilization of American financial resources. The desire to reduce taxes, for example, circumscribed policymakers' ability to use the war debts as a lever to elicit European concessions on such matters as reparations and disarmament. This was true because any decrease in European war debt payments had to be borne by American taxpayers so long as the American government had to liquidate its own wartime obligations to private American bondholders.[32] Similarly, in their quest to prevent inflation and restrain speculation, Federal Reserve officials had to manage discount rates and undertake operations in the open market in ways that sometimes conflicted with the financial needs of European nations.[33] Furthermore, protective tariffs, which were designed to

Douglas Dakin, and M. E. Lambert, eds., *Documents on British Foreign Policy, 1919–1939*, Series IA, Vol. I (London, 1966), 8ff., 16 [hereafter this source will be cited as *DBFP*].

31. For Stresemann's statement, see Sutton, *Stresemann*, II, 263; for D'Abernon's comment, see Viscount D'Abernon, *The Diary of an Ambassador* (London, 1929), I, 19.

32. Melvyn P. Leffler, "The Origins of Republican War Debt Policy, 1921–1923: A Case Study in the Applicability of the Open Door Interpretation," *Journal of American History*, 59 (1973), 585–602.

33. For the conflicting national and international pressures bearing on Federal Reserve

safeguard the home market from goods produced in nations with lower standards of living, tended to impede the growth of European exports and to exacerbate the exchange problems facing European nations.[34]

The emphasis of Republican officials on lowering taxes, maintaining price stability, and protecting the home market reflected their belief that the domestic market and the internal economy were the principal determinants of American prosperity and therefore ought to receive primary consideration. Even Hoover's Commerce Department, well known for its efforts to expand American exports, focused the major portion of its attention on managing and organizing the domestic economy.[35] The rapid recovery from the economic recession of 1921 was interpreted by Hoover and Mellon to reveal that American prosperity could be fostered even in spite of ominous European developments. "It has been made evident," the Treasury Department concluded in 1923, "that with fairly balanced relations between our own industries this country may enjoy a good deal of prosperity even when very unsatisfactory conditions prevail abroad."[36] This did not mean that American policymakers abandoned the goals of stabilizing Europe and cultivating new foreign markets. In fact, Republican officials endeavored to find appropriate institutional mechanisms, like the War Debt Commission and the Tariff Commission, to reconcile the needs of the domestic economy with the requirements of the European economy.[37] But internal fiscal, economic, and political priorities continued to infringe upon the foreign policymaking process and to cause chronic inconsistencies between the conceptualization of diplomatic goals and the ability to achieve those goals.

Likewise, the hierarchy of importance attached to diplomatic objectives themselves often complicated the implementation of policy and restricted the American contribution to European stability. For example, keeping the United

---

policy, see, for example, Strong to Moreau, June 20, 1927, 261.1 (French Stabilization), Federal Reserve Bank Papers (Federal Reserve Bank of New York); Strong to James H. Case, August 25, 1925, 1000.6 (Strong's Trips, 1925), Strong Papers; Clarke, *Central Bank Cooperation*, pp. 29–42.

34. Prominent Americans, preoccupied with the task of stabilizing Europe, complained to Republican officials about the harmful impact of United States tariff policies. See, for example, Young to Hoover, January 5, 1926, 1–73, Owen D. Young Papers (Van Hornesville, New York); Gilbert to Winston, October 16, 1925, 1012.1 (Gilbert), Strong Papers.

35. Department of Commerce, *Annual Reports*, 1921–1927. In 1925, the Commerce Department indicated that the domestic construction industry was "the greatest balance wheel in our economic system." See ibid., 1925, p. 32; also see the essay by Ellis Hawley, in J. Joseph Huthmacher and Warren I. Sussman, eds., *Herbert Hoover and the Crisis of American Capitalism* (Cambridge, 1973), pp. 1–27.

36. Treasury Department, *Annual Report*, 1923, p. 2; for Hoover's attitude, see Will Payne, "Income Tax Dividends," *Saturday Evening Post*, 196 (September 1, 1923), 122.

37. Leffler, "The United States and European Stability."

States aloof from Europe's chronic political squabbles sometimes assumed more importance than contributing to European economic stability. As a result, American officials, especially Hoover, refused to link the war debt and reparation issues because they feared that the United States might become Germany's de facto sole creditor. In this capacity, the United States might have had to assume the responsibility for collecting German indemnity payments and for enforcing the punitive provisions of the Treaty of Versailles.[38]

The myriad of internal factors affecting foreign policy decisions together with the unresolved conflict between diplomatic goals themselves prevented the United States from exerting consistent financial pressure in behalf of European stabilization. In addition, the aura of prosperity and stability that prevailed during the mid-1920s generated a false sense of security and of accomplishment. In November 1925, for example, Hoover magnified the extent of European progress since 1919. In a letter to Charles Hebberd, he emphasized that

> the standards of living have increased in every country. Unemployment has been greatly remedied. Practically all of the important countries except France are now either on the gold standard or are rapidly stabilizing their currency on a gold basis. The League of Nations has unquestionably developed great strength in the suppression of conflicts between the smaller nations. The Locarno agreement is the most forward step and will undoubtedly further decrease armament.[39]

Such optimistic appraisals inclined Republican officials to reject proposals calling for additional American financial sacrifices in behalf of European stability. In 1926 and 1927, Mellon cautioned against reopening the debt question lest such action undermine the prevailing state of stability. Existing conditions of peace, prosperity, and stability, he claimed, would generate further economic growth and would make the debt accords financially viable.[40]

Despite this complacency, American attempts to use financial resources to help stabilize European affairs did not cease in the middle of the decade. The Treasury Department continued to support the efforts of the Federal Reserve System to ease European financial problems and to bolster American exports

38. Hoover to Harding, June 9, 1922, box 88, File 57, Folder 3, PCF, Harding Papers; Memorandum of Conversation between Ogden Mills and George Harrison, May 18, 1929, 2013.1 George Harrison Papers (copies deposited in the Federal Reserve Bank of New York); diary entry, August 28, 1930, volume 10, Henry L. Stimson Diaries (Sterling Library, Yale University).

39. Hoover to Charles Hebberd, November 24, 1925, box 21, "Economic Situation in Europe," PF, HHCD.

40. World War Foreign Debt Commission, *Combined Annual Reports of the World War Foreign Debt Commission with Additional Information Regarding Foreign Debts Due the United States* (Washington, D.C., 1927), pp. 59–60; Treasury Department, *Annual Report*, 1927, pp. 321–325.

through the management of discount rates.[41] The State Department approved the private American participation in the Young Plan negotiations,[42] the private American cooperation with the Bank for International Settlements,[43] and the private flotation of the Young bonds in the American market.[44] Moreover, the worsening of economic conditions in 1930 and 1931 actually accelerated the use of financial resources to help stabilize European monetary, economic, and political affairs. This was evidenced by the declaration of the Hoover moratorium, by the consummation of the standstill agreements, by the preoccupation with the gold standard, and by the Hoover administration's request for authority to recreate the War Debt Commission.[45] Indeed, by the end of the summer of 1931, American involvement in Europe had become so extensive that the *Journal of the American Bankers Association* editorialized that "the last vestige, the last pretense, of following Washington's advice to avoid European entanglements [has been] thrown aside. . . . Our isolation is at an end, we sit in the seats of the mighty."[46]

American actions, however, were not bold initiatives in the sense that they eliminated all the inconsistencies in American foreign economic policies. Nor did they provide European statesmen with the means to resolve all the economic and political problems confronting the Old World. Indeed, two fundamental tenets of American foreign policy remained intact: the United States would not totally cancel the war debts and thereby be saddled with the entire remaining financial costs of the Great War;[47] in addition, European leaders would have to share the major responsibility to iron out their own political differences.[48] But the moratorium, the standstill, and these other measures were constructive efforts to promote American self-interest by contributing to European recovery within the limitations imposed by domestic political considerations and internal financial and fiscal factors. They were sincere at-

41. See, for example, Ogden Mills, "An Explanation of Federal Reserve Policy," *Review of Reviews*, 78 ( July 1928), 259–260.

42. *FR*, 1928, II, 873ff.

43. Ibid., 1929, II, 1072.

44. Under Secretary of State Joseph Cotton insisted, however, that the American participation not exceed one-third of the total flotation. See Jay E. Crane to Harrison, Mardi 28, 1930, and Harrison to Crane, March 29, 1930, Bureau of Accounts, box 218 (unmarked folder), RG 39.

45. For a survey of these developments, see *FR*, 1931, I, x–xi, xxiv–xxv, 1–358.

46. See "The End of Isolation," *Journal of the American Bankers Association*, 24 (August 1931), 78–79.

47. If all war debts and reparations were canceled, the United States government would still have had to pay off the Liberty Bonds. Thus, cancellation would have saddled the American taxpayers with the burden of financing the remaining costs of World War I. This was unacceptable to American officials. See, for example, Myers, *State Papers*, II, 488–489.

48. See, for example, Memorandum of Conversation between Henderson and Stimson, July 15, 1931, General Records of the Department of State, 462.00R296/45061/2; *FR*, 1931, I, 275, 280, 549.

tempts to restore confidence, to preserve the gold standard, to reinvigorate trade, and to provide time for European governments to grapple realistically with the problems before them.[49] Insofar as these actions were aimed at facilitating European peace and prosperity through the extension of American capital resources without too deeply embroiling the United States in European political affairs, they were a logical continuation of postwar American policies toward Europe.[50]

## III. Disarmament

When the Depression began to erode American financial power and to intensify European political dissension, however, the Hoover administration relied increasingly upon disarmament proposals as the primary means to restore confidence and eliminate uncertainty.[51] This emphasis on arms limitation, of course, was not a new departure for the Republican administrations of the interwar era. Throughout the 1920s, whenever the French clamored for additional guarantees of French security, American officials retorted that increased disarmament meant increased security. By the early 1930s, American officials were convinced that with some French disarmament European tensions could be alleviated, French security insured, and world stability enhanced. Stimson, for example, told the House Committee on Foreign Affairs in 1932 that Germany's disarmament in the midst of well-armed neighbors had

> produced an instability of attitude in the midst of Europe, which attitude had produced repercussions of a political and financial nature which extend far beyond Europe itself, and has produced an instability in the whole world, because, naturally, the nations that have been disarmed are restless under the inequality of their situation with respect to the others.[52]

49. For official thinking on the debt moratorium and the standstill agreements, see, for example, Herbert C. Hoover, *The Memoirs of Herbert Hoover* (New York, 1951–1952), III, 61–79; Statements by Mills and Stimson, in House, Committee on Ways and Means, *Moratorium on Foreign Debts*, Part I (Washington, 1931); Senate, Committee on Finance, *Postponement of Inter-Governmental Debts* (Washington, 1931); see also Hoover's moratorium statement in William Starr Myers and Walter H. Newton, *The Hoover Administration* (New York, 1936), pp. 93–94; *FR*, 1931, I, 275–278, 280–282.

50. See, for example, Carter, "America's Present Role in World Affairs," pp. 161–166.

51. For Hoover's interest in disarmament, see, for example, *FR*, 1931, I, 163, 493–495. In April 1931, Stimson decided to plan a vacation in European capitals. His purpose, at least in part, was to discuss the issue of disarmament. See General Records of the Department of State, File 033.1140 Stimson/1, RG 59.

52. See statement by Stimson, Committee on Foreign Affairs, *Disarmament Conference*, p. 24; for the American thesis that increased disarmament meant increased security, see, for example, *FR*, 1927, I, 164–165.

American officials supported disarmament agreements in the post–World War I era because they viewed arms limitation in its economic bearings upon peace. Secretary of State Hughes opened the Washington Disarmament Conference in 1921 by insisting that "if there is to be economic rehabilitation . . . competition in armament must stop." The cost of armaments not only imposed an insuperable burden on government budgets, but also contributed to inflation, to unstable exchange rates, to depreciating currencies, and to a more restricted world trade. Since American officials believed peace to be based upon foundations of economic progress and not of military strength, they constantly reiterated that disarmament itself was a guarantee of security.[53]

Herbert Hoover was the policymaker who most consistently and most forcefully attacked the belief that peace could be safeguarded through the force of arms. In May 1931 he told the International Chamber of Commerce:

> International confidence cannot be builded [*sic*] upon fear—it must be builded upon good will. The whole history of the world is filled with chapter after chapter of the failure to secure peace through either competitive arms or intimidation.[54]

Such sentiments had long been an integral part of Hoover's conceptual framework of international behavior. Exactly a decade earlier he had written President Warren Harding that arms expenditures were "the first and primary obstruction" to the restoration of commercial prosperity and world stability.[55] Such attitudes were common in the upper echelons of the American government. In January 1926, for example, President Coolidge told Congress:

> The conviction that competitive armaments constitute a powerful factor in the promotion of war is more widely and justifiably held than ever before, and the necessity for lifting the burden of taxation from the peoples of the world by limiting armaments is becoming daily more imperative.[56]

When American policymakers talked of disarmament during the 1920s and early 1930s, however, they were not indulging in idealistic or utopian rhetoric. In the context of the times, they accurately perceived armaments as a source of political unrest and financial strain.[57] But they never contemplated

53. See Hughes, *Pathway of Peace*, pp. 24–25; see also, for example, Calvin Coolidge, "Promoting Peace through the Limitation of Armaments," *Ladies' Home Journal*, 48 (May 1929), 3–4, 93; Stimson, "Our Foreign Relations," p. 21, General Records of the Department of State, File 711.00/400½, RG 59; Ogden Mills, "Our Foreign Policy: A Republican View," *Foreign Affairs*, 6 (July 1928), 559ff.; Alanson Houghton, "Disarmament and Depression," *The Nation*, 133 (December 1931), 695.

54. Myers, *State Papers*, I, 560.

55. Quoted in Van Meter, "The United States and European Recovery," p. 299.

56. See *FR*, 1926, I, 42–44.

57. For the financial strain caused by armaments, see, for example, "The Burden of Armaments," *The Index*, 12 (August 1932), 153–159.

the reduction of armaments to the point where American defenses might be adversely affected. At the Washington Conference in 1921, the United States secured mathematical parity in capital ships with the world's leading naval power.[58] In 1928, the Coolidge administration contemplated embarking upon a large-scale naval program unless other nations, especially Britain, assumed a more cooperative attitude regarding limitation of auxiliary craft.[59] In addition, in the late 1920s and early 1930s, the United States was spending more money on armaments than any other nation in the world. American expenditures on land forces, small as they were in comparison with post–World War II standards, exceeded even those of France! In 1929, President Hoover reminded Americans "that current expenditures on strictly military activities of the army and navy constitute the largest military budget of any nation in the world today." In fact, despite its relatively advantageous geographic location, the United States was spending a larger proportion of its total budget (17.47%) on national defense in 1930 than was Great Britain (14.45%), and only six percent less than was France (23.56%).[60]

During the late 1920s, military studies concluded that the international environment was calm and that there was no need for immediate military preparations for war.[61] Nevertheless, American officials always were careful to protect American strategic interests in the Western Hemisphere and to oppose arms limitation accords that might undermine American preparedness. The traditional European "threat" to United States strategic interests in Latin America was eliminated as a result of the military emasculation of Germany and of the efforts of American officials, bankers, and businessmen to gain predominant control over cables, petroleum resources, and capital supplies.[62] At the same time, the United States government opposed any international

58. For a good recent appraisal of the Washington Conference, see Thomas H. Buckley, *The United States and the Washington Conference, 1921–1922* (Knoxville, Tenn., 1970); also see Ernest Andrade, Jr., "The United States Navy and the Washington Conference," *The Historian*, 31 (1969), 345–364.

59. Raymond G. O'Connor, *Perilous Equilibrium: The United States and the London Naval Conference* (Lawrence, Kan., 1962), pp. 20–23.

60. For Hoover's quotation, see Arthur A. Ekirch, Jr., *The Civilian and the Military* (New York, 1956), p. 215; for a statistical analysis of comparative arms expenditures, see Memorandum for the President, "Maintenance of International Order by the Army as Affected by Budgetary Limitation of Armaments," Exhibit H ("Per Cent of Total National Budget for National Defense—F.Y. 1930"), August 1931, in box 866 ("Foreign Affairs-Disarmament"), Herbert Hoover Presidential Papers (Herbert Hoover Presidential Library, West Branch, Iowa); also see "The Burden of Armaments," pp. 157–159. The absolute military expenditures of the United States appear disproportionately large because the cost of weapons and the pay of military personnel were considerably higher in the United States than elsewhere. This is why the armed services prepared computations in terms of the percentage of the total budget expended on military items.

61. Greene, "Military View of American National Policy," p. 368.

62. See Joseph Tulchin, *The Aftermath of War: World War I and U. S. Policy toward Latin America* (New York, 1971).

agreement regulating trade in armaments that might impair its ability to influence political events in Latin America.[63] In addition, American diplomats scrutinized developments at Geneva to insure that American strategic planning was not compromised by European disarmament plans, especially by proposals to limit armaments on the basis of budgetary expenditures or industrial capacity.[64] And it was no coincidence that Stimson's interest in the Geneva Disarmament Conference slackened as conditions in the Far East deteriorated in 1931–1932. Even Hoover was not unmindful of tailoring his disarmament proposals in June 1932 to accommodate possible future contingencies in Asia.[65] Arms limitation was an American policy objective during the Republican ascendancy, but government officials and their business supporters tried to formulate and implement disarmament proposals in a pragmatic and hardheaded way that would leave American defenses unimpaired.

## IV. Security

In the debates over disarmament, French policy assumed special importance because France was the most vigorous opponent of American proposals. The French doubted the long-term benefits of arms limitation accords unless they were accompanied by guarantees of French security. The real problem, however, was in the definition of French security. Did it mean French hegemony on the European continent? Did it mean the maintenance of the status quo as instituted by the Treaty of Versailles? Or did it mean a reconciliation with Germany? For the most part, the French identified their security, at least in the short run, with the preservation of the status quo. They made concessions reluctantly and only as a result of Anglo-American financial pressure, French financial weakness, skillful German diplomacy, and the apparent failure of independent French action in the Ruhr. The slowness of these concessions, however, coupled with the punitive nature of some of the provisions of the peace treaty, generated constant friction in Franco-German relations. The Depression eventually magnified German grievances, exacerbated German discontent, and intensified German demands for revision of the reparation, disarmament, and eastern boundary sections of the Versailles treaty. Faced

63. See, for example, Hughes to Harding, August 2, 1922, box 119, File 74, Folder 2, PCF, Harding Papers; *FR*, 1924, I, 79.

64. The careful reader of the appropriate sections of Volume I of the *Foreign Relations* series from 1926 through 1933 will see that American diplomats were entirely conscientious about protecting the strategic interests of the United States. Also see Fred H. Winkler, "The War Department and Disarmament, 1926–1935," *The Historian*, 28 (1966), 426–446.

65. For Stimson's preoccupation with the Far East situation and for Hoover's disarmament proposals, see Nancy Hooker, ed., *The Moffat Papers* (Cambridge, 1956), pp. 68–71; *FR*, 1932, I, 153–156, 182–186.

with these demands, the French continued to reiterate their willingness to reduce their arms, but only if they first received additional guarantees of their security.[66]

American policymakers considered arms limitation a key to the economic stabilization and political pacification of Europe, but they rejected French pleas for guarantees of French security. Public opinion, of course, limited the flexibility of elected American officials. A sense of disillusionment with the results of the recent conflict, a belief that Europe would forever remain incorrigible, and a feeling of revulsion at the horrors and excesses of war all merged into a pervasive public sentiment that opposed entanglement in European affairs. In December 1922, for example, Frederick H. Gillett, speaker of the House of Representatives, wrote friends that though he personally had favored guarantees of French security, "the great majority here now would be opposed to any such guaranty [sic] on our part. The horrible confusion and discord in Europe has made us more averse than ever to being implicated and has given . . . to the feeling against being embroiled a greatly added strength."[67]

American officials, however, did not just succumb to public and congressional opinion. Despite their concern with European disarmament, they also maintained a real antipathy to political and strategic commitments. They particularly did not want to guarantee French security because they disagreed with the French on what constituted French security. This critical problem of definition, often not precisely articulated but always of major importance, clearly emerged during an all-day conference of top American decision-makers in October 1931. They agreed that France was entitled to security. But:

> the rub came in the definition of the word "security." If the French meant the perpetual freezing of the postwar status quo, including the maintenance of unjust and bitterly resented treaty provisions, and a preponderant

66. For standard sources on the course of Franco-German relations in the 1920s and early 1930s, see, for example, Arnold Wolfers, *Britain and France between Two Wars: Conflicting Strategies of Peace since Versailles* (New York, 1940); W. M. Jordan, *Great Britain, France, and the German Problem, 1918–1939: A Study of Anglo-French Relations in the Making and Maintenance of the Versailles Settlement* (London, 1943); Henry Bretton, *Stresemann and the Revision of Versailles* (Stanford, 1953); Hans Gatzke, *Stresemann and the Rearmament of Germany* (Baltimore, 1954); Jon Jacobson, *Locarno Diplomacy: Germany and the West, 1925–1929* (Princeton, 1972); William J. Newman, *The Balance of Power in the Interwar Years, 1919–1939* (New York, 1968). For some general statements of the French position on security and disarmament, see Louis Aubert, "Security, Key to French Policy," *Foreign Affairs*, 11 (October 1932), 122–136, André Géraud, "The London Naval Conference: A French View," ibid., 8 (July 1930), 519–533; Richard D. Challener, "The French Foreign Office: The Era of Philippe Berthelot," in Craig and Gilbert, *The Diplomats*, pp. 48–83; Judith M. Hughes, *To the Maginot Line: The Politics of French Military Preparation in the 1920's* (Cambridge, 1971).

67. Gillett to Herrick, December 26, 1922, box 11, Herrick Papers; Gillett to Fletcher, December 26, 1922, box 9, Fletcher Papers.

military force to guarantee it, then we could not agree with them. Our idea was a tranquilized Europe, which meant the solution, one by one, and by peaceful means, of the problems that were preventing it from settling down.[68]

In essence, then, American policymakers did not feel that American security and American interests were reconcilable with the French vision of French security. American officials realized that, in a broad sense, American self-interest extended to the Rhine, but their conception of this self-interest was linked to a concept of European stability and not of French hegemony. In other words, American officials were basically sympathetic to German revisionism during the 1920s and early 1930s. They assumed that the economic stabilization of Europe and, to a lesser extent, the economic well-being of the United States depended upon the existence of a prosperous, republican, and contented Germany. In March 1921, in a long and carefully written letter, Norman Davis, former assistant secretary of the treasury and undersecretary of state in the Wilson administration, explained to Secretary of State Hughes:

> Through the highly industrial developments of Europe prior to the war, Germany had become the axis, and the rehabilitation of Europe and its continued prosperity is most dependent upon that of Germany. Unless Germany is at work and prosperous, France can not be so, and the prosperity of the entire world depends upon the capacity of industrial Europe to produce and purchase.

Hughes, himself, came to believe that "there could be no economic recuperation in Europe unless Germany recuperates." In fact, Democrats and Republicans, bankers and farmers, internationalists and isolationists all agreed that European prosperity depended upon the resuscitation of the German economy.[69]

Many American officials also believed that a satisfied and republican Germany would be a peaceful nation. They argued that French efforts to extract huge reparation payments and to impose sanctions would cause economic chaos, social dislocation, and political upheaval in Germany. If this occurred, the development of democratic institutions in Germany would be retarded and the economic rehabilitation of all of Europe would be delayed. These

68. Memorandum, October 2, 1931, General Records of the Department of State, File 033.5111 Laval/257, RG 59.

69. Davis to Hughes, March 12, 1921, box 27, Norman H. Davis Papers (Manuscript Division, Library of Congress); Hughes, *Pathway to Peace*, p. 55; see also, for example, statement by Senator Borah, in *Cong. Record*, 67 Cong., 2 Sess., 1684 (January 25, 1922); Dawes, *Journal of Reparations*, p. 30; Frank Vanderlip, *What Next in Europe?* (New York, 1922), p. 87; also see many of the references listed in footnote 17.

developments, in turn, would endanger France's own security.[70] In the autumn of 1923, Hughes asked French Ambassador Jules Jusserand, "If Germany broke up, would France be secure?" The secretary of state did not think so.[71] He shared the views of Dwight Morrow, the prominent banker, diplomat, and presidential adviser. In July 1924, Morrow wrote Hughes that it was shortsighted for the French to balance reparations "against security as though the two things are contradictory. . . . Such an antithesis really defines security as keeping your adversary weak. There is no real security that way."[72]

Many influential American diplomats recognized that French policies toward Germany were motivated by fear and not by a desire for aggrandizement. In March 1923, for example, Ambassador Houghton emphasized to Secretary Hughes that France used reparations only as an excuse. "Her real policy," he reported, "is based upon fear of what a strong and powerful Germany could and perhaps would do. And if she can prevent it, there will never again be a strong and powerful Germany."[73] American emissaries nonetheless believed that French actions would prove harmful whether their motives were justified or not. James Logan, the influential assistant unofficial American delegate to the Reparations Commission, urgently wrote Hughes in February 1923:

> We cannot emphasize too much or too strongly that any form of the present policy [of military sanctions] . . . is disastrous for reparations, for Germany, for France, and for all outside nations, both from the point of view of economics and of peace, which is one of the most important factors of economics.[74]

While understanding the sources of French conduct and perceiving the results of French behavior, American officials did not think that any conceivable American strategic or political commitment would either influence the French to act very differently or persuade them to alter their conception of national security. Roland Boyden, the unofficial American delegate to the Reparations Commission in the early 1920s, emphasized that "this state of mind [French fear of German military and economic power] cannot be eradicated by the ratification of a treaty or any other guarantee of safety to France."

70. Hoover, *Memoirs*, II, 182; Bernard Baruch, *The Making of the Reparation and Economic Sections of the Treaty* (New York, 1970), p. 50; Thomas W. Lamont, *Across World Frontiers* (New York, 1950), p. 125.

71. Memorandum of Conversation between Hughes and Jusserand, November 5, 1923, box 174 (France), Hughes Papers.

72. Morrow to Hughes, July 12, 1924, box 56 (Dawes Plan), ibid.

73. Houghton to Hughes, March 6, 1923, box 43, ibid.; also see Fletcher to Hughes, November 28, 1922, box 9, Fletcher Papers.

74. Logan to Hughes, February 2, 1923, box 10, Fletcher Papers.

Hoover, too, assumed that the French would use a military alliance with the United States to maintain the status quo, to stifle progress, and to prevent the redress of grievances. Such feelings about French intentions persisted into the early 1930s. In August 1931, Secretary of State Stimson felt that when France talked about peace guaranteed by military action, "she was also seeking by this to freeze into permanency the extreme oscillation in her favor and against Germany which had resulted from the last war. . . . In other words, while she was ready to accept cooperation she wanted this cooperation to secure her hegemony as against Germany."[75]

Since key American officials believed that French security and European stability depended upon "taking Germany into camp" rather than upon maintaining the status quo,[76] they remained highly suspicious of French efforts to include the United States in European security accords. Americans worried that the extension of political and strategic commitments might envelop the United States in a European conflict over such issues as the payment of reparations, the stationing of French troops in Germany, the revision of Germany's eastern boundaries, and the demilitarization of the Rhineland. In the context of the 1920s and early 1930s, a war over these matters, undesirable as it might have been, did not seem to bear directly on American strategic interests.[77] Some American diplomats, like Hugh Wilson, moreover, felt a conflict over one or another of these issues was never far off. As a result, he warned against the United States becoming attached to European mutual assistance treaties whose very purpose was to uphold the status quo. He condemned French disarmament proposals because they were carefully framed to insure French security through concerted European action, but "failed to provide adequate facilities for altering by orderly processes a status where justice and the maintenance of peace require a change."[78]

American officials would not agree to guarantee French security because they fundamentally disagreed with the French on what constituted French

75. See Boyden to Harrison, March 25, 1921, box 2, Harrison Papers; Hoover, *Memoirs*, II, 11; *FR*, 1931, I, 515. While skeptical of their impact, Boyden did not oppose American guarantees of French security.

76. The quote appears in a letter from George Harvey (ambassador to Britain) to Harding, October 3, 1921, Presidential Personal File (PPF) 60, Harding Papers. Hughes concurred. See Hughes to Harding, October 25, 1921, ibid.

77. See, for example, the scenario for a European war that was in the mind of the isolationist senator James Reed, in Senate, Committee on Foreign Relations, *General Pact for the Renunciation of War*, Part I (Washington, 1928), 20. In the context of the 1920s, it was not unrealistic to assume that even a war between Germany and Poland might be contained and thus not threaten the security of England, let alone the United States. See Newman, *Balance of Power*, pp. 106–110; for the perspective of the American military, also see Greene, "Military View of American National Policy," p. 366.

78. See *FR*, I, 398–399.

security. In addition, they recognized their inability to impose their own definition of French security upon the French. In other words, American leaders had few illusions about the omnipotence of American power. They felt that the United States could not resolve the incendiary issues separating France and Germany simply by guaranteeing the integrity of French borders. In fact, American policymakers, including Hughes, Hoover, Harding, Stimson, and William Castle, understood that in Europe the United States was dealing with major powers whose national security in the most immediate sense was at stake in the discussions over disarmament, sanctions, mutual assistance, and reparations. It seemed imperative that these nations themselves settle their outstanding differences. Lasting peace depended upon mutual accommodation. Senator Irvine Lenroot best expressed the opinion of many American officials:

> Most of the problems of war and peace arise in Europe and they must be settled by the peoples most directly concerned, for while it is true that the United States is profoundly affected by war in any part of the world, it is also true that we cannot settle questions giving rise to such wars.[79]

While the United States refused to guarantee French "security," many American friends of France, as well as many Americans who were simply concerned with European stability, recognized that in certain contingencies the United States might have to defend France, perhaps even with military force.[80] They wanted the United States to reserve the right to determine when a threat to French "security" was a threat to American "security." Such a policy minimized the chances of the United States becoming involved in a European conflict that did not relate to vital American interests.[81] Moreover, by withholding

79. Irvine L. Lenroot, "Disarmament and the Present Outlook for Peace," *Annals of the American Academy of Political and Social Science*, 126 (July 1926), 145; also see Hughes to White, November 22, 1923, box 48, Hughes Papers; Harding to Richard W. Child, October 9, 1922, PPF 60, Harding Papers; Statement by Coolidge, in Howard H. Quint and Robert Ferrell, *The Talkative President: The Off-the-Record Press Conferences of Calvin Coolidge* (Amherst, 1964), p. 208; Memorandum of Conversation between Stimson and Arthur Henderson, July 15, 1931, General Records of the Department of State, File 462.00R296/4506½, RG 59.

80. See, for example, the survey of American press sentiment in "What Will We Do if France is Attacked Again?" *Literary Digest*, 71 (December 31, 1921), 50ff.; also see Lloyd E. Ambrosius, "Wilson, the Republicans, and French Security after World War I," *Journal of American History*, 59 (1972), 341–353.

81. In the 1920s, it was no doubt difficult for American officials to envision when a threat to French security might also be a threat to American security. Certainly, at least until 1933, German revisionism did not constitute a direct threat to American security. It is easy to understand, however, why the French felt it constituted a threat to French security. It was up to American policymakers in the middle 1930s to determine when the parameters of French and American security coincided.

their commitment and by staying outside of the League of Nations, some American leaders, including such "internationalists" as Stimson and Felix Frankfurter, believed that they were maximizing their influence in European affairs.[82]

During the 1920s and early 1930s, American officials had reason to look askance at French requests to guarantee French "security." Having obtained an American commitment, would the French have felt more or less inclined to make concessions? Would the influence and leverage of the United States in European affairs have been increased or decreased by commitments to French "security," especially if "security" were defined as the maintenance of the status quo? And if it were not defined in this way, would the French have been satisfied?[83] These questions cannot, of course, be answered with precision, but they must be considered before dismissing American policy during the Republican ascendancy as naive or moralistic. And it should not be forgotten that during this period American officials were dealing for the most part with Stresemann and Heinrich Brüning, with a republican and relatively disarmed Germany; not with Hitler and the Nazis, and not with a militaristic and bellicose Germany.

Indeed, the apparent existence of an intransigent and belligerent French leadership on the one hand and a moderate and conciliatory, if not always cooperative, German leadership on the other hand significantly influenced the way in which many American leaders perceived their options. Not long after the French occupation of the Ruhr, Senator Borah denounced French officials as "enemies of humanity, enemies of peace, and of good order throughout Europe." He went on to depict French Premier Raymond Poincaré's program as "vicious and as untenable as anything which has been announced in international affairs in the last one hundred years." Borah's statement, though an exaggerated expression of American sentiment, reflected the way in which many Americans tended to view the policies of the French government during the 1920s and early 1930s.[84] Diplomats like Hugh Wilson "could not escape the

82. See, for example, Allen Klots to Castle, October 2, 1931, General Records of the Department of State, File 033.5111 Laval/256½, RG 59; *FR*, 1931, I, 544–545; Frankfurter to Stimson, October 13, 1931, Stimson to Frankfurter, October 15, 1931, box 103, Felix Frankfurter Papers (Manuscript Division, Library of Congress).

83. The British also were reluctant to increase their commitments on the European continent lest France use these as a means of consolidating and institutionalizing a rigid and unnatural balance of power, especially in Eastern Europe. See Newman, *Balance of Power*, pp. 65–66, 92–97, 103–110, 164–165, 180.

84. For Borah's statement, see Borah to Charles R. Smith, February 2, 1923, box 227 (Europe), William E. Borah Papers (Manuscript Division, Library of Congress); for American attitudes toward France, see Elizabeth Brett White, *American Opinion of France* (New York, 1927), pp. 272–303.

impression that [with the one exception of the Herriot ministry of 1932] no other government of France had the faintest intention of surrendering or impairing its power to dictate to Germany."[85] Such interpretations of French intentions discouraged any American inclination to assume positive military commitments to alleviate French anxieties.

In contrast, German leaders, especially Stresemann, succeeded in convincing American policymakers that their goals were legitimate and their tactics peaceful. Stresemann's very prompt and positive response to the provisions of the Kellogg-Briand Pact typified his efforts throughout the 1920s to reap American goodwill, to procure American loans, and to elicit American support in behalf of the peaceful revision of the Treaty of Versailles.[86] Though American officials often were disgruntled with what they considered to be shortsighted and selfish German financial policies,[87] many of them nevertheless sympathized with German efforts to secure territorial adjustments on their eastern frontier, to achieve equality of rights under the Treaty of Versailles, and to effect some French disarmament. During 1931, Hoover, Stimson, Herbert Feis, and other prominent officials acknowledged that the resolution of the Polish Corridor issue in Germany's favor was a precondition for the stabilization of European affairs. German demands for such changes did not appear unreasonable or threatening while Brüning was in power and Germany still was relatively disarmed. In fact, satisfying Germany's legitimate grievances was considered a means of salvaging the Weimar Republic.[88]

In this framework, French and Polish recalcitrance served only to exasperate American officials. In December 1930, Ambassador Hugh Gibson wrote President Hoover that the French ought to "be realistic enough to know that

85. Hugh R. Wilson, *Diplomat between Wars* (New York, 1941), p. 266; also see, for example, Herbert Hoover and Hugh Gibson, *The Problems of Lasting Peace* (New York, 1942), pp. 143–145.

86. For Stresemann's reaction to Kellogg's proposals, see *FR*, 1928, I, 30–31, 42–44; Sutton, *Stresemann*, III, 376.

87. During the late 1920s, S. Parker Gilbert, the American agent-general for reparations, often criticized German financial policies. See, for example, Memorandum for the Reparations Commission, by the Agent-General, February 24, 1928, Records of the Bureau of Accounts, box 85, RG 39; for American attitudes during the financial crisis of 1931, see, for example, Walter Newton (from Hoover) to Henry Robinson, July 27, 1931, box 28, "Individual File, Henry Robinson," Herbert Hoover Presidential Library.

88. For evidence of American sympathy with many of Germany's revisionist aims, see diary entries, September 30, 1931, October 6, 12, 23, 1931, volume 18. Stimson Diaries; *FR*, 1931, I, 524–525; Feis to Shotwell, October 27, 1931, box 26, Herbert Feis Papers (Manuscript Division, Library of Congress); Memorandum, by Moffat, October 5, 1931, General Records of the Department of State, File 033.5111 Laval/257, RG 59. For Stimson's desire to help the Brüning government, see, for example, Memorandum of Conversation between Castle, Stimson, and Hoover, July 24, 1931, box 875, "Foreign Affairs—Financial," Herbert Hoover Presidential Library.

they can't hold Germany down permanently and that if they persist in trying there is going to be an explosion as soon as Germany is strong enough to explode."[89] Less than a year later, when the Polish ambassador warned the president that if Polish rights in the Corridor were tampered with, Poland might resort to the use of force, Stimson was infuriated.[90] Threats of this sort and rumors of impending war[91] reinforced the desire of American officials to avoid firm guarantees of French "security" lest they become militarily committed to preserving a status quo that they considered unrelated to the vital interests of the United States.

## V. The Kellogg-Briand Pact, American Neutrality, and Mutual Assistance

During the period 1921–1933, many influential American businessmen, bankers, and government officials deplored the refusal of Frenchmen "to look at Europe as a whole, to comprehend that the welfare of France is related to the welfare of Europe."[92] However, since France's preoccupation with security complicated the settlement of other European issues, prominent Americans eventually began to consider various means by which the United States could make a strategic contribution to French security and to European stability without incurring binding military commitments. The Kellogg-Briand Treaty of 1928 served as the focal point for the ensuing debate.

In early 1927, French Foreign Minister Aristide Briand was anxious both to improve the image of France in America and to link the United States, however indirectly, to the French alliance system. Therefore, he proposed that the two nations sign a bilateral accord renouncing the use of war. Initially, the Coolidge administration responded coolly to the Briand proposal. The American peace movement, however, exerted tremendous pressure in behalf of some concrete action to outlaw war and to stabilize international relations. By the autumn of 1927, Coolidge and Kellogg succumbed to public pressure and decided to seek a multilateral pact outlawing war. Senator Borah, the powerful chairman of the Foreign Relations committee, supported this multilateral approach, but vigorously objected to any accord providing for the use of sanctions to enforce the treaty. Kellogg accepted Borah's view. Then, by patiently negotiating outstanding differences with the major powers, the secretary of

89. Gibson to Hoover, December 31, 1930, box 849, "Foreign Affairs—France," ibid.

90. Diary entry, October 21, 1931, volume 18, Stimson Diaries.

91. Castle to Frederic H. Sackett, October 23, 1931, December 14, 1931, box 5, William Castle Papers (Herbert Hoover Presidential Library, West Branch, Iowa).

92. For the quotation, see Vanderlip, *What Next in Europe?* p. 151; also see, for example, Hoover and Gibson, *Problems of Lasting Peace*, p. 143; Henry L. Stimson and McGeorge Bundy, *On Active Service in Peace and War* (New York, 1948), p. 272.

state secured their adherence to a multilateral pact renouncing the use of armed force as an instrument of national policy.[93]

The Kellogg-Briand Treaty, as it was molded by the secretary of state and the chairman of the Senate Foreign Relations Committee, reflected certain significant aspects of American policy in the 1920s. Borah's insistence on the absence of sanctions revealed his skepticism about the utility of force, his fear of unknown commitments, and his emphasis on attacking the sources rather than the manifestations of discontent. He and Kellogg were both anxious to maintain America's independence of action and America's distance from the French alliance system. Rather than use alliances to guarantee the status quo, they hoped to see the emergence of a stable community of great nations adjusting peacefully to necessary changes. Borah spoke frequently of finding alternative means of adjudicating disputes, and Kellogg maintained a real interest in consummating conciliation and arbitration treaties. But Borah in particular was skeptical of the inclination of European nations to renounce force. He suspected Briand's motives and, like other American officials, he saw no reason why France should be singled out for special treatment. With Europe never far from war, he was determined to keep the United States out of any conflict that did not affect vital American interests.[94]

While desiring to maintain America's independence of action and eschewing the utility of force, Borah and Kellogg were neither idealists nor moralists. Indeed, there was an acute streak of pragmatism that characterized their thinking. Though they were opposed to using force to maintain peace wherever it was threatened and consequently excluded enforcement machinery from the pact, they were not averse to using force to safeguard the national self-interest. And they understood that such terms as "national self-interest" and "national self-defense" could be interpreted in diverse ways. Borah told the Senate Foreign Relations Committee that "every nation . . . will construe this treaty in any way it regards as justifying self-defense." Likewise, Kellogg emphasized that "any nation [including the United States] has the right [under the pact] to defend its interests anywhere in the world."[95]

93. Ferrell, *Peace in Their Time,* pp. 66–192; Ellis, *Kellogg,* pp. 193–208; Jean-Baptiste Duroselle, *From Wilson to Roosevelt: Foreign Policy of the United States, 1913–1945* (Cambridge, 1963), pp. 174–181.

94. For Borah's views, see Vinson, *Borah,* especially pp. 16, 24, 61–66, 97, 100, 102–103, 122–131, 161; for Kellogg's dislike for alliances in general and for French alliances in particular, see, for example, *FR,* 1928, I, 36; for Kellogg's interest in arbitration treaties, see Ellis, *Kellogg,* pp. 222–225; for American policymakers' objection to renouncing war with only one nation, see "The Security Question," by Noel Field (Division of Western European Affairs), December 1931, box 17, Davis Papers; for a more critical appraisal of Borah's motives, see Robert James Maddox, "William E. Borah and the Crusade to Outlaw War," *The Historian,* 29 (1967), 200–220.

95. For the statements of Borah and Kellogg, see U.S. Senate, Foreign Relations, *Renunciation of War,* pp. 5–6, 16, 26.

The heart of the matter, then, was the ensuing debate over what consti-tuted national defense and over what means should be taken to protect the national self-interest. This was not a dispute between idealists and realists, but a controversy between practical men who disagreed on vital issues. Borah, Kellogg, Hoover, and others, while concerned with European stability, doubted whether the benefits of an increased political involvement would outweigh the dangers inherent in political commitments. Probably suspecting that changes in French behavior would not be commensurate with the risks assumed by the United States, they opposed efforts to define "aggression" and to insert sanctions into the proposed pact.[96] They felt little sympathy for the French quest for security. Indeed, Borah and Hoover believed that the French commitment to the Treaty of Versailles was an inherently destabilizing influence.[97]

On the other hand, prominent individuals like Norman Davis, James Shot-well, Arthur Capper, and subsequently Henry Stimson and Dwight Morrow felt that the United States could play a more constructive role in stabilizing European affairs without incurring dangerous commitments. They, too, dis-agreed with the French definition of security, but they nevertheless empa-thized with French anxieties and assumed that the French would act in the interests of long-term European stability if they felt more secure. Conse-quently, these more "internationally oriented" individuals wished not only to define "aggression," but also to alter American neutrality policy when aggres-sion occurred. This was not an effort to involve the United States in European political affairs in a large way. Ironically, it was an attempt to act constructively by taking negative action, that is, by not insisting upon respect for American neutral rights when aggression occurred and when other nations were acting collectively to punish an aggressor. And once the Kellogg-Briand Pact de-clared aggressive war a crime, there was increasing justification for changing the whole concept of neutrality.[98]

96. For the attitudes of Kellogg, Borah, and Hoover toward sanctions, see, for example, ibid., pp. 7, 21; Vinson, *Borah*, pp. 137ff.; Myers, *State Papers*, II, 260, 475–476; also see Borah to Oscar S. Straus, January 9, 1923, box 227 (Europe), Borah Papers.

97. Vinson, *Borah*, pp. 99–100, 179; Hoover, *Memoirs*, II, 11; also see Borah to Hoover, July 23, 1931, box 874, "Foreign Affairs—Financial," Herbert Hoover Presidential Library.

98. See James T. Shotwell, "The Problem of Disarmament," *Annals of the American Acad-emy of Political and Social Science*, 126 (July 1926), 51–55; Shotwell, *War as an Instrument*, pp. 220–223; Arthur Capper, "Making the Peace Pact Effective," *Annals of the American Academy of Political and Social Science*, 144 (July 1929), 59–65; for Davis's thinking on the pact, see Davis to Pat Harrison, December 17, 1928, box 27, Davis Papers; Memorandum, no date [late 1928], ibid.; for efforts to revise American neutrality policies in the mid-1920s, see Charles DeBene-detti, "The Origins of Neutrality Revision: The American Plan of 1924," *The Historian*, 35 (1972), 75–89.

The Kellogg-Briand Pact, therefore, must be understood in relation to the ongoing European negotiations regarding regional security agreements, and especially in relation to the discussions between Britain and France over the responsibility of Britain to cooperate in the application of sanctions against an aggressor nation. Since the early 1920s, the British had been trying to avoid additional commitments to enforce sanctions. They rationalized their position by explaining that if the British navy were called upon to enforce an economic embargo and if the American government insisted on respect for its neutral rights, an Anglo-American confrontation might ensue. This claim was not unfounded since Secretary of State Hughes had refused to modify the traditional American stand on neutrality during the debate over the Geneva Protocol in 1924.[99]

The Kellogg-Briand Treaty, however, raised the possibility of eventual revisions in American neutrality policies. Many European statesmen realized this. As a result, although they looked upon the pact somewhat cynically, they still considered it a hopeful omen of future American collaboration in European attempts to maintain peace. Walter Lippmann accurately noted that the Kellogg-Briand Treaty "alters the expectation of Europe as to what the United States will do in the event of a breach of the Covenant or of the Locarno treaties."[100]

Thus, in the context of the 1920s, the Kellogg-Briand Pact was an important step toward increasing American participation in European affairs. It constituted a foundation for additional initiatives to build a stable international order. Though it was also a sop to the public and though some may have been taken in by the absence of sanctions, Coolidge, Hoover, Stimson, and most senators, including Borah, were not. In fact, shortly after his inauguration, Hoover suggested amending the pact in order "to make it more potent." Stimson subsequently tried to use the treaty to lay "the foundations of a constructive policy of world stabilization."[101]

99. In June 1933, Lord Tyrrell, the British ambassador to France, bluntly acknowledged that "it was always believed in France that the key to action by Great Britain was the abandonment of neutrality by the United States." See *DBFP*, II, V, 333; for the issue of American neutrality during the discussions over the Geneva Protocol, see David D. Burks, "The United States and the Geneva Protocol of 1924: 'A New Holy Alliance?'" *American Historical Review*, 64 (1959), 891–905; *FR*, 1925, I, 16–20.

100. Walter Lippmann, "Public Opinion and the Renunciation of War," *Proceedings of the Academy of Political Science*, 13 (January 1929), 50–51; Shotwell, *War as an Instrument*, pp. 221ff.; see also *DDB*, II, 527; Roland Stromberg, *Collective Security and American Foreign Policy* (New York, 1963), pp. 58ff.; also see Robert B. Dockhorn, "The Wilhelmstrasse and the Search for a New Diplomatic Order, 1926–30" (unpub. PhD diss., University of Wisconsin, 1972), pp. 153–204.

101. Hoover, *Memoirs*, II, 336, 343–344; Stimson, "Bases of American Foreign Policy," pp.

It was not until the London Naval Conference of 1930, however, that American officials grasped the full significance of the Kellogg-Briand Pact for French security. At London, the American delegation realized that the French request for a consultative pact with the United States was only important to the French insofar as it would facilitate an Anglo-French understanding on mutual assistance. Dwight Morrow, one of the American delegates, emphasized to Stimson that the French were not asking the United States "to enter into any entangling alliances in Europe, but merely to assure Great Britain that America would not impede her in the performance of her continental obligations." The object of a consultative pact, then, was to provide a framework for discussions between Britain and the United States over the latter's attitude toward measures recommended by the League Council in cases of aggression. If the league urged the application of sanctions, the United States government would advise Britain whether American neutrality rights had to be respected. In an article in *Foreign Affairs*, André Géraud, the influential French journalist, explained:

> It had long been well known that no conceivable British Government would jump at the throat of an aggressor, on the League's request, unless it had ascertained beforehand that America was not determined to uphold her neutral rights upon the seas. But what was merely understood has now . . . become a fixed principle of British policy.[102]

The great failure of American policy, however, was that almost nothing was done for over a year after the London Conference. Hoover and Stimson, though very much interested in disarmament on the land and the seas, made little effort to convince the public or the Congress of the need to revise the nation's neutrality practices. The administration's negligence on this matter can only be explained in terms of the more pressing domestic economic issues and international financial questions posed by the Depression.

This did not mean that American policymakers had lost interest in the European political situation. Stimson kept urging European leaders to grapple realistically with the problems before them.[103] And officials in the State De-

---

389–391; Vinson, *Borah*, pp. 133–135, 171–177; also see Calvin Coolidge, "Promoting Peace through Renunciation of War," p. 161.

102. For the quotations, see Harold Nicolson, *Dwight Morrow* (New York, 1935), p. 368; Géraud, "London Naval Conference," pp. 530–531; also see Stimson to Cotton, March 23, 1930, box 849, "Foreign Affairs—France," Herbert Hoover Presidential Library; Walter Lippmann, "The London Naval Conference: An American View," *Foreign Affairs*, 8 (July 1930), 514; Philip Kerr, "Europe and the United States," *Journal of the Royal Institute of International Affairs*, 9 (May 1930), 295, 301, 308–313, 317.

103. See, for example, *FR*, 1931, I, 321–322, 542–548, 552, 561.

partment continued to ponder the problem of dealing with the French obsession with security. "The feeling is there and cannot be ignored, however unreasonable it may seem to us," commented Pierrepont Moffat, chief of the Division of Western European Affairs. Rather than guarantee a vision of security they found unacceptable, top policymakers in the State Department proceeded to reexamine the efficacy of revising American neutrality policy. Their aim was to alleviate the French fear "that the United States might interfere in its own interest against some common action against an aggressor . . . and thus set the present structure on which [France's] security is based at naught."[104] Significantly, while Stimson was in England in August 1931, he told British Prime Minister Ramsay MacDonald that the American navy would never be used to enforce an extreme doctrine of neutrality. On September 10, he reiterated this to the French chargé with unusual clarity.[105]

Nevertheless, when Premier Pierre Laval visited Washington in October 1931, Hoover said he could neither sign a consultative pact nor declare a change in American neutrality policy. The president claimed that these were political impossibilities. Instead, he simply told Laval that the United States would never be found on the side of an aggressor.[106] Hoover might have been more flexible had he not felt that the French were purposely withdrawing gold from the United States and thus exacerbating the domestic financial crisis. This infuriated him, as it came not long after the acrimonious dispute over the debt moratorium. To Hoover, France seemed not only intransigent, but totally irresponsible. He confided to Stimson that "France always goes through this cycle. After she is done and begins to recuperate . . . she gets rich, militaristic, and cocky; and nobody can get on with her until she has to be thrashed again."[107]

When the Geneva Conference convened in early 1932, however, Hugh Gibson and Norman Davis, the two key American delegates, reported that the French were not intransigent. French Premier André Tardieu and French delegate Louis Aubert emphasized to the Americans that they did not expect security guarantees from the United States. Tardieu claimed that he only

104. See Memorandum, by Moffat, October 5, 1931, General Records of the Department of State, File 711.0012 Anti-War/1189½, RG 59; Klots to Castle, October 2, 1931, ibid., 033.5111 Laval/256½.

105. *FR*, 1931, I, 514–516, 524–525.

106. For accounts of the Hoover-Laval conversations, see diary entries, October 22–25, 1931, volume 18, Stimson Diaries; Memorandum of Conversation between Stimson and Ronald Lindsay, October 26, 1931, General Records of the Department of State, File 033.5111 Laval/168, RG 59; *DBFP*, II, II, 307–308, 317–318.

107. Diary entry, October 24, 1931, volume 18, Stimson Diaries; for Hoover's suspicions that the French were withdrawing gold, see diary entry, October 20, 1931, ibid.; for the dispute over the debt moratorium, see *FR*, 1931, I, 42–164.

wanted assurances that the United States "would refrain from cutting across the course of action determined on by the League, that would be a maximum which could be hoped for from America." Davis believed that the French premier finally had realized that France could not dominate the continent by military force. Shortly thereafter, when the more moderate Radical-Socialists emerged victorious in the May elections, the American delegates became increasingly convinced that the time was propitious for the Hoover administration to launch a disarmament offensive.[108]

In Washington, throughout the spring of 1932, American policymakers agonized over what should be done. Stimson was preoccupied with the Far East situation and was reluctant to undertake any action that might lead to the weakening of the American navy.[109] With regard to Europe, the secretary of state believed that the crux of the impasse was the British reluctance to provide France with additional guarantees of security. Accordingly, when he was in Geneva in April, Stimson told the British that they had no reason to justify their policies on the grounds of American neutrality.[110] In June, however, under the constant prodding of the American delegation, and as a result of fiscal and political considerations, Hoover assumed the initiative and presented a list of American proposals to the Disarmament Conference. The Hoover Plan of June 22 provided for the abolition of tanks, bombing planes, chemical warfare, and large mobile guns, for the reduction of land armies (above a certain minimum size) by one-third, and for the further diminution of naval tonnage.[111]

Though Hoover's proposals did not refer to American neutrality policies, they were a serious, albeit unsuccessful, effort to inject life into the disarmament talks.[112] The introduction of an American plan revealed that the United States was embarking upon an active course to try to make the conference a success and to contribute to European stability. Soon thereafter, Stimson also indicated that the United States was prepared to reconsider its position on the technical, but very important, questions of inspection and budgetary limitation.[113] At the same time, the administration succeeded in getting both the

---

108. For the quotation, see *FR*, 1932, I, 55ff.; also see ibid., 34–39, 62–67, 142–143, 145–150; Aubert to Davis, March 16, 1932, box 20, Davis Papers.

109. Hooker, *Moffat Papers*, pp. 59–72.

110. *FR*, 1932, I, 104–108, 112–119; *DBFP*, II, III, 516.

111. For Hoover's disarmament proposals, see *FR*, 1932, I, 212–214.

112. After the presentation of the Hoover plan, the American delegates told Stimson and Hoover that "it has been without doubt the biggest day we have ever had at Geneva." See *FR*, 1932, I, 215; also see Wilson, *Diplomat between Wars*, p. 273; Hooker, *Moffat Papers*, pp. 74–75.

113. For the issue of inspection, see *FR*, 1932, I, 249; Ministère des Affaires Étrangères, *Documents diplomatiques français*, Series I, Volume I (Paris, 1964), 136 [hereafter this source will be cited as *DDF*]. For the discussions over budgetary limitations, see *FR*, 1932, I, 295ff.; also see

Republican and Democratic parties to accept the principle of consultation.[114] Even more significantly, on August 8, 1932, in a major public address to the Council on Foreign Relations, the secretary of state proclaimed that the Kellogg-Briand Pact altered many legal precedents and made consultation inevitable.[115] For the first time, then, there was the real prospect that the United States might revise its neutrality practices.

Hoover's disarmament proposals and Stimson's speech had a positive impact on the French government. Premier Édouard Herriot made a concerted effort to influence the French press and to mold French public opinion in favor of a positive reaction to the American initiatives.[116] Within the highest councils of the French government, Herriot and Joseph Paul-Boncour, the minister of war, pleaded with Generals Weygand and Pétain to allow the ministry to try to reconcile French security requirements with the American disarmament program.[117] Thus, the French plan that was submitted to the Disarmament Conference in November 1932 was a compromise proposal. On the one hand, it tried to satisfy the French military and the French right; on the other hand, it tried to placate the Americans and the British. What was especially significant was the French attempt to insure French security without demanding action from the United States that was beyond the realm of possibility, that is, without asking the United States to promise to use force to deter aggression. The French only wanted a triple American commitment to consult, to refuse to recognize the fruits of aggression, and to refrain from trading with and financing an aggressor nation.[118]

On the whole, the American delegates were disappointed with the French plan.[119] Republican officials, however, kept trying to participate constructively in the disarmament negotiations, but within the bounds set by Ameri-

---

Thomas Casey Irvin, "Norman H. Davis and the Quest for Arms Control, 1931–1938" (unpub. PhD diss., Ohio State University, 1963), pp. 78ff.

114. See, for example, Claude Swanson to Joseph T. Robinson, March 7, 1932, box 20, Davis Papers; Robinson to Swanson, March 15, 1932, ibid.; Stimson to Swanson, June 22, 1932, General Records of the Department of State, File 711.0012 Anti-War/1261, RG 59.

115. *FR*, 1932, I, 575–583. American policy, of course, was also reacting to events in the Far East. But when Stimson began preparing his speech, he certainly had the European crisis as well as the Asian imbroglio in mind. See, for example, diary entries, June 29, 30, 1932, July 14, 1932, volume 23, Stimson Diaries.

116. For Herriot's efforts, see Norman Armour to Stimson, August 12, 1932, General Records of the Department of State, File 711.0012 Anti-War/1284, RG 59; "Walter Edge to Stimson, August 19, 1932, ibid., 711.0012 Anti-War/1320; Edge to Stimson, July 29, 1932, box 17, Davis Papers.

117. See the documents in *DDF*, I, I, 435–437, 439–462, 476–490, 499–503, 509–525, 544–553, 560–584, 614–641.

118. For the French plan, see *FR*, 1932, I, 180–186. For some comments on the French plan by the American delegates, see ibid., pp. 348–350, 356–358, 360–361.

119. Ibid., pp. 389–390, 399–401; Davis to Stimson, January 16, 1933, box 32, Davis Papers.

can public opinion and American strategic interests. Accordingly, Stimson told visiting Frenchmen that the United States would never interfere with league action against an aggressor.[120] And Hoover asked Congress for authority to control the shipment of arms from the United States in order to cooperate in maintaining world peace.[121] But at the same time, American officials insisted on the right to determine for themselves who was the aggressor and when aggression had occurred. Likewise, Stimson and Davis told the French that though the United States government felt obligated to consult, this could not be put in treaty form. The most the French could expect was a unilateral declaration of American policy.[122]

During the spring of 1933, President Franklin D. Roosevelt tried to move more decisively to accommodate the French and to effect a disarmament accord. In late April, he told Herriot that he supported automatic and continuous inspection to insure that violations of a disarmament agreement did not occur. The president also reaffirmed his opposition to any German rearmament. Subsequently, on May 16, his address to world leaders probably had a moderating impact on Hitler's intent to embark upon a course of immediate and overt rearmament. And finally, on May 21, Davis's public presentation of the revised American position on consultation and neutrality represented the culmination of the continuous American involvement in the security-disarmament controversy.[123]

When these initiatives failed to break the impasse at Geneva and when the Senate Foreign Relations Committee refused to report out a satisfactory neutrality bill, Democratic policymakers began intimating their intent to withdraw from European affairs. Such inclinations were intensified by the pervasive discord over international economic issues and by the acrimonious developments at the London Economic Conference.[124] By the middle of October, it was evident that Roosevelt had decided upon a course of domestic

120. Memorandum of conversation between Stimson and Stanislas de la Rochefoucauld, November 15, 1932, General Records of the Department of State, File 800.51W89/587, RG 59.

121. Myers, *State Papers*, II, 565–566, 599.

122. Memorandum of Conversation between Davis and Herriot, November 18, 1932, box 17, Davis Papers; *FR*, 1932, I, 359–360; also see *DDF*, I, II, 51–52.

123. For Roosevelt's policy in the spring of 1933, see Robert Divine, "F.D.R. and Collective Security, 1933," *Mississippi Valley Historical Review*, 48 (1961), 42–58; for Roosevelt's talks with Herriot, see *DDF*, I, III, 314, 316–317, 326–327; *FR*, 1933, I, 106–107, 110–112; for Roosevelt's opposition to German rearmament, see Memorandum of Conversation between Hjalmar Schacht and Roosevelt, May 6, 1933, General Records of the Department of State, File 550.S1 Washington/408, RG 59; for Roosevelt's address of May 16 and Davis's speech on May 21, see *FR*, 1933, I, 143–145, 154–158.

124. See, for example, *DDF*, I, III, 465–466, 616–621; Divine, "F.D.R. and Collective Security," pp. 57–59; also see Edgar G. Nixon, ed., *Franklin D. Roosevelt and Foreign Affairs* (Cambridge, 1969–), I, 291–294.

reform and reconstruction. He did not wish to risk a divisive debate over foreign policy. Assuming that the nation's security was not threatened by developments in Europe, the president, in part, concurred with and, in part, acquiesced in the isolationist sentiment overrunning the country.[125] He no longer tried to reconcile the imperatives of domestic recovery with the exigencies of European stability. He had come to believe, at least temporarily, that it was possible to bring about economic recovery regardless of political and economic conditions in Europe.[126]

This marked a turning point in American policy toward Western Europe in the interwar period. With the nation's financial and economic power emasculated by the Depression, Democratic policymakers could find no alternative means to exert a stabilizing influence in Europe.[127] The new object of American policy, at least for several years, was to insure America's isolation from a European war. Consequently, all attempts to exert pressure in behalf of a moderate disarmament accord ceased.[128]

## VI. Conclusion

Ironically, American efforts to participate constructively in the struggle for European stability came to an end when that struggle had greater ramifications for American security than ever before. But the purpose of this essay has not been to review Republican foreign policies in order to compare them favorably with Democratic policies in the 1930s. Rather, the intent has been to shed some light on two related questions: To what extent did American policy toward Western Europe constitute political isolationism, economic expansionism, or diplomatic realism in the context of the 1920s and early 1930s? To what extent did the desire to restore Germany, to stabilize Europe, and to effect disarmament through the application of financial power and the revision of American neutrality practices constitute a shrewd effort to expand the American empire or a naive attempt to escape the realities of international politics?

There can be little doubt that William A. Williams's incisive and suggestive article on the legend of isolationism in the 1920s opened up an important area of research and correctly emphasized certain salient aspects of American di-

125. Robert Dallek, "Franklin Roosevelt as World Leader," *American Historical Review*, 75 (1971), 1504.

126. See, for example, Herbert Feis, *1933: Characters in Crisis* (Boston, 1966), pp. 279–306; Elmus Wicker, "Roosevelt's 1933 Monetary Experiment" *Journal of American History*, 57 (1971), 864–879.

127. Jules Henry, the well-informed French chargé d'affaires in Washington, noted the impact of the Depression on American influence in Europe. See *DDF*, II, II, 675–676.

128. See, for example, *FR*, 1933, I, 299–300, 331.

plomacy during the era of the Republican ascendancy.[129] It is important, however, not to draw erroneous conclusions from that essay. The growth of American industry and commerce did foster an appreciation of the importance of the international economy to American well-being. Likewise, the expansion of overseas investments and foreign loans did generate a desire to create a community of economic interests among the industrialized powers. But these trends did not generate a consensus of business opinion regarding the necessity of foreign markets for the viability of the American capitalist system. Indeed, even Hoover occasionally cautioned against overestimating the extent to which the American economy was dependent upon the international economy. The related beliefs that the United States could survive, if not prosper, in relative economic self-containment and that the United States could recover independently from any economic setback were deeply embedded in the American business community and in policymaking circles.[130] In fact, these views help to explain why Republican officials often were slow to work out the inconsistencies in American foreign economic policies and why they remained reluctant to become more deeply involved in European political affairs. Thus, it is misleading to stress only the expansionist elements of American diplomacy, to discount the significance of political isolationism, or to overlook the elements of economic nationalism in American economic policies.

On the other hand, the so-called realists must try to overcome the Munich syndrome and to consider American foreign policy in proper perspective. In the 1920s, there was no threat to American security. Recognizing this, Republican officials wanted to create a prosperous international economy that would redound to the benefit of all nations, including the United States. Although American policymakers also believed in law and moral suasion as important instruments for reconciling international disputes, their real hope was to deter serious international tensions from arising in the first place. This task, they felt, might be accomplished by dealing with the economic causes of conflict and by redressing Germany's legitimate grievances. It was not the naiveté of American diplomatic goals, but the breakdown of the international

129. Williams, "Legend of Isolationism," pp. 1–20.

130. For some references to the nation's relative economic self-containment and to the ability of the United States to recover independently from the rest of the world, see, for example, Herbert Hoover, "A Year of Cooperation," *Nation's Business*, 10 (June 5, 1922), 13; Julius Barnes, "The Treatment of the Allied Debts," *Commercial and Financial Chronicle*, 115 (October 28, 1922), 1884; Herbert Hoover, "The Question of Stability is a Great Human Problem," *Journal of the American Bankers Association*, 23 (October, 1930), 257; also see NAM, *Proceedings*, 1927, 82; Department of Commerce, *Commerce Yearbook*, 1924 (Washington, 1924), pp. 460, 514–516; ibid., 1928, pp. 92ff.; ibid., 1930, pp. 88ff.; "Final Declaration," in NFTC, *Official Report*, 1931, p. viii; Lamont, "Prospects of United States Foreign Trade," ibid., 1929, pp. 13–20; Charles E. Mitchell, *Back to First Principles* (New York, 1922), p. 17; also see references in footnote 36.

economy and the resulting social and political chaos, that had such disastrous consequences.

This is not to say that Republican policy toward Western Europe was bold or imaginative. But it was realistic in the sense that there were continuous (though sometimes belated and misguided) efforts to establish diplomatic policies that were commensurate with the value attributed to diplomatic goals. Linking means and ends, however, was an extraordinarily complex task because of the multitude of conflicting economic and political factors bearing on the decision-making process and because of the dispute between French and American officials over what constituted French security and European stability.

The reluctance of Republicans to incur strategic commitments and their antipathy to using force to uphold the status quo, however, did not reflect any lack of concern with American national security. Instead, they realized that the outbreak of hostilities anywhere in the world did not necessarily involve vital American interests and justify the armed intervention of the United States. They also understood that major powers might resort to war for limited purposes if their grievances were not redressed. Such conflicts might or might not affect crucial American interests. It was the task of American officials to judge when aggression elsewhere impinged upon the national security. Such situations were not likely to be clear-cut. This was especially true while the Weimar Republic survived (and while it appeared that Japanese ambitions might be confined to Manchuria and North China).

Republican officials did not reject the use of force in international affairs. But it was to be used only in the last resort. Accordingly, President Hoover declared in a campaign speech in Salt Lake City on November 7, 1932: "I should be the last man in the world to say that war is never justified. . . . There are issues which it is right that men, if need be, should sacrifice their lives to defend." But he went on to admit that the Great War and its aftermath

> have impressed upon my mind with ineradicable vividness the colossal error of war as an instrument of national policy. I have learned the futility of war as a solvent of great human problems, and I have perceived the fearful toll that war takes of the generations succeeding the one which fought the battles.[131]

As a result of such perceptions, American officials between 1921 and 1933 tried to develop alternative means of fostering European stability and of promoting American interests. They resorted to the use of economic power, to the application of financial leverage, to the advocacy of disarmament, and, ultimately, to the modification of traditional neutrality practices. Even in

131. Myers, *State Papers*, II, 474–475.

early 1933, President Hoover still hoped that some means would be found to restore stability and to forestall another conflict.[132] Meanwhile, however, he did not ignore his obligation to safeguard the nation's security. National defense, he declared, "is the first and most solemn obligation" of the federal government.[133] But Hoover defined the nation's security perimeter in a relatively narrow sense.[134] And he did not equate all diplomatic goals, e.g., the open door, with the national security.[135]

Did these policies in the 1920s and early 1930s constitute a form of realism? Were they rational attempts to cultivate American self-interest in an international environment not yet beset by powers clearly intent on world domination? Or did they establish precedents that invited subsequent fascist expansion? To raise such questions anew is to emphasize the importance of studying foreign policy in the proper historical context. Only then will it be possible to draw proper conclusions from past events and to conduct a meaningful debate on the evolution of American foreign policy.

132. Ibid., pp. 586–595.

133. Ibid., p. 388.

134. Hoover apparently believed that security meant the ability to resist either a foreign attack on the territorial integrity of the United States or a foreign assault against the Western Hemisphere. See ibid., pp. 18, 257; John M. R. Wilson, "Herbert Hoover and the Armed Forces: A Study of Presidential Attitudes and Policy" (unpub. PhD diss., Northwestern University, 1971), pp. 7–10, 30, 32, 67.

135. This helps to explain why Hoover opposed the use of sanctions against Japan in 1931–1932. See, for example, Hoover to Stimson, June 3, 1936 (including undated memorandum from 1931–1932), box 178, "Stimson, Individual File," Herbert Hoover Post-Presidential Papers (Herbert Hoover Presidential Library, West Branch, Iowa).

# 4

# The American Conception of National Security and the Beginnings of the Cold War, 1945–1948

When I shifted my attention to studying U.S. policy after World War II, I wanted to know why the United States involved itself so quickly in European political controversies, offered governmental aid like the Marshall Plan, and assumed strategic obligations like the North Atlantic Treaty when it had not done so after World War I. My examination of U.S. policy in the interwar years had alerted me to the importance of threat perception as a key interpretive lens to view the unfolding of U.S. foreign policy. It was not clear to me why U.S. officials in 1945 and 1946 were so worried about the Soviet Union when that country was so much weaker than the United States and when it had suffered so much damage during the war itself. Why were policymakers in Washington feeling so fearful when the potential adversary had no strategic air force, no real navy, and no atomic bomb? I realized that to examine the

Research on this article was made possible by generous support from the Woodrow Wilson International Center, the Council on Foreign Relations, the Harry S. Truman Institute, and the Vanderbilt University Research Council. The author wishes to express his gratitude for the incisive comments and constructive criticism of Samuel Walker, Michael Hogan, Walter LaFeber, Thomas G. Paterson, Charles Eagles, Cecilia Stiles, Eduard Mark, Robert Pollard, Rajon Menon, Ernest May, and Andrew Goodpaster. Special thanks go to David Rosenberg for his unceasing efforts to declassify documents pertaining to atomic strategy.

threat perceptions of these U.S. policymakers, I had to grasp their views of vital interests. I had to understand what it was that seemed endangered to them and why.

I was fortunate that in the late 1970s the U.S. government declassified millions of pages of military documents. I could examine the records of the Joint Chiefs of Staff and those of leading military and civilian officials in the Army, Navy, Air Force, and the newly created Department of Defense.

Previously, few diplomatic historians had looked extensively at military records; indeed, military history and diplomatic history often were regarded as two distinct fields. But the military records I looked at offered me a magnificent lens to understand the unfolding of U.S. foreign policy and the beginnings of the Cold War. These records illuminated how the concept of national security evolved and clarified its essential ingredients. Equally important, these documents demonstrated (to my great surprise) that U.S. military officers and their civilian leaders did not think that the Kremlin was poised to engage in premeditated military aggression. They did not think Soviet dictator Joseph Stalin wanted to begin another war. They grasped Stalin's view of his own military vulnerabilities and intuited that he wished to avoid military conflict.

Nonetheless, U.S. officials felt threatened.

They felt threatened precisely because of the lessons they had learned from World War II itself and the definition of America's vital interests that waging World War II had taught them. They had learned that an adversary, or coalition of adversaries, that conquered other countries could assimilate their resources into their own military machine, wage aggressive war, and challenge America's vital interests. Although the Kremlin seemed unlikely to wage war, it nevertheless had the capacity to gain indirect leverage or control over many countries in Europe and Asia because of the political ferment, economic chaos, social strife, and revolutionary nationalist fervor that existed in the aftermath of war. American officials believed that communist ideology and Marxist-Leninist rhetoric had great appeal to peoples who had suffered so much and who yearned for something better in the aftermath of depression, war, genocide, and forced migration. Policymakers in Washington believed they had to act quickly to prevent the Soviet Union from exploiting the vacuums of power and political ferment, thereby thwarting its ability to gain a preponderance of power in Europe and Asia—that was the defining lesson of World War II. United States officials had to thwart the appeal of communism, defeat the forces of the political left, and deter the adventurism of the Kremlin. They had to expedite the recovery of Western Europe, co-opt key potential power centers like West Germany and Japan, and compete for influence in the emerging "Third World." The American concept of national security, not the behavior of the Kremlin, mandated these initiatives.

My article ignited a storm of controversy and garnered much criticism from traditional scholars like John Lewis Gaddis and Bruce Kuniholm. It challenged some of the most basic assumptions about the origins of the Cold War: it demonstrated that the United States was neither naive nor reactive. It argued that although it was not the intention of the United States to challenge the vital security interests of the Soviet Union, it nevertheless did so as officials in Washington built positions of strength in Europe and Asia. The article demonstrated that fear and power were critical aspects of U.S. policymaking, thus underscoring some of the important claims among realist theorists of international relations.

This article initially appeared in *The American Historical Review* 89 (April 1984): 346–381.

——

In an interview with Henry Kissinger in 1978 titled "The Lessons of the Past," Walter Laqueur observed that during World War II "few if any people thought . . . of the structure of peace that would follow the war except perhaps in the most general terms of friendship, mutual trust, and the other noble sentiments mentioned in wartime programmatic speeches about the United Nations and related topics." Kissinger concurred, noting that no statesman, except perhaps Winston Churchill, "gave any attention to what would happen after the war." Americans, Kissinger stressed, "were determined that we were going to base the postwar period on good faith and getting along with everybody."[1]

That two such astute and knowledgeable observers of international politics were so uninformed about American planning at the end of the Second World War is testimony to the enduring mythology of American idealism and innocence in the world of realpolitik. It also reflects the state of scholarship on the interrelated areas of strategy, economy, and diplomacy. Despite the publication of several excellent overviews of the origins of the Cold War,[2] despite the outpouring of incisive monographs on American foreign policy in

1. Henry Kissinger, *For the Record: Selected Statements, 1977–1980* (Boston, 1980), 123–24.

2. For recent overviews of the origins of the Cold War that seek to go beyond the heated traditionalist-revisionist controversies of the 1960s and early 1970s, see, for example, John L. Gaddis, *The United States and the Origins of the Cold War* (New York, 1972); Daniel Yergin, *Shattered Peace: The Origins of the Cold War and the National Security State* (Boston, 1978); Thomas G. Paterson, *On Every Front: The Making of the Cold War* (New York, 1979); and Roy Douglas, *From War to Cold War, 1942–48* (New York, 1981).

many areas of the world,[3] and despite some first-rate studies on the evolution of strategic thinking and the defense establishment,[4] no comprehensive ac-

3. For some of the most important and most recent regional and bilateral studies, see, for example, Bruce Kuniholm, *The Origins of the Cold War in the Near East: Great Power Conflict and Diplomacy in Iran, Turkey, and Greece* (Princeton, 1980); Lawrence S. Wittner, *American Intervention in Greece* (New York, 1982); Aaron Miller, *Search for Security: Saudi Arabian Oil and American Foreign Policy, 1939–1949* (Chapel Hill, N.C., 1980); Michael B. Stoff, *Oil, War, and American Security: The Search for a National Policy on Foreign Oil, 1941–47* (New Haven, 1980); Timothy Ireland, *Creating the Entangling Alliance: The Origins of the North Atlantic Treaty Organization* (Westport, Conn., 1981); William W. Stueck, Jr., *The Road to Confrontation: American Policy toward China and Korea* (Chapel Hill, N.C., 1981); Charles M. Dobbs, *The Unwanted Symbol: American Foreign Policy, the Cold War, and Korea, 1945–50* (Kent, Ohio, 1981); Dorothy Borg and Waldo Heinrichs, eds., *Uncertain Years: Chinese-American Relations, 1947–50* (New York, 1980); Robert J. McMahon, *Colonialism and Cold War: The United States and the Struggle for Indonesian Independence* (Ithaca, N.Y., 1981); Robert M. Blum, *Drawing the Line: The Origin of the American Containment Policy in East Asia* (New York, 1982); Russell D. Buhite, *Soviet-American Relations in Asia, 1945–1954* (Norman, Okla., 1981); Bruce Cumings, *The Origins of the Korean War: Liberation and the Emergence of Separate Regimes, 1945–47* (Princeton, 1982); Geir Lundestaad, *America, Scandinavia, and the Cold War, 1945–49* (New York, 1980); Kenneth Ray Bain, *March to Zion: United States Foreign Policy and the Founding of Israel* (College Station, Texas, 1979); Evan M. Wilson, *Decision on Palestine: How the U.S. Came to Recognize Israel* (Stanford, 1979); Robert M. Hathaway, *Ambiguous Partnership: Britain and America, 1944–47* (New York, 1981); Terry H. Anderson, *The United States, Great Britain, and the Cold War, 1944–47* (Columbia, Mo., 1981); Eduard Mark, "American Policy toward Eastern Europe and the Origins of the Cold War, 1941–46: An Alternative Interpretation," *Journal of American History* [hereafter, *JAH*], 68 (1981–82): 313–36; Michael Schaller, "Securing the Great Crescent: Occupied Japan and the Origins of Containment in Southeast Asia," ibid., 69 (1982–83): 392–414; Scott Jackson, "Prologue to the Marshall Plan," ibid., 65 (1978–79): 1043–68; and Michael J. Hogan, "The Search for a 'Creative Peace': The United States, European Unity, and the Origins of the Marshall Plan," *Diplomatic History*, 6 (1982): 267–85.

4. For recent works on strategy, the national military establishment, and the emergence of the national security bureaucracy, see, for example, Richard Haynes, *The Awesome Power: Harry S. Truman as Commander in Chief* (Baton Rouge, La., 1973); Alfred D. Sander, "Truman and the National Security Council, 1945–1947," *JAH*, 59 (1972–73): 369–88; Michael S. Sherry, *Preparing for the Next War: American Plans for Postwar Defense, 1941–45* (New Haven, 1977); Brian L. Villa, "The U.S. Army, Unconditional Surrender, and the Potsdam Declaration ," *JAH*, 63 (1976–77): 66–92; James F. Schnaebel, *The History of the Joint Chiefs of Staff: The Joint Chiefs of Staff and National Policy,* volume 1: *1945–1947* (Wilmington, Del., 1979); Kenneth W. Condit, *The History of the Joint Chiefs of Staff: The Joint Chiefs of Staff and National Policy: 1947–49,* volume 2 (Wilmington, Del., 1979); Gregg Herken, *The Winning Weapon: The Atomic Bomb and the Cold War, 1945–1950* (New York, 1980); David Alan Rosenberg, "American Atomic Strategy and the Hydrogen Bomb Decision," *JAH,* 66 (1979–80): 62–87; Harry R. Borowski, *A Hollow Threat: Strategic Air Power and Containment before Korea* (Westport, Conn., 1982); Mark Stoler, "From Continentalism to Globalism: General Stanley D. Embick, the Joint Strategic Survey Committee, and the Military View of American National Policy during the Second World War," *Diplomatic History,* 6 (1982): 303–21; Walter S. Poole, "From Conciliation to Containment: The Joint Chiefs of Staff and the Coming of the Cold War," *Military Affairs,* 42 (1978): 12–16; Thomas H. Etzold, "The Far East in American Strategy, 1948–1951," in Etzold, ed., *Aspects of Sino-American Relations since 1784*

count yet exists of how American defense officials defined national security interests in the aftermath of World War II. Until recently, the absence of such a study was understandable, for scholars had limited access to records pertaining to national security, strategic thinking, and war planning. But in recent years documents relating to the early years of the Cold War have been declassified in massive numbers.[5]

---

(New York, 1978), 102–26; Paolo E. Coletta, *The United States Navy and Defense Unification, 1947–1953* (East Brunswick, N.J., 1981); Douglas Kinnard, *The Secretary of Defense* (Lexington, Ky., 1980); Anna K. Nelson, "National Security I: Inventing a Process, 1945–1960," in Hugh Heclo and Lester M. Salamon, eds., *The Illusion of Presidential Government* (Boulder, Colo., 1981), 229–45; Larry D. O'Brien, "National Security and the New Warfare: Defense Policy, War Planning, and Nuclear Weapons, 1945–50" (PhD diss., Ohio State University, 1981); John T. Greenwood, "The Emergence of the Post-War Strategic Air Force, 1945–1955," paper delivered at the Eighth Military History Symposium, held at the United States Air Force Academy in October 1978; and Robert F. Futrell, *Ideas, Concepts, Doctrine: A History of Basic Thinking in the United States Air Force, 1907–1964* (Maxwell Air Force Base, Ala., 1971).

5. For the records of the Joint Chiefs of Staff, see Record Group 218, National Archives, Washington [hereafter, RG 218]; for the records of the Office of the Secretary of Defense, see Record Group 330, National Archives, Washington [hereafter, RG 330]; and, for the records of the National Security Council, see Record Group 273, Judicial, Fiscal, and Social Branch, National Archives, Washington. (I used this special collection of declassified National Security Council documents prior to their receiving a record group number within the Judicial, Fiscal, and Social Branch of the National Archives.) There are important National Security Council materials in the Harry S. Truman Papers, President's Secretary's File, Harry S. Truman Presidential Library, Independence Missouri [hereafter, HTL, HSTP, PSF], boxes 191–208. For assessments by the CIA, including those prepared for meetings of the National Security Council (NSC), especially see ibid., boxes 249–60, 203–07. For a helpful guide to War and Army department records in the National Archives, see Louis Galambos, ed., *The Papers of Dwight David Eisenhower*, 9 vols. (Baltimore, 1970–78), 9: 2262–70. Of greatest utility in studying the views of civilian and military planners in the Army and War Department are Record Group 165, Records of the Operations Division (OPD) and Records of American-British Conversations (ABC); Record Group 319, Records of the Plans and Operations Division (P&O); Record Group 107, Records of the Office of the Secretary of War, Robert P. Patterson Papers (RPPP), safe file and general decimal file, and Records of the Office of the Assistant Secretary of War, Howard C. Petersen Papers (HCPP), classified decimal file; and Record Group 335, Records of the Under-Secretary of the Army, Draper/Voorhees files, 1947–50. The records of the navy's Strategic Plans Division (SPD) and the Politico-Military Division (PMD) are divided into many subseries; helpful indexes are available at the Naval Historical Center (NHC). The center also contains, among many other collections, the records of the Office of the Chief of Naval Operations (CNO, double zero files) as well as the manuscript collections of many influential naval officers, including Chester Nimitz, Forrest Sherman, Louis Denfeld, and Arthur Radford. For air force records, I tried—with only moderate success—to use the following materials at the National Archives: Record Group 107, Records of the Office of the Assistant Secretary of War for Air, Plans, Policies, and Agreements, 1943–47; Records of the Office of the Assistant Secretary of War for Air, Establishment of Air Fields and Air Bases, 1940–45; and Incoming and Outgoing Cablegrams, 1942–47; and Record Group 18, Records of the Office of the Chief of Air Staff, Headquarters Army Air Forces: Office of the Air Adjutant General, confidential and secret decimal correspondence file, 1945–48. For the records

This documentation now makes it possible to analyze in greater depth the perceptions, apprehensions, and objectives of those defense officials most concerned with defining and defending the nation's security and strategic interests.[6] This essay seeks neither to explain the process of decision-making on any particular issue nor to dissect the domestic political considerations and fiscal constraints that narrowed the options available to policymakers. Furthermore, it does not pretend to discern the motivations and objectives of the Soviet Union.[7] Rather, the goal here is to elucidate the fundamental strategic and economic considerations that shaped the definition of American national security interests in the postwar world. Several of these considerations—especially as they related to overseas bases, air transit rights, and a strategic sphere of influence in Latin America—initially were the logical result of technological developments and geostrategic experiences rather than directly related to postwar Soviet behavior.[8] But American defense officials also con-

---

of the State-War-Navy Coordinating Committee and its successor, the State-Army-Navy-Air Force Coordinating Committee, see Record Group 353, National Archives, Washington, and, for the important records of the Committee of Three (meetings of the secretaries of state, war, and navy), see Record Group 107, RPPP, safe file.

6. I use the term "defense officials" broadly in this essay to include civilian appointees and military officers in the departments of the Army, Navy, and Air Force, in the office of the secretary of defense, in the armed services, in the intelligence agencies, and on the staff of the National Security Council. While purposefully avoiding a systematic analysis of career diplomats in the Department of State, who have received much attention elsewhere, the conclusions I draw here are based on a consideration of the views of high-ranking officials in the State Department, including James F. Byrnes, Dean Acheson, George C. Marshall, and Robert Lovett. For an excellent analysis of the views of career diplomats, see Hugh DeSantis, *The Diplomacy of Silence: The American Foreign Service, the Soviet Union, and the Cold War, 1933–1947* (Chicago, 1980). Also see, for example, Robert L. Messer, "Paths Not Taken: The United States Department of State and Alternatives to Containment, 1945–1946," *Diplomatic History*, 1 (1977): 297–319; and W. W. Rostow, *The Division of Europe after World War II: 1946* (Austin, Texas, 1981). Many of the references in note 3 deal extensively with the views of State Department officials.

7. For recent studies of Soviet policy during this era, see, for example, Adam Ulam, *The Rivals: America and Russia since World War II* (New York, 1971), 3–151, and *Stalin: The Man and His Era* (New York, 1973), 604–99; William Zimmerman, "Choices in the Postwar World, 1: Containment and the Soviet Union," in Charles Gati, ed., *Caging the Bear: Containment and the Cold War* (Indianapolis, 1974), 85–108; Vojtech Mastny, *Russia's Road to the Cold War* (New York, 1979); William O. McCagg, *Stalin Embattled, 1943–1948* (Detroit, 1978); William Taubman, *Stalin's American Policy: From Entente to Detente to Cold War* (New York, 1982); Werner G. Hahn, *Postwar Soviet Policies: The Fall of Zhadanov and the Defeat of Moderation* (Ithaca, N.Y., 1982); and Alvin Z. Rubinstein, *Soviet Foreign Policy since World War II: Imperial and Global* (Cambridge, Mass., 1981), 2–70.

8. Any assessment of postwar national security policy must also take note of the role of the atomic bomb in U.S. strategy and diplomacy. But, since nuclear weapons have received extensive attention elsewhere, I deal with this issue rather briefly. For excellent work on the atomic bomb, see, for example, Martin J. Sherwin, *A World Destroyed: The Atomic Bomb and the Grand Alliance*

sidered the preservation of a favorable balance of power in Eurasia as fundamental to U.S. national security. This objective impelled defense analysts and intelligence officers to appraise and reappraise the intentions and capabilities of the Soviet Union. Rather modest estimates of the Soviets' ability to wage war against the United States generated the widespread assumption that the Soviets would refrain from military aggression and seek to avoid war. Nevertheless, American defense officials remained greatly preoccupied with the geopolitical balance of power in Europe and Asia, because that balance seemed endangered by communist exploitation of postwar economic dislocation and social and political unrest. Indeed, American assessments of the Soviet threat were less a consequence of expanding Soviet military capabilities and of Soviet diplomatic demands than a result of growing apprehension about the vulnerability of American strategic and economic interests in a world of unprecedented turmoil and upheaval. Viewed from this perspective, the Cold War assumed many of its most enduring characteristics during 1947–48, when American officials sought to cope with an array of challenges by implementing their own concepts of national security.

American officials first began to think seriously about the nation's postwar security during 1943–44. Military planners devised elaborate plans for an overseas base system. Many of these plans explicitly contemplated the breakdown of the wartime coalition. But, even when strategic planners postulated good postwar relations among the Allies, their plans called for an extensive system of bases. These bases were defined as the nation's strategic frontier. Beyond this frontier the United States would be able to use force to counter any threats or frustrate any overt acts of aggression. Within the strategic frontier, American military predominance had to remain inviolate. Although plans for an overseas base system went through many revisions, they always presupposed American hegemony over the Atlantic and Pacific oceans. These plans received President Franklin D. Roosevelt's endorsement in early 1944. After his death, army and navy planners presented their views to President Harry S.

———————

(New York, 1973); Barton J. Bernstein, "The Quest for Security: American Foreign Policy and International Control of Atomic Energy, 1942–1946," *JAH*, 60 (1973–74): 1003–44; Herken, *The Winning Weapon*; and Rosenberg, "American Atomic Strategy and the Hydrogen Bomb Decision." For older but still very important accounts, see P.M.S. Blackett, *Fear, War, and the Bomb* (New York, 1949); Richard G. Hewlett and Oscar G. Anderson, *The New World: A History of the United States Atomic Energy Commission, 1939–1946* (University Park, Pa., 1962); Richard G. Hewlett and Francis Duncan, *Atomic Shield: A History of the United States Atomic Energy Commission, 1947–52* (University Park, Pa., 1969); Gar Alperovitz, *Atomic Diplomacy: Hiroshima and Potsdam* (New York, 1965); and Herbert Feis, *The Atomic Bomb and the End of World War II* (Princeton, 1966).

Truman, and Army Chief of Staff George C. Marshall discussed them extensively with Secretary of State James C. Byrnes.[9]

Two strategic considerations influenced the development of an overseas base system. The first was the need for defense in depth. Since attacks against the United States could only emanate from Europe and Asia, the Joint Chiefs of Staff concluded as early as November 1943 that the United States must encircle the Western Hemisphere with a defensive ring of outlying bases. In the Pacific this ring had to include the Aleutians, the Philippines, Okinawa, and the former Japanese mandates. Recognizing the magnitude of this strategic frontier, Admiral William E. Leahy, chief of staff to the president, explained to Truman that the joint chiefs were not thinking of the immediate future when, admittedly, no prospective naval power could challenge American predominance in the Pacific. Instead, they were contemplating the long term, when the United States might require wartime access to the resources of southeast Asia as well as "a firm line of communications from the West Coast to the Asiatic mainland, plus denial of this line in time of war to any potential enemy."[10] In the Atlantic, strategic planners maintained that their minimum requirements included a West African zone, with primary bases in the Azores or Canary Islands. Leahy went even further, insisting on primary bases in West Africa itself—for example, at Dakar or Casablanca. The object of these defensive bases was to enable the United States to possess complete control of the Atlantic and Pacific oceans and keep hostile powers far from American territory.[11]

9. Plans for America's overseas base system may be found in RG 218, Combined Chiefs of Staff (CCS) series 360 (12-9-42): Joint Strategic Survey Committee [hereafter, JSSC], "Air Routes across the Pacific and Air Facilities for International Police Force," March 15, 1943, JSSC 9/1; Joint Chiefs of Staff [hereafter, JCS], "United States Military Requirements for Air Bases, Facilities, and Operating Rights in Foreign Territories," November 2, 1943, JCS 570/2; Joint War Plans Committee [hereafter, JWPC], "Overall Examination of the United States Requirements for Military Bases," August 25, 1943, JWPC 361/4; and JWPC, "Overall Examination of United States Requirements for Military Bases," September 13, 1945, JWPC 361/5 (revised). For Roosevelt's endorsement, see Roosevelt to the Department of State, January 7, 1944, ibid., JWPC 361/5; for civilian-military discussion of base requirements following the president's death, see OPD, "Extract of Conversation—Adm. Duncan and Gen. Lincoln," June 18, 1945, RG 165, OPD 336 (top secret); OPD, Memorandum for the Record, June 30, 1945, ibid.; General George A. Lincoln, "Memorandum concerning U.S. Post-War Pacific Bases," June 30, 1945, ibid.; and George C. Marshall to James F. Byrnes, July 23, 1945, ibid.

10. For Leahy's explanation, see JCS, "Strategic Areas and Trusteeships in the Pacific," October 10, 18, 1946, RG 218, ser. CCS 360 (12-9-42), JCS 1619/15, 19; JCS, "United States Military Requirements for Air Bases," November 2, 1943; JCS, "Overall Examination of United States Requirements for Military Bases and Base Rights," October 25, 1945, ibid., JCS 570/40.

11. JCS, "United States Military Requirements for Air Bases," November 2, 1943; JCS, Minutes of the 71st meeting, March 30, 1943, RG 218, ser. CCS 360 (12-9-42); Leahy, Memorandum for the President, November 15, 1943, ibid.; Nimitz, Memorandum, October 16, 1946, ibid., JCS

Defense in depth was especially important in light of the Pearl Harbor experience, the advance of technology, and the development of the atomic bomb. According to the Joint Chiefs of Staff, "Experience in the recent war demonstrated conclusively that the defense of a nation, if it is to be effective, must begin beyond its frontiers. The advent of the atomic bomb reemphasizes this requirement. The farther away from our own vital areas we can hold our enemy through the possession of advanced bases . . . , the greater are our chances of surviving successfully an attack by atomic weapons and of destroying the enemy which employs them against us." Believing that atomic weapons would increase the incentive to aggression by enhancing the advantage of surprise, military planners never ceased to extol the utility of forward bases from which American aircraft could seek to intercept attacks against the United States.[12]

The second strategic consideration that influenced the plan for a comprehensive overseas base system was the need to project American power quickly and effectively against any potential adversary. In conducting an overall examination of requirements for base rights in September 1945, the Joint War Plans Committee stressed that World War II demonstrated the futility of a strategy of static defense. The United States had to be able to take "timely" offensive action against the adversary's capacity and will to wage war. New weapons demanded that advance bases be established in "areas well removed from the United States, so as to project our operations, with new weapons or otherwise, nearer the enemy." Scientists, like Vannevar Bush, argued that "regardless of the potentialities of these new weapons [atomic energy and guided missiles], they should not influence the number, location, or extent of strategic bases now considered essential." The basic strategic concept underlying all American war plans called for an air offensive against a prospective enemy from overseas bases. Delays in the development of the B-36, the first intercontinental bomber, only accentuated the need for these bases.[13]

---

1619/16; and Joint Planning Staff [hereafter, JPS], "Basis for the Formulation of a Post-War Military Policy," August 20, 1945, RG 218, ser. CCS 381 (5-13-45), JPS 633/6.

12. JCS, "Statement of Effect of Atomic Weapons on National Security and Military Organization," March 29, 1946, RG 165, ser. ABC 471.6 Atom (8-17-45), JCS 477/10. Also see JCS, "Guidance as to the Military Implications of a United Nations Commission on Atomic Energy," January 12, 1946, ibid., 1567/26; and JCS, "Over-All Effect of Atomic Bomb on Warfare and Military Organization," October 30, 1945, ibid., JCS 1477/1.

13. For the emphasis on "timely" action, see JWPC, "Overall Examination of Requirements for Military Bases" (revised), September 13, 1946; for the need for advance bases, see JCS, "Strategic Concept and Plan for the Employment of United States Armed Forces," September 19, 1945, RG 218, ser. CCS 381 (5-13-45), JCS 1518; for Bush's view, see JWPC, "Effect of Foreseeable New Developments and Counter-Measures on a Post-War Strategic Concept and Plan," August 22, 1945, ibid., JWPC 394/1/M. Also see, for the evolution of strategic war plans, many of the materials in RG 218, ser. CCS 381 USSR (3-2-46).

In October 1945, the civilian leaders of the War and Navy departments carefully reviewed the emerging strategic concepts and base requirements of the military planners. Secretary of the Navy James Forrestal and Secretary of War Robert P. Patterson discussed them with Admiral Leahy, the Joint Chiefs of Staff, and Secretary of State Byrnes. The civilian secretaries fully endorsed the concept of a far-flung system of bases in the Atlantic and Pacific oceans that would enhance the offensive capabilities of the United States.[14] Having expended so much blood and effort capturing Japanese-held islands, defense officials, like Forrestal, naturally wished to devise a base system in the Pacific to facilitate the projection of American influence and power. The Philippines were the key to southeast Asia, Okinawa to the Yellow Sea, the Sea of Japan, and the industrial heartland of northeast Asia. From these bases on America's "strategic frontier," the United States could preserve its access to vital raw materials in Asia, deny these resources to a prospective enemy, help preserve peace and stability in troubled areas, safeguard critical sea lanes, and, if necessary, conduct an air offensive against the industrial infrastructure of any Asiatic power, including the Soviet Union.[15]

Control of the Atlantic and Pacific oceans through overseas bases was considered indispensable to the nation's security regardless of what might happen to the wartime coalition. So was control over polar air routes. Admiral Leahy criticized a Joint Strategic Survey Committee report of early 1943 that omitted Iceland and Greenland as primary base requirements. When General S. D. Embick, the senior member of that committee, continued to question the desirability of a base in Iceland, lest it antagonize the Russians, he was overruled by Assistant Secretary of War John McCloy. McCloy charged that Embick had "a rather restricted concept of what is necessary for national defense." The first postwar base system approved by both the Joint Chiefs of Staff and the civilian secretaries in October 1945 included Iceland as a primary base

14. For the discussions and conclusions of civilian officials, see Leahy to Patterson and Forrestal, October 9, 1945, RG 165, OPD 336 (top secret); Robert Lovett to Chief of Staff, October 12, 1945, ibid.; Patterson to the Secretary of Navy, October 17, 1945, ibid.; and Forrestal to Byrnes, October 4, 1945, RG 218, ser. CCS 360 (12-9-42). For Forrestal's views, also see Forrestal to James K. Vardaman, September 14, 1945, Mudd Library, Princeton University, James Forrestal Papers [hereafter ML, JFP], box 100; Forrestal to Byrnes, October 4, 1945, RG 218, ser. CCS 360 (12-9-42); and Vincent Davis, *Postwar Defense Policy and the U.S. Navy, 1943–1946* (Chapel Hill, N.C., 1962), 157–206, 259–66.

15. For the Philippines, see, for example, Strategy Section, OPD, "Post-War Base Requirements in the Philippines," April 23, 1945, RG 165, OPD 336 (top secret), and "Report on the Military Base Requirements in the Philippines," October 20, 1945, ibid. For Okinawa, see JCS, "Disposition of the Ryukyu Islands," September 10, 1946, RG 218, ser. CCS 360 (12-9-42), JCS 1619/9; JCS, "Review of United States Control Needed over the Japanese Islands," August 26, 1947, ibid., JCS 1619/24; and Lincoln, "Memorandum concerning U.S. Post-War Pacific Bases," June 30, 1945.

area. The Joint War Plans Committee explained that American bases must control the air in the Arctic, prevent the establishment of enemy military facilities there, and support America's own striking forces. Once Soviet-American relations began to deteriorate, Greenland also was designated as a primary base for American heavy bombers and fighters because of its close proximity to the industrial heartland of the potential enemy. As the United States sought rights for bases along the polar route in 1946 and 1947, moreover, American defense officials also hoped to thwart Soviet efforts to acquire similar rights at Spitzbergen and Bear Island.[16]

In the immediate postwar years, American ambitions for an elaborate base system encountered many problems. Budgetary constraints compelled military planners to drop plans for many secondary and subsidiary bases, particularly in the South Pacific and Caribbean. These sacrifices merely increased the importance of those bases that lay closer to a potential adversary. By early 1948, the joint chiefs were willing to forgo base rights in such places as Surinam, Curaçao-Aruba, Cayenne, Nouméa, and Viti-Levu if "joint" or "participating" rights could be acquired or preserved in Karachi, Tripoli, Algiers, Casablanca, Dharan, and Monrovia. Budgetary constraints, then, limited the depth of the base system but not the breadth of American ambitions.[17] Furthermore, the governments of Panama, Iceland, Denmark, Portugal, France, and Saudi Arabia often rejected or abolished the exclusive rights the United States wanted and sometimes limited the number of American personnel on such bases. Washington, therefore, negotiated a variety of arrangements to meet the objections of host governments. By early 1948, for example, the base in Iceland was operated by a civilian company under contract to the United States Air Force; in the Azores, the base was manned by a detachment of

16. For Leahy's views, see JCS, Minutes of the 71st meeting, March 30, 1943. For the differences between Embick and McCloy, see Embick to John Hickerson, June 8, 1945, RG 165, OPD 336 (top secret); and Harrison A. Gerhardt, Memorandum for General Hull, June 16, 1945, ibid. For the utility of Iceland and Greenland as bases, see JWPC, "Attributes of United States Overseas Bases," November 2, 1945, RG 218, ser. CCS 360 (12-9-42), JWPC 361/10; NSC, "Report by the NSC on Base Rights in Greenland, Iceland, and the Azores," November 25, 1947, ibid., NSC 2/1; and Albert C. Wedemeyer to Secretary of Defense, March 6, 1948, RG 330, box 19, CD 6-1-44 (decimal correspondence file). And, for the dilemma posed by prospective Soviet demands for similar base rights at Spitzbergen, see, for example, JCS, "Foreign Policy of the United States," February 10, 1946, RG 218, ser. CCS 092 US (12-21-45), JCS 1519/2; Department of State, *Foreign Relations of the United States* [hereafter, *FRUS*], 1947, 8 vols. (Washington, 1971–73), 1: 708–12, 766–70, and 3: 657–87, 1003–18; and Lundestad, *America, Scandinavia, and the Cold War*, 63–76.

17. See, for example, Report of the Director, Joint Staff, March 18, 1948, RG 218, ser. CCS 360 (12-9-42), Joint Strategic Plans Group [hereafter JSPG] 503/1. For the special emphasis on North African bases, see, for example, Forrestal to Truman, January 6, 1948, HTL, HSTP, PSF, box 156. And, for further evidence regarding plans for the development of the base system in 1947–48, see notes 70–71, below.

Portuguese military personnel operating under the Portuguese flag, but an Air Force detachment serviced the American aircraft using the base. In Port Lyautey, the base was under the command of the French navy, but under a secret agreement an American naval team took care of American aircraft on the base. In Saudi Arabia, the Dharan air strip was cared for by 300 U.S. personnel and was capable of handling B-29s. Because these arrangements were not altogether satisfactory, in mid-1948 Secretary of Defense Forrestal and Secretary of the Army Kenneth Royall advocated using American economic and military assistance as levers to acquire more permanent and comprehensive base rights, particularly in Greenland and North Africa.[18]

Less well known than the American effort to establish a base system, but integral to the policymakers' conception of national security, was the attempt to secure military air transit and landing rights. Military planners wanted such rights at critical locations not only in the Western Hemisphere but also in North Africa, the Middle East, India, and southeast Asia. To this end they delineated a route from Casablanca through Algiers, Tripoli, Cairo, Dharan, Karachi, Delhi, Calcutta, Rangoon, Bangkok, and Saigon to Manila.[19] In closing out the African–Middle East theater at the conclusion of the war, General H. W. Aurand, under explicit instructions from the secretary of war, made preparations for permanent rights at seven airfields in North Africa and Saudi Arabia.[20] According to a study by the Joint Chiefs of Staff, "Military air transit rights for the United States along the North African–Indian route were most desirable in order to provide access to and familiarity with bases from which offensive and defensive action might be conducted in the event of a major war, and to provide an alternate route to China and to United States Far Eastern

18. For the situation in Iceland, the Azores, and Port Lyautey, see Edmond T. Wooldridge to the General Board of the Navy, April 30, 1948, NHC, Records of the General Board 425 (ser. 315); for Saudi Arabia, see G. R. Cooper et al., "Joint Report on Pertinent Observations during Recent Trip to the Mediterranean–Middle East Area," September 25, 1948, NHC, SPD, central files, 1948, A8; for more information on the Dharan base, also see *FRUS*, 1948, 5: 209–63; James L. Gormly, "Keeping the Door Open in Saudi Arabia: The U.S. and the Dharan Airfield, 1945–46," *Diplomatic History*, 4 (1980): 189–206; and, for aspirations to secure more permanent and comprehensive base rights, see Royall to Forrestal, July 28, 1948, RG 330, box 119, CD 27-1-21; and Forrestal to Royall, August 7, 1948, ibid. The State Department's concern with base rights in Iceland and Greenland was evident throughout the exploratory talks on a security pact; see *FRUS*, 1948, 3: 169–351. For North Africa, also see ibid., 682–715.

19. JCS, "Over-All Examination of United States Requirements for Military Bases and Rights," September 27, 1945, RG 218, ser. CCS 360 (12-9-42), JCS 570/34; JPS, "Over-All Examination of Requirements for Transit Air Bases in Foreign Countries," January 8, 1946, ibid., JPS 781; and JCS, "Over-All Examination of Requirements for Transit Air Bases and Air Base Rights in Foreign Countries," June 30, 1946, ibid., JCS 570/52.

20. Aurand to Patterson, February 7, 1946, Dwight David Eisenhower Presidential Library, Abilene, Kansas [hereafter, DDEL], H. S. Aurand Papers, box 28; Secretary of War to Secretary of State, March 17, 1946, ibid.

bases." In other words, such rights would permit the rapid augmentation of American bases in wartime as well as the rapid movement of American air units from the eastern to the western flank of the U.S. base system. In order to maintain these airfields in a state of readiness, the United States would have to rely on private airlines, which had to be persuaded to locate their operations in areas designated essential to military air transit rights. In this way, airports "in being" outside the formal American base system would be available for military operations in times of crisis and war. Assistant Secretary McCloy informed the State Department at the beginning of 1945 that a "strong United States air transport system, international in scope and readily adapted to military use, is vital to our air power and future national security." Even earlier, the joint chiefs had agreed not to include South American air bases in their strategic plans so long as it was understood that commercial fields in that region would be developed with a view to subsequent military use.[21]

In Latin America, American requirements for effective national security went far beyond air transit rights. In a report written in January 1945 at Assistant Secretary McCloy's behest, the War Department urged American collaboration with Latin American armed forces to insure the defense of the Panama Canal and the Western Hemisphere. Six areas within Latin America were considered of special significance either for strategic reasons or for their raw materials: the Panama Canal and approaches within 1,000 miles; the Straits of Magellan; northeast Brazil; Mexico; the river Plate estuary and approaches within 500 miles; and Mollendo, Peru–Antofagasta, Chile. These areas were so "important," Secretary of War Patterson explained to Secretary of State Marshall in early 1947, "that the threat of attack on any of them would force the United States to come to their defense, even though it were not certain that attack on the United States itself would follow." The resources of these areas were essential to the United States, because "it is imperative that our war potential be enhanced . . . during any national emergency."[22]

While paying lip service to the United Nations and worrying about the impact of regional agreements in the Western Hemisphere on Soviet actions and American influence in Europe, the Joint Chiefs of Staff insisted that in

21. JPS, "Over-All Examination of Requirements for Transit Air Bases . . . ," January 20, 1946, RG 218, ser. CCS 360 (10-9-42), JPS 781/1; and McCloy, Memorandum to the Department of State, January 31, 1945, RG 165, OPD 336 (top secret). Also see JPS, "Over-All Examination of Requirements for Transit Air Bases," January 8, 1946; and, for the joint chiefs' view on South American air fields, see JCS, Minutes of the 69th meeting, March 23, 1943, RG 218, CCS 360 (12-9-42).

22. P&O, "The Strategic Importance of Inter-American Military Cooperation" [January 20, 1947], RG 319, 092 (top secret). Also see H. A. Craig, "Summary," January 5, 1945, RG 107, Records of the Assistant Secretary of War for Air, Establishment of Air Fields and Air Bases, box 216 (Latin America); and War Department, "Comprehensive Statement" [January 1945], ibid.

practice non-American forces had to be kept out of the Western Hemisphere and the Monroe Doctrine had to be kept inviolate. "The Western Hemisphere is a distinct military entity, the integrity of which is a fundamental postulate of our security in the event of another world war."[23] Developments in aviation, rockets, guided missiles, and atomic energy had made "the solidarity of the Hemisphere and its united support of the principles of the Monroe Doctrine" more important than before. Patterson told Marshall that effective implementation of the Monroe Doctrine now meant "that we not only refuse to tolerate foreign colonization, control, or the extension of a foreign political system to our hemisphere, but we take alarm from the appearance on the continent of foreign ideologies, commercial exploitation, cartel arrangements, or other symptoms of increased non-hemispheric influence. . . . The basic consideration has always been an overriding apprehension lest a base be established in this area by a potentially hostile foreign power." The United States, Patterson insisted, must have "a stable, secure, and friendly flank to the south, not confused by enemy penetration, political, economic, or military."[24]

The need to predominate throughout the Western Hemisphere was not a result of deteriorating Soviet-American relations but a natural evolution of the Monroe Doctrine, accentuated by Axis aggression and new technological imperatives.[25] Patterson, Forrestal, and Army Chief of Staff Dwight D. Eisenhower initially were impelled less by reports of Soviet espionage, propaganda, and infiltration in Latin America than by accounts of British efforts to sell cruisers and aircraft to Chile and Ecuador, Swedish sales of antiaircraft artillery to Argentina, and French offers to build cruisers and destroyers for both Argentina and Brazil.[26] To foreclose all foreign influence and to insure

23. JCS, "Foreign Policy of the United States," February 10, 1946, RG 218, ser. CCS 092 United States (12-21-45), JCS 1592/2; and JCS to the Secretary of the Navy and Secretary of War, September 19, 1945, ibid., ser. CCS 092 (9-10-45), JCS 1507/2. For JCS views on the Western Hemisphere, also see JCS to the Secretary of the Navy and Secretary of War, February 11, 1945, ibid., ser. CCS 092 (1-18-45); JCS, "International Organization for the Enforcement of World Peace and Security," April 14, 1945, ibid., ser. CCS 092 (4-14-45), JCS 1311; and JCS, "Guidance as to Command and Control of the Armed Forces to be Placed at the Disposal of the Security Council of the United Nations," May 26, 1946, ibid., JCS 1670/5.

24. For Patterson's views, see P&O, "Strategic Importance of Inter-American Military Cooperation" [January 20, 1947]; and Patterson to Byrnes, December 18, 1946, RG 107, RPPP, safe file, box 3.

25. This evaluation accords with the views of Chester J. Pach, Jr.; see his "The Containment of United States Military Aid to Latin America, 1944–1949," *Diplomatic History*, 6 (1982): 232–34.

26. For fears of foreign influence, see, for example, [no signature] "Military Political Cooperation with the Other American Republics," June 24, 1946, RG 18, 092 (International Affairs), box 567; Patterson to the Secretary of State, July 31, 1946, RG 353, State-War-Navy Coordinating Committee (SWNCC), box 76; Eisenhower to Patterson, November 26, 1946, RG 107, HCPP, general decimal file, box 1 (top secret); S. J. Chamberlin to Eisenhower, November 26, 1946, ibid.;

United States strategic hegemony, military officers and the civilian secretaries of the War and Navy departments argued for an extensive system of United States bases, expansion of commercial airline facilities throughout Latin America, negotiation of a regional defense pact, curtailment of all foreign military aid and foreign military sales, training of Latin American military officers in the United States, outfitting of Latin American armies with U.S. military equipment, and implementation of a comprehensive military assistance program.[27]

The military assistance program, as embodied in the Inter-American Military Cooperation Act, generated the most interagency discord. Latin American experts in the State Department maintained that military assistance would stimulate regional conflicts, dissipate Latin American financial resources, and divert attention from economic and social issues. Before leaving office, Byrnes forcefully presented the State Department position to Forrestal and Patterson. Instead of dwelling on the consequences of military assistance for Latin America, Byrnes maintained that such a program would be too costly for the United States, would focus attention on a region where American interests were relatively unchallenged, and would undermine more important American initiatives elsewhere on the globe. "Greece and Turkey are our outposts," he declared.[28]

The secretary of state clearly did not think that Congress would authorize funds for Latin America as well as for Greece and Turkey. Although Truman favored military assistance to Latin America, competing demands for American resources in 1947 and 1948 forced both military planners and U.S. senators to give priority to Western Europe and the Near East. In June 1948 the Inter-American Military Cooperation Act died in the Senate. But this signified no diminution in American national security imperatives; indeed, it underscored Byrnes's statement of December 1946 that the "outposts" of the nation's security lay in the heart of Eurasia.[29]

---

Minutes of the meeting of the Secretaries of State, War, and Navy, December 11, 1946, ibid., RPPP, safe file, box 3; and Director of Intelligence to Director of P&O, February 26, 1947, RG 319, P&O, 091 France. For reports on Soviet espionage, see, for example, Military Intelligence Service [hereafter, MIS], "Soviet-Communist Penetration in Latin America," March 24, 1945, RG 165, OPD, 336 (top secret); and MIS, "Summary of a Study . . . on Soviet-Communist Penetration in Latin America," September 27, 1945, ibid.

27. See, for example, Craig, "Summary," January 5, 1945; JPS, "Military Arrangements Deriving from the Act of Chapultepec Pertaining to Bases," January 14, 1946, RG 218, ser. CCS 092 (9-10-45), JPS 761/3; Patterson to Byrnes, December 18, 1946; and P&O, "Strategic Importance of Inter-American Military Cooperation" [January 20, 1947].

28. Minutes of the meeting of the Secretaries of State, War, and the Navy, December 18, 1946, April 23, May 1, 1947, RG 107, RPPP, safe file, box 3; and M. B. Ridgway, Memorandum for the Assistant Secretary of War, February 1947, ibid., HCPP, 092 (classified).

29. Pach, "Military Aid to Latin America," 235–43.

From the closing days of World War II, American defense officials believed that they could not allow any prospective adversary to control the Eurasian land mass. This was the lesson taught by two world wars. Strategic thinkers and military analysts insisted that any power or powers attempting to dominate Eurasia must be regarded as potentially hostile to the United States.[30] Their acute awareness of the importance of Eurasia made Marshall, Thomas Handy, George A. Lincoln, and other officers wary of the expansion of Soviet influence there. Cognizant of the growth in Soviet strength, General John Deane, head of the United States military mission in Moscow, urged a tougher stand against Soviet demands even before World War II had ended. While acknowledging that the increase in Soviet power stemmed primarily from the defeat of Germany and Japan, postwar assessments of the Joint Chiefs of Staff emphasized the importance of deterring further Soviet aggrandizement in Eurasia.[31] Concern over the consequences of Russian domination of Eurasia

30. This view was most explicitly presented in an army paper examining the State Department's expostulation of U.S. foreign policy. See S. F. Giffin, "Draft of Proposed Comments for the Assistant Secretary of War on 'Foreign Policy'" [early February 1946], RG 107, HCPP 092 international affairs (classified). The extent to which this concern with Eurasia shaped American military attitudes is illustrated at greater length below. Here I should note that in March 1945 several of the nation's most prominent civilian experts (Frederick S. Dunn, Edward M. Earle, William T. R. Fox, Grayson L. Kirk, David N. Rowe, Harold Sprout, and Arnold Wolfers) prepared a study, "A Security Policy for Postwar America," in which they argued that the United States had to prevent any one power or coalition of powers from gaining control of Eurasia. America could not, they insisted, withstand attack by any power that had first subdued the whole of Europe or of Eurasia; see Frederick S. Dunn et al., "A Security Policy for Postwar America," NHC, SPD, ser. 14, box 194, A1–2.

The postwar concept of Eurasia developed out of the revival of geopolitical thinking in the United States, stimulated by Axis aggression and strategic decision-making. See, for example, the reissued work of Sir Halford F. Mackinder. Mackinder, *Democratic Ideals and Reality* (1919; reprint edn., New York, 1942), and "The Round World and the Winning of Peace," *Foreign Affairs*, 21 (1943): 598–605. Mackinder's ideas were modified and widely disseminated in the United States, especially by intellectuals such as Nicholas John Spykman, Hans W. Weigert, Robert Strausz-Hupé, and Isaiah Bowman. Spykman flatly took exception to Mackinder's dictum, "Who controls eastern Europe rules the heartland; who rules the Heartland rules the World Island; and who rules the World Island rules the World." Instead, Spykman emphasized, "Who controls the rimland rules Eurasia; who rules Eurasia controls the destinies of the world." Spykman, *The Geography of Peace* (New York, 1944), 43. Also see Spykman, *America's Strategy in World Politics: The United States and the Balance of Power* (New York, 1942); Weigert, *Generals and Geographers: The Twilight of Geopolitics* (New York, 1942); Strausz-Hupé, *Geopolitics: The Struggle for Space and Power* (New York, 1942); Russell H. Fifield and G. Etzel Pearcy, *Geopolitics in Principle and Practice* (Boston, 1944); and Alfred C. Eckes, *The United States and the Global Struggle for Minerals* (Austin, Texas, 1979), 104–08.

31. For views of influential generals and army planners, see OPD, Memorandum, June 4, 1945, RG 165, OPD 336 (top secret). Also see the plethora of documents from May and June 1945, U.S. Military Academy, West Point, New York [hereafter, USMA], George A. Lincoln Papers [hereafter, GLP], War Department files. For Deane's advice, especially see Deane, "Revi-

helps explain why in July 1945 the joint chiefs decided to oppose a Soviet request for bases in the Dardanelles; why during March and April 1946 they supported a firm stand against Russia in Iran, Turkey, and Tripolitania; and why in the summer of 1946 Clark Clifford and George Elsey, two White House aides, argued that Soviet incorporation of any parts of Western Europe, the Middle East, China, or Japan into a communist orbit was incompatible with American national security.[32]

Yet defense officials were not eager to sever the wartime coalition. In early 1944, Admiral Leahy noted the "phenomenal development" of Soviet power but still hoped for Soviet-American cooperation. When members of the Joint Postwar Committee met with their colleagues on the Joint Planning Staff in April 1945, Major General G. V. Strong argued against using U.S. installations in Alaska for staging expeditionary forces, lest such a move exacerbate Russo-American relations. A few months later, Eisenhower, Lincoln, and other officers advised against creating a central economic authority for Western Europe that might appear to be an anti-Soviet bloc.[33] The American objective, after all, was to avoid Soviet hegemony over Eurasia. By aggravating Soviet fears, the United States might foster what it wished to avoid. American self-restraint, however, might be reciprocated by the Soviets, providing time for Western Europe to recover and for the British to reassert some influence on the Continent.[34] Therefore, many defense officials in 1945 hoped to avoid an open rift with the Soviet Union. But at the same time they were

---

sion of Policy with Relation to Russia," April 16, 1945, RG 218, ser. CCS 092 USSR (3-27-45), JCS 1313, and *The Strange Alliance: The Story of Our Efforts at Wartime Co-operation with Russia* (New York, 1946), 84–86. For the JCS studies, see, for example, JPS, "Strategic Concept and Plan for the Employment of United States Armed Forces," September 14, 1945, RG 218, ser. CCS 381 (5-13-45), JPS 744/3; and JCS, "United States Military Policy," September 17, 1945, ibid., JCS 1496/2.

32. For the decision on the Dardanelles, see the attachments to JCS, "United States Policy concerning the Dardanelles and Kiel Canal" [July 1945], RG 218, ser. CCS 092 (7-10-45), JCS 1418/1; for the joint chiefs' position on Iran, Turkey, and Tripolitania, see JCS, "U.S. Security Interests in the Eastern Mediterranean," March 1946, ibid., ser. CCS 092 USSR (3-27-45), JCS 1641 series; and Lincoln, Memorandum for the Record, April 16, 1946, RG 165, ser. ABC 336 Russia (8-22-43); and, for the Clifford memorandum, see Arthur Krock, *Memoirs: Sixty Years on the Firing Line* (New York, 1968), 477–82.

33. Leahy, excerpt from letter, May 16, 1944, RG 59, lot 54D394 (Records of the Office of European Affairs), box 17. For Strong's opinion, see JPS, Minutes of the 199th meeting, April 25, 1945, RG 218, ser. CCS 334 (3-28-45); and, for the views of Eisenhower and Lincoln, see Lincoln, Memorandum for Hull, June 24, 1945, USMA, GLP, War Dept. files; and Leahy, Memorandum for the President [late June 1945], ibid.

34. For the emphasis on expediting recovery in Western Europe, see, for example, McCloy, Memorandum for Matthew J. Connelly, April 26, 1945, HTL, HSTP, PSF, box 178; and, for the role of Britain, see, for example, Joint Intelligence Staff [hereafter, JIS], "British Capabilities and Intentions," December 5, 1945, RG 218, ser. CCS 000.1 Great Britain (5-10-45), JIS 161/4.

determined to prevent the Eurasian land mass from falling under Soviet and communist influence.

Studies by the Joint Chiefs of Staff stressed that, if Eurasia came under Soviet domination, either through military conquest or political and economic "assimilation," America's only potential adversary would fall heir to enormous natural resources, industrial potential, and manpower. By the autumn of 1945, military planners already were worrying that Soviet control over much of Eastern Europe and its raw materials would abet Russia's economic recovery, enhance its war-making capacity, and deny important foodstuffs, oil, and minerals to Western Europe. By the early months of 1946, Secretary Patterson and his subordinates in the War Department believed that Soviet control of the Ruhr-Rhineland industrial complex would constitute an extreme threat. Even more dangerous was the prospect of Soviet predominance over the rest of Western Europe, especially France.[35] Strategically, this would undermine the impact of any prospective American naval blockade and would allow Soviet military planners to achieve defense in depth. The latter possibility had enormous military significance, because American war plans relied so heavily on air power and strategic bombing, the efficacy of which might be reduced substantially if the Soviets acquired outlying bases in Western Europe and the Middle East or if they "neutralized" bases in Great Britain.[36]

Economic considerations also made defense officials determined to retain American access to Eurasia as well as to deny Soviet predominance over it. Stimson, Patterson, McCloy, and Assistant Secretary Howard C. Petersen agreed with Forrestal that long-term American prosperity required open markets, unhindered access to raw materials, and the rehabilitation of much—if not all—of Eurasia along liberal capitalist lines. In late 1944 and 1945, Stimson

35. Joint Logistic Plans Committee [hereafter, JLPC], "Russian Capabilities," November 15, 1945, RG 218, ser. CCS 092 USSR (3-27-45), JLPC 35/9/RD; Military Intelligence Division [hereafter, MID], "Intelligence Estimate of the World Situation and Its Military Implications," June 25, 1946, RG 319, P&O 350.05 (top secret); Joint Intelligence Committee [hereafter, JIC], "Intelligence Estimate Assuming that War between the Soviet Union the Non-Soviet Powers Breaks Out in 1956," November 6, 1946, RG 218, ser. CCS 092 USSR (3-27-45), JIC 374/1; and JIC, "Capabilities and Military Potential of Soviet and Non-Soviet Powers in 1946," January 8, 1947, ibid., JIC 374/2. For concern with the Ruhr-Rhineland industrial complex, especially see Patterson to the Secretary of State, June 10, 1946, RG 107, HCPP, 091 Germany (classified); and, for the concern with Western Europe, especially France, see, for example, JCS, "United States Assistance to Other Countries from the Standpoint of National Security," April 29, 1947, in *FRUS*, 1947, 1: 734–50, esp. 739–42. Also see the General Board, "National Security and Navy Contributions Thereto for the Next Ten Years," Enclosure D, June 25, 1948, NHC, General Board 425 (ser. 315).

36. See, for example, JIS, "Military Capabilities of Great Britain and France," November 13, 1945, RG 218, ser. CCS 000.1 Great Britain (5-10-45), JIS 211/1; JIS, "Areas Vital to Soviet War Effort," February 12, 1946, ibid., ser. CCS 092 (3-27-45), JIS 226/2; and JIS, "Supplemental Information Relative to Northern and Western Europe," April 18, 1947, ibid., JIS 275/1.

protested the prospective industrial emasculation of Germany, lest it undermine American economic well-being, set back recovery throughout Europe, and unleash forces of anarchy and revolution. Stimson and his subordinates in the Operations Division of the army also worried that the spread of Soviet power in northeast Asia would constrain the functioning of the free enterprise system and jeopardize American economic interests. A report prepared by the staff of the Moscow embassy and revised in mid-1946 by Ambassador (and former General) Walter Bedell Smith emphasized that "Soviet power is by nature so jealous that it has already operated to segregate from world economy almost all of the areas in which it has been established." While Forrestal and the navy sought to contain Soviet influence in the Near East and to retain American access to Middle East oil, Patterson and the War Department focused on preventing famine in occupied areas, forestalling communist revolution, circumscribing Soviet influence, resuscitating trade, and preserving traditional American markets especially in Western Europe.[37] But American economic interests in Eurasia were not limited to Western Europe, Germany, and the Middle East. Military planners and intelligence officers in both the army and navy expressed considerable interest in the raw materials of southeast Asia, and, as already shown, one of the purposes of the bases they wanted was to maintain access to those resources and deny them to a prospective enemy.[38]

While civilian officials and military strategists feared the loss of Eurasia, they did not expect the Soviet Union to attempt its military conquest. In the early Cold War years, there was nearly universal agreement that the Soviets, while eager to expand their influence, desired to avoid a military engagement. In October 1945, for example, the Joint Intelligence Staff predicted that the Soviet Union would seek to avoid war for five to ten years. In April 1946, while

37. Moscow embassy staff, "Russia's International Position at the Close of the War with Germany," enclosed in Smith to Eisenhower, July 12, 1946, DDEL, Dwight David Eisenhower Papers, file 1652, box 101. Also see, for example, Stimson to Roosevelt, September 15, 1944, ML, JFP, box 100; Stimson to Truman, May 16, 1945, HTL, HSTP, PSF, box 157; McCloy, Memorandum for Connelly, April 26, 1945, ibid., box 178; MID, "Intelligence Estimate of the World Situation," June 25, 1946; numerous memoranda, June 1945, USMA, GLP, War Dept. files; numerous documents, 1946 and 1947, RG 107, HCPP, 091 Germany (Classified); and Rearmament Subcommittee, Report to the Special Ad Hoc Committee, July 10, 1947, RG 165, ser. ABC 400.336 (3-20-47). For Forrestal's concern with Middle Eastern oil, see, for example, "Notes in Connection with Navy's 'Line' on Foreign Oil" [late 1944 or early 1945], ML, JFP, box 22; Minutes of the meeting of the Secretaries of State, War, and the Navy, April 17, 1946, RG 107, RPPP, safe file, box 3; and Walter Millis, ed., *The Forrestal Diaries* (New York, 1951), 272, 356–58.

38. Strategy Section, OPD, "Post-War Base Requirements in the Philippines," April 23, 1945; JCS, "Strategic Areas and Trusteeships in the Pacific," October 18, 1946; MID, "Positive U.S. Action Required to Restore Normal Conditions in Southeast Asia," July 3, 1947, RG 319, P&O, 092 (top secret); and Lauris Norstad to the Director of Intelligence, July 10, 1947, ibid.

Soviet troops still remained in Iran, General Lincoln, the army's principal war planner, concurred with Byrnes's view that the Soviets did not want war. In May, when there was deep concern about a possible communist uprising in France, military intelligence doubted the Kremlin would instigate a coup, lest it ignite a full scale war. At a high-level meeting at the White House in June, Eisenhower stated that he did not think the Soviets wanted war; only Forrestal dissented. In August, when the Soviet note to Turkey on the Dardanelles provoked consternation in American policymaking circles, General Hoyt Vandenberg, director of central intelligence, informed President Truman that there were no signs of unusual Soviet troop movements or supply buildups. In March 1947, while the Truman Doctrine was being discussed in Congress, the director of army intelligence maintained that the factors operating to discourage Soviet aggression continued to be decisive. In September 1947, the CIA concluded that the Soviets would not seek to conquer Western Europe for several reasons: they would recognize their inability to control hostile populations; they would fear triggering a war with the United States that could not be won; and they would prefer to gain hegemony by political and economic means. In October 1947, the Joint Intelligence Staff maintained that for three years at least the Soviet Union would take no action that would precipitate a military conflict.[39]

Even the ominous developments during the first half of 1948 did not alter these assessments. Despite his alarmist cable of March 5, designed to galvanize congressional support for increased defense expenditures, General Lucius Clay, the American military governor in Germany, did not believe war imminent. A few days later, the CIA concluded that the communist takeover in Czechoslovakia would not increase Soviet capabilities significantly and reflected no alteration in Soviet tactics. On March 16, the CIA reported to the president, "The weight of logic, as well as evidence, also leads to the conclusion that the Soviets will not resort to military force within the next sixty days." While this assessment was far from reassuring, army and navy intelligence experts concurred that the Soviets still wanted to avoid war; the question was whether war would erupt as a result of "miscalculation" by either the United States or Russia. After talking to Foreign Minister V. M. Molotov in

39. JIS, "Russian Military Capabilities," October 25, 1945, RG 218, ser. CCS 092 USSR (3-27-45), JIS 80/10; Lincoln to M. B. Gardner and F. F. Everest, April 10, 1946, RG 165, ser. ABC 336 Russia (8-22-43); O.S.P., Memorandum for Hull, May 3, 1946, ibid., ser. ABC 381 (9-1-45); S.W.D., Memorandum for the Record, June 12, 1946, RG 319, P&O, 092 (top secret); Vandenberg, Memorandum for the President, August 24, 1946, HTL, HSTP, PSF, box 249; Chamberlin, "Reevaluation of Soviet Intentions," March 27, 1947, RG 165, Records of the Chief of Staff, 091 Russia (top secret); CIA, "Review of the World Situation as It Relates to the Security of the United States," September 26, 1947, HTL, HSTP, PSF, box 203; and JIC, "Soviet Military Objectives and Capabilities, 1947–50," October 27, 1947, RG 165, ser. ABC 381 USSR (3-2-46), JIC 391/1.

June, Ambassador Smith concluded that Soviet leaders would not resort to active hostilities. During the Berlin blockade, army intelligence reported few signs of Soviet preparations for war; naval intelligence maintained that the Soviets desired to avoid war yet consolidate their position in East Germany. In October 1948, the Military Intelligence Division of the army endorsed a British appraisal that "all the evidence available indicates that the Soviet Union is not preparing to go to war in the near future." In December, Acting Secretary of State Robert Lovett summed up the longstanding American perspective when he emphasized that he saw "no evidence that Soviet intentions run toward launching a sudden military attack on the western nations at this time. It would not be in character with the tradition or mentality of the Soviet leaders to resort to such a measure unless they felt themselves either politically extremely weak, or militarily extremely strong."[40]

Although American defense officials recognized that the Soviets had substantial military assets, they remained confident that the Soviet Union did not feel extremely strong. Military analysts studying Russian capabilities noted that the Soviets were rapidly mechanizing infantry units and enhancing their firepower and mobility. It was estimated during the winter of 1946–47 that the Soviets could mobilize six million troops in thirty days and twelve million in six months, providing sufficient manpower to overrun all important parts of Eurasia. The Soviets were also believed to be utilizing German scientists and German technological know-how to improve their submarine force, develop rockets and missiles, and acquire knowledge about the atomic bomb. During 1947 and 1948, it was reported as well that the Soviets were making rapid progress in the development of high performance jet fighters and already possessed several hundred intermediate range bombers comparable to the American B-29.[41]

40. CIA, "Special Evaluation No. 27," March 16, 1948, RG 319, P&O, 350.05 (top secret); MID, "Intelligence Division Daily Briefing," October 18, 1948, ibid.; and Lovett to John L. Sullivan, December 20, 1948, NHC, double zero files, 1948, box 2. Also see Jean Edward Smith, *The Papers of General Lucius D. Clay: Germany, 1945–1949*, 2 vols. (Bloomington, Ind., 1974), 2: 564–65, 568–69, 602; CIA, "Review of the World Situation," March 10, HTL, HSTP, PSF, box 203; R. H. Hillenkoetter, Memorandum for the President, March 16, 1948, ibid., box 249; Chamberlin, Memorandum to the Chief of Staff, March 14, 1948, RG 319, P&O, 092 (top secret); Thomas B. Inglis, Memorandum of Information, March 16, September 28, 1948, NHC, SPD, central files, 1948, A8 and EF 30; Smith to Kennan, June 11, 1948, ML, George F. Kennan Papers [hereafter, GFKP], box 28; and Carter Clarke to the Chief of Staff, August 6, 1948, RG 330, CD 2-2-2, box 4.

41. For reports on Soviet mobilization capabilities and conventional strength on the land, see, for example, Chamberlin, Memorandum to the Chief of Staff, March 14, 1948; Carter Clarke, "Present Capability of the U.S.S.R. Armed Forces," September 16, 1946, RG 319, P&O, 091 Russia (top secret); and P&O, "Capabilities (Ground) and Intentions of the USSR for Overruning Northern and Western Europe in 1947, 1948, and 1949," February 28, 1947, ibid., 350.05 (top secret).

Even so, American military analysts were most impressed with Soviet weaknesses and vulnerabilities. The Soviets had no long-range strategic air force, no atomic bomb, and meager air defenses. Moreover, the Soviet navy was considered ineffective except for its submarine forces.[42] The Joint Logistic Plans Committee and the Military Intelligence Division of the War Department estimated that the Soviet Union would require approximately fifteen years to overcome wartime losses in manpower and industry, ten years to redress the shortage of technicians, five to ten years to develop a strategic air force, fifteen to twenty-five years to construct a modern navy, ten years to refurbish military transport, ten years (or less) to quell resistance in occupied areas, fifteen to twenty years to establish a military infrastructure in the Far East, three to ten years to acquire the atomic bomb, and an unspecified number of years to remove the vulnerability of the Soviet rail-net and petroleum industry to long-range bombing.[43] For several years at least, the Soviet capability for sustained attack against North America would be very limited. In January 1946, the Joint Intelligence Staff concluded that "the offensive capabilities of the United States are manifestly superior to those of the U.S.S.R. and any war between the U.S. and the U.S.S.R. would be far more costly to the Soviet Union than to the United States."[44]

Key American officials like Lovett, Clifford, Eisenhower, Bedell Smith, and Budget Director James Webb were cognizant of prevailing Soviet weak-

---

The war plans of the Joint Chiefs of Staff outline the extensive ground capabilities of Soviet forces. See especially the documents in RG 218, ser. CCS 381 USSR (3-2-46); for information on Soviet use of German scientists, see, for example, JIS, "Capabilities and Intentions of the USSR in the Postwar Period," July 9, 1946, ibid., ser. CCS 092 USSR (3-27-45), JIS 80/26; MID, "Ability of Potential Enemies to Attack the Continental United States," August 8, 1946, RG 319, P&O 381 (top secret); and JIC, "Soviet Capabilities to Launch Air Attacks against the United Kingdom," November 29, 1946, RG 218, ser. CCS 092 USSR (3-27-45), JIC 375/1. For assessments of the improvements in Soviet air power, see, for example, Patterson to Truman, June 23, 1947, HTL, HSTP, PSF, box 157; JIC, Moscow Embassy, "Soviet Intentions," April 1, 1948, RG 330, box 4, CD 2-2-2.

42. See, for example, JIS, "Russian Military Capabilities," October 25, 1945; JIS, "Estimate of Soviet Postwar Military Capabilities and Intentions," November 8, 1945, RG 218, ser. CCS 092 USSR (3-27-45), JIS 80/14; JIS, "Military Capabilities of Great Britain and France," November 13, 1945; JWPC, "Military Position of the United States in Light of Russian Policy," January 8, 1946, RG 218, ser. CCS 092 USSR (3-27-45), JWPC 416/1; and Inglis, Memorandum of Information, January 21, 1946, ML, JFP, box 24.

43. JLPC, "Russian Capabilities," November 15, 1945; and MID, "Intelligence Estimate of the World Situation for the Next Five Years," August 21, 1946, RG 319, P&O, 350.05 (top secret). For a contemporary analysis of the Soviet transport network, also see Paul Wohl, "Transport in the Development of Soviet Policy," *Foreign Affairs*, 24 (1946): 466–83.

44. JIS, "Soviet Post-War Military Policies and Capabilities," January 15, 1946, RG 218, ser. CCS 092 USSR (3-27-45), JIS 80/24; MID, "Ability of Potential Enemies to Attack the Continental United States," August 8, 1946; and P&O, "Estimate of the Situation Pertaining to the Northeast Approaches to the United States," August 12, 1946, RG 319, P&O, 381 (top secret).

nesses and potential American strength. Despite Soviet superiority in man-power, General Eisenhower and Admiral Forrest P. Sherman doubted that Russia could mount a surprise attack, and General Lincoln, Admiral Cato Glover, and Secretaries Patterson and Forrestal believed that Soviet forces would encounter acute logistical problems in trying to overrun Eurasia—especially in the Near East, Spain, and Italy. Even Forrestal doubted reports of accelerating Soviet air capabilities. American experts believed that most Soviet planes were obsolescent, that the Soviets had insufficient airfields and aviation gas to use their new planes, and that these planes had serious problems in their instrumentation and construction.[45]

In general, improvements in specific areas of the Soviet military establishment did not mean that overall Soviet capabilities were improving at an alarming rate. In July 1947, the Military Intelligence Division concluded, "While there has been a slight overall improvement in the Soviet war potential, Soviet strength for total war is not sufficiently great to make a military attack against the United States anything but a most hazardous gamble." This view prevailed in 1946 and 1947, even though the American nuclear arsenal was extremely small and the American strategic bombing force of limited size. In the spring of 1948, the Joint Intelligence Committee at the American embassy in Moscow explained why the United States ultimately would emerge victorious should a war erupt in the immediate future. The Soviets could not win because of their "inability to carry the war to U.S. territory. After the occupation of Europe, the U.S.S.R. would be forced to assume the defensive and await attacks by U.S. forces which should succeed primarily because of the ability of the U.S. to outproduce the U.S.S.R. in materials of war."[46]

45. For the views of Eisenhower and Sherman, see S.W.D., Memorandum for the Record, June 12, 1946; Galambos, *Papers of Dwight David Eisenhower*, 7: 1012–13, 1106–07; Sherman, "Presentation to the President," January 14, 1947, NHC, Forrest E. Sherman Papers, box 2; for the views of Lincoln, Glover, Patterson, Forrestal, and others on Soviet logistical problems, see JPS, Minutes of the 249th meeting, May 22, 1946, RG 218, ser. CCS 381 USSR (3-2-46); Glover to Lincoln and Kissner, June 24, 1947, NHC, SPD, ser. 4, box 86; Louis Denfeld, Memorandum, March 29, 1948, ibid., central files, 1948, A16-3 (5); and Millis, *The Forrestal Diaries*, 272. For assessments of Soviet air power, see, for example, JIS, "Estimate of Soviet Postwar Military Capabilities and Intentions," November 8, 1945; JIC, "Soviet Capabilities to Launch Air Attacks against the United Kingdom," November 29, 1946; Office of Naval Intelligence [hereafter, ONI], "A Study of B-29 Airfields with a Capacity in Excess of 120,000 Pounds" [Spring 1948], NHC, General Board 425 (ser. 315); General Board, "National Security and Navy," Enclosure B, June 25, 1945, ibid., page 16; Forrestal and Clarence Cannon, Excerpt of Conversation, April 9, 1948, ML, JFP, box 48; Inglis to Op-30, December 1, 1948, NHC, SPD, central files, 1948, A8; and Robert Lovett, Diary Entry, December 16, 1947, New York Historical Society, Robert Lovett MS Diaries. For a recent assessment of Soviet conventional strength, see Matthew A. Evangelista, "Stalin's Postwar Army Reappraised," *International Security*, 7 (1982–83): 110–38.

46. MID, "Estimate of the Possibility of War between the United States and the USSR Today from a Comparison with the Situation as it Existed in September 1946," July 21, 1947, RG 319, P&O, 350.05 (top secret); and JIC, Moscow Embassy, "Soviet Intentions," April 1, 1948.

Awareness of Soviet economic shortcomings played a key role in the American interpretation of Soviet capabilities. Intelligence reports predicted that Soviet leaders would invest a disproportionate share of Russian resources in capital goods industries. But, even if such Herculean efforts enjoyed some success, the Soviets still would not reach the pre–World War II levels of the United States within fifteen to twenty years. Technologically, the Soviets were behind in the critical areas of aircraft manufacturing, electronics, and oil refining. And, despite Russia's concerted attempts to catch up and to surpass the United States, American intelligence experts soon started reporting that Soviet reconstruction was lagging behind Soviet ambitions, especially in the electronics, transportation, aircraft, construction machinery, nonferrous metals, and shipping industries. Accordingly, throughout the years 1945–48, American military analysts and intelligence experts believed that Soviet transportation bottlenecks, industrial shortcomings, technological backwardness, and agricultural problems would discourage military adventurism.[47]

If American defense officials did not expect a Soviet military attack, why, then, were they so fearful of losing control of Eurasia? The answer rests less in American assessments of Soviet military capabilities and short-term military intentions than in appraisals of economic and political conditions throughout Europe and Asia. Army officials in particular, because of their occupation roles in Germany, Japan, Austria, and Korea, were aware of the postwar plight of these areas. Key military men—Generals Clay, Douglas MacArthur, John Hilldring, and Oliver P. Echols, and Colonel Charles H. Bonesteel—became alarmed by the prospects of famine, disease, anarchy, and revolution. They recognized that communist parties could exploit the distress and that the Russians could capitalize upon it to spread Soviet influence. As early as June 1945, Rear Admiral Ellery Stone, the American commissioner in Italy, wrote that wartime devastation had created fertile soil for the growth of communism in Italy and the enlargement of the Soviet sphere. MacArthur also feared that, if the Japanese economy remained emasculated and reforms were not undertaken, communism would spread. Clay, too, was acutely aware that

47. For assessments of the interrelationships between the state of the Soviet economy and Soviet military capabilities, see, for example, JIS, "Postwar Economic Policies and Capabilities of the USSR," November 1, 1945, RG 218, ser. CCS 092 USSR (3-27-45), JIS 80/12; JIS, "Soviet Postwar Economic Capabilities and Policies," January 8, 1946, ibid., JIS 80/22; JIS, "Soviet Post-War Military Policies and Capabilities," January 15, 1946; W. B. Shockley, "Relative Technological Achievements in Weapons Characteristics in USSR and USA," January 30, 1946, RG 107, RPPP, safe file, box 6; MID, "Ability of Potential Enemies to Attack the United States," August 8, 1946; U.S. Military Attaché (Moscow) to Chamberlin, March 21, 1947, NHC, Operations Division, ser. 2 (secret and under), box 33, EF 61; JIC, "Soviet Military Objectives and Capabilities," October 27, 1947; and JIC, Moscow Embassy, "Soviet Intentions," April 1, 1948.

German communists were depicting themselves and their beliefs as their country's only hope of salvation. In the spring of 1946, military planners, working on contingency plans for the emergency withdrawal of American troops from Germany, should war with Russia unexpectedly occur, also took note of the economic turmoil and political instability in neighboring countries, especially France. Sensitivity to the geopolitical dimensions of the socioeconomic crisis of the postwar era impelled Chief of Staff Eisenhower to give high priority in the army budget to assistance for occupied areas.[48]

Civilian officials in the War, Navy, and State departments shared these concerns. In the autumn of 1945, McCloy warned Patterson that the stakes in Germany were immense and economic recovery had to be expedited. During the first half of 1946, Secretary Patterson and Assistant Secretary Petersen continually pressed the State Department to tackle the problems beleaguering occupation authorities in Germany and pleaded for State Department support and assistance in getting the Truman administration to provide additional relief to the devastated areas of Europe. On Petersen's urging, Acheson wrote Truman in April 1946, "We have now reached the most critical period of the world food crisis. We must either immediately greatly increase the exports of grain from the United States or expect general disorder and political upheaval to develop in [most of Eurasia]."[49] Forrestal had already pressed for a reassessment of occupation policies in Germany and Japan. In May, Clay suspended reparation payments in order to effect an accord on German economic unity. In June, Patterson began to support the merger of the American and British zones. The man most responsible for this latter undertaking was William Draper, Forrestal's former partner in Dillon, Read, and Co., and Clay's chief economic assistant. Draper firmly believed that "economic collapse in either

48. Stone to Admiral H. R. Stark, June 25, 1945, NHC, double zero files, 1942–47, folder 23. For MacArthur's view, see J. W. Dower, *Empire and Aftermath: Yoshida Shigeru and the Japanese Experience* (Cambridge, Mass., 1979), 292–303; for the situation in Germany, see Patterson to Byrnes, February 25, 1946, RG 107, RPPP, general decimal file, box 8; materials in RG 165, ser. ABC 387 Germany (12-18-43), sects. 4D, 4E; Smith, *Papers of General Lucius D. Clay*, 1: 165–66, 184, 187–89, 196–98, 201–02, 207–08, 217; Galambos, *Papers of Dwight David Eisenhower*, 7: 892; and, for the relationship between the situation in France and American war planning, see, for example, JPS, Minutes of the 249th and 250th meetings, May 22, 29, 1946, RG 218, ser. CCS 381 USSR (3-2-46). For evolving war plans in the Pincher series, see ibid., sects. 1, 2; also see Forrestal, "French Situation," May 6, 1946, ML, JFP, box 20; and *FRUS*, 1946, 5: 434–40; and, for Eisenhower's concern, see Galambos, *Papers of Dwight David Eisenhower*, 8: 1516–20.

49. Acheson to Truman, April 30, 1946, RG 107, HCPP, general subject file, box 1. Also see McCloy to Patterson, November 24, 1945, ibid., RPPP, safe file, box 4. For pressure on the State Department, see Patterson to Byrnes, December 10, 1945, RG 165, Civil Affairs Division [hereafter, CAD], ser. 014 Germany; Patterson to Byrnes, February 25, 1946; OPD and CAD, "Analysis of Certain Political Problems Confronting Military Occupation Authorities in Germany," April 10, 1946, RG 107, HCPP, 091 Germany (classified); and "Combined Food Board" file, spring 1946, ibid., HCPP, general subject file, box 1.

[France or Germany] with probable political break-down and rise of communism would seriously threaten American objectives in Europe and in the world."[50]

American defense officials, military analysts, and intelligence officers were extremely sensitive to the political ferment, social turmoil, and economic upheaval throughout postwar Europe and Asia. In their initial postwar studies, the Joint Chiefs of Staff carefully noted the multiplicity of problems that could breed conflict and provide opportunities for Soviet expansion. In the spring of 1946, army planners, including General Lincoln, were keenly aware that conflict was most likely to arise from local disputes (for example, in Venezia Giulia) or from indigenous unrest (for example, in France), perhaps even against the will of Moscow. A key War Department document submitted to the State-War-Navy Coordinating Committee in April 1946 skirted the issue of Soviet military capabilities and argued that the Soviet Union's strength emanated from totalitarian control over its satellites, from local communist parties, and from worldwide chaotic political and economic conditions. In October 1946, the Joint Planning Staff stressed that for the next ten years the major factor influencing world political developments would be the East-West ideological conflict taking place in an impoverished and strife-torn Europe and a vacuum of indigenous power in Asia. "The greatest danger to the security of the United States," the CIA concluded in mid-1947, "is the possibility of economic collapse in Western Europe and the consequent accession to power of Communist elements."[51]

50. William Draper, Memorandum [early 1947], RG 107, HCPP, 091 Germany (classified); and Forrestal to Acheson, January 14, 1946, ML, JFP, box 68. For Clay's initiative, see Smith, *Papers of General Lucius D. Clay*, 1: 203–04, 213–14, 218–23; John F. Gimbel, *The American Occupation of Germany: Politics and the Military, 1945–1949* (Stanford, 1968), 35–91; John H. Backer, *The Decision to Divide Germany: American Foreign Policy in Transition* (Durham, N.C., 1978), 137–48; and Bruce Kuklick, *American Policy and the Division of Germany: The Clash with Russia over Reparations* (Ithaca, N.Y., 1972), 205–35. For Patterson's concerns and his support of Bizonia, see Patterson to Byrnes, June 11, 1946, RG 107, HCPP, 091 Germany (classified); Patterson to Truman, November 20, 1946, ibid., RPPP, safe file, box 4; Minutes of the War Council meeting, December 5, 1946, ibid., box 7; and Patterson to Palmer Hoyt, December 27, 1946, ibid., box 4. For the merger of the zones, also see *FRUS*, 1946, 5: 579–659; Smith, *Papers of General Lucius D. Clay*, 1: 245, 248–49; and, for Draper's importance, also see Carolyn Eisenberg, "U.S. Social Policy in Post-War Germany: The Conservative Restoration," paper delivered at the Seventy-Fourth Annual Meeting of the Organization of American Historians, held in April 1981, in Detroit.

51. CIA, "Review of the World Situation as it Relates to the Security of the United States," September 26, 1947. Also see, for example, JCS, "Strategic Concept and Plan for the Employment of United States Armed Forces," Appendix A, September 19, 1945; JPS, Minutes of the 249th and 250th meetings; Lincoln to Wood, May 22, 1946, RG 165, ser. ABC 381 (9-1-45); [Giffin (?)] "U.S. Policy with Respect to Russia" [early April 1946], ibid., ser. ABC 336 (8-22-43); JPS, "Estimate of Probable Developments in the World Political Situation up to 1956," October 31, 1946, RG 218,

In brief, during 1946 and 1947, defense officials witnessed a dramatic unraveling of the geopolitical foundations and socioeconomic structure of international affairs. Britain's economic weakness and withdrawal from the eastern Mediterranean, India's independence movement, civil war in China, nationalist insurgencies in Indochina and the Dutch East Indies, Zionist claims to Palestine and Arab resentment, German and Japanese economic paralysis, communist inroads in France and Italy—all were ominous developments. Defense officials recognized that the Soviet Union had not created these circumstances but believed that Soviet leaders would exploit them. Should communists take power, even without direct Russian intervention, the Soviet Union, it was assumed, would gain predominant control of the resources of these areas because of the postulated subservience of communist parties everywhere to the Kremlin. Should nationalist uprisings persist, communists seize power in underdeveloped countries, and Arabs revolt against American support of a Jewish state, the petroleum and raw materials of critical areas might be denied the West. The imminent possibility existed that, even without Soviet military aggression, the resources of Eurasia could fall under Russian control. With these resources, the Soviet Union would be able to overcome its chronic economic weaknesses, achieve defense in depth, and challenge American power—perhaps even by military force.[52]

In this frightening postwar environment, American assessments of Soviet long-term intentions were transformed. When World War II ended, military planners initially looked upon Soviet aims in foreign affairs as arising from the Kremlin's view of power politics, Soviet strategic imperatives, historical Russian ambitions, and Soviet reactions to moves by the United States and Great Britain. American intelligence analysts and strategic planners most frequently discussed Soviet actions in Eastern Europe, the Balkans, the Near East, and Manchuria as efforts to establish an effective security system. Despite enormous Soviet gains during the war, many assessments noted that, in fact, the Soviets had not yet achieved a safe security zone, especially on their southern periphery. While Forrestal, Deane, and most of the planners in the army's

ser. CCS 092 (10-9-46), JPS 814/1; MID, "World Political Developments Affecting the Security of the United States during the Next Ten Years," April 14, 1947, RG 319, P&O, 350.05 (top secret).

52. See, for example, JIS, "Soviet Postwar Economic Capabilities," January 8, 1946; MID, "Intelligence Estimate of the World Situation," June 25, 1946; JCS, "Presidential Request for Certain Facts and Information Regarding the Soviet Union," July 25, 1946, RG 218, ser. CCS 092 USSR (3-27-45), JCS 1696; H. D. Riley to Op-30, February 7, 1947, NHC, SPD, ser. 5, box 111, A16-3 (5); MID, "Capabilities (Ground) and Intentions of the USSR for Overruning Northern and Western Europe," February 28, 1947; P&O, "Strategic Study of Western and Northern Europe," May 21, 1947, RG 319, P&O, 092 (top secret); and Wooldridge to the General Board, April 30, 1948.

Operations Division possessed a skeptical, perhaps even sinister, view of Soviet intentions, the still-prevailing outlook at the end of 1945 was to dismiss the role of ideology in Soviet foreign policy yet emphasize Soviet distrust of foreigners; to stress Soviet expansionism but acknowledge the possibility of accommodation; to abhor Soviet domination of Eastern Europe but discuss Soviet policies elsewhere in terms of power and influence; and to dwell upon the Soviet preoccupation with security yet acknowledge doubt about ultimate Soviet intentions.[53]

This orientation changed rapidly during 1946. In January, the Joint War Plans Committee observed that "the long-term objective [of the Soviet Union] is deemed to be establishment of predominant influence over the Eurasian land mass and the strategic approaches thereto." Reports of the new military attaché in Moscow went further, claiming that "the ultimate aim of Soviet foreign policy seems to be the dominance of Soviet influence throughout the world" and "the final aim . . . is the destruction of the capitalist system." Soon thereafter, American diplomat George Kennan's "long telegram" was widely distributed among defense officials, on whom it had considerable impact. Particularly suggestive was his view that Soviet leaders needed the theme of capitalist encirclement to justify their autocratic rule. Also influential were Kennan's convictions that the Soviet leaders aimed to shatter the international authority of the United States and were beyond reason and conciliation.[54]

53. For assessments of Soviet intentions, see, for example, JIC, "Estimate of Soviet Post-War Capabilities and Intentions," February 2, 1945, RG 218, ser. CCS 000.1 USSR (10-2-44), JIC 250/2; John S. Wise to Hull, April 3, 1945, RG 319, P&O, 350.05, State Department red file (top secret); JSSC to JCS, April 5, 1945, RG 218, ser. CCS 092 USSR (3-27-45); Deane, "Revision of Policy with Relation to Russia," April 16, 1945 (JCS 1313); Secretary of War to Secretary of State [early July 1945], RG 165, ser. ABC 093 Kiel (7-6-45); Marshall to McCloy, July 3, 1945, ibid., OPD 336 (top secret); OPD, "Soviet Intentions," July 6, 1945, ibid., ser. ABC 092 USSR (11-15-44); JCS, "United States Policy concerning the Dardanelles" [July 1945]; JCS, "Military Position of the United States in the Light of Russian Policy," October 8, 1945, RG 218, ser. CCS 092 USSR (3-27-45), JCS 1545; JIS, "Soviet Postwar Foreign Policy," October 25, 1945, ibid., JIS 80/9; JIS, "Russian Military Capabilities," October 25, 1945; Ritchie, "Report of the United States Mission to Moscow, 18 October 1943 to 31 October 1945" [October 31, 1945], RG 165, OPD 336 (top secret); ONI, "Basic Factors in World Situation," December 1945, NHC, SPD, ser. 5, box 106, A8; JIS, "Capabilities and Intentions of the USSR in the Post-War Period," January 2, 1946, RG 218, ser. CCS 092 USSR (3-27-45), JIS 80/20; Forrestal, Notes for remarks to the Harvard Club, January 18, 1946, JL, JFP, box 29; Inglis, Memorandum of Information, January 21, 1946; Stoler, "Continentalism to Globalism," 315–21; and Sherry, *Preparing for the Next War*, 159–90.

54. JWPC, "Military Position of the United States in Light of Russian Policy," January 8, 1946; and U.S. Military Attaché (Moscow), "Estimate of the Situation as of February 1," February 18, 1946, RG 165, ser. ABC 381 Germany (1-29-43). For Kennan's telegram, see *FRUS*, 1946, 4: 696–709; and, for the distribution of Kennan's telegram, see R. L. Vittrup, Memorandum for Craig, February 26, 1946, RG 107, RPPP, safe file, box 5; Vittrup to Lincoln, March 1, 1946, RG 319, P&O, 350.05, State Department red file (top secret); and Bruce Hopper to Kennan, March 29, 1946, ML, GFKP, box 28.

During the spring and summer of 1946, defense officials found these no-tions persuasive as an interpretation of Soviet intentions because of the vola-tile international situation, the revival of ideological fervor within the Soviet Union, and the domestic political atmosphere and legislative constraints in the United States. President Truman wished to stop "babying the Soviets," and his predilection for a tougher posture probably led his subordinates to be less inclined to give the Soviets the benefit of any doubt when assessing Rus-sian intentions.[55] Forrestal believed the Soviet communist threat had become more serious than the Nazi challenge of the 1930s; General John E. Hull, direc-tor of the Operations Division, asserted that the Soviets were "constitutionally incapable of being conciliated"; and Clark Clifford and George Elsey consid-ered Soviet fears "absurd." A key subcommittee of the State-War-Navy Coor-dinating Committee declared that Soviet suspicions were "not susceptible of removal," and in July 1946 the Joint Chiefs of Staff declared the Soviet objec-tive to be "world domination." By late 1946, it was commonplace for intelli-gence reports and military assessments to state, without any real analysis, that the "ultimate aim of Soviet foreign policy is Russian domination of a com-munist world."[56] There was, of course, plentiful evidence for this appraisal of Soviet ambitions—the Soviet consolidation of a sphere of influence in Eastern Europe; the incendiary situation in Venezia Giulia; Soviet violation of the agreement to withdraw troops from Iran; Soviet relinquishment of Japanese arms to the Chinese communists; the Soviet mode of extracting reparations from the Russian zone in Germany; Soviet diplomatic overtures for bases in the Dardanelles, Tripolitania, and the Dodecanese; Soviet requests for a role in the occupation of Japan; and the Kremlin's renewed emphasis on Marxist-Leninist doctrine, the vulnerability of capitalist economies, and the inevitabil-ity of conflict.

Yet these assessments did not seriously grapple with contradictory evi-dence. While emphasizing Soviet military capabilities, strategic ambitions, and diplomatic intransigence, reports like the Clifford-Elsey memorandum of September 1946 and the Joint Chiefs of Staff report 1696 (upon which the

55. Robert L. Messer, *The End of an Alliance: James F. Byrnes, Roosevelt, Truman, and the Origins of the Cold War* (Chapel Hill, N.C., 1982), 152–94, and "Paths Not Taken," 297–319.

56. Forrestal to Clarence Dillon, April 11, 1946, ML, JFP, box 11; Hull to Theater Command-ers, March 21, 1946, RG 165, ser. ABC 336 (8-22-43); for the Clifford-Elsey viewpoint, see Krock, *Memoirs: Sixty Years on the Firing Line*, 428; and SWNCC, "Resume of Soviet Capabilities and Possible Intentions," August 29, 1946, NHC, SPD, ser. 5, box 106, A8. For the SWNCC estimate, see JCS, "Political Estimate of Soviet Policy for Use in Connection with Military Studies," April 5, 1946, RG 218, ser. CCS 092 USSR (3-27-45), JCS 1641/4; and JCS, "Presidential Request for Certain Facts and Information Regarding the Soviet Union," July 25, 1946. Some of the most thoughtful studies on Soviet intentions, like that of the Joint Intelligence Staff in early January 1946 (JIS 80/20), were withdrawn from consideration. See the evolution of studies and reports in RG 218, ser. CCS 092 USSR (3-27-45), sects. 5–7.

Clifford-Elsey memorandum heavily relied) disregarded numerous signs of Soviet weakness, moderation, and circumspection. During 1946 and 1947, intelligence analysts described the withdrawal of Russian troops from northern Norway, Manchuria, Bornholm, and Iran (from the latter under pressure, of course). Numerous intelligence sources reported the reduction of Russian troops in Eastern Europe and the extensive demobilization going on within the Soviet Union. In October 1947, the Joint Intelligence Committee forecast a Soviet army troop strength during 1948 and 1949 of less than two million men. Soviet military expenditures appeared to moderate. Other reports dealt with the inadequacies of Soviet transportation and bridging equipment for the conduct of offensive operations in Eastern Europe. And, as already noted, assessments of the Soviet economy revealed persistent problems likely to restrict Soviet adventurism.[57]

Experience suggested that the Soviet Union was by no means uniformly hostile or unwilling to negotiate with the United States. In April 1946, a few days after a State-War-Navy subcommittee issued an alarming political estimate of Soviet policy (for use in American military estimates), Ambassador Smith reminded the State Department that the Soviet press was not unalterably critical of the United States, that the Russians had withdrawn from Bornholm, that Stalin had given a moderate speech on the United Nations, and that Soviet demobilization continued apace. The next month General Lincoln, who had accompanied Byrnes to Paris for the meeting of the council of foreign ministers, acknowledged that the Soviets had been willing to make numerous concessions regarding Tripolitania, the Dodecanese, and Italian reparations. In the spring of 1946, General Echols, General Clay, and Secretary Patterson again maintained that the French constituted the major impediment to an agreement on united control of Germany. At the same time, the Soviets

---

57. For the withdrawal of Soviet troops, see, for example, MID, "Soviet Intentions and Capabilities in Scandinavia as of 1 July 1946," April 25, 1946, RG 319, P&O, 350.05 (top secret); and [Giffin (?)] "U.S. Policy with Respect to Russia" [early April 1946]. For reports on reductions of Russian troops in Eastern Europe and demobilization within the Soviet Union, see MID, "Review of Europe, Russia, and the Middle East," December 26, 1945, RG 165, OPD, 350.05 (top secret); Carl Espe, weekly calculations of Soviet troops, May–September 1946, NHC, SPD, ser. 5, box 106, A8; MID, "Soviet Capabilities in Germany and West Europe," December 26, 1946, RG 319, P&O, 350.05 (top secret); JIC, "Movement of Russian Troops Outside of USSR except in the Far East," December 31, 1946, RG 218, ser. CCS 092 USSR (3-27-5), JIC Memorandum of Information no. 237; MID, "Estimate of the Possibility of War," July 21, 1947; and JIC, "Soviet Military Objectives and Capabilities," October 27, 1947. For references to Soviet military expenditures, see Patterson to Julius Adler, November 2, 1946, RG 107, RPPP, safe file, box 5; and Abram Bergson, "Russian Defense Expenditures," *Foreign Affairs*, 26 (1948): 373–76. And, for assessments of the Soviet transport system, see R. F. Ennis, Memorandum for the P&O Division, June 24, 1946, RG 165, ser. ABC 336 (8-22-43); U.S. Military Attaché (Moscow) to Chamberlin, March 21, 1947; Op-32 to the General Board, April 28, 1948, NHC, General Board 425 (ser. 315); and Wohl, "Transport in the Development of Soviet Policy," 475–76, 483.

ceased pressing for territorial adjustments with Turkey. After the diplomatic exchanges over the Dardanelles in the late summer of 1946 the Soviets did not again ask for either a revision of the Montreux Convention or the acquisition of bases in the Dardanelles. In early 1947, central intelligence delineated more than a half-dozen instances of Soviet moderation or concessions. In April, the Military Intelligence Division noted that the Soviets had limited their involvement in the Middle East, diminished their ideological rhetoric, and given only moderate support to Chinese communists. In the months preceding the Truman Doctrine, Soviet behavior—as noted by American military officials and intelligence analysts—hardly justified the inflammatory rhetoric Acheson and Truman used to secure congressional support for aid to Greece and Turkey. Perhaps this is why General Marshall, as secretary of state, refrained from such language himself and preferred to focus on the socioeconomic aspects of the unfolding crisis.[58]

In their overall assessments of Soviet long-term intentions, however, military planners dismissed all evidence of Soviet moderation, circumspection, and restraint. In fact, as 1946 progressed, these planners seemed to spend less time analyzing Soviet intentions and more time estimating Soviet capabilities.[59] Having accepted the notion that the two powers were locked in an

58. For the SWNCC estimate, see JCS, "Political Estimate of Soviet Policy," April 5, 1946; for Smith's despatch, see Smith to the Secretary of State, April 11, 1946, RG 165, Records of the Chief of Staff, 091 Russia; and, for Soviet negotiating concessions, see Lincoln, Memorandum for the Chief of Staff, May 20, 1946, USMA, GLP, War Dept. files; James F. Byrnes, *Speaking Frankly* (New York, 1947), 129–37; Patricia Dawson Ward, *The Threat of Peace: James F. Byrnes and the Council of Foreign Ministers* (Kent, Ohio, 1979), 95–102. For the situation in Germany, see OPD and CAD, "Analysis of Certain Political Problems Confronting Military Occupation Authorities in Germany," April 10, 1946, RG 107, HCPP, 091 Germany (classified); Patterson to Truman, June 11, 1946, RG 165, Records of the Chief of Staff, 091 Germany. For Clay's references to French obstructionism, see, for example, Smith, *Papers of General Lucius D. Clay*, 1: 84–85, 88–89, 151–52, 189–90, 212–17, 235–36; for American perceptions of the situation in Turkey, see Melvyn P. Leffler, "Strategy, Diplomacy, and the Cold War: The United States, Turkey, and N.A.T.O.," paper delivered at the Seventy-Fifth Annual Meeting of the Organization of American Historians, held in April 1983, in Cincinnati; for overall intelligence assessments, see Central Intelligence Group [hereafter, CIG], "Revised Soviet Tactics in International Affairs," January 6, 1947, HTL, HSTP, PSF, box 254; MID, "World Political Developments Affecting the Security of the United States during the Next Ten Years," April 14, 1947; and Walter E. Todd to the Director of P&O, April 25, 1947, RG 319, P&O, 350.05 (top secret); for background on the Truman Doctrine, see Joseph Jones, *The Fifteen Weeks* (New York, 1955), esp. 138–70; and, for Marshall's emphasis on the economic roots of the European crisis, see ibid., 203–06, 220–24; and Charles Bohlen, *The Transformation of American Foreign Policy* (New York, 1969), 87–89.

59. Both the quantity and the quality of JCS studies on Soviet intentions seem to have declined during 1946. In "Military Position of the United States in Light of Russian Policy" (January 8, 1946), strategic planners of the Joint War Plans Committee maintained that it was more important to focus on Soviet capabilities than on Soviet intentions. During a key discussion at the White House, Admiral Leahy also was eager to dismiss abstract evaluations of Russian psychology and

ideological struggle of indefinite duration and conscious of the rapid demobilization of American forces and the constraints on American defense expenditures, they no longer explored ways of accommodating a potential adversary's legitimate strategic requirements or pondered how American initiatives might influence the Soviet Union's definition of its objectives.[60] Information not confirming prevailing assumptions either was ignored in overall assessments of Soviet intentions or was used to illustrate that the Soviets were shifting tactics but not altering objectives. Reflective of the emerging mentality was a report from the Joint Chiefs of Staff to the president in July 1946 that deleted sections from previous studies that had outlined Soviet weaknesses. A memorandum sent by Secretary Patterson to the president at the same time was designed by General Lauris Norstad, director of the War Department's Plans and Operations Division, to answer questions about relations with the Soviet Union "without ambiguity." Truman, Clark Clifford observed many years later, liked things in black and white.[61]

During 1946 and early 1947, the conjunction of Soviet ideological fervor and socioeconomic turmoil throughout Eurasia contributed to the growth of a myopic view of Soviet long-term policy objectives and to enormous apprehension lest the Soviet Union gain control of all the resources of Eurasia, thereby endangering the national security of the United States. American assessments of Soviet short-term military intentions had not altered; Soviet military capabilities had not significantly increased, and Soviet foreign policy positions had not greatly shifted. But defense officials were acutely aware of America's own rapidly diminishing capabilities, of Britain's declining military strength, of the appeal of communist doctrine to most of the underdeveloped world, and of the opportunities open to communist parties throughout most of Eurasia as a result of prevailing socioeconomic conditions. War Depart-

---

to focus on Russian capabilities; S.W.D., Memorandum for the Record, June 12, 1946. My assessment of the quality of JCS studies is based primarily on my analysis of the materials in RG 218, ser. CCS 092 USSR (3-27-45); ser. CCS 381 USSR (3-2-46); RG 319, P&O, 350.05 (top secret); and NHC, SPD, central files, 1946–48, A8.

60. During 1946 it became a fundamental tenet of American policymakers that Soviet policy objectives were a function of developments within the Soviet Union and not related to American actions. See, for example, Kennan's "long telegram," in *FRUS*, 1946, 4: 696–709; JCS, "Political Estimate of Soviet Policy," April 5, 1946; JCS, "Presidential Request," July 25, 1946; and the Clifford/Elsey memorandum, in Krock, *Memoirs*, esp. 427–36.

61. For Norstad's comment, see Norstad, Memorandum, July 25, 1946, RG 319, P&O, 092 (top secret). For references to shifting tactics and constant objectives, see Vandenberg, Memorandum for the President, September 27, 1946, HTL, HSTP, PSF, box 249; CIG, "Revised Soviet Tactics," January 6, 1947; and, for the JCS report to the president, compare JCS 1696 with JIC 250/12. Both studies may be found in RG 218, ser CCS 092 USSR (3-27-45). For Clifford's recollection, Clark Clifford, HTL, oral history, 170.

ment papers, studies of the joint chiefs, and intelligence analyses repeatedly described the restiveness of colonial peoples that had sapped British and French strength, the opportunities for communist parties in France, Italy, and even Spain to capitalize upon indigenous conditions, and the ability of the Chinese communists to defeat the nationalists and make the resources and manpower of Manchuria and North China available to the Soviet Union. In this turbulent international arena, the survival of liberal ideals and capitalist institutions was anything but assured. "We could point to the economic benefits of Capitalism," commented one important War Department paper in April 1946, "but these benefits are concentrated rather than widespread, and, at present, are genuinely suspect throughout Europe and in many other parts of the world."[62]

In this environment, there was indeed no room for ambiguity or compromise. Action was imperative—action aimed at safeguarding those areas of Eurasia not already within the Soviet sphere. Even before Kennan's "long telegram" arrived in Washington, the joint chiefs adopted the position that "collaboration with the Soviet Union should stop short not only of compromise of principle but also of expansion of Russian influence in Europe and in the Far East."[63] During the spring and summer of 1946, General Lincoln and Admiral Richard L. Conolly, commander of American naval forces in the eastern Atlantic and Mediterranean, worked tirelessly to stiffen Byrnes's views, avert

62. [Giffin] "U.S. Policy with Respect to Russia" [early April 1946]. Also see Giffin, Draft of Proposed Comments for Assistant Secretary of War on "Foreign Policy," [early February 1946]; MID, "Intelligence Estimate," June 25, 1946; JPS, "Estimate of Probable Developments in the World Political Situation," October 31, 1946, RG 218, ser. CCS 092 (10-9-46), JPS 814/1; Special Ad Hoc Committee of SWNCC, "Study on U.S. Assistance to France," April 9, 1947, RG 165, ser. ABC 400.336 France (3-20-47); MID, "World Political Developments," April 14, 1947; JWPC, "The Soviet Threat against the Iberian Peninsula and the Means Required to Meet It," May 8, 1947, RG 218, ser. CCS 381 USSR (3-2-46), JWPC 465/1; and CIA, "Review of the World Situation," September 26, 1947. With regard to China, the Joint Chiefs of Staff stressed the importance of Soviet aid to Chinese communist forces in late 1945. But both naval and army intelligence were fully cognizant of the corruption and ineptness of nationalist forces and of the indigenous appeal of the Chinese Communist Party. The important point, from the perspective of American defense officials, was that Chinese communist victories would offer the Soviets control over critical resources and enable them to achieve greater defense in depth in parts of Asiatic Russia. See, for example, Patterson, Notes on Cabinet Meeting, August 2, 1946, RG 107, RPPP, safe file, box 2; Minutes of the meetings of the Secretaries of State, War, and Navy, September 11, 1946, February 12, 1947, June 20, 1947, ibid., box 3; Lincoln, Proposed Memorandum for the Secretaries of War and Navy [September 1946], NHC, SPD, ser. 12, box 158, C2 (4); Richard M. Phillips. Memorandum, September 6, 1946, ibid.; Charles J. Rend, Memorandum of Information, June 3, 1947, ibid., ser. 5, box 110, A8; Nimitz to JCS, June 9, 1947, ibid., box 109, Al; JWPC, "Moonrise," June 16, 1947, RG 218, ser. CCS 381 USSR (3-2-46), JWPC 476/1; MID, "Soviet Influence in China," June 16, 1947, RG 319, P&O, 350.05 (top secret); and SWNCC, "United States Policy toward China," June 11, 1947, *FRUS*, 1947, 7: 838–48.

63. JCS, "Foreign Policy of the United States," February 10, 1946.

American diplomatic concessions, and put the squeeze on the Russians.[64] "The United States," army planners explained, "must be able to prevent, by force if necessary, Russian domination of either Europe or Asia to the extent that the resources of either continent could be mobilized against the United States." Which countries in Eurasia were worth fighting over remained unclear during 1946. But army and navy officials as well as the joint chiefs advocated a far-reaching program of foreign economic assistance coupled with the refurbishment of American military forces.[65]

During late 1946 and early 1947, the Truman administration assumed the initiative by creating German Bizonia, providing military assistance to Greece and Turkey, allocating massive economic aid to Western Europe, and reassessing economic policy toward Japan. These initiatives were aimed primarily at tackling the internal sources of unrest upon which communist parties capitalized and at rehabilitating the industrial heartlands of Eurasia. American defense officials supported these actions and acquiesced in the decision to give priority to economic aid rather than rearmament. Service officers working on foreign assistance programs of the State-War-Navy Coordinating Committee supported economic aid, showed sensitivity to the socioeconomic sources of unrest, and recognized that economic aid was likely to be the most efficacious means of preserving a favorable balance of power in Eurasia.[66] Because they judged American military power to be superior and war to be unlikely, Forrestal, Lovett, and Webb insisted that military spending not interfere with the implementation of the Marshall Plan, rehabilitation of Germany, and revival of Japan. "In the necessarily delicate apportioning of our available resources," wrote Assistant Secretary of War Petersen, "the time element permits present emphasis on strengthening the economic and social dikes against

64. Lincoln to Hull [April 1946], RG 59, Office of European Affairs, box 17; Lincoln, Memorandum for the Record, April 16, 1946; Lincoln to Hull, April 16, 1946, RG 165, ser. ABC 092 USSR (11-15-44); Lincoln to Cohen, June 22, 1946, ibid., ABC 381 (9-1-45); Richard L. Conolly, oral history (Columbia, 1960), 293–304; Lincoln, Memorandum for Chief of Staff, May 20, 1946; and Lincoln, Memorandum for Norstad, July 23, 1946, USMA, GLP, War Department files.

65. Giffin, "Draft of Proposed Comments" [early February 1946]. Also see, for example, JCS, "Foreign Policy of the United States," February 10, 1946; [Giffin] "U.S. Policy with Respect to Russia" [early April 1946]; JCS, "Political Estimate of Soviet Policy," April 5, 1946; and Sherman, Memorandum for Forrestal, March 17, 1946, ML, JFP, box 24.

66. See, for example, SWNCC, "Policies, Procedures, and Costs of Assistance by the United States to Foreign Countries," April 21, 1947, *FRUS*, 1947, 3: 204–20; ibid., 1: 725–34; JCS, "United States Assistance to Other Countries," ibid., 734–50, 762–63; and Lincoln to Petersen, May 2, 1947, RG 165, ser. ABC 400.336 (3-20-47). Also see the many SWNCC subcommittee reports on individual countries, ibid.: Report of the Working Group on Economic Aid to the Special Ad Hoc Committee of the SWNCC, "Foreign Needs for United States Economic Assistance during the Next Three to Five Years" [July 1947], RG 353, box 134; and Report of Rearmament Subcommittee to Special Ad Hoc Committee, July 10, 1947, RG 165, ser. ABC 400.336 (3-20-47).

Soviet communism rather than upon preparing for a possibly eventual, but not yet inevitable, war."[67]

Yet if war should unexpectedly occur, the United States had to have the capability to inflict incalculable damage upon the Soviet Union. Accordingly, Truman shelved (after some serious consideration) proposals for international control of atomic energy. The Baruch Plan, as it evolved in the spring and summer of 1946, was heavily influenced by defense officials and service officers who wished to avoid any significant compromise with the Soviet Union. They sought to perpetuate America's nuclear monopoly as long as possible in order to counterbalance Soviet conventional strength, deter Soviet adventurism, and bolster American negotiating leverage. When negotiations at the United Nations for international control of atomic energy languished for lack of agreement on its implementation, the way was clear for the Truman administration gradually to adopt a strategy based on air power and atomic weapons. This strategy was initially designed to destroy the adversary's will and capability to wage war by annihilating Russian industrial, petroleum, and urban centers.[68] After completing their study of the 1946 Bikini atomic tests, the Joint Chiefs of Staff in July 1947 called for an enlargement of the nuclear arsenal. While Truman and Forrestal insisted on limiting military expenditures, government officials moved vigorously to solve problems in the production of plutonium, to improve nuclear cores and assembly devices, and to increase the number of aircraft capable of delivering atomic bombs. After much initial postwar disorganization, the General Advisory Committee to the Atomic Energy Commission could finally report to the president at the end of 1947 that "great progress" had been made in the atomic program. From June 30, 1947, to June 30, 1948, the number of bombs in the stockpile increased

67. Petersen, as quoted in Chief of Staff, Memorandum [July 1947], RG 165, ser. ABC 471.6 Atom (8-17-45). Also see, for example, Lovett diaries, December 16, 1947, January 5, 15, 1948; Baruch to Forrestal, February 7, 1948, ML, JFP, box 78; Forrestal to Baruch, February 10, 1948, ibid.; and Excerpt of Phone Conversation between Forrestal and C. E. Wilson, April 2, 1948, ibid., box 48.

68. These generalizations are based on the following materials: Stimson, Memorandum for the President, September 11, 1945, RG 107, RPPP, safe file, box 1; Forrestal, Memorandum, September 21, 1945, ML, JFP, box 48; Mathia F. Correa to Forrestal, September 27, 1945, ibid., box 28; Forrestal, Memorandum for the President, October 1; 1945, HTL, HSTP, PSF, box 158; documents in HTL, HSTP, PSF, box 199; RG 165, ser. ABC 471.6 Atom (8-17-45); "Brief of Letters Addressed to Mr. Baruch by Each of the Members of the JCS" [June 1946], Bernard Baruch Papers [hereafter, BBP], ML, box 65; Dennison, Draft Reply to Letter from Mr. Baruch, June 4, 1946, NHC, CNO, double zero files, folder 31; and Minutes of the meeting of the Secretaries of State, War, and Navy, January 29, 1947, RG 107, RPPP, safe file, box 3. For the negotiations at the United Nations, see FRUS, 1947, 1: 327–614; also see Herken, Winning Weapon; Larry G. Gerber, "The Baruch Plan and the Origins of the Cold War," Diplomatic History, 6 (1982): 69–95; Bernstein, "Quest for Security," 1033–44; and Rosenberg, "Hydrogen Bomb Decision," 66–71.

from thirteen to fifty. Although at the time of the Berlin crisis the United States was not prepared to launch a strategic air offensive against the Soviet Union, substantial progress had been made in the development of the nation's air-atomic capabilities. By the end of 1948, the United States had at least eighteen nuclear-capable B-50s, four B-36s, and almost three times as many nuclear-capable B-29s as had been available at the end of 1947.[69]

During late 1947 and early 1948, the administration also responded to pleas of the Joint Chiefs of Staff to augment the overseas base system and to acquire bases in closer proximity to the Soviet Union. Negotiations were conducted with the British to gain access to bases in the Middle East, and an agreement was concluded for the acquisition of air facilities in Libya. Admiral Conolly made a secret deal with the French to secure air and communication rights and to stockpile oil, aviation gas, and ammunition in North Africa.[70] Plans also were discussed for postoccupation bases in Japan, and considerable progress was made in refurbishing and constructing airfields in Turkey. During 1948, the Turks also received one hundred eighty F-47 fighter-bombers, thirty B-26 bombers, and eighty-one C-47 cargo planes. The F-47s and B-26s, capable of reaching the vital Ploesti and Baku oil fields, were more likely to be used to slow down a Soviet advance through Turkey or Iran, thereby af-

69. For the views of the General Advisory Committee, see Robert Oppenheimer to Truman, December 31, 1947, HTL, HSTP, PSF, box 200; for the views of the JCS, see, for example, JCS, "Guidance on Military Aspects of United States Policy to be Adopted in Event of Continuing Impasse in Acceptance of International Control of Atomic Energy," July 14, 1947, RG 165, ser. ABC 471.6 Atom (8-17-45), JCS 1764/1; and Leahy to the Secretaries of War and the Navy, August 13, 1947, NHC, CNO, double zero files, 1947, folder 13; and, for the size and quality of the stockpile and the number of nuclear-capable aircraft, see especially David Alan Rosenberg, "U.S. Nuclear Stockpile, 1945 to 1950," *Bulletin of Atomic Scientists*, 38 (1982); 25–30. The number of nuclear-capable B-29s grew with great rapidity at the end of 1948. One memorandum in early 1949 enumerated eighty-three such planes; see O. S. Picher, Memorandum for Colonel Page, February 14, 1949, RG 330, box 126, CD 33-1-4. Both Borowski and Rosenberg have stressed the problems beleaguering the Strategic Air Command until the Korean War, but their work also illustrates the significant changes and improvements that began to occur late in 1947 and especially during 1948. See Borowski, *Hollow Threat*; David Alan Rosenberg, "The Origins of Overkill: Nuclear Weapons and American Strategy, 1945–1960," *International Security*, 7 (1983): 11–27.

70. For negotiations with the British over Middle East strategy and bases, see *FRUS*, 1947, 5: 485–626; and Sullivan to the Acting Secretary of State, September 26, 1947, NHC, SPD, ser. 5, box 110, A14; for facilities in Libya, see, for example, Leahy to the Secretary of Defense, March 18, 1948, RG 319, P&O, 092 (top secret); and *FRUS*, 1948, 3: 906–07; and, for negotiations with the French, see Spaatz to Symington [October 1947], RG 107, Office of the Assistant Secretary of War for Air, 1947, 090, box 187B; Symington to Spaatz, October 30, 1947, ibid.; Wooldridge, Memorandum for Op-09, October 13, 1948, NHC, CNO, double zero files, 1948, box 4 (29); and Wooldridge, Memorandum for Op-09, October 25, 1948, ibid., SPD, central files, 1948, A14. For bases in North Africa, see Forrestal to Truman, January 6, 1948, HTL, HSTP, PSF, box 156; also see *FRUS*, 1948, 1: 603–04, 674–76.

fording time to activate a strategic air offensive from prospective bases in the Cairo-Suez area.[71]

Despite these developments, the joint chiefs and military planners grew increasingly uneasy with the budgetary constraints under which they operated. They realized that American initiatives, however necessary, placed the Soviet Union on the defensive, created an incendiary situation, and made war more likely—though still improbable. In July 1947, intelligence analysts in the War Department maintained that the Truman Doctrine and the Marshall Plan had resulted in a more aggressive Soviet attitude toward the United States and had intensified tensions. "These tensions have caused a sharper line of demarcation between West and East tending to magnify the significance of conflicting points of view, and reducing the possibility of agreement on any point." Intelligence officers understood that the Soviets would perceive American efforts to build strategic highways, construct airfields, and transfer fighter bombers to Turkey as a threat to Soviet security and to the oilfields in the Caucasus. The latter, noted the director of naval intelligence, "lie within easy air striking range of countries on her southern flank, and the Soviet leaders will be particularly sensitive to any political threat from this area, however remote." Intelligence analysts also recognized that the Soviets would view the Marshall Plan as a threat to Soviet control in Eastern Europe as well as a death knell to communist attempts to capture power peacefully in Western Europe. And defense officials were well aware that the Soviets would react angrily to plans for currency reform in German Trizonia and to preparations for a West German republic. "The whole Berlin crisis," army planners informed Eisenhower, "has arisen as a result of . . . actions on the part of the Western Powers." In sum, the Soviet clampdown in Eastern Europe and the attempt to blockade Berlin did not come as shocks to defense officials, who anticipated hostile and defensive Soviet reactions to American initiatives.[72]

71. For references to Japanese bases, see, for example, "Discussion of Need of Obtaining Long-Term Rights for a U.S. Naval Operating Base in Japan" (approved by Nimitz) [Autumn 1947], NHC, SPD, ser. 4, box 86; Nimitz to Under Secretary of the Navy, December 12, 1947, ibid., ser. 5, box 110; and Denfeld, Memorandum for Schuyler, February 20, 1948, ibid., central files, 1948, box 245, EF37; for the transfer of planes to Turkey, see Report No. 29, March 12, 1949, RG 59, 867.00/5–1249; and, for the uses of military assistance to Turkey, see Leffler, "The United States, Turkey, and NATO, 1945–52."

72. MID, "Estimate of the Possibility of War," July 21, 1947, RG 319, P&O, 350.05 (top secret); Op-32 to General Board, April 28, 1948, NHC, General Board 425 (serial 315); and "National Military Establishment Views on Germany" [appended to memorandum for Maddocks], June 30, 1948, RG 319, P&O, 092 (top secret). For the repercussions of the Truman Doctrine and Marshall Plan, see Chamberlin to Chief of Staff, July 9, 1947, RG 165, Records of the Chief of Staff, 091 Greece; and Hillenkoetter, Memorandum for the President, November 7, 1947, HTL, HSTP, PSF, box 249; and, for a similar view in the State Department, see FRUS, 1947, 1: 770–75. For prospective Soviet reactions to American assistance to Turkey, also see General Board, "National

The real consternation of the Joint Chiefs of Staff and other high-ranking civilian and military officials in the defense agencies stemmed from their growing conviction that the United States was undertaking actions and assuming commitments that now required greater military capabilities. Recognizing that American initiatives, aimed at safeguarding Eurasia from further communist inroads, might be perceived as endangering Soviet interests, it was all the more important to be ready for any eventuality. Indeed, to the extent that anxieties about the prospects of war escalated in March and April 1948, these fears did not stem from estimates that the Soviets were planning further aggressive action after the communist seizure of power in Czechoslovakia but from apprehensions that ongoing American initiatives might provoke an attack. On March 14, General S. J. Chamberlin, director of army intelligence, warned the chief of staff that "actions taken by this country in opposition to the spread of Communism . . . may decide the question of the outbreak of war and of its timing." The critical question explicitly faced by the intelligence agencies and by the highest policymakers was whether passage of the Selective Service Act, or of universal military training, or of additional appropriations for the air force, or of a military assistance program to Western European countries, or of a resolution endorsing American support for West European Union would trigger a Soviet attack. Chamberlin judged, for example, that the Soviets would not go to war just to make Europe communist but would resort to war if they felt threatened. The great imponderable, of course, was what, in the Soviet view, would constitute a security threat justifying war.[73]

Recognizing the need to move ahead with planned initiatives but fearing Soviet countermeasures, the newly formed staff of the National Security Council undertook its first comprehensive assessment of American foreign policy. During March 1948, after consulting with representatives of the army, navy, air force, State Department, CIA, and National Security Resources

---

Security and the Navy," enclosure D, June 25, 1948; and Conolly to CNO, December 4, 1947, NHC, Operations Division, ser. 1, A4/FF7. For assessments of Soviet reactions to Western initiatives in Germany, also see Hillenkoetter, Memoranda for the President, March 16, 1948, and June 9, 1948, HTL, HSTP, PSF, box 249; CIA, "Possible Program of Future Soviet Moves in Germany," April 28, 1948, ibid., box 255; and Inglis, Memorandum of Information, April 3, 1948, NHC, Operations Division, ser. 1, box 3.

73. For Chamberlin's views, see, for example, Chamberlin, Memorandum to the Chief of Staff, March 14, 1948; and Chamberlin, Memorandum for Wedemeyer, April 14, 1948, RG 319, P&O, 092 (top secret). For the view from Moscow, see JIC, "Soviet Intentions," April 1, 1948 (extracts of this report are printed in *FRUS*, 1948, 1: 550–57); also see, for example, Hillenkoetter, Memorandum for the President, March 16, 1948; CIA, Special Evaluation No. 27, March 16, 1948; Inglis, Memorandum of Information, March 16, 1948; CIA, "Possibility of Direct Soviet Military Action during 1948," April 2, 1948, HTL, HSTP, PSF, box 255; and CIA, "Review of the World Situation," April 8, 1948, ibid., box 203.

Board, the National Security Council staff produced NSC 7, "The Position of the United States with Respect to Soviet-Dominated World Communism." This study began with the commonplace assumption that the communist goal was "world conquest." The study then went on to express the omnipresent theme behind all conceptions of American national security in the immediate postwar years. "Between the United States and the USSR there are in Europe and Asia areas of great potential power which if added to the existing strength of the Soviet world would enable the latter to become so superior in man-power, resources, and territory that the prospect for the survival of the United States as a free nation would be slight." Accordingly, the study called, first, for the strengthening of the military potential of the United States and, second, for the arming of the non-Soviet world, particularly Western Europe. Al-though this staff study was never formally approved, the national security bureaucracy worked during the spring and summer of 1948 for West Euro-pean unity, military assistance to friendly nations, currency reform in Trizo-nia, revitalization of the Ruhr, and the founding of the Federal Republic of Germany.[74]

The priority accorded to Western Europe did not mean that officials ig-nored the rest of Eurasia. Indeed, the sustained economic rejuvenation of Western Europe made access to Middle Eastern oil more important than ever. Marshall, Lovett, Forrestal, and other defense officials, including the joint chiefs, feared that American support of Israel might jeopardize relations with Arab nations and drive them into the hands of the Soviet Union. Al-though Truman accepted the partition of Palestine and recognized Israel, the United States maintained an embargo on arms shipments and sought to avoid too close an identification with the Zionist state lest the flow of oil to the West be jeopardized.[75] At the same time, the Truman administration moved swiftly in June 1948 to resuscitate the Japanese economy. Additional funds

74. For NSC 7, see *FRUS*, 1948, 1: 545–50; for reactions and reservations of the State De-partment and the JCS, see ibid., 557–64; and, for the support of Western Union, see ibid., 3: 1–351. Also see, for example, materials in RG 218, Leahy Papers, boxes 5, 6; ibid., ser. CCS 092 Western Europe (3-12-48). For military assistance, see *FRUS*, 1948, 1: 585–88; also see materials in RG 330, boxes 22 and 24, CD 6-2-46 and 6-2-49; RG 319, P&O, 092 (top secret); Lawrence S. Kaplan, *A Community of Interests: NATO and the Military Assistance Program, 1948–1951* (Wash-ington, 1980); Condit, *History of the JCS*, 2: 409–36; and Chester J. Pach, "Arming the Free World: The Origins of the United States Military Assistance Program, 1945–1949" (PhD diss., Northwestern University, 1981). For Germany, see especially *FRUS*, 1948, 2: 1–1340; and Smith, *Papers of General Lucius D. Clay*, 2: 527–969.

75. See, for example, *FRUS*, 1948, 5: 545–54, 972–76, 1005–07, 1021–22, 1380–81; CNO to the Secretary of the Navy, January 24, 1948, NHC, CNO, double zero files, 1948, box 2; Leahy, Memorandum for the Secretary of Defense, October 10, 1947, RG 330, box 20, CD 6-1-8; Millis, *Forrestal Diaries*, 344–49, 356–65, 376–77; Bain, *March to Zion*, 137–213; and Miller, *Search for Security*, 173–203.

were requested from Congress to procure imports of raw materials for Japanese industry so that Japanese exports might also be increased. Shortly thereafter, Draper, Tracy S. Voorhees, and other army officials came to believe that a rehabilitated Japan would need the markets and raw materials of Southeast Asia. They undertook a comprehensive examination of the efficacy and utility of a Marshall Plan for Asia. Integrating Japan and Southeast Asia into a viable regional economy, invulnerable to communist subversion and firmly ensconced in the Western community, assumed growing significance, especially in view of the prospect of a communist triumph in China.[76] But communist victories in China did not dissuade policymakers from supporting, for strategic as well as domestic political considerations, the appropriation of hundreds of millions of dollars in additional aid to the Chinese nationalists in the spring of 1948. And the American commitment to preserve the integrity of South Korea actually increased, despite the planned withdrawal of occupation forces.[77]

The problem with all of these undertakings, however, was that they cost large sums, expanded the nation's formal and informal commitments, and necessitated larger military capabilities. Yet on March 24, 1948, just as NSC 7 was being finished, Truman's Council of Economic Advisors warned that accelerating expenditures might compel the president "to set aside free market practices—and substitute a rather comprehensive set of controls." Truman was appalled by this possibility and carefully limited the sums allocated for a buildup of American forces.[78] Key advisers, like Webb, Marshall, Lovett, and

76. For the rehabilitation of Japan, see Special Ad Hoc Committee [of SWNCC], Country Report on Japan, August 8, 1947, RG 353, box 109; Blum to Ohly, December 22, 1947, RG 330, box 9, CD 3-1-9; Blum to Forrestal, December 29, 1947, ibid.; Royall to Forrestal, April 28, 1948, ibid.; Royall, Memorandum for the Secretary of Defense, May 18, 1948, HTL, HSTP, PSF, box 182; and CIA, "Strategic Importance of Japan," May 24, 1948, ibid., box 255. Also see *FRUS*, 1948, 6: 654–56, 694–95, 712–17, 733–34, 750–51, 964–65. For Japan and Southeast Asia, see Ad Hoc Committee, "Study of a United States Aid Program for the Far East," February 16, 1949, RG 319, P&O, 092 Pacific (top secret); and Schaller, "Securing the Great Crescent," 392–414.

77. In recent years scholars have shown that the limited aid to China was not simply a consequence of the influence of the China lobby and the administration's concern with the legislative fate of the European Recovery Program. Some policymakers (especially military officers) also were motivated by fear of the strategic and geopolitical consequences of a communist takeover in China, even though they fully recognized the ineptitude of the Chinese nationalists. See, for example, John H. Feaver, "The China Aid Bill of 1948: Limited Assistance as a Cold War Strategy," *Diplomatic History*, 5 (1981): 107–20; Russell D. Buhite, "Major Interests: American Policy toward China, Taiwan, and Korea, 1945–50," *Pacific Historical Review*, 47 (1978): 425–51; and Thomas G. Paterson, "If Europe, Why Not China? The Containment Doctrine, 1947–49," *Prologue*, 13 (1981): 19–38. For a fine analysis of developments in both China and Korea, see Stueck, *Road to Confrontation*, 31–110; and, for aid to China, also see *FRUS*, 1948, 8: 1–269, 442–601.

78. Edwin G. Nourse, Leon Keyserling, and Clark to Truman, March 24, 1948, HTL, HSTP, PSF, box 143; Truman to Nourse, March 25, 1948, ibid.; Statement by the President to the Sec-

Clifford, supported this approach because they perceived too much fat in the military budget, expected the Soviets to rely on political tactics rather than military aggression, postulated latent U.S. military superiority over the Soviet Union, and assumed that the atomic bomb constituted a decisive, if perhaps short-term, trump card. For many American policymakers, moreover, the Iranian crisis of 1946, the Greek civil war, and the ongoing Berlin airlift seemed to demonstrate that Russia would back down when confronted with American determination, even if the United States did not have superior forces-in-being.[79]

As secretary of defense, however, Forrestal was beleaguered by pressures emanating from the armed services for a buildup of American military forces and by his own apprehensions over prospective Soviet actions. He anguished over the excruciatingly difficult choices that had to be made between the imperatives of foreign economic aid, overseas military assistance, domestic rearmament, and fiscal orthodoxy. In May, June, and July 1948, he and his assistants carefully pondered intelligence reports on Soviet intentions and requested a special State Department study on how to plan American defense expenditures in view of prospective Soviet policies. He also studied carefully the conclusions of an exhaustive study of the navy's contribution to national security undertaken by the General Board of the navy under the direct supervision of Captain Arleigh Burke. Still not satisfied, Forrestal asked the president to permit the National Security Council to conduct another comprehensive examination of American policy objectives. Forrestal clearly hoped that this reassessment would show that a larger proportion of resources should be allocated to the military establishment.[80]

---

retary of Defense, the Secretaries of the Three Departments, and the Three Chiefs of Staff, May 13, 1948, ibid., box 146; and Truman to Forrestal, July 13, 1948, RG 330, box 18, CD 5-1-20.

79. For the views of Lovett and Webb, see Lovett diaries, December 16, 1947, January 15, 1948, April 21, 1948; for Clifford's view of the importance of the atomic bomb, see Clifford, Oral History, 88; and, for Marshall's reliance on the atomic bomb, see McNarney, Memorandum for the JCS, November 2, 1948, HTL, HSTP, PSF, box 114. Also see Policy Planning Staff [hereafter, PPS], "Factors Affecting the Nature of the U.S. Defense Arrangements in the Light of Soviet Policies," June 23, 1948, RG 330, box 4, CD 2-2-2; and Lovett to Forrestal, June 25, 1948, ibid. For the lessons derived from crisis decision making over Iran, Greece, and Turkey, see John R. Oneal, *Foreign Policy Making in Times of Crises* (Columbus, 1982).

80. For the conflicting pressures on Forrestal and his own uncertainties, see, for example, Excerpt of Phone Conversation between Forrestal and C. E. Wilson, April 2, 1948, ML, JFP, box 48; Excerpt of Phone Conversation between Forrestal and Cannon, April 9, 1948, ibid.; and Forrestal to Ralph Bard, November 20, 1948, ibid., box 78; for Forrestal's intense interest in the assessments of Soviet intentions, see Forrestal to Charles A. Buchanan [July 1948], RG 330, box 4, CD 2-2-2; and John McCone to Forrestal, July 7, 1948, ibid.; for Forrestal's request for a State Department study, see Lovett to Forrestal, June 25, 1948; for the naval study and Forrestal's interest therein, see General Board, "National Security and Navy," June 25, 1948;

The Policy Planning Staff of the Department of State prepared the initial study that Forrestal requested and Truman authorized. Extensively redrafted, it reappeared in November 1948 as NSC 20/4 and was adopted as the definitive statement of American foreign policy. Significantly, this paper reiterated the longstanding estimate that the Soviet Union was not likely to resort to war to achieve its objectives. But war could erupt as a result of "Soviet miscalculation of the determination of the United States to use all the means at its command to safeguard its security, through Soviet misinterpretation of our intentions, and through U.S. miscalculation of Soviet reactions to measures which we might take." Immediately following this appraisal of the prospects of war, the National Security Council restated its conception of American national security: "Soviet domination of the potential power of Eurasia, whether achieved by armed aggression or by political and subversive means, would be strategically and politically unacceptable to the United States."[81]

Yet NSC 20/4 did not call for a larger military budget. With no expectation that war was imminent, the report emphasized the importance of safeguarding the domestic economy and left unresolved the extent to which resources should be devoted to military preparations. NSC 20/4 also stressed "that Soviet political warfare might seriously weaken the relative position of the United States, enhance Soviet strength and either lead to our ultimate defeat short of war, or force us into war under dangerously unfavorable conditions." Accordingly, the National Security Council vaguely but stridently propounded the importance of reducing Soviet power and influence on the periphery of the Russian homeland and of strengthening the pro-American orientation of non-Soviet nations.[82]

Language of this sort, which did not define clear priorities and which projected American interests almost everywhere on the globe, exasperated the joint chiefs and other military officers. They, too, believed that the United States should resist communist aggression everywhere, "an overall commitment which in itself is all-inclusive." But to undertake this goal in a responsible and effective fashion it was necessary "to bring our military strength to a level commensurate with the distinct possibility of global warfare." The Joint Chiefs of Staff still did not think the Soviets wanted war. But, given the long-term

Arleigh Burke, Oral History, NHC, 2: 30; and, for Forrestal's request and for a comprehensive study of American policy and Truman's responses, see Truman to Forrestal, July 13, 1948, RG 330, box 18, CD 5-1-20; Truman to Forrestal, July 15, 1948, HTL, HSTP, PSF, box 150; and *FRUS*, 1948, 1: 589–93.

81. NCS 20/1 and 20/4 may be found in Gaddis and Etzold, *Containment*, 173–211 (the quotations appear on page 208). Also see *FRUS*, 1948, 1: 589–93, 599–601, 609–11, 615–24, 662–69.

82. Gaddis and Etzold, *Containment*, 209–10.

intentions attributed to the Soviet Union and given America's own aims, the chances for war, though still small, were growing.[83]

Particularly worrisome were studies during 1948 suggesting that, should war occur, the United States would have difficulty implementing basic strategic undertakings. Although the armed services fought bitterly over the division of funds, they concurred fully on one subject—the $15 billion ceiling on military spending set by Truman was inadequate. In November 1948, military planners argued that the $14.4 billion budget would jeopardize American military operations by constricting the speed and magnitude of the strategic air offensive, curtailing conventional bombing operations against the Soviet Union, reducing America's ability to provide naval assistance to Mediterranean allies, undermining the nation's ability to control Middle East oil at the onset of a conflict, and weakening initial overall offensive capabilities. On November 9, the joint chiefs informed the secretary of defense that the existing budget for fiscal 1950 was "insufficient to implement national policy in any probable war situation that can be foreseen."[84]

From the viewpoint of the national military establishment, the deficiency of forces-in-being was just one of several problems. Forrestal told Marshall that he was more concerned about the absence of sufficient strength to support international negotiations than he was about the availability of forces to combat overt acts of aggression, which were unlikely in any case. During 1948,

83. NSC 35, "Existing International Commitments Involving the Possible Use of Armed Forces," November 17, 1948, *FRUS*, 1948, 1: 656–62. For assessments of Soviet intentions and the prospects of war, see the citations in note 74 above; also see CIA, "Possibility of Direct Soviet Military Action during 1948–49," September 16, 1948, HTL, HSTP, PSF, box 255; CIA, "Threats to the Security of the United States," September 28, 1948, ibid., box 256; COMNAVFORGER, Intelligence Report, September 30, 1948, NHC, SPD, central files, 1948, box 245, EF61; JSPC, "Revised Brief of Short-Range Emergency Plan; Fleetwood," October 14, 1948, RG 218, ser. CCS 381 USSR (3-2-46), JSPC 877/23; and *FRUS*, 1948, 1:648–50, and 5: 942–47.

84. JCS, Denfeld, Memorandum for the Secretary of Defense, November 8, 1948, RG 218, ser. CCS 370 (8-19-45), JCS 1800/14. For the impact of the $14.4 billion budget on strategic plans, see JCS, "Allocation of Forces and Funds for the FY 1950 Budget," November 22, 1948, RG 330, box 16, "Draper: Budget File," JCS, 1800/18; for overall problems facing strategic planners, see the voluminous studies in RG 218, ser. CCS 381 USSR (3-2-46); and, for a few examples of the problems in implementing strategic plans, see Joint Logistics Planning Group (JLPG), "Quick Feasibility Test of JSPG 496/4," March 19, 1948, ibid., JLPG 84/5; JCS, "The Logistic Feasibility of Doublestar," August 12, 1948, ibid., JCS 1844/15; JLPG, "Supply Priorities, for Fleetwood," October 15, 1948, ibid., JLPG 84/31; and JLPC, "The Correction of Deficiencies Revealed by the Limited Feasibility test of ABC 101," December 23, 1948, ibid., JLPC 416/36. In late 1948 and 1949 the navy challenged fundamental aspects of the strategic air offensive. See the studies in ibid., ser. CCS 373 (10-23-48); also see Rosenberg, "Hydrogen Bomb Decision," 71–75. For service rivalries and the budgetary process, see, for example, Warner R. Schilling, "The Politics of National Defense: Fiscal 1950," in Schilling et al., *Strategy, Politics, and Defense Budgets* (New York, 1962), 5–266.

the joint chiefs also grew increasingly agitated over the widening gap between American commitments and interests on the one hand and American military capabilities on the other. In November, the Joint Chiefs of Staff submitted to the National Security Council a comprehensive list of the formal and informal commitments that already had been incurred by the United States government. According to the joint chiefs, "current United States commitments involving the use or distinctly possible use of armed forces are very greatly in excess of our present ability to fulfill them either promptly or effectively." Limited capabilities meant that the use of American forces in any specific situation—for example, in Greece, Berlin, or Palestine—threatened to emasculate the nation's ability to respond elsewhere.[85]

Having conceived of American national security in terms of Western control and of American access to the resources of Eurasia outside the Soviet sphere, American defense officials now considered it imperative to develop American military capabilities to meet a host of contingencies that might emanate from further Soviet encroachments or from indigenous communist unrest. Such contingencies were sure to arise because American strategy depended so heavily on the rebuilding of Germany and Japan, Russia's traditional enemies, as well as on air power, atomic weapons, and bases on the Soviet periphery.[86] Such contingencies also were predictable because American strategy depended so heavily on the restoration of stability in Eurasia, a situation increasingly unlikely in an era of nationalist turmoil, social unrest, and rising economic expectations.[87] Although the desire of the national military establishment for large increases in defense expenditures did not prevail in the tight budgetary environment and presidential election year of 1948, the mode of thinking about national security that subsequently accelerated the arms race and precipitated military interventionism in Asia was already widespread among defense officials.

Indeed, the dynamics of the Cold War after 1948 are easier to comprehend when one grasps the breadth of the American conception of national security that had emerged between 1945 and 1948.[88] This conception included a stra-

85. For the position of the JCS, see NSC 35, "Existing International Commitments," November 17, 1948, *FRUS*, 1948, 1: 656–62. For Forrestal's view, see ibid., 644–46. For background, see William A. Knowlton, Memorandum for the Chief of Staff, October 21, 1948, RG 319, P&O, 092 (top secret); for the reference to Greece, see JCS, "The Position of the United States with Respect to Greece," April 13, 1948, RG 218, ser. CCS 092 Greece (12-30-47), JCS 1826/8.

86. See, for example, the citations in notes 72–73, above.

87. See, for example, CIA, "The Break-Up of the Colonial Empires and Its Implications for U.S. Security," September 3, 1948, HTL, HSTP, PSF, box 255; CIA, "Review of the World Situation," September 16, 1948; and Inglis, Memorandum of Information, February 16, 1949, NHC, SPD, central files, 1949, box 249, All.

88. The view presented here of the expansive American conception of national security

tegic sphere of influence within the Western Hemisphere, domination of the Atlantic and Pacific oceans, an extensive system of outlying bases to enlarge the strategic frontier and project American power, an even more extensive system of transit rights to facilitate the conversion of commercial air bases to military use, access to the resources and markets of most of Eurasia, denial of those resources to a prospective enemy, and the maintenance of nuclear superiority. Not every one of these ingredients, it must be emphasized, was considered vital. Hence, American officials could acquiesce, however grudgingly, to a Soviet sphere in Eastern Europe and could avoid direct intervention in China. But cumulative challenges to these concepts of national security were certain to provoke a firm American response. This occurred initially in 1947–48 when decisions were made in favor of the Truman Doctrine, Marshall Plan, military assistance, Atlantic alliance, and German and Japanese rehabilitation. Soon thereafter, the "loss" of China, the Soviet detonation of an atomic bomb, and the North Korean attack on South Korea intensified the perception of threat to prevailing concepts of national security. The Truman administration responded with military assistance to southeast Asia, a decision to build the hydrogen bomb, direct military intervention in Korea, a commitment to station troops permanently in Europe, expansion of the American alliance system, and a massive rearmament program in the United States. Postulating a long-term Soviet intention to gain world domination, the American conception of national security, based on geopolitical and economic imperatives, could not allow for additional losses in Eurasia, could not risk a challenge to its nuclear supremacy, and could not permit any infringement on its ability to defend in depth or to project American force from areas in close proximity to the Soviet homeland.

To say this is neither to exculpate the Soviet government for its inhumane treatment of its own citizens nor to suggest that Soviet foreign policy was idle or benign. Indeed, Soviet behavior in Eastern Europe was often deplorable; the Soviets sought opportunities in the Dardanelles, northern Iran, and Manchuria; the Soviets hoped to orient Germany and Austria toward the East; and the Soviets sometimes endeavored to use communist parties to expand Soviet influence in areas beyond the periphery of Russian military power. But, then again, the Soviet Union had lost twenty million dead during the war, had experienced the destruction of 1,700 towns, 31,000 factories, and 100,000 collective farms, and had witnessed the devastation of the rural economy with

---

conflicts in part with the one presented by John L. Gaddis's *Strategies of Containment: A Critical Appraisal of Postwar American National Security Policy* (New York, 1981), 3–88. Gaddis's argument is thoughtful and insightful but relies too heavily on the recommendations of Kennan and his Policy Planning Staff. Indeed, the adoption of NSC 68 and the massive military buildup that accompanied the Korean War are much easier to understand if one grasps the expansive conception of national security that was pervasive in defense circles after World War II.

the Nazi slaughter of twenty million hogs and seventeen million head of cattle. What is remarkable is that after 1946 these monumental losses received so little attention when American defense analysts studied the motives and intentions of Soviet policy; indeed, defense officials did little to analyze the threat perceived by the Soviets. Yet these same officials had absolutely no doubt that the wartime experiences and sacrifices of the United States, though much less devastating than those of Soviet Russia, demonstrated the need for and entitled the United States to oversee the resuscitation of the industrial heartlands of Germany and Japan, establish a viable balance of power in Eurasia, and militarily dominate the Eurasian rimlands, thereby safeguarding American access to raw materials and control over all sea and air approaches to North America.[89]

To suggest a double standard is important only insofar as it raises fundamental questions about the conceptualization and implementation of American national security policy. If Soviet policy was aggressive, bellicose, and ideological, perhaps America's reliance on overseas bases, air power, atomic weapons, military alliances, and the rehabilitation of Germany and Japan was the best course to follow, even if the effect may have been to exacerbate Soviet anxieties and suspicions. But even when one attributes the worst intentions to the Soviet Union, one might still ask whether American presuppositions and apprehensions about the benefits that would accrue to the Soviet Union as a result of communist (and even revolutionary nationalist) gains anywhere in Eurasia tended to simplify international realities, magnify the breadth of American interests, engender commitments beyond American capabilities, and dissipate the nation's strength and credibility. And, perhaps even more importantly, if Soviet foreign policies tended to be opportunist, reactive, nationalistic, and contradictory, as some recent writers have claimed and as some contemporary analysts suggested, then one might also wonder whether America's own conception of national security tended, perhaps unintentionally, to engender anxieties and to provoke countermeasures from a proud, suspicious, insecure, and cruel government that was at the same time legitimately apprehensive about the long-term implications arising from the rehabilitation of traditional enemies and the development of foreign bases on the

---

89. For Soviet losses, see Nicholas V. Riasanovsky, *A History of Russia* (3rd edn., New York, 1977), 584–85. While Russian dead totaled almost twenty million and while approximately 25 percent of the reproducible wealth of the Soviet Union was destroyed, American battlefield casualties were 300,000 dead, the index of industrial production in the United States rose from 100 to 196, and the gross national product increased from $91 billion to $166 billion. See Gordon Wright, *The Ordeal of Total War* (New York, 1968), 264–65. For an analysis of Soviet threat perception in the aftermath of World War II, see Michael McGwire, "The Threat to Russia: An Estimate of Soviet Military Requirements" (manuscript in preparation at the Brookings Institution [title tentative]).

periphery of the Soviet homeland. To raise such issues anew seems essential in the 1980s, when a correct understanding of an adversary's intentions, a shrewd grasp of an adversary's perceptions of vital interests, and a sound assessment of America's own national security imperatives seem to be indispensable prerequisites for the avoidance of nuclear war and the establishment of a safer climate for great power competition.

# 5

## Strategy, Diplomacy, and the Cold War

### THE UNITED STATES, TURKEY, AND NATO, 1945–1952

My research in military records provided me with insights into some of the key diplomatic events of the early Cold War years. Of central importance to the early Cold War was the Truman Doctrine. In a speech on March 12, 1947, the president announced that the United States must "support free peoples who are resisting subjugation by armed minorities or by outside pressures." Greece, President Truman said, was endangered by civil war, and Turkey was endangered by external threats to its territorial integrity. Both countries required assistance and advisers.

My research, however, suggested that the threats to Turkey were hugely exaggerated. In fact, the interest in Turkey stemmed not from Soviet threats, but from American war planning. Looking through Joint Chiefs of Staff records, I learned that U.S. war planning, although crude, began in the early months of 1946. If war erupted, for whatever reasons, the war plans called for the United States to strike the Soviet Union. Expecting Soviet armies to overrun most of Europe very quickly, planners assumed that the United States would launch its attack primarily from bases in the United Kingdom and the British-controlled Cairo-Suez base in the Middle East. To protect the latter, it would be essential to slow down Soviet armies marching southward to conquer the Middle East. The United States needed the Turkish army to thwart Soviet military advances and required Turkish airfields to insure the success of the strategic offensive against targets inside the USSR.

Some historians, like Eduard Mark, challenged my claims that U.S. officials did not feel endangered by Soviet threats to Turkey in 1946. (See Eduard Mark, "The War Scare of 1946 and Its Consequences," *Diplomatic History*, 21 [Summer 1997]: 383–413). Yet, most scholars acknowledged the importance of Turkey to U.S. strategic plans and to the enlargement of NATO after it was founded in early 1949. The important point was that strategy and diplomacy were intimately interrelated, and that neither the diplomacy of the Cold War nor Soviet (nor American) threat perception could be understood without an understanding of the Cold War's military dimensions. Indeed, the concept of national security presupposed the integration of economic, military, and diplomatic initiatives to achieve vital interests.

This article first appeared in *Journal of American History* 71 (March 1985): 807–25.

—————

On March 12, 1947, President Harry S. Truman appeared before a joint session of Congress and made one of the most momentous addresses of the postwar era. Requesting $400 million in aid for Greece and Turkey, he emphasized that a "fateful hour" had arrived and that nations had to "choose between alternative ways of life." The United States, Truman insisted, had to support "free peoples who are resisting attempted subjugation by armed minorities or by outside pressures." Greece, of course, was then beleaguered by civil war. Turkey, while enjoying remarkable internal stability, supposedly was subject to pressure from the Soviet Union, a constant war of nerves, and the prospect of outright Soviet aggression. Undersecretary of State Dean G. Acheson warned that if the United States did not act, three continents could fall prey to Soviet domination.[1]

The international situation, of course, was far more complex than that described by Truman or Acheson. The president and his closest advisers simplified international realities in order to generate public support for unprecedented peacetime foreign-policy initiatives.[2] Many scholars have demonstrated that the Greek civil war did not fall neatly into the category of Soviet

1. *Public Papers of the Presidents of the United States: Harry S. Truman, 1947* (Washington, 1963), 178–79; Dean Acheson, *Present at the Creation: My Years in the State Department* (New York, 1969), 219; Joseph M. Jones, *Fifteen Weeks (February 21–June 5, 1947)* (New York, 1955), 39–198.

2. President Harry S. Truman said that he confronted "the greatest selling job ever facing a President." Dean Acheson admitted: "No time was left for measured appraisal." Matthew J.

aggression–American response. Developments in Turkey, however, have received far less attention.[3]

The purpose of this article is to examine the policy of the United States toward Turkey in the postwar era, to elucidate United States policymakers' assessments of Soviet intentions toward Turkey, and to explain the reasons for and the consequences of Turkey's inclusion in the Truman Doctrine. Rather than expecting an imminent Soviet attack on Turkey, United States officials sought to take advantage of a favorable opportunity to enhance the strategic interests of the United States in the Middle East and the eastern Mediterranean. Assistance under the Truman Doctrine was designed to improve the military capabilities of both Turkey and the United States to wage war against the Soviet Union should conflict unexpectedly erupt. Although United States officials hoped to capitalize on Turkey's geographic location without assuming specific guarantees to defend Turkey's territorial integrity, they soon found that their investment in Turkey might be wasted and their hopes for strategic gain unrealized if they did not accept more binding commitments in the form of Turkey's admission into the North Atlantic Treaty Organization (NATO). This article, then, underscores the important and often unexplained role of strategic imperatives in the shaping of foreign policy actions and alli-

---

Connelly, notes on cabinet meeting, March 7, 1947, box 1, Matthew J. Connelly Papers (Harry S. Truman Library, Independence, Mo.); Acheson, *Present at the Creation*, 219.

3. Lawrence S. Wittner, *American Intervention in Greece, 1943–1949* (New York, 1982); John R. Oneal, *Foreign Policy Making in Times of Crisis* (Columbus, 1982), 137–215; George Martin Alexander, *The Prelude to the Truman Doctrine: British Policy in Greece, 1944–1947* (New York, 1982); John O. Iatrides, *Revolt in Athens: The Greek Communist "Second Round," 1944–1945* (Princeton, 1972); C. M. Woodhouse, *The Struggle for Greece, 1941–1949* (London, 1976). Turkish-American relations are covered briefly in most of the standard accounts of the origins of the Cold War and of United States policy in the Middle East. See, for example, Daniel Yergin, *Shattered Peace: The Origins of the Cold War and the National Security State* (Boston, 1977), 233–35; John Lewis Gaddis, *The United States and the Origins of the Cold War, 1941–1947* (New York, 1972), 336–52; Thomas G. Paterson, *Soviet-American Confrontation: Postwar Reconstruction and the Origins of the Cold War* (Baltimore, 1973), 174–206; Joyce Kolko and Gabriel Kolko, *The Limits of Power: The World and United States Foreign Policy, 1945–1954* (New York, 1972), 242–45, 336–46; George Kirk, *The Middle East, 1945–1950* (London, 1954), 21–56; John C. Campbell, *Defense of the Middle East: Problems of American Policy* (New York, 1958), 154–82; and George Lenczowski, *Soviet Advances in the Middle East* (Washington, 1972), 37–49. For a recent account of United States policy in the region prior to the Truman Doctrine, see Bruce Robellet Kuniholm, *The Origins of the Cold War in the Near East: Great Power Conflict and Diplomacy in Iran, Turkey, and Greece* (Princeton, 1980). For the controversy over the Dardanelles, see Harry N. Howard, *Turkey, the Straits and U.S. Policy* (Baltimore, 1974); Anthony R. De Luca, "Soviet-American Politics and the Turkish Straits," *Political Science Quarterly*, 92 (Fall 1977), 503–24; and David J. Alvarez, *Bureaucracy and Cold War Diplomacy: The United States and Turkey, 1943–1946* (Thessaloniki, 1980). For an analysis of Truman's perceptions of Soviet intentions regarding Turkey, see J. Garry Clifford, "President Truman and Peter the Great's Will," *Diplomatic History*, 4 (Fall 1980), 371–85.

ance relationships. More indirectly, it seeks to stimulate a reconsideration of how the relationship between the United States and Turkey might have interacted with other variables to escalate tensions during the formative years of the Cold War.

In the immediate aftermath of World War II, United States policymakers did not believe that Soviet leaders intended to use force to achieve their goals vis-à-vis Turkey. State Department and military officials assumed that the Soviet Union's desire to revise the Montreux Convention, to establish bases in the Dardanelles, and to acquire Kars and Ardahan constituted threats to long-term Anglo-American interests in the Mediterranean. Foreign Service officers such as George F. Kennan and Elbridge Durbrow and strategic planners such as General George A. Lincoln, however, maintained that Soviet leaders felt too weak to engage in military aggression and thereby to risk a general war.[4]

Those assessments were based on appraisals of Soviet actions that were, in fact, carefully modulated. In June 1945, for example, Soviet Foreign Minister Vyacheslav M. Molotov informed the Turkish ambassador that Soviet acceptance of a new treaty of friendship was contingent on the revision of the Montreux Convention, frontier readjustments, and greater security in the straits, including a base. Yet even hard-line United States officials, such as Loy W. Henderson, director of the Office of Near Eastern and African Affairs, acknowledged that the Soviets had not made formal demands, had acted with restraint, and had invited further discussion. When Joseph Stalin discussed these issues with Winston S. Churchill and Truman at Potsdam and when he reviewed them with Ambassador Walter Bedell Smith in Moscow in April 1946, the Soviet leader was neither intransigent nor intemperate. Soviet diplomats made it clear that they were flexible on the territorial issue and that it was of secondary importance. After the spring of 1946, the Soviets stopped raising the matter of frontier readjustments, and the issue faded from the diplomatic scene.[5]

4. Expanded draft of letter from Secretary of War to Secretary of State, "U.S. Position re Soviet Proposals on Kiel Canal and Dardanelles," July 8, 1945, sec. 1-A, American-British Conversations (ABC) 093 Kiel (6 July 1945), Records of the War Department General and Special Staffs, RG 165 (National Archives); George A. Lincoln to Stanley D. Embick, July 7, 1945, ibid.; Lincoln to John E. Hull, April 11, 1945, OPD 336 TS, ibid.; Joint Chiefs of Staff [JCS] 1418/1, enclosure "B," JCS to Secretary of State, July 30, 1945, CCS 092 (7-10-45), Records of the Joint Chiefs of Staff, RG 218 (National Archives); JCS 1641, "U.S. Security interests in the Eastern Mediterranean," March 10–13, 1946, sec. 6, CCS 092 USSR (3-27-45), ibid.; *Foreign Relations of the United States, 1946* (11 vols., Washington, 1969–1972), VII, 840–42; George F. Kennan to Secretary of State, March 17, 1946, box 63, George M. Elsey Papers (Harry S. Truman Library); Elbridge Durbrow to Secretary of State, Aug. 5, 1946, file 761.67/8-546, Records of the Department of State, RG 59 (National Archives).

5. Memorandum regarding Soviet-Turkish Relations, June 29, 1945, FW 761.6711/6–1845, Records of the Department of State; Edwin C. Wilson to Secretary of State, April 19, 1946, file

In their relations with Turkey, the Soviets gave priority to enhancing their security in the straits and in the Black Sea. Because that matter has received extensive attention, there is no reason to dwell on it here. In brief, United States officials acknowledged the legitimacy of the Soviet desire to revise the Montreux Convention but opposed Soviet acquisition of bases. Truman and Churchill agreed at Potsdam that the Soviets ought to raise the question of revision at a subsequent time. In their informal and nonacrimonious discussions with Turkish officials in 1945 and early 1946, Soviet diplomats emphasized the need to enhance Soviet security in the Dardanelles and in the Black Sea. They were usually vague about what they wanted, but occasionally they intimated that they might be satisfied with less than permanent bases in the straits.[6]

When the Soviets finally raised the issue of the straits in a formal diplomatic note in August 1946, the furor engendered in Washington was out of proportion to the diplomatic event. Edwin C. Wilson, the United States ambassador to Turkey, interpreted the Soviet proposals, including a request for joint defense of the Dardanelles, as a smoke screen for destroying Turkey's independence. Wilson acknowledged, however, that the Soviet note itself was not threatening in tone. Nor were Turkish officials particularly alarmed. They did not expect a Soviet attack, and they had anticipated a more bellicose Soviet diplomatic initiative. Moreover, they considered the second Soviet note, circulated in September, even milder and more restrained. The Soviet quest for bases in the Dardanelles, in fact, was similar to ongoing United States efforts to negotiate base rights in Iceland, Greenland, Panama, the Azores, and the western Pacific. Several months earlier Henderson had emphasized precisely this point when he had advised against raising a formal objection to Soviet requests of Turkey.[7]

---

761.67/4–1946, ibid.; James F. Byrnes, memorandum for the president, July 4, 1945, box 175, President's Secretary's File, Harry S. Truman Papers (Harry S. Truman Library); Walter Bedell Smith to Secretary of State, April 5, 1946, box 188, ibid.; *Foreign Relations of the United States, Diplomatic Papers: The Conference of Berlin (The Potsdam Conference), 1945* (2 vols., Washington, 1960), I, 1010–54, II, 257–58, 266–67, 301–305, 312–14, 320, 365–67, 372–73, 393, 606, 1427–28, 1439–40; *Foreign Relations of the United States, 1946*, VII, 809–810; "Russian-Turkish Frontier," March 11, 1946, box 11, William D. Leahy Papers, Records of the Joint Chiefs of Staff. It is difficult to find any reference to the Soviets' raising the territorial issue anew after the middle of 1946. In May 1953 the Soviets assured Turkey that they no longer laid claim to Kars and Ardahan. Stephen G. Xydis, "The 1945 Crisis over the Turkish Straits," *Balkan Studies*, 1 (1960), 90.

6. Howard, *Turkey, the Straits and U.S. Policy*; Xydis, "1945 Crisis over the Turkish Straits," 65–90; Byrnes, memorandum for the president, July 4, 1945, box 175, President's Secretary's File, Truman Papers; Smith to Secretary of State, April 5, 1946, box 188, ibid.; *Foreign Relations of the United States, 1946*, VII, 812–13, 816, 826. Despite occasional vituperous press and radio announcements by both the Turks and the Soviets, United States officials knew that Turkish-Soviet diplomatic talks took place in a correct, if not a cordial, manner. Ibid., 810–18; *Foreign Relations of the United States, 1945* [9 vols., Washington, 1967–1969), VIII, 1219.

7. *Foreign Relations of the United States, 1946*, VII, 827–29, 835, 837, 859, 860, 867–68, 869;

What supposedly distinguished Soviet actions toward Turkey was Soviet bellicosity. Diplomats and historians often have focused on Soviet troop movements to support their contention that the Soviets were preparing or threatening to use force to dominate Turkey. On March 18, 1946, for example, in a frequently cited dispatch, Ambassador Wilson informed Washington of new Soviet troop dispositions and suggested that the Soviets might soon be in a position to strike at Turkey. In the most recent and widely acclaimed analysis of developments in the Near East, Bruce Robellet Kuniholm fully accepts Wilson's appraisal of Soviet actions and intentions.[8]

There is, however, considerable reason to question that view of Soviet behavior and to reassess the motivations behind subsequent actions of the United States. Throughout late 1945 and 1946, for example, United States officials received intelligence that Soviet troops were being withdrawn in substantial numbers from eastern and southeastern Europe. Although troop rotations and maneuvers did occur, those actions were considered normal. In October 1945, a report from the joint intelligence subcommittee in London emphasized that there was no appreciable buildup of troops in Bulgaria and no concentration of aircraft, either in Bulgaria or in the Caucasus, capable of sustaining a Soviet attack on Turkey. In late December 1945, United States Army intelligence reported that stories of Soviet troop concentrations in Bulgaria had been alarmist. Some increase in Soviet troops in Bulgaria probably did occur briefly in early 1946, but United States military analysts concurred with Turkish officials that it did not portend a Soviet attack. Indeed, at the very time that Wilson sent his alarming dispatch on March 18 warning of impending Soviet aggression, both the Turkish prime minister and the secretary-general of the Turkish Foreign Office were discounting that possibility. According to United States intelligence, between May and September 1946, Soviet troops in Europe decreased from about 2 million men to about 1.5 million; within the Soviet Union, from about 5 million to 2.7 million. During the crisis of August 1946, General Hoyt S. Vandenberg, director of the Central Intelligence Group, reassured President Truman that there were no unusual Soviet troop concentrations, troop movements, or supply buildups.[9]

---

Thomas T. Handy to Dwight D. Eisenhower, Aug. 15, 1946, Records of the Plans and Operations Division [hereafter, P&O] 092 TS, Records of the United States Army Staff, RG 319 (National Archives); JCS 1704/1, "Military Implications of the Current Turkish Situation," Aug. 24, 1946, sec. 1, CCS 092 (8-22-46), Records of the Joint Chiefs of Staff; Loy W. Henderson to H. Freeman Matthews, Jan. 30, 1946, box 17, Lot 54D394, Records of the Department of State.

8. Edwin C. Wilson's stress on Soviet troop movements can be found in his frequently cited dispatch to the Secretary of State. Bruce Robellet Kuniholm uses that document as a framework for much of his analysis regarding Turkey. *Foreign Relations of the United States, 1946,* VII, 818–19; Kuniholm, *Origins of the Cold War in the Near East,* 316–17, 356.

9. For weekly calculations of Soviet troop dispositions, see Carl Espe, memoranda, 1946, A8, box 106, series V, Strategic Plans Division (Naval Historical Center, Washington Navy Yard);

Why, then, were United States officials so exercised by Soviet policy toward Turkey? Although they did not expect the Soviets to apply military force, policymakers worried that the Soviet demand for bases in the Dardanelles might be a ruse for the eventual projection of Soviet power into the eastern Mediterranean and the Near East. Bases in the straits, United States military experts argued, would not suffice to keep the waterway open in wartime against modern air power; hence, the Soviets were likely to seek additional bases in the Aegean and the eastern Mediterranean. If Soviet influence expanded in that region, vital British petroleum supplies and communication networks might be jeopardized. And if the British Empire disintegrated, Soviet prospects for gaining control of Eurasia would be greatly enhanced, and the United States might be left vulnerable and exposed. At a meeting with the president on August 15, 1946, Acting Secretary of State Acheson, Secretary of the Navy James V. Forrestal, Assistant Secretary of War Kenneth C. Royall, and top military leaders presented those arguments and urged resistance to Soviet demands. Truman fully concurred with their advice.[10]

The decision to encourage Turkish opposition to Soviet overtures constituted part of the overall toughening of United States policy toward the Soviet Union during 1946. Truman began the year determined to stop babying the Soviets; in his "long telegram" in February, Kennan laid out an elaborate rationale for resisting Soviet pressure; during the Iranian crisis in the spring, United States officials learned that if they assumed a determined posture, the Soviets would back down. Rankled by domestic criticism and by division within his administration, beleaguered by a host of domestic and international problems, exasperated by the tedious negotiations over the minor peace treaties, and cognizant of traditional Soviet ambitions in the Near East, Truman was in no mood to enter into negotiations with the Soviet Union over the Dardanelles.[11]

---

Joint Intelligence Committee (JIC) (45) 289 (0) (FINAL), Report by Joint Intelligence Subcommittee, "The Russian Threat to Turkey," Oct. 6, 1945, ABC 092 USSR (15 November 1944), Records of the War Department General and Special Staffs; Joint Intelligence Committee, "Russian Troop Movements in South East Europe and Persia," May 15, 1946, ibid.; Military Intelligence Division, "Review of Europe, Russia, and the Middle East," Dec. 26, 1945, sec. 2, Records of the Operations Division (OPD) 350.05 TS, ibid.; John Weckerling to Deputy Chief of Staff, March 19, 1946, ibid.; SACMED AFHQ, Caserta, Italy, to War Department, March 9, 1946, box 1, Leahy Papers, Records of the Joint Chiefs of Staff; William M. Robertson to War Department, June 13, 1946, ibid.; Hoyt S. Vandenberg, memorandum for the President, Aug. 24, 1946, box 249, President's Secretary's File, Truman Papers. For Wilson's cables noting the Turkish belief that the Soviets were not planning an attack, see Wilson to Secretary of State, March 19, 1946, file 761.67/3–1946, Records of the Department of State.

10. *Foreign Relations of the United States, 1946*, VII, 840–58.

11. Robert L. Messer, *The End of an Alliance: James F. Byrnes, Roosevelt, Truman, and the*

During the summer the president asked Clark M. Clifford, one of his assistants in the White House, to write a paper outlining Soviet violations of international commitments. Clifford and George M. Elsey, another White House aide, took the opportunity to consult with all the leading members of the administration, including top military officers, and to write a comprehensive report calling for the global containment of Soviet influence. The rapid, decisive, and unanimous accord to stiffen Turkish resistance to Soviet demands reflected a consensus that new initiatives had to be taken to shore up United States influence in areas of vital importance.[12]

Top officials suspected, however, that the American public would not understand the strategic importance of Turkey. At their August meeting with the president, Royall and Forrestal emphasized the importance of properly briefing the press. Shortly thereafter, Royall informed Secretary of War Robert P. Patterson that Acheson was ready to discuss means "of conditioning the public mind." Exactly what was done is uncertain, but the news media did begin to explain to the attentive public that the dispute over the straits was assuming central importance in the overall rivalry between the Soviet Union and the United States. For example, *Time* noted that the Soviet proposals on the Dardanelles, coupled with Bulgaria's request for part of Thrace, represented the Soviet Union's effort to gain access to the Aegean, to seal off the straits, and to threaten Greece and Turkey. At the same time, the *Saturday Evening Post* reproached left-wingers, isolationists, and appeasers for their indifference to the Soviet Union's ominous attempt to exclude the shipping of other nations from the Black Sea. *United States News*, quoting administration officials, reported that the Soviet goal was to gain control of the eastern Mediterranean, to secure access to oil in the Middle East, and to establish a "flanking position on India and China."[13]

What top officials did not tell the press and what the media did not explain were the precise strategic calculations that underlay United States determination to contain Soviet influence in the Near East. Indeed, on the very day that Acheson, Forrestal, and Royall met with Truman, military planners on the Joint War Plans Committee were putting the final touches on a strategic study,

*Origins of the Cold War* (Chapel Hill, 1982), 137–94; *Oneal, Foreign Policy Making*, 68–136; Clifford, "President Truman and Peter the Great's Will."

12. Arthur Krock, *Memoirs: Sixty Years on the Firing Line* (New York, 1968), 421–82; box 63, Elsey Papers; boxes 14, 15, Clark M. Clifford Papers (Harry S. Truman Library).

13. Walter Millis, ed., *The Forrestal Diaries* (New York, 1951), 191–92; Kenneth C. Royall to Robert P. Patterson, n.d. [mid-August 1946], box 9, general decimal file, Robert P. Patterson Papers, Records of the Office of the Secretary of War, RG 107 (National Archives); *Time*, Sept. 2, 1946, p. 22; "Our Left Wingers Go Isolationist," *Saturday Evening Post*, Oct. 12, 1946, p. 160; "U.S. Stand on Dardanelles: High Stakes in the Middle East," *United States News*, Aug. 30, 1946, pp. 16–17.

known as "Griddle," that emphasized the importance of Turkey as a base for Allied operations against the Soviet Union should war unexpectedly erupt. Those civilian and military officials who met with Truman on August 15, including Admiral Chester W. Nimitz, General Carl Spaatz, and General Thomas T. Handy, were very aware of Turkey's prospective strategic importance to the West in wartime.[14]

In fact, despite the rhetoric about the Soviet expansionist thrust southward, military analysts and civilian officials acknowledged that Soviet demands on Turkey had a substantial defensive component. "Soviet pressure in the Middle East," concluded the Joint Chiefs of Staff (JCS) in March 1946, "has for its primary objective the protection of the vital Ploesti, Kharkov and Baku areas." Three months later, in a comprehensive assessment of Soviet intentions in the Middle East, British intelligence emphasized Soviet efforts to move the center of Soviet industry eastward, to safeguard the Caucasian oil fields, and to protect the development of Soviet resources from prospective attack. In their report to the president, Clifford and Elsey also noted that "the Near East is an area of great strategic interest to the Soviet Union because of the shift of Soviet industry to southeastern Russia, within range of air attack from much of the Near East." And in November 1946, in a still more detailed assessment of the region, United States war planners stressed that the Soviet Union wanted to control the eastern Mediterranean and Persian Gulf areas in order "to deny them as possible enemy air, sea, and ground offensive bases. By this increase in the depth of her southerly territorial border, the Soviets would greatly increase the security of their vital areas from air attack and from seizure by ground forces."[15]

It was this very vulnerability that United States strategic planners hoped to capitalize on. In fact, United States interest in Turkey accelerated as war planners began to develop a strategic concept for the postwar era and as overall United States–Soviet relations deteriorated sharply in early 1946. In September 1945 strategic planners emphasized "the necessity of keeping a prospective enemy at the maximum possible distance, and conversely of projecting our advance bases into areas well removed from the United States, so as to project our operations with new weapons or otherwise nearer the enemy." With regard

14. Joint War Plans Committee [hereafter, JWPC] 467/1, Aug. 15, 1946, sec. 11, CCS 092 USSR (3-27-45), Records of the Joint Chiefs of Staff. See also citations in footnote 18.

15. JCS 1641/1, "U.S. Security Interests in the Eastern Mediterranean," March 10, 1946, sec. 6, CCS 092 USSR (3-27-45), Records of the Joint Chiefs of Staff; JWPC 475/1, "Strategic Study of the Area between the Alps and the Himalayas," Nov. 2, 1946, sec. 3, pt. 1, CCS 381 USSR (3-2-46), ibid.; Joint Intelligence Committee [of the British Staff Mission], Memorandum for Information No. 223, "Russia's Strategic Interests and Intentions in the Middle East," June 28, 1946, sec. 1-C, ABC 336 Russia (22 August 1943), Records of the War Department General and Special Staffs; Krock, *Memoirs*, 434.

to a prospective war with the Soviet Union, the aim was "to oppose, as far as possible, Russian advances beyond her own borders and to obtain such strategic positions as are required to destroy her war potential rather than to overrun the USSR." Later in the autumn of 1945, the first efforts were made to define Soviet industrial-urban centers of critical strategic importance. In order of priority, planners focused on oil-producing centers in the Caucasus and in Rumania and, secondarily, on industrial complexes in the Urals, Ukraine, Upper Silesia and Czechoslovakia, Moscow, and Mukden areas. "Destruction by air of the Caucasian and Ploesti oil fields and the Ukraine and Ural industrial centers would prevent Soviet prosecution of war."[16]

Turkey's special role emerged in March 1946 when, during the Iranian crisis, State Department officials pressed military planners to define more clearly the importance of Turkey and when strategic analysts were forced to come to terms with the effects of Western Europe's military weakness and the United States's rapid demobilization. Assuming that Soviet troops would easily overrun all of Western Europe and that United States forces would be evacuated from the continent, the utilization of air power took on more significance than ever before. Turkey was seen as a key to the effective application of air power.[17] During the spring and summer of 1946, prior to the Soviet note on the straits, strategic planners decided that other than Great Britain, the Cairo-Suez area was the most desirable place on the globe from which to launch an air attack against Soviet targets. Should war erupt, Turkey's great importance would be that it provided a cushion, absorbing the initial Soviet blow and deterring Soviet advances, while the United States prepared to undertake the counteroffensive, particularly from the Cairo-Suez area. In April 1946, General Lincoln repeatedly emphasized that strategy to Benjamin V. Cohen, Secretary of State James F. Byrnes's closest aide; in July Admiral Richard L. Conolly, commander of United States naval forces in the eastern Atlantic and

16. Joint Planning Staff [hereafter, JPS] 744/3, "Strategic Concept and Plan for the Employment of United States Armed Forces," Sept. 14, 1945, sec. 1, CCS 381 (5-13-45), Records of the Joint Chiefs of Staff; Joint Intelligence Staff [hereafter, JIS] 80/8, "Strategic Vulnerability of Russia to a Limited Air Attack," Oct. 25, 1945, sec. 2, CCS 092 USSR (3-27-45), ibid.; JIS 226/2, "Areas Vital to Soviet War Effort," Feb. 12, 1946, sec. 5, ibid.; JIS 226/3, "Areas Vital to Soviet War Effort," March 4, 1946, ibid.

17. Byrnes to JCS, March 6, 1946, sec. 5, CCS 092 USSR (3-27-45), ibid.; memo for the Joint Staff Planners, March 8, 1946, ibid.; JCS 1641/1, "U.S. Security Interests in the Eastern Mediterranean," March 10, 1946, sec. 6, ibid.; JPS 789, "Concept of Operations for Pincher," enclosure "B," sec. 1, CCS 381 USSR (3-2-46), ibid.; JWPC 453, "Disposition of Occupation Forces in Europe and the Far East in the Event of Hostilities in Europe, and the Importance of Certain Areas of Eurasia," March 27, 1946, sec. 5, CCS 092 USSR (3-27-45), ibid.; Operations Division, "Adequate Governmental Machinery to Handle Foreign Affairs," March 13, 1946, P&O 092 TS, Records of the United States Army Staff; meeting of the Secretaries of State, War, and Navy, March 6, 1946, box 3, safe file, Patterson Papers.

the Mediterranean, almost certainly discussed the strategy with Byrnes and other State Department officials when he served with them on the United States delegation to the Paris Peace Conference; and later in the month Secretary of War Patterson explained the same strategy to President Truman. By the time of the August 1946 crisis, it was evident to high-level civilian policymakers, not just to military planners, that "Turkey must be preserved for reasons of Middle East strategy" as well as to prevent the falling of other dominoes in Western Europe and in the Far East.[18]

While State Department officials labored over an answer to the Soviet note on the Dardanelles, military planners insisted that "every practicable measure should be undertaken to permit the utilization of Turkey as a base for Allied operations in the event of war with the USSR." If war occurred Turkey could slow down a Soviet advance to Suez and North Africa, attack Soviet oil resources, provide fighter cover for bombers heading toward Moscow, bottle up Soviet submarines in the Black Sea, destroy Soviet shipping, and launch a possible ground offensive into the Soviet heartland. It was indispensable, then, to encourage Turkey to resist Soviet demands in peacetime and to thwart Soviet advances in wartime. Accordingly, military planners began advocating the allocation of military assistance to Turkey, including fighter aircraft, automatic weapons, ammunition, and small arms. They believed that previous studies had exaggerated Soviet logistic capabilities and that Turkey could mount an effective resistance, especially if provided with aid prior to hostilities. With that in mind, initial United States Army Air Force plans for launching a strategic offensive assumed the deployment to the Cairo-Suez area of three heavy bomber groups and the commencement of sustained conventional bombing of Soviet Russia from that location within 120 days after the onset of hostilities. On January 14, 1947, Admiral Forrest Sherman made a detailed presentation of those evolving strategic concepts to President Truman.[19]

18. JPS 789/1, appendix "B," April 13, 1946, sec. 1, CCS 381 USSR (3-2-46), Records of the Joint Chiefs of Staff; Pincher plans and discussions on JWPC 432 series, April–July 1946, sec. 2, ibid.; JCS 1704/1, "Military Implications of the Current Turkish Situation" Aug. 24, 1946, sec. 1, CCS 092 (8-22-46), ibid.; S.W.D., memorandum for the record, June 12, 1946, P&O 092 TS, Records of the United States Army Staff; Patterson to Truman, July 27, 1946, ibid.; Lincoln, memorandum for the record, April 16, 1946, sec. 1-C, ABC 336 Russia (22 August 1943), Records of the War Department General and Special Staffs; James McCormack, memorandum for Charles H. Bonesteel, April 20, 1946, sec. 1-A, ABC 093 Kiel (6 July 1945), ibid.; H.C.P. [Howard C. Petersen], memorandum for Patterson, April 22, 1946, box 1, safe file, Patterson Papers; "Possible Program in Connection with Turkey," Aug. 15, 1946, box 9, general decimal file, ibid.; Richard L. Conolly interview, 1960, transcript, pp. 293–303, Columbia Oral History Collection (Butler Library, Columbia University, New York City).

19. JWPC 467/1, "Griddle," Aug. 15, 1946, sec. 11, CCS 092 USSR (3-27-45), Records of the Joint Chiefs of Staff; Joint Logistic Plans Committee [hereafter, JLPC] 35/23, "Request for Lo-

By early 1947 almost all civilian and military officials agreed on the need to furnish military assistance to Turkey. Left uncertain were whether this assistance would be provided by the United States or by Great Britain, the precise purposes for which the assistance would be used, and the means of garnering support in the United States. After extensive interagency discussions in the autumn of 1946, Henderson noted the opposition of the Export-Import Bank to large-scale financial assistance to Turkey; yet he encouraged continued consultation between the State, War, and Navy departments so that "we will be prepared to move when conditions are propitious." The British notes in February 1947, announcing their intent to withdraw from Greece and their inability to continue military assistance to Turkey, provided the rationale to mobilize congressional and public support.[20]

Nevertheless, United States policymakers had considerable difficulty making their case for aid to Turkey. Turkey was not experiencing dire economic conditions, nor was it facing financial stringencies. The Soviets had not recently exerted pressure on Turkey, nor did American officials expect an imminent attack. Hence, the most effective argument that could be made in public was that the Turkish military establishment constituted a serious burden on the Turkish economy; that burden had to be eased to ensure that the Turks would not acquiesce to Soviet demands. During executive sessions of the Committee on Foreign Relations, however, senators' skepticism about whether the Turkish crisis constituted an emergency compelled Acheson to acknowledge the strategic motivations behind the United States's initiative. Similar questions forced Ambassador Wilson to answer so frankly that his testimony had to be stricken even from the executive hearings. In his classic personal account of the period, Joseph M. Jones acknowledges that "the

---

gistic Information relative to Turkey," Oct. 10. 1946, sec. 12, pt. 1, ibid.; JWPC 475/1, "Strategic Study of the Area between the Alps and the Himalayas," Nov. 2, 1946, sec. 3, CCS 381 USSR (3-2-46), ibid.; JCS 1704/1, "Military Implications of the Current Turkish Situation," Aug. 24, 1946, sec. 1, CCS 092 (8-22-46), ibid.; A. R. Pefley to Op-30, Aug. 21, 1946, box 68, series III, Strategic Plans Division; "Air Plan for Makefast," n.d., sec. 3, ABC 381 USSR (2 March 1946), Records of the War Department General and Special Staffs; Forrest P. Sherman, "Presentation to the President," Jan. 14, 1947, box 2, Forrest P. Sherman Papers (Naval Historical Center).

20. William Clayton to Byrnes, Sept. 12, 1946, P&O 092 TS, Records of the United States Army Staff; Meetings of the Secretaries of State, War, and Navy, Nov. 5, Nov. 13, box 3, safe file, Patterson Papers; *Foreign Relations of the United States, 1946*, VII, 894–97, 916–17; Henderson to R. L. Dennison, Dec. 18, 1946, EF-70, series 1, Records of the Politico-Military Division (Naval Historical Center); Henderson, memorandum, "Aid to Turkey," Nov. 24, 1946, ibid.; David LeBreton, memorandum of conversation, Nov. 18, 1946, file 867.20/11–1846, Records of the Department of State; *Foreign Relations of the United States, 1947* (8 vols., Washington, 1971–1973), V, 35–37. Secretary of War Robert P. Patterson did consistently question the wisdom of military assistance to Turkey. See, for example, Patterson to Acting Secretary of State, Sept. 12, 1946, box 7, safe file, Patterson Papers.

strategic importance of Turkey ranked high in discussions within the executive branch and in discussions with congressional leaders. They were, however, consciously played down in the President's message, in the public sessions of the congressional committees, and in the public approach generally." That long-term strategic calculations rather than short-term expectations of Soviet aggression prompted concern with Turkey was evident several months later when United States officials supported a partial demobilization of Turkish forces because "no immediate danger of an armed clash between Turkey and Russia" was foreseen.[21]

Although planned Soviet aggression was not anticipated, war could erupt as a result of a miscalculation in a diplomatic crisis. Accordingly, under the auspices of the Truman Doctrine, United States officials designed the aid program to enhance the fighting capabilities of the Turkish army, air force, and navy, to help build strategic roads, and to restock Turkish arsenals and war reserves. American military advisers, however, were most concerned with the Turkish army. They desired to reorganize and modernize the army, to build up its combat effectiveness, to provide it with much greater mobility and firepower, to develop its transportation and communication infrastructure, and to bolster its logistical capabilities.[22] United States military advisers hoped that the Turkish army would play a key role in retarding a Soviet land offensive in the Middle East should war occur, thereby affording time for the United States and Great Britain to activate and utilize bases in the Cairo-Suez region. The Turkish army was given equipment that would enable it initially to resist a three-pronged Soviet attack across the Bosporus, the Black Sea, and the

21. Henderson, memorandum, "Aid to Turkey," Nov. 24, 1946, EF-70, series 1, Records of the Politico-Military Division; *Foreign Relations of the United States, 1946*, VII, 921–22; *Foreign Relations of the United States, 1947*, V, 61–62, 90–91, 95, 364–65; Wilson to Secretary of State, Feb. 26, 1947, file 761.67/2–2647, Records of the Department of State; LeBreton to Henderson, Oct. 8, 1947, file 867.20/10–447, ibid.; "Summary of Costs of U.S. Assistance to Greece and Turkey until 30 June 1948," n.d. [early March 1947], box 65, Elsey Papers; Lincoln to Secretary of War, March 12, 1947, box 1, general subject file, Howard C. Petersen Papers, Records of the Office of the Secretary of War; U.S. Congress, Senate, Committee on Foreign Relations, *Legislative Origins of the Truman Doctrine: Hearings Held in Executive Session before the Committee on Foreign Relations* (Washington, 1973), 7–10, 48–53, 55–61, 84, 105; Jones, *Fifteen Weeks*, 162.

22. Minutes of the Executive Committee, Turkish General Staff/U.S. Mission, May 27–July 10, 1947, file 867.20/7-1047, Records of the Department of State; Wilson to Secretary of State, Jan. 30, 1948, file 867.20/1-3048, ibid.; *Foreign Relations of the United States, 1947*, V, 233–36; "Call for Estimates, FY 1950, MAP," Sept. 23, 1949, P&O 092 Europe TS, Records of the United States Army Staff; Joint American Military Mission for Aid to Turkey [JAMMAT], "Major Items of Equipment: Aid to Turkey Program," March 1952, box 56, Records of the Assistant Secretary of Defense, International Security Affairs, Office of the Secretary of Defense, RG 330 (National Archives). Many monthly progress reports on the arrival of assistance and on the courses of instruction may be found in decimal file series 867.00, Records of the Department of State.

Caucasus. Recognizing that Turkish forces could not hold those positions, United States military assistance sought to provide the Turkish army with the mobility and logistical capability to fall back gradually, to carry on guerrilla activity behind advancing Soviet forces, and to make a final, large-scale stand in southern Turkey in the Iskenderon pocket. Much of the road construction undertaken in Turkey with United States funds was designed to facilitate that strategy. From the military perspective, a concentrated Turkish defense in the Iskenderon area was a key to maintaining access to Middle Eastern oil as well as to defending vital strategic airports and communication facilities in Egypt.[23]

From air bases in Turkey, fighter bombers and attack planes could not only aid Turkish ground forces inside Turkey but also interdict Soviet troops moving through Iran and Iraq toward Persian Gulf oil or sweeping widely toward Cairo-Suez. Accordingly, next to the army, the Turkish air force was the largest recipient of United States assistance. During 1948, for example, the United States transferred over one hundred eighty F-47s, thirty B-26s, and eighty-six C-47s. Smaller numbers of jet fighters began arriving in 1950 and 1951. At the same time, the United States placed a great deal of stress on reconstructing and resurfacing Turkish airfields at places such as Bandirma and Diyarbakir. As a result, Turkey began to develop the capability to attack vital Soviet petroleum resources in Rumania and in the Caucasus; Ploesti and Baku, for example, came within range of the F-47s and the B-26s. Even more important, the rehabilitation of Turkish airfields and the construction of new ones, at Adana for example, meant that if war erupted the United States would be able to bring in its own B-29s to bomb the Soviet Union. Secretary of the Air Force W. Stuart Symington and Secretary of Defense Forrestal were contemplating that contingency in early 1948. A more systematic effort to achieve such bombing capability was inaugurated in late 1949; significant progress toward that goal was expected during 1952.[24]

23. Central Intelligence Agency, "The Current Situation in Turkey," Oct. 20, 1947, box 254, President's Secretary's File, Truman Papers; Joint Strategic Plans Committee [JSPC] 868/1, "Guidance for the Coordinator, Armed Forces Groups, American Mission for Aid to Turkey [AMAT]," March 26, 1948, P&O 091 Turkey TS, Records of the United States Army Staff; Chief of Staff, U.S. Army, memorandum, "Turkish and Iranian Military Effort in War," Feb. 25, 1950, 381 Middle East TS, ibid.; Robert B. Carney, memorandum for Secretary of Defense, Sept. 29, 1948, CD 2-2-5, box 4, Records of the Office of the Secretary of Defense; Subcommittee for the Near and Middle East, memorandum for the State-Army-Navy-Air Force Coordinating Committee, Dec. 15, 1948, box 134, TS file, Records of the State-War-Navy Coordinating Committee [SWNCC], RG 353 (National Archives).

24. Ambassador's Report on Aid to Turkey, July 15, 1947, Annex D, Part Three, P&O 091 Turkey, Records of the United States Army Staff; Chief of Staff, U.S. Army, memorandum, "Turkish and Iranian Military Effort in War," Feb. 25, 1950, 381 Middle East TS, ibid.; "Proposal for Continuing Aid to the Turkish Air Force," appended to Wilds to Robert A. Lovett, Jan. 23, 1948, file 867.20/1–2348, Records of the Department of State; John H. Ohly to Llewellyn E. Thompson,

United States assistance to the Turkish navy aimed primarily at enhancing Turkey's ability to close the Dardanelles and to prevent Soviet submarines from entering the Mediterranean. The United States also wanted to help the Turkish navy plan the defense of the Bosporus and develop the capability of destroying Soviet Black Sea shipping. But the latter mission also was within the purview of the United States Navy. Aircraft from United States carriers would leapfrog to Turkish air bases, refuel, and attack oil cargoes on Soviet ships in the Black Sea. To achieve that capability, Admiral Conolly, with the support of the secretary of defense, sought funds for the storage of aviation gas in Turkey.[25]

Throughout the period 1947–1950, United States military planners were eager to use assistance as a lever to bring Turkish military planning into line with United States desires. United States Army officers feared that Turkey would try to make a full-scale stand at the Bosporus and would lose much of its army; such a possibility conflicted with the United States emphasis on the Iskenderon pocket. United States naval officials, despairing of the Turkish navy's elementary strategy, its reliance on a pre–World War I German battleship, and its focus on protecting Turkish coastal shipping in the Black Sea, sought a Turkish commitment to mine the straits and to close the Bosporus on receiving instructions from the commander of United States naval forces in the Mediterranean. United States Air Force advisers, frustrated by the defensive mentality of Turkish officers, wanted to use Turkey's air assets to attack enemy airfields, refineries, and communication and rail centers in Bulgaria, Rumania, and the Caucasus. United States officers also were uncertain whether Turkey would permit their use of its airfields. In order to clarify mat-

---

Nov. 22, 1949, box 1, Lot 484, ibid.; USTAP Report No. 29, March 12, 1949, file 867.00/5–1249, ibid.; Stuart Symington to James V. Forrestal, March 9, 1948, CD 6-2-38, box 35, Records of the Office of the Secretary of Defense; Lyman L. Lemnitzer to James H. Burns, March 6, 1950, CD 6-2-46, box 23, ibid.; National Security Council [NSC] 42, "U.S. Objectives with Respect to Greece and Turkey to Counter Soviet Threats to U.S. Security," March 4, 1949, Records of the National Security Council, RG 273 (National Archives); *Foreign Relations of the United States, 1950* (7 vols., Washington, 1976–1980), V, 1234, 1250; *Foreign Relations of the United States, 1951* (6 vols., Washington, 1977–1983), V, 1124–25.

25. JCS 1704/8, enclosure "A," memorandum for the coordinator, Armed Forces Group, AMAT n.d. [Sept. 1948], P&O 091 Turkey TS, Records of the United States Army Staff; J.R.D., memo for the record, Feb. 18, 1949, ibid.; Ray T. Maddocks, memorandum for Horace L. McBride, March 1, 1949, ibid.; Louis Denfeld, memorandum for JCS, Aug. 9, 1948, JJ7, box 245, Strategic Plans Division; E. T. Wooldridge, memorandum for Op-03, Jan. 10, 1949, A19, box 251, ibid.; Elliott B. Strauss, memorandum for Op-30, June 17, 1949, A14, box 249, ibid.; JCS 1887/20, Carney to CNO, Jan. 30, 1951, sec. 4, CCS 381 Eastern Mediterranean and Middle East Area [hereafter, EMMEA] (11-19-47), Records of the Joint Chiefs of Staff; Forrestal, memorandum for the NSC, n.d. [early 1949], CD 19-2-21, box 92, Records of the Office of the Secretary of Defense.

ters and to achieve United States goals, Arthur W. Radford, the vice chief of naval operations, Admiral Conolly, and other military officers desired to institutionalize strategic coordination with Turkey.[26]

State Department officials, however, would not permit formal strategic collaboration without prior treaty commitments. During 1948 and 1949, the formation of the NATO alliance riveted American attention on Western Europe and unexpectedly reoriented United States strategic priorities. In July 1948, Undersecretary of State Robert A. Lovett told the Turkish ambassador that Americans "must be careful not to over-extend ourselves. We lack sufficient financial and economic resources simultaneously to finance the economic recovery of Europe, to furnish arms and equipment to all individual countries or groups of countries which request them, and to build up our own military strength." When Acheson assumed the office of secretary of state, he reiterated those views. The United States, he maintained, was assuming unprecedented obligations in Western Europe; those commitments had to be worked out in all their complexity before the United States could offer additional guarantees elsewhere. Throughout 1949, Acheson repeatedly rebuffed Turkish pleas to be included in the alliance.[27]

Toiling over the problem of meeting expanding commitments with extremely circumscribed resources, stemming from budgetary restrictions, the JCS vigorously supported Acheson's desire to limit the alliance and to give priority to assistance to Western Europe. United States war planners were overwhelmed by the difficulties of figuring out how to defend Western Europe. They modified emergency war plans and placed a much greater emphasis on defense of the western Mediterranean and the launching of the strategic offensive primarily from Great Britain. Had a war erupted in 1949 or 1950, the

26. *Foreign Relations of the United States, 1950*, V, 1249–50; McBride to Director, Plans and Operations Division, May 18, 1948, P&O 091 Turkey TS, Records of the United States Army Staff; J. R. D., memorandum for the Record, Feb. 18, 1949, ibid.; JCS 1704/7, McBride, memorandum for the JCS, Feb. 19, 1948, ibid.; JSPC 868/1, Guidance for the Coordinator, Armed Forces Groups, AMAT, March 26, 1948, ibid.; Chief of Staff, U.S. Army, memorandum, n.d. [Feb. 25, 1950], 381 ME TS, ibid.; A. D. Struble, memo for CNO, Oct. 4, 1948, A19, box 244, Strategic Plans Division; Carney, memorandum for Op-03, March 22, 1949, EF, box 252, ibid.; Strauss, memorandum for Op-30, March 25, 1949, ibid.; C. V. Johnson, memorandum for Op-30, Sept. 16, 1949, A8, box 249, ibid.; Carney to Struble, March 31, 1949, A16-1, ibid.; CNO, memorandum, March 13, 1950, sec. 1, CCS 337 (2-20-50), Records of the Joint Chiefs of Staff; JCS 2105 series, "Proposed Positions to be Taken in Conversations with Political and Military Authorities of Near and Middle East Countries," February–April 1950, ibid.; Arthur W. Radford to Richard L. Conolly, Jan. 17, 1949, drawer 1, safe A, Arthur W. Radford Papers (Naval Historical Center).

27. *Foreign Relations of the United States, 1948* (9 vols., Washington, 1972–1975), III, 197, IV, 84–85, 114–15, 148–49, 172–73, 214; *Foreign Relations of the United States, 1949* (9 vols., Washington, 1974–1978), IV, 120, 177–78, 234–35, 243–44, 270–71, 359–60, VI, 1647–53, 1656–57; *Foreign Relations of the United States, 1950*, V, 1238–40.

United States would not have had the means to aid Turkey directly or even to secure Cairo-Suez. Defense of the Middle East, although recognized as critically important, was assigned to Great Britain despite that nation's limited capabilities. Yet United States war planners never relinquished the hope of capitalizing on Turkey's geopolitical position and on the opportunities emanating from military assistance. During 1949, for example, Forrestal still sought appropriations to help build up bases in the Cairo-Suez region. And during 1951, the JCS made clear its determination to retain control over strategic planning and coordination in Greece, Turkey, and Iran despite Great Britain's overall military responsibility for the rest of the Middle Eastern region.[28]

Turkish officials, however, were offended by rebuffs to their requests for concrete military guarantees and for inclusion in the NATO alliance. Ambassador Wilson feared that the Turkish government might conclude that the United States was downgrading the importance of Turkey and might adopt a more neutral posture. The Central Intelligence Agency (CIA) agreed that Turkey felt exposed and vulnerable. The great imponderable, then, was what Turkey would do if a Soviet attack took place beyond Turkey's borders. The United States air attaché emphasized to naval planners that Turkey would resist if attacked but otherwise would attempt to remain neutral. In March 1950, Admiral Conolly beseeched Sherman, now chief of naval operations, to get the JCS to support an alliance with Turkey. "It is of utmost importance," Conolly wrote,

> to engage Turkey's certain participation [in a war]. Although it can be assumed that Turkey would fight if attacked it is almost as certain that Turkey would not fight if not attacked and very probable that USSR would not immediately attack Turkey. It would therefore be greatly to our national interest considering money we have spent on her military establishment to have Turkey bound to us formally by mutual defense treaty, to include an engagement for her to go to war in case of attack upon her own territory or upon or through any neighboring contiguous state.[29]

28. *Foreign Relations of the United States, 1949*, I, 285–87; *Foreign Relations of the United States, 1951*, V, 36–37. The views of the Joint Chiefs of Staff are best found in the JCS 2105 series cited in footnote 26. See especially JCS 2105/2, Report by the Joint Strategic Survey Committee, March 17, 1950, sec. 1, CCS 337 (2-20-50), Records of the Joint Chiefs of Staff. For the evolution of United States war plans from 1948 to 1950, see especially the JCS 1844 series, secs. 10–45, CCS 381 USSR (3-2-46), ibid.; and documents in secs. 1, 2, CCS 381 EMMEA (11-19-47), ibid.

29. Joseph C. Satterthwaite to Secretary of State, March 31, 1949, file 711.67/3–3149, Records of the Department of State; Robertson to George McGhee, July 26, 1949, box 1, Lot 484, ibid.; Central Intelligence Agency, "Review of the World Situation," April 20, 1949, box 206, President's Secretary's File, Truman Papers; Johnson, memorandum to Op-30, Sept. 16, 1949, A8, box 249, Strategic Plans Division; Conolly to CNO, March 9, 1950, box 6, Sherman Papers.

In the spring of 1950, however, neither State Department officials nor the JCS were ready to make commitments to Turkey. These policymakers feared that the capabilities of the United States to defend vital interests in Europe still were not adequate. A memorandum prepared in the State Department's Office of Near Eastern and African Affairs emphasized that only after Western Europe's defensive strength was augmented would the United States consider additional security arrangements elsewhere. The outbreak of the Korean War initially intensified those views. Faced with the emergency in the Far East, fearing a full-scale war in Europe, and not foreclosing the possibility of a diversionary trap by a Soviet satellite, policymakers did not wish to incur commitments that might embroil the United States in another localized conflict and sap the nation's strength.[30]

The real dilemma for the United States was to find a means to ensure the availability of Turkey's strategic assets to the West without extending commitments that might be both beyond the capabilities of the United States and disproportionate to the advantages that might accrue from a formal alliance. Both the JCS and the Near East division of the State Department studied the problem throughout the late summer of 1950. Acheson prodded Secretary of Defense Louis A. Johnson to consider how new arrangements with Turkey might deter or provoke the Soviet Union, might offer military advantages, or might pose military liabilities by adding new administrative or command problems to the NATO alliance. The JCS believed, however, that immediate enlargement of NATO might upset the substantial progress then under way within the alliance and might add new distractions just at the time that the United States was committing forces-in-being to Western Europe.[31]

But to rebuff Turkey completely risked the loss of a key prospective ally in wartime. Hence, the JCS concluded that the United States ought to try "to obtain the benefits of Turk and Greek participation in the North Atlantic Treaty Organization and at the same time minimize the disadvantages thereof by according to these two nations an associate status—such a status would permit their representatives to participate in coordinated planning against Soviet aggression." Acheson presented this position to the British and the French in September 1950. Shortly thereafter, the Defense Committee of the

30. JCS 2105/6, enclosure "B," Office of Near Eastern and African Affairs, Department of State, "Regional Security Arrangements in the Mediterranean and Near Eastern Areas," April 18, 1950, sec. 1, CCS 337 (2-20-50), Records of the Joint Chiefs of Staff; *Foreign Relations of the United States, 1950*, I, 353–57, 376–87, III, 975–76, 1218, V, 153–57.

31. Paul H. Nitze to Philip Jessup, Aug. 14, 1950, box 1, Lot 484, Records of the Department of State; JCS to Secretary of Defense, Sept. 9, 1950, ibid.; Johnson to Acheson, Sept. 11, 1950, ibid.; Office of Near Eastern and African Affairs, "Security Problem in the Near East and Africa," Aug. 29, 1950, CD 092.3 NATO–Council of Ministers, box 184, Records of the Office of the Secretary of Defense; *Foreign Relations of the United States, 1950*, III, 257–61.

North Atlantic Council voted to invite Turkey and Greece to coordinate their military planning with appropriate NATO commanders.[32]

The Turkish government immediately agreed but again expressed disappointment in not securing full membership. When Assistant Secretary of State George C. McGhee visited Turkey in February 1951, President Celal Bayar emphasized that he was affronted by NATO's refusal to offer full membership to Turkey, especially in view of Turkey's direct military contribution in Korea. Speaking bluntly, President Bayar told McGhee that Turkey was unhappy with its status and sought reciprocal guarantees; Turkey would not be content with anything less. McGhee then discussed Turkish sentiments with all the United States chiefs of mission in the Middle East who were gathered in Istanbul for a conference with the assistant secretary of state. They strongly supported a guarantee of Turkey's security. McGhee wired the State Department that "there is reason to believe that Turkey will veer towards a policy of neutralism, which will always have a strong basic appeal; and, until a commitment is extended to Turkey, there is no assurance that Turkey will declare war unless it is attacked. In order to assure Turkey's immediate cobelligerency, utilization in collective security action of the military potential which Turkey is building, and immediate United States and Allied utilization of Turkish bases . . . a commitment on the part of United States is required." At about the same time, Henry S. Villard, of the Policy Planning Staff, urged Paul H. Nitze, the staff's director, to focus attention on meeting Turkey's desire for security guarantees. In general, State Department officials believed that new United States initiatives in the Middle East could and ought to be taken because the military buildup in the United States already had reached significant proportions, organizational progress had been achieved in Western Europe, and "the chances of the Middle East remaining tranquilly on the side of the West without some practical evidence of Western interest have greatly declined."[33]

United States defense officials, however, remained ambivalent. While the JCS still feared any agreement that might imply the commitment of forces to the region in the event of hostilities, Admiral Robert B. Carney, commander in chief of United States forces in the Mediterranean, urged officials to reexamine the question of security commitments to Turkey. Carney agreed with McGhee's assessment of the situation, feared Turkish neutrality, and sought

32. JCS to Secretary of Defense, Sept. 9, 1950, box 1, Lot 484, Records of the Department of State; *Foreign Relations of the United States, 1950*, III, 1218–20, 1284–85; Matthews to Burns, Oct. 3, 1950, CD 092.3 NATO–Defense Committee, box 184, Records of the Office of the Secretary of Defense. For references to apprehensions over losing a prospective ally in wartime, see citations in footnote 31.

33. Memorandum of conversation, Feb. 12, 1951, CD 092.3 NATO-GEN, box 243, Records of the Office of the Secretary of Defense; *Foreign Relations of the United States, 1950*, V, 1321; *Foreign Relations of the United States, 1951*, V, 4–11, 21–27, 51–76, 1117–19.

substantial military aid "predicated on the Turkish capacity for great resistance and the possibility of generating some limited Turkish offensive." At NATO headquarters, a separate study, conducted under the authority of Vice Admiral Jerauld Wright, also stressed that there was a "real danger" of Turkish neutrality "stemming from the Turks' gnawing feeling of frustration and isolation." And at the end of February 1951, the CIA completed the coordination of a new National Intelligence Estimate (NIE) of "Turkey's Position in the East-West Struggle." Emphasizing Turkey's strong antipathy to the Soviet Union as well as Turkey's desire to facilitate a Western victory should war erupt elsewhere, the NIE nevertheless noted that "the commitment of Turkish troops or the provision of Turkish bases would . . . be contingent upon a firm assurance of U.S. armed support in event of Soviet attack."[34]

Fear of Turkey's neutrality, then, played a decisive role in compelling another appraisal of Turkey's relationship to NATO. Officials in the State Department, not those in the Defense Department, continued to be the most vigorous proponents of expanding military assistance and commitments throughout the Middle East. In their view, the forces of nationalism and neutralism were making headway, partly because of a pervasive feeling of insecurity. Military assistance would help strengthen United States influence on existing governments; security guarantees to Turkey would bolster confidence in that country, the linchpin of efforts to defend the Middle East. When Secretary Acheson asked the Defense Department to reconsider Turkey's admission into NATO, he emphasized that a security arrangement might induce Turkey to undertake certain measures that would redound to the military advantage of the entire anti-Soviet coalition. He specifically alluded to the peacetime mining of the straits that the Navy Department had been advocating for several months. A security agreement also would facilitate conclusion of an agreement on the use of forward air bases in Turkey. Fearing the loss of those opportunities, McGhee summed up the view of the State Department when he returned from the Middle East and met with the JCS. He emphasized that "there is a real danger that the Turks will choose neutrality if they cannot obtain a security commitment. We cannot be sure that we will have Turkey as an ally unless we extend a security commitment."[35]

In May 1951 the JCS finally decided to accede to an expansion of United States commitments. Military officers recognized the critical role Turkey could play in protecting the West's southern flank in Europe, in diverting large

34. *Foreign Relations of the United States, 1951*, V, 27–42, 103–104, 113–18, 1118, 1119–26, esp. 1120; JCS 2009/12, "Factors Involving the Inclusion of Greece and Turkey as Full Members of the North Atlantic Treaty Organization," March 16, 1951, sec. 1, CCS 337 (2-20-50), Records of the Joint Chiefs of Staff.

35. *Foreign Relations of the United States, 1951*, III, 501–505, V, 4–11, 21–42, 80–83, 113–20, esp. 117; memorandum for the Secretary of Defense, Feb. 27, 1951, CD 092 Turkey, box 236, Records of the Office of the Secretary of Defense.

numbers of Soviet troops to the Turkish theater, and in facilitating defense of the Mediterranean and the Middle East. If the Soviets decided to sweep around Turkey through Iran and Iraq and if Turkey opted for neutrality, military planners recognized that the West would have great difficulty closing the straits to Soviet submarines, protecting NATO's lines of communication in the Mediterranean, and destroying Soviet shipping in the Black Sea. Even more disillusioning was the prospect of wasting the millions of dollars that had been spent on the construction of airfields in Turkey. With that in mind, the army chief of staff circulated a memorandum to the other chiefs underscoring the importance of readying Turkish airports for use by heavy bombers and jet fighters and urging a treaty commitment with Turkey. Cognizant that United States capabilities had been expanding rapidly, the JCS now endorsed Turkey's inclusion in NATO. The National Security Council formally adopted that position in May 1951. During the following summer and autumn, United States officials persuaded NATO allies to admit Turkey and Greece into the alliance.[36]

From the time of the Truman Doctrine until Turkey's entry into NATO, strategic considerations exerted an important influence on the course of United States policy toward Turkey. Turkey became first the object of assistance from and then the formal ally of the United States, not because of the expectation of any imminent Soviet attack on Turkey, but because of Turkey's potential utility in waging war, protecting air bases, and safeguarding Middle Eastern oil resources. In March 1951, as had been the case in March 1947, United States officials realized that the Soviet threat to Turkey was "relatively quiescent." Soviet policy seemed ominous in other areas of the world, however, and if hostilities erupted elsewhere, United States war planners wanted to use Turkish facilities and manpower to neutralize the Soviet submarine threat in the Mediterranean, to tie up large numbers of Soviet troops, and to launch air attacks on vital Soviet petroleum resources. Estimates that Soviet air defenses in the south were meager and ineffective were added inducements to establish a strategic air base in the region.[37]

36. JCS 1704/49, memorandum by the Chief of Staff, U.S. Army, May 1, 1951, sec. 53, CCS 092 (8-22-46), Records of the Joint Chiefs of Staff; "Summary Views and Bases for Joint Chiefs of Staff Position on Security Arrangements for Greece and Turkey," n.d. [April 1951], CD 092.3 NATO, box 243, Records of the Office of the Secretary of Defense; *Foreign Relations of the United States, 1951*, V, 1148–62. The negotiations on the inclusion of Turkey and Greece into the North Atlantic Treaty Organization were complicated by differences over the command structure in the Middle East. *Foreign Relations of the United States, 1951*, III, 479–85, 505–506, 551–55, 558, 567, 569–71, 574–613, 621–32, 661–63, 669, 678–81, 744, 1265–67, 1302.

37. JCS 2009/12, "Factors Involving the Inclusion of Greece and Turkey as Full Members of the North Atlantic Treaty Organization," March 16, 1951, sec. 1, CCS 337 (2-20-50), Records of the Joint Chiefs of Staff. For the situation in March 1947, see citation in footnote 21. For weak-

What effect did all of this have on relations between the United States and the Soviet Union? From the middle of 1947, the Soviets bitterly condemned United States military assistance to Turkey. Soviet diplomats insisted that the United States was undertaking aggressive action and establishing bases from which attacks on the Soviet Union could be launched easily and effectively.[38] United States war plans and military-assistance programs demonstrate that Soviet military planners had reason to worry about the ramifications of United States aid to Turkey. A major object of United States policy was to enhance Turkey's military capabilities and, if military conflict occurred, to integrate those capabilities into the war effort. This is not to say or even to intimate that the United States was planning aggressive war. But if war broke out as a result of a miscalculation in a diplomatic crisis—and that was considered the most probable cause of war—then Turkey would play an important role in American offensive as well as defensive actions.

The Soviets had cause to worry about developments in Turkey; just as the United States feared Soviet inroads in Cuba in 1962. The difference, of course, was that in 1962 the United States had the military wherewithal to stop the emergence of an offensive threat on its southern border. In 1947–1948 the Soviets had no such power. Although they had exerted rather little pressure on Turkey, they now had to contemplate the development of a more modern military infrastructure in Turkey, to grapple with the latent ability of the United States to project power from the Middle East, and to deal with the global geopolitical policy inherent in the Truman Doctrine. That challenge, along with other concurrent developments, may well have served to intensify their suspicions of United States intentions and to magnify their sense of weakness.[39]

---

nesses of Soviet air defenses in the south, see JCS 1952/1, Chief of Staff, United States Air Force, memorandum, Dec. 21, 1948, sec. 1, CCS 373 (10-23-48), Records of the Joint Chiefs of Staff. In an assessment of Soviet radar nets, the chief of naval intelligence stressed the likelihood that by 1950 the Soviets would have integrated early-warning nets in the west, north, and east. He made no mention of such nets in the south. Op-32 to General Board, May 12, 1948, 425 (serial 315), Records of the General Board (Naval Historical Center).

38. Wilson to Secretary of State, July 29, 1947, file 861.20267/7-2947, Records of the Department of State; Smith to Secretary of State, Aug. 2, 1947, file 867.00/8-247, ibid.; Wilson to Secretary of State, Sept. 11, 1947, file 861.20267/8-2947, ibid.; Bursley to Secretary of State, Nov. 18, Nov. 25, 1947, file 861.20267/11-1847, 10-3147, ibid.; Wilson to Secretary of State, Dec. 1, 1947, file 761.67/11-2147, ibid.; Smith to Secretary of State, April 30, 1948, file 861.20267/4-3048, ibid.; *Foreign Relations of the United States, 1950*, IV, 1254–55; [Nikita S. Khrushchev], *Khrushchev Remembers*, ed. Edward Crankshaw and Strobe Talbott (Boston, 1970), 494, 514.

39. Although this is not the place for a discussion of Soviet foreign policy, two recent studies suggest the defensive and reactive character of Joseph Stalin's actions in 1947 and 1948. William O. McCagg, Jr., *Stalin Embattled, 1943–1948* (Detroit, 1978); William Taubman, *Stalin's American Policy: From Entente to Détente to Cold War* (New York, 1982), esp. 128–92.

A study of American policy toward Turkey in the aftermath of World War II highlights the role of strategic imperatives both in the expansion of United States global interests and in the formation of the nation's alliance system. It also helps to elucidate the matrix of considerations that accelerated distrust between the Soviet Union and the United States and generated the Cold War.

# 6

# Adherence to Agreements

## YALTA AND THE EXPERIENCES
## OF THE EARLY COLD WAR

This article arose from my concern with ongoing events in the early and mid-1980s. Secretary of Defense Caspar W. Weinberger and other influential policymakers charged the Kremlin with violations of arms control agreements like the first Strategic Arms Limitation Treaty (SALT I) and the Anti-Ballistic Missile (ABM) Treaty. In his very first press conference as president, Ronald Reagan assailed the Kremlin for seeking world domination and for wantonly engaging in "treachery, deceit, destruction, and bloodshed." (See Kiron K. Skinner, Annelise Anderson, and Martin Anderson, eds., *Reagan in His Own Hand* [New York: Simon & Schuster, 2001], 10–15.) These accusations served as justification for extricating the United States from the restraints it had accepted in previous arms control accords and for moving ahead with the Strategic Defense Initiative (known as SDI or Star Wars).

These developments in the mid-1980s reminded me of the recriminations of the early Cold War years. In his first meeting with Foreign Minister V. M. Molotov, President Harry Truman denounced Soviet violations of the Yalta agreements and warned that future cooperation depended on Soviet adherence to wartime promises. About a year later he asked his trusted aides, Clark Clifford and George Elsey, to assess the record of Soviet compliance. They concluded that it was dismal. Soviet leaders, they insisted, were inspired by

I would like to thank Sam Walker, Dave Painter, Tom Paterson, and John Arthur for their constructive comments on previous drafts of this article. I am grateful to the Woodrow Wilson International Center, the Council on Foreign Relations, and the Harry S. Truman Library for research support.

Marxist-Leninist dogma and were determined to spread their system around the world. In their view, Soviet transgressions legitimized America's own unilateral actions to build American strength, shore up its potential friends, and redress the balance of power. (Their report appears in Arthur Krock, *Memoirs: Sixty Years on the Firing Line* [New York: Funk and Wagnalls, 1968], 417–482.)

The rhetoric of American innocence and Soviet duplicity were staples of early American scholarship on the Cold War. By the 1980s, however, many revisionist scholars had rebutted these allegations and had illuminated the expansionist impulses that shaped U.S. foreign policy in the months and years immediately following the defeat of the Axis powers. My intent here was to chart a middle road between traditional and revisionist scholars and to high-light how ambiguities and uncertainties influenced the behavior of both Washington and Moscow. The Yalta agreements were vague, purposefully so, because Joseph Stalin, Franklin D. Roosevelt, and British Prime Minister Winston Churchill were seeking to pave over their differences, sustain the wartime alliance, and establish a framework for postwar cooperation. Once victory was assured, the impulse to cooperate waned as new circumstances and new fears intensified mutual distrust and catalyzed unilateral moves to insure security. These actions were coupled with harsh condemnations of one another's treachery. Yet neither the Americans nor the Russians really wanted to antagonize the potential rival; they wanted to seize upon ambiguities in the wartime agreements to enhance their respective notions of security. By engaging in rhetorical overkill, leaders in both capitals made compromise and accommodation more difficult. Few Americans, however, understood how their own rhetoric, charges, and actions contributed to the collapse of the wartime alliance.

This article appeared in *International Security* 11 (Summer 1986): 88–123.

———

On April 23, 1945, President Harry S. Truman had a stormy meeting with Soviet Foreign Minister V. M. Molotov. In what many historians consider the first round of the Cold War, Truman denounced Soviet violations of the Yalta agreements. When Molotov sought to defend Soviet actions, Truman bluntly retorted that the Soviets would have to adhere to their agreements if cooperation were to continue.[1]

During the next year Truman lost faith in the Kremlin. He grew frustrated with the tedious deliberations among the foreign ministers; he became

1. Harry S. Truman, *Memoirs: Year of Decisions, 1945* (New York: Signet, 1955), pp. 96–99; and Department of State, *Foreign Relations of the United States, 1945*, 9 vols. (Washington, D.C., 1967–1969), Vol. 5, pp. 256–258 [hereinafter cited as *FRUS*].

alarmed by the Soviet consolidation of power in Eastern Europe; and he was frightened by the sociopolitical turmoil throughout much of the world. In July 1946, he ordered two White House aides, Clark Clifford and George Elsey, to write an assessment of Soviet compliance with wartime and postwar agreements. If the Kremlin did not adhere to past accords, it made little sense to try to reach new agreements. Knowing the chief executive's wishes, Clifford and Elsey solicited the views of top officials in the Truman administration and wrote a devastating critique of Soviet adherence to wartime and postwar agreements. Interpreting their assignment very broadly, they went on to attribute Soviet actions to Marxist-Leninist ideology, to claim that the Soviets sought world domination, and to recommend adoption of a series of measures to assist prospective allies, augment American strength, and redress the balance of power.[2]

Taking another look at these early Cold War developments seems appropriate at a time when influential policymakers are using allegations of Soviet duplicity and noncompliance to extricate the United States from the SALT II and ABM treaties, to thwart progress toward new arms control agreements, and to help justify the Strategic Defense Initiative (SDI). On the eve of the 1985 Geneva Summit, Secretary of Defense Caspar W. Weinberger denounced the Soviet record of adherence to recent accords. He urged President Ronald Reagan to resist any new commitments that would obligate the United States to observe the SALT II agreement, that would limit SDI research, development, or testing, or that would obscure the pattern of Soviet arms control violations. According to Assistant Secretary of Defense Richard Perle, one of Weinberger's closest advisers, it is "a great mistake" for the United States to honor past accords when the Soviets disregard their key provisions. Although the administration thus far has been reluctant to renounce the SALT II and ABM treaties formally, the temptation to do so will mount as new nuclear submarines are deployed, as "Star Wars" research generates new demands for testing and development, and as additional B-52 bombers are converted to carry cruise missiles.[3]

In effect, Weinberger and Perle are claiming that Soviet noncompliance constitutes a threat to vital American interests, justifies unilateral measures to enhance American security, and obviates the utility of negotiation. This line of reasoning closely resembles the arguments of Clifford, Elsey, and Truman

2. For the Clifford–Elsey report, see Arthur Krock, *Memoirs: Sixty Years on the Firing Line* (New York: Funk & Wagnalls, 1968), pp. 422–482. For input into this report, see especially the materials in the George Elsey Papers, Harry S. Truman Library [hereafter, HSTL], Independence, Missouri, box 63; Clark Clifford Papers, HSTL, boxes 14 and 15; also see Clark Clifford, Oral History, HSTL, pp. 11–17, 75–90, 180–186.

3. *The New York Times*, November 16, 1985, pp. 1, 7; *The New York Times*, February 26, 1985, pp. 1, 4; *The Washington Post*, June 11, 1985, pp. A1, A10, A11.

at the onset of the Cold War. Accordingly, it is worthwhile to look at the historical events surrounding the disintegration of the great wartime coalition in order to clarify the records of compliance of the United States and of the Soviet Union. In fact, the Soviet pattern of adherence was not qualitatively different from the American pattern; both governments complied with some accords and disregarded others. American policymakers often exaggerated Soviet malfeasance and disregarded the strategic calculations that may have influenced Soviet actions. Driven by the need to safeguard vital American interests and impelled by a sense of power afforded by the atomic bomb, Truman administration officials themselves sometimes violated key provisions of wartime agreements. And these transgressions could be construed as endangering vital Soviet interests just as Soviet violations may have imperilled critical American interests.

Of course, Clifford, Elsey, and Truman did not see things this way. They were convinced of Soviet duplicity and American innocence. Their self-deception could serve as a lesson to contemporary officials. By their very nature, great power agreements demand compromise and are wrapped in ambiguities. Pressures to interpret provisions, even unambiguous ones, to comport with national self-interest are relentless on both American and Soviet officials. Leaders of both countries tend to act opportunistically yet demand punctilious behavior from their adversaries. Their sense of expediency and self-righteous hypocrisy endanger efforts to regulate competition through international agreement. If competition is to be channeled into constructive avenues and conflict contained, both great powers must abandon the temptation to use the issue of adherence to agreements as a morality play or a propaganda ploy; both sides must wish to define their security in terms of compliance and accommodation rather than in terms of other priorities that compete with and may take ascendancy over a cooperative relationship.

## The Transition from Roosevelt to Truman

During World War II, the major allied governments—the United States, the United Kingdom, and the Soviet Union—signed agreements with one another and with many less powerful governments regarding postwar military, political, and economic developments. The most controversial of these were the agreements signed at the Yalta Conference in February 1945 by Franklin D. Roosevelt, Winston Churchill, and Joseph Stalin. Because the Yalta accords have assumed almost mythic proportions in the history of the Cold War, they shall receive primary attention in this analysis. But what can be observed in the record of adherence to the Yalta accords can be reconfirmed by carefully scrutinizing the pattern of compliance with other wartime agreements. In this respect, the treaties obligating Britain and the Soviet Union to withdraw from

Iran six months after the war and similar ones calling for American withdrawal from advance bases in the Azores, Iceland, and elsewhere are of particular interest. Finally, because the Potsdam accords on Germany gave rise to so many recriminations, it will be worthwhile to look at them, if only in a cursory fashion.

The Yalta agreements have received much scholarly and popular attention. During the McCarthy era, partisan critics charged that alleged communist advisers, like Alger Hiss, were instrumental in undermining the American bargaining position and extending unnecessary concessions. Even sympathizers of President Franklin D. Roosevelt acknowledged shortcomings in the Yalta accords and attributed these flaws to Roosevelt's declining health. After the Department of State published many of the confidential papers and memoranda regarding Yalta in 1955, a number of scholars put together a collection of essays on the Crimean meeting. John Snell, Forrest C. Pogue, Charles F. Delzell, and George A. Lensen provided a careful scholarly assessment of the negotiating trade-offs at Yalta and emphasized the constraints on American actions. The desire for Soviet intervention in the Pacific War, the reality of the Soviet military presence in Eastern Europe, and the hope for postwar cooperation within a United Nations circumscribed the options available to American officials.[4]

The Snell volume constituted a first-rate assessment of Yalta by a group of eminent scholars whose reputation for objectivity was beyond dispute. Their analysis led to the conclusion that the Yalta agreements were not inherently flawed. These accords reflected power realities in Eastern Europe and wartime exigencies in the Far East. What went wrong, they concluded, was subsequent Soviet violation of these agreements.

However, as scholars have probed more deeply into the immediate post-Yalta period, the meaning of the agreements has become ever more difficult to assess. During the last twenty years, historians have come to emphasize the reciprocal concessions made by Roosevelt and Stalin at the Crimea Conference. These concessions were dictated by the realities of the military situation and by Roosevelt's complex aspirations for the postwar era. The president realized that the Kremlin had legitimate interests in Eastern Europe that had to be accommodated if there were to be any hope for postwar cooperation. He desired a cooperative relationship not because he was complacent about Soviet intentions, but because he was altogether well aware of the imponderables that lay ahead. He thought accommodation of legitimate Soviet

4. For background on interpretations of Yalta, see Athan G. Theoharis, *The Yalta Myths: An Issue in U.S. Politics, 1945–1955* (Columbia, Mo.: University of Missouri Press, 1970). For the key primary documents, see Department of State, *FRUS: The Conferences of Malta and Yalta, 1945* (Washington, 1955); and John L. Snell, ed., *The Meaning of Yalta: Big Three Diplomacy and the New Balance of Power* (Baton Rouge, La.: Louisiana State University Press, 1956).

objectives might enable him to safeguard at less cost more vital American (and British) interests elsewhere around the globe. But Roosevelt also desired to preserve the nation's atomic and financial leverage should the Kremlin prove recalcitrant on matters of critical importance to the United States.

In his dealings with the Kremlin, however, Roosevelt felt it imperative to cloak his concessions in the ambiguous language of the Declaration on Liberated Europe. In this way, he hoped to satisfy Stalin without disappointing domestic constituencies whose support he still needed for many legislative enactments, including American participation in the United Nations, the International Monetary Fund, and the World Bank. Paradoxically, then, Roosevelt's carefully concealed concessions were prompted by a desire to cooperate with the Kremlin, by a recognition of Soviet preponderance in Eastern Europe, and by a desire to ensure active American participation in world affairs, which, if necessary, could take the direction of the containment of Soviet power. Roosevelt evidently hoped that Yalta might allow Stalin to safeguard Soviet strategic interests without too overtly violating American principles. Elections in Eastern Europe were promised, but they were to be held without allied supervision and under the aegis of provisional governments that were for the most part the creation of Soviet occupation forces. Democratic forms would be adhered to, thereby satisfying American predilections, but the results would comport with the Kremlin's need for friendly governments. In return, the Soviets would be expected to restrain their ambitions elsewhere and to respect Anglo-American interests.[5]

Roosevelt's goals were difficult to implement. Scholars have shown how Roosevelt refused to acknowledge his Yalta concessions to the American public lest he trigger a wave of cynicism and a return to the isolationism of the interwar era. Moreover, when he died on April 12, 1945, he left his foreign policy in the hands of Vice President Harry S. Truman, a man with whom Roosevelt almost never discussed foreign policy. Truman, by his own repeated admissions, had absolutely no idea of the intricacies of the Yalta agreements and knew very little about the motivations that lay behind Roosevelt's diplomatic and domestic posturing. The new president had to rely on Roosevelt's advisers to explain to him the meaning of the Yalta agreements and the objectives of Roosevelt's diplomacy. Yet because of the improvised way in which Roosevelt used his advisers, because of the bureaucratic morass and the

---

5. The two preceding paragraphs rely heavily on Diane Shaver Clemens, *Yalta* (New York: Oxford University Press, 1970); Robert Dallek, *Franklin D. Roosevelt and American Foreign Policy* (New York: Oxford University Press, 1979), especially pp. 502–529; James MacGregor Burns *Roosevelt: The Soldier of Freedom, 1940–1945* (New York: Harcourt Brace Jovanovich, 1979), pp. 564–579; Martin Sherwin, *A World Destroyed: The Atomic Bomb and the Grand Alliance* (New York: Vintage Books, 1973), pp. 85–140; and Brian L. Villa, "The Atomic Bomb and the Normandy Invasion," *Perspectives in American History*, Vol. 11 (1977–1978), pp. 463–502.

wartime subordination of the State Department, and because of Roosevelt's own deceptive behavior, no one could convey to Truman the full meaning of Roosevelt's concessions and aspirations. Although historians have made substantial progress in putting together a picture of Roosevelt's intentions, few of his contemporaries grasped the multifaceted dimensions of his policies.[6]

During his first months in office, Truman received a set of explanations and advice from one group of advisers, including Secretary of State Edward R. Stettinius, Ambassador to the Soviet Union W. Averell Harriman, Secretary of the Navy James Forrestal, and Admiral William Leahy, the president's chief of staff. He often received contrasting opinions from Secretary of War Henry L. Stimson, Army Chief of Staff General George C. Marshall, Secretary of Commerce Henry A. Wallace, Anna Boettiger, Roosevelt's daughter, and Joseph Davies, former ambassador to the Soviet Union and prominent Democratic fund-raiser. Ironically, Truman came to rely heavily on James F. Byrnes, former senator, supreme court justice, and wartime director of mobilization and reconversion. Although Byrnes had been spurned by Roosevelt as a vice presidential candidate at the Democratic convention in 1944, he reluctantly agreed to accompany Roosevelt to Yalta and to serve as public salesman of the Crimean accords before retiring to his native South Carolina. As Robert Messer has shown, Byrnes was not privy to all the discussions at Yalta, partly because he had to rush back to Washington to lead the domestic media blitz before the final settlements were reached between Roosevelt, Stalin, and Churchill. Nevertheless, Truman looked to Byrnes, who had had little previous familiarity with Roosevelt's foreign policy, for the most definitive explanation of the meaning of Yalta. His dependence upon Byrnes was revealed by his decision to designate him secretary of state as soon as Stettinius completed work on the founding of the United Nations at the San Francisco Conference.[7]

6. In addition to the citations above, see John Lewis Gaddis, *The United States and the Origins of the Cold War, 1941–1947* (New York: Columbia University Press, 1972), pp. 133–173; Daniel Yergin, *Shattered Peace: The Origins of the Cold War and the National Security State* (Boston: Houghton Mifflin, 1978), pp. 61–68; Robert L. Messer, *The End of an Alliance: James F. Byrnes, Roosevelt, Truman, and the Origins of the Cold War* (Chapel Hill, N.C.: University of North Carolina Press, 1982), pp. 1–92; and Lisle Rose, *Dubious Victory: The United States and the End of World War II* (Kent, Ohio: Kent State University Press, 1973).

7. Messer, *End of an Alliance*, pp. 31–92. The most revealing primary sources include the Henry L. Stimson Diaries (Yale University); Joseph Davies Diaries (Library of Congress); William Leahy Diaries (Library of Congress). Also see Robert H. Ferrell, ed., *Off the Record: The Private Papers of Harry S. Truman* (New York: Harper & Row, 1980), pp. 14–48; W. Averell Harriman and Elie Abel, *Special Envoy to Churchill and Stalin, 1941–1946* (New York: Random House, 1975), pp. 418–475; Thomas M. Campbell and George C. Herring, eds., *The Diaries of Edward R. Stettinius, Jr., 1943–1946* (New York: New Viewpoints, 1975), pp. 310–407; John Morton Blum, *The Price of Vision: The Diary of Henry A. Wallace* (Boston: Houghton Mifflin, 1973), pp. 431–464; and Walter Millis, *The Forrestal Diaries* (New York: Viking, 1951), pp. 31–85.

The above depiction of events is well known to historians who have examined the closing events of World War II and the succession from Roosevelt to Truman. The implications of these developments, however, have not been fully explored. Although recent historians like John Lewis Gaddis and Robert Messer fully acknowledge the chasm between Roosevelt's concessions at Yalta and the information disseminated to the American people, they focus attention on the American public's growing disillusionment with Soviet behavior.[8] But the purposeful misrepresentation of the Yalta compromises, the unilateral interpretation of some of the Yalta provisions, and the clear abrogation of others had an important bearing on Soviet-American relations because these developments represented American efforts to extricate the United States from commitments and restraints that were no longer considered desirable. At the same time, the unqualified American denunciations of Soviet compliance with the Yalta accords and with other agreements constituted American efforts to define permissible Soviet behavior in as narrow a way as possible in order to circumscribe Soviet influence in Europe and Asia.

## Differing Interpretations of the Yalta Accords

The Yalta agreements addressed five important topics: Poland, liberated Europe, Germany, the Far East, and the United Nations. Initial rancor revolved around the provisions for Poland and liberated Eastern Europe. With the definition of Poland's eastern border pretty well resolved at Yalta, the post-Yalta dispute focused on the procedures for establishing and the composition of the provisional government for Poland. When Soviet armies advanced through Poland in late 1944, the Kremlin put together and recognized the government of procommunist Poles at Lublin as the Provisional National Government; the British and the Americans, however, still carried on wartime relations with the Polish government-in-exile in London. The State Department favored the establishment of a "fully representative" government inside Poland, to consist primarily of non-Lublin Poles from outside and inside Poland. When British Prime Minister Winston Churchill advocated this position at Yalta, Stalin was obdurate. Emphasizing the need for a Polish government friendly to the Soviet Union in order to guarantee future Soviet security and to safeguard lines of communication to Soviet armies in Germany, he wanted Churchill and Roosevelt to recognize the Lublin Poles.

Wisely or unwisely, Roosevelt mediated the Churchill-Stalin dispute. The final agreement stipulated that "the Provisional Government which is now functioning in Poland [i.e., the Lublin Government] should therefore be reorganized on a broader democratic basis with the inclusion of democratic lead-

8. Gaddis, *Origins of the Cold War*; Messer, *End of an Alliance*.

ers from Poland itself and from Poles abroad." There was no mention of this government becoming "fully representative." Although there was a reference to the holding of free elections, it could not conceal the critical importance of acceding to short-term Lublin control and of eliminating language calling for supervised elections. Roosevelt had made a critical concession that he understood at the time and that he again acknowledged, however unhappily, in a letter to Churchill on March 29, 1945. "You will recall," Roosevelt wrote,

> that the agreement on Poland at Yalta was a compromise. . . . The wording of the resulting agreement reflects this compromise, but if we attempt to evade the fact that we placed, as clearly shown in the agreement, somewhat more emphasis on the Lublin Poles than on the other two groups from which the new government is to be drawn I feel we will expose ourselves to the charges that we are attempting to go back on the Crimea decision.[9]

In other words, the language of the Yalta agreement did concede Lublin predominance in a provisional government, albeit a reorganized one.

Notwithstanding this admission, Roosevelt assented to efforts to try to dilute the meaning of his Yalta concession. Churchill and many American officials sought to regain what had been given away by underscoring the importance of the post-Yalta talks in Moscow. The Crimean accord authorized Harriman, Molotov, and British Ambassador Archibald Clark Kerr "to consult in the first instance in Moscow with members of the present Provisional Government and with other Polish democratic leaders from within Poland and from abroad, with a view to the reorganisation of the present Government along the above lines [that is, on a broader democratic basis]." Churchill, under great criticism in Parliament for the Yalta provisions on Poland, sought to use these deliberations in Moscow to circumvent the Yalta language. Our goal, he wrote Roosevelt, is "to promote the formation of a new reorganised Polish government sufficiently representative of all Poland for us to recognise it."[10] Harriman, too, struggled tenaciously to narrow the preeminence of the Lublin Poles. He demanded that consultations take place with leaders from outside

9. For background on the Polish issue at the Yalta Conference, see Clemens, *Yalta*, pp. 173–215; Snell, *Meaning of Yalta*, pp. 75–126; Martin F. Herz, *Beginnings of the Cold War* (New York: McGraw-Hill, 1966), pp. 38–92; Richard C. Lukas, *The Strange Allies: The United States and Poland, 1941–1945* (Knoxville: University of Tennessee Press, 1978), pp. 128–142. For the quotation revealing Roosevelt's recognition of the concession he made, see Warren F. Kimball, *Roosevelt and Churchill: The Complete Correspondence*, 3 vols. (Princeton, N.J.: Princeton University Press, 1984), Vol. 3, p. 593. Also see Harriman and Abel, *Special Envoy*, pp. 406–414; and Charles Bohlen, *Witness to History, 1929–1969* (New York: Norton, 1973), pp. 188–192. For the precise phrasing of the Yalta agreement on Poland, see Clemens, *Yalta*, p. 306.

10. For Churchill's letter, see Kimball, *Roosevelt and Churchill*, Vol. 3, p. 564. For the Yalta language on the consultations in Moscow, see Clemens, *Yalta*, p. 306.

Poland, and that the Lublin government have no veto over who could participate in these talks. Molotov argued that conversations should be held initially
with representatives of the Lublin government and that Poles who opposed
Yalta should not be consulted. Whatever the merits of the Anglo-American
and Soviet positions on the procedural matter, the real dispute was over the
composition of the reorganized provisional government. Harriman and Clark
Kerr sought to establish a new government "broadly representative of Democratic elements of the Polish State," while Molotov sought reaffirmation that
the Lublin government would constitute the "basis" for the reorganized
government.[11]

The deadlock on the formation of the Polish provisional government was
complete when Roosevelt died. Harriman immediately rushed to Washington
to brief Truman on Soviet perfidy and treachery in Poland and Eastern Europe. Before the ambassador reached Washington, the new president took his
first look at the Yalta agreements and expressed shock and disappointment
that they were not more clear-cut. On the very morning of the president's
acrimonious interview with Molotov, Truman's advisers discussed the meaning of Yalta regarding Poland. Admiral Leahy, the chief of staff to the president, although well known for his tough-nosed, conservative, and anti-Soviet
views, acknowledged that the Yalta language on Poland was susceptible to
contrasting interpretations. Previously, he had told Roosevelt that the language was so vague that the Soviets "could stretch it all the way from Yalta to
Washington without ever technically breaking it." Thus, when Truman met
with Molotov later that same day, the president knew that the Soviet position
was not an unreasonable interpretation of Yalta. But fearful of the Kremlin's
growing strength and the emerging vacuum of power in central Europe, Truman unqualifiedly accused Molotov of transgressing the Yalta provisions on
Poland. "The United States Government," Truman insisted, "cannot be party
to any method of consultation with Polish leaders which would not result in
the establishment of a new Provisional Government of National Unity genuinely representative of the democratic elements of the Polish people."[12] By
focusing on results and calling for a new and "genuinely representative" government, Truman shifted attention from the procedural issue of the Moscow
consultations, on which the United States position was reasonable, to the substantive question regarding the makeup of the provisional government, on
which the American interpretation was unfounded.

11. *FRUS*, 1945, Vol. 5, pp. 134–252; for the quotations, see pp. 180–181. Also see Harriman
and Abel, *Special Envoy*, pp. 426–431; and Lukas, *Strange Allies*, pp. 147–151.
12. Truman, *Memoirs: Years of Decisions*, pp. 85–99 (for Truman's quotation, see p. 97). For
Truman's shock at the ambiguity of the Yalta accords, see Herring and Campbell, *Stettinius*, pp.
324–325. For the morning meeting on April 23, at which Truman's top advisers discussed Soviet
policy toward Poland, see Millis, *Forrestal Diaries*, pp. 49–51. For Leahy's views, see Leahy Diaries, April 23, 1945; and Snell, *Meaning of Yalta*, p. 124. Also see Stimson Diaries, April 23, 1945.

Soviet leaders were angered by the American interpretation. Before Roosevelt's death, Stalin charged that the American position amounted to a claim for "the establishment of an entirely new government." This thesis, Stalin argued, was "tantamount to direct violation of the Crimean Conference decisions." The day before Molotov listened to President Truman's dressing-down, he met privately with Joseph Davies. Molotov explained that Poland was an absolutely vital interest to the Soviet Union, and expressed dismay that Roosevelt's subordinates and successor were seeking to reverse and redefine the meaning of Yalta. From the Soviet perspective, Truman's attempt to force Soviet acceptance of the American interpretation reflected America's failure to adhere to the substantive concessions accepted by Roosevelt. At the Crimea Conference, Stalin wrote Truman on April 24, 1945, the signatories had agreed that the government now functioning in Poland "should be the core, that is, the main part of a new, reconstructed Polish Government of National Unity." American abrogation of the understanding, Stalin insisted, manifested American indifference to Soviet strategic imperatives: "Poland is to the security of the Soviet Union what Belgium and Greece are to the security of Great Britain."[13]

Davies agreed with Molotov's and Stalin's viewpoint. Moreover, during the next two months, Davies spent many hours with Truman at the White House seeking to explain how the Soviets viewed their vital interests in Eastern Europe. Meanwhile, Byrnes, too, endeavored to ascertain more information about the last minute concessions made by Roosevelt at the Crimea meeting. By early June, Byrnes confidentially admitted to Davies, "There was no justification under the spirit or letter of the agreement for insistence by Harriman and the British ambassador that an entirely new Government should be created."[14]

When Harry Hopkins visited Moscow at the end of May and listened to Stalin's strenuous defense of the Kremlin's Polish policy, the American emissary did not seek to justify the American position with a legal or textual analysis of the Yalta accords. Instead, Hopkins alluded, rather lamely, to the sensibilities of American public opinion. In effect, Hopkins conceded that the Soviet position on the preponderant role of the Lublin Poles in any new provisional government comported with the substantive compromises worked out at Yalta. Truman acquiesced to this bitter reality.[15]

13. Herz, *Beginnings of the Cold War*, pp. 91–92; diary entry, April 23, 1945, Davies Papers, box 16; Ministry of Foreign Affairs of the USSR, *Stalin's Correspondence with Roosevelt and Truman, 1941–1945* (New York: Capricorn Books, 1965), pp. 219–220.

14. Diary entry, June 6, 1945, Davies Papers, box 17. Walter Lippmann told Davies that Clark Kerr also disagreed with the Anglo-American interpretation of the Yalta provisions on Poland. But Churchill had squelched his ambassador's view. See diary entry, June 9, 1945, ibid.; also see Messer, *End of an Alliance*, pp. 64–84.

15. The Hopkins-Stalin negotiations and the ensuing efforts to reorganize the Polish Provi-

The recognition of the Lublin Poles meant acceptance of predominant Soviet influence in postwar Poland. This point Roosevelt had conceded at Yalta, but he hoped to elicit at least minimal Soviet adherence to democratic forms. The Soviets, however, had little tolerance for such symbols, as reflected by their arrest and imprisonment of antifascist leaders inside Poland. Nor did the Kremlin ever show any willingness to support free elections or tolerate basic freedoms. The resilience of the anti-Soviet Polish underground and the persistent American pleas for open trade, economic data, and Polish coal (for Western Europe) helped to perpetuate Soviet suspicions about the future orientation of postwar Poland and reinforced the Kremlin's determination to have a friendly government susceptible to Soviet influence notwithstanding the democratic trappings of the Yalta provisions.[16] Neither Moscow nor Washington, then, demonstrated much inclination to adhere to the meaning of Yalta regarding Poland, but American policymakers paid almost no attention to the significance of their own desire to disengage from one of the most significant aspects of the Yalta accords, that is, the provision on the composition of the Polish provisional government.

After the Yalta Conference, rancorous disputes also emerged over the implementation of the Declaration on Liberated Europe. The declaration contained no mechanisms for the enforcement of its lofty principles on self-government and self-determination. Indeed, during the discussions at Yalta, Molotov inserted language that weakened even the implication of great power collaboration in the enforcement of the declaration. The Yalta agreement simply obligated the signatories to "consult together on the measures necessary to discharge the joint responsibilities set forth in this declaration." And this consultation would occur only "when in the opinion of the three governments, conditions . . . make such action necessary." Nothing Roosevelt said or did at Yalta suggested that he had much concern for developments in Eastern Europe except insofar as they might influence the political climate in the United States. With no language to implement its rhetorical flourishes, the Declaration on Liberated Europe did little to dispel the sphere of influence arrangements that had been incorporated into the armistice agreements and that had been sanctioned in the Churchill-Stalin percentages agreement of October 1944.[17]

---

sional Government can be followed in *FRUS*, 1945, Vol. 5, pp. 299–361. Also see Robert E. Sherwood, *Roosevelt and Hopkins: An Intimate History* (New York: Harper & Brothers, 1948), pp. 883–916.

16. For the anti-Soviet Polish underground, see Richard Lukas, *Bitter Legacy: Polish–American Relations in the Wake of World War II* (Lexington, Ky.: University of Kentucky Press, 1982), pp. 29–32; and Kimball, *Churchill and Roosevelt*, Vol. 3, p. 461. For American concerns with open trade and Polish coal, see, for example, *FRUS*, 1945, Vol. 5, pp. 374–376, 402–404.

17. The Declaration on Liberated Europe may be found in Clemens, *Yalta*, pp. 303–304;

The armistice accords denied the Soviet Union any significant influence in Italy and gave the Kremlin the preeminent role in Rumania, Finland, Bulgaria, and Hungary. For all intents and purposes, Soviet officials had a legal claim to run things as they wished in Rumania and Finland until peace treaties were completed and in Bulgaria and Hungary at least until the war was over. The Churchill-Stalin deal complemented the armistice accords and assigned the Kremlin 90 percent influence in Rumania, 80 percent in Bulgaria, and 80 percent in Hungary, while allotting the British predominant influence in Greece and allaying British apprehensions over Soviet support for the leftist partisans in northern Italy. Notwithstanding its inspirational language, the Declaration on Liberated Europe never received much attention at Yalta and never superseded the clarity of the armistice agreements or the realpolitik encompassed in the Churchill-Stalin accords. And despite Churchill's self-serving disclaimers in his magisterial history of World War II, the documents now demonstrate beyond any reasonable doubt that the percentage agreement was neither designed as a temporary accord pending the end of the war nor contingent upon American acceptance.[18]

Yet shortly after the Yalta meeting, Churchill sought to renege on the meaning of these previous concessions and to circumscribe Soviet domination. By the spring of 1945, British forces had put down the insurrection in Greece. Stalin said nothing. He even withdrew Bulgarian troops, now under Soviet tutelage, from Thrace and Macedonia. But when Stalin's emissary, Andrei Vyshinsky, forced the Rumanians to reshuffle their government and sign a bilateral trade agreement with the Kremlin, Churchill remonstrated and the State Department protested. Roosevelt, however, cautioned Churchill to tread carefully because "Rumania is not a good place for a test case. The Russians have been in undisputed control from the beginning, and with Rumania lying athwart the Russian lines of communication it is moreover difficult to contest the plea of military necessity and security." Although Roosevelt had not signed the percentages accord and was not obligated to abide by it, he knew that Soviet actions could not be construed as incompatible with the armistice agreement, especially while the war against Germany was still being waged.[19]

---

also see ibid., pp. 204–207, 262–264; Dallek, *Roosevelt*, pp. 503–516; and Gaddis, *Origins of the Cold War*, pp. 163–164.

18. Albert Resis, "The Churchill-Stalin Secret Percentages Agreement on the Balkans, Moscow, October, 1944," *American Historical Review*, Vol. 83 (April 1978), pp. 368–387; Warren F. Kimball, "Naked Reverse Right: Roosevelt, Churchill, and Eastern Europe from TOLSTOY to Yalta—and a Little Beyond," *Diplomatic History*, Vol. 9 (Winter 1985), pp. 1–24; and Michael M. Boll, *Cold War in the Balkans: American Foreign Policy and the Emergence of Communist Bulgaria, 1943–1947* (Lexington, Ky.: University of Kentucky Press, 1984), pp. 37–51.

19. For Roosevelt's quotation, see Kimball, *Churchill and Roosevelt*, Vol. 3, p. 562. Also see

After Roosevelt died, however, Truman sought to constrict Soviet predominance in Eastern Europe. American policy was more circumspect but no less intent than the British on reversing the real meaning of the Churchill-Stalin agreement, the armistice accords, and the Yalta compromises. Pending Soviet retrenchment in Eastern Europe, the State Department initially decided to refrain from discussing a postwar loan to the Soviet Union and to stiffen the conditions of lend-lease assistance. Truman refused to recognize the provisional governments set up by the Kremlin in Rumania and Bulgaria until they were reorganized and made more representative. At Potsdam, Byrnes endeavored to enlarge the influence of Anglo-American officials within the Allied Control Commissions in occupied Eastern Europe. After Potsdam, American diplomats pressed the Bulgarians to postpone their impending and obviously rigged elections. While rejecting proposals to monitor elections in Eastern Europe and disregarding pleas from American diplomats to intervene more directly in internal Rumanian affairs, Byrnes nonetheless continually prodded Molotov to reorganize the Rumanian and Bulgarian governments, to hold free elections, and to accept self-determination in Eastern Europe. At the London Conference of Foreign Ministers in September 1945, Molotov bluntly told Byrnes that the Kremlin interpreted his requests as efforts to establish unfriendly governments in Rumania and Bulgaria and to jeopardize Soviet security.[20]

Byrnes disclaimed any such intention. From his perspective, he sought no more than Soviet adherence to the language of the Yalta Declaration on Liberated Europe that emphasized "the right of all peoples to choose the form of government under which they will live." Byrnes did not dispute the Soviet claim to a sphere of influence. Prodded by Charles Bohlen, one of the ablest Kremlinologists in the State Department, Byrnes publicly declared that the United States sought neither to impose hostile governments on the Soviet Union's periphery nor to encourage behavior unfriendly to it. Indeed, Byrnes

---

Kimball's editorial comments in ibid., pp. 545–547; *FRUS*, 1945, Vol. 5, pp. 470–526; Herz, *Beginnings of the Cold War*, pp. 121–136; and Resis, "Churchill-Stalin Agreement," pp. 376–377. For the armistice agreement on Rumania, see U.S. Senate, Committee on Foreign Relations, *A Decade of American Foreign Policy; Basic Documents, 1941–1949*, 81st Congress, 1st Session (Washington, 1950), pp. 487–492.

20. For financial assistance, see *FRUS*, 1945, Vol. 5, pp. 836–846. For developments in Eastern Europe, see, for example, Thomas G. Paterson, *Soviet-American Confrontation: Post-War Reconstruction and the Origins of the Cold War* (Baltimore: Johns Hopkins University Press, 1973), pp. 99–143; Boll, *Cold War in the Balkans*, especially pp. 102–155; Lynn Davis, *The Cold War Begins: Soviet-American Conflict over Eastern Europe* (Princeton, N.J.: Princeton University Press, 1974), pp. 255–319; Geir Lundestad, *The American Non-Policy towards Eastern Europe, 1943–1947: Universalism in an Area not of Essential Interest to the United States* (Tromso: Universitets Forlaget, Norway, 1978), especially pp. 231–245, 263–271. For key discussions at the London meeting of the Council of Foreign Ministers, see *FRUS*, 1945, Vol. 2, pp. 246–247, 266–267, 292–295.

proclaimed a willingness to accept the notion of an "open sphere," wherein Eastern European governments would conduct their foreign and defense policies within parameters set by the Kremlin (much as Latin American nations had to mold their policies within the confines established by Washington). The caveat, however, was that the Kremlin had to refrain from intervention in the strictly internal affairs of these countries and to accept the principles of open and nondiscriminatory trade, free elections, and the unimpeded movement of Western journalists.[21]

In the abstract, this orientation constituted a means of reconciling the Soviet interpretation of Yalta as mandating a Soviet sphere with the American claim that Yalta underscored the principles of self-determination and personal freedom. But throughout Eastern Europe, except perhaps Bulgaria, free elections portended the emergence of anti-Soviet governments; open trade meant the eventual influx of Western capital, goods, and influence. Indeed, the planning documents for the Yalta meeting reveal that American officials conceptualized the open door and self-determination as means to exercise leverage and to maintain some influence within a Soviet sphere. Harriman, for example, advocated free elections as a means to circumscribe Soviet predominance. Likewise, U.S. State Department officials championed the right of journalists to travel in Eastern Europe because they anticipated that reports of Soviet repression might generate public support in the United States for a more sustained diplomatic effort to achieve American objectives.[22]

Although Eduard Mark has made a persuasive case for the view that American policy was designed to support an "open sphere," it was an illusion to think that the conflicting interpretations of Yalta could be reconciled through this concept.[23] Wartime ravages, historical experiences, and traditional ethnic rivalries confounded the notion that free elections could lead to governments

21. Memorandum, by Charles E. Bohlen, October 18, 1945, National Archives (NA), Record Group (RG) 59, Charles E. Bohlen Papers, box 8; James F. Byrnes, "Neighboring Nations in One World," October 31, 1945, *Department of State Bulletin*, Vol. 13 (November 4, 1945), pp. 709–711; and Eduard Mark, "Charles E. Bohlen and the Acceptable Limits of Soviet Hegemony in Eastern Europe: A Memorandum of 18 October 1945," *Diplomatic History*, Vol. 3 (Spring 1979), pp. 201–214. For the language of the Declaration, see Clemens, *Yalta*, p. 303.

22. Harriman realized, for example, that his interpretation of Yalta would mean the demise of the Lublin Poles and other pro-Soviet governments. See, for example, the memorandum of his conversation with Truman, April 20, 1945, *FRUS, 1945*, Vol. 5, p. 233; and Harriman and Abel, *Special Envoy*, p. 517. For the use of journalists to mobilize support for American goals, see *FRUS, Conference of Berlin (Potsdam)*, 2 vols. (Washington, 1960), Vol. 1, p. 319 [hereinafter cited as *FRUS, Potsdam*]. For the planning documents on Yalta, see *FRUS, Yalta*, pp. 230–248.

23. Eduard Mark, "American Policy toward Eastern Europe and the Origins of the Cold War, 1941–1946: An Alternative Interpretation," *Journal of American History*, Vol. 68 (September 1981), pp. 313–336. Also see Thomas G. Paterson, *On Every Front: The Making of the Cold War* (New York: Norton, 1979), pp. 33–68.

friendly to the Soviet Union. "A freely elected government in any of these countries," Stalin acknowledged at Potsdam, "would be anti-Soviet, and that we cannot allow." At the Moscow Conference in December 1945, the Soviet dictator reminded Byrnes that Rumanian troops had marched to the Volga, Hungarian armies had reached the Don, and Nazi naval vessels had moved unhindered through Bulgarian waters. Nor was Stalin unaware of the potential political leverage inherent in the principle of equal commercial opportunity. The open door was no different from a foreign military invasion, Stalin told Chiang Kai-shek's son. And unlike Truman, who suspected that German power was unlikely to revive very quickly, Stalin anticipated a German economic resurgence and expected another conflict within ten or fifteen years.[24]

Leaders in Moscow and Washington, then, had reason to feel exasperated with one another's actions and attitudes toward Eastern Europe. However restrained might have been the use of American leverage on behalf of an open sphere and the Yalta Declaration on Liberated Europe, the constant American allusions to free elections, self-government, and open trade, the American eagerness to conclude peace treaties, and the American desire to expedite the withdrawal of Soviet troops cast doubt on the American commitment to accept a Soviet sphere, as defined in the Kremlin.[25] But at the same time, Moscow's refusal to ensure free elections and to establish representative governments constituted clear-cut violations of wartime agreements and engendered legitimate consternation in Washington.

While officials in Moscow and Washington could charge one another with violations of the meaning of Yalta in Poland and Eastern Europe, the situation in Germany was initially less ambiguous. At Yalta, Stalin and Churchill argued heatedly over the amount of German reparations. Ultimately they agreed to create a reparation commission in Moscow. The commission was to apply the principles under which Germany was obligated to "pay in kind for the losses caused by her to the Allied nations in the course of the war." The United States and the Soviet Union concurred that the "Moscow Reparation Commission should take in its initial studies as a basis for discussion the suggestion of the

24. For Stalin's remark at Potsdam, see Herz, *Beginnings of the Cold War*, p. 140. For his comments at Moscow, see *FRUS*, 1945, Vol. 2, pp. 753–754. For his view of the open door, see Harriman and Abel, *Special Envoy*, p. 538. For his expectation of a German revival, see Milovan Djilas, *Conversations with Stalin* (New York: Harcourt, Brace & World, 1962), p. 114. For Truman's view of German enfeeblement, see Memorandum of Conversation between Truman and Charles De-Gaulle, August 22, 1945, HSTL, Harry S. Truman papers (HSTP), President's Secretary's File (PSF), box 177.

25. Once it was clear to Byrnes that he could not persuade the Soviets to accept free elections in Eastern Europe, his major focus switched to the negotiation of the peace treaties with Germany's ex-satellites, upon the ratification of which he hoped to secure Soviet troop withdrawals from Eastern Europe. With a diminished Soviet military presence, Byrnes believed prospects for the autonomy of Eastern European governments would improve. See "Political Aspects of the Meetings of the Council on Foreign Ministers," by Bohlen, no date, RG 59, Bohlen Papers, box 6.

Soviet Government that the total sum . . . should be 20 billion dollars and that 50% of it should go to the Union of Soviet Socialist Republics." Churchill still refused to accept this compromise, but Roosevelt supported it. Based on the discussions at Yalta, Stalin had good reason to believe that the American government sympathized with his desire for large reparations, so long as they were not paid in cash. Moreover, American officials knew that Stalin expected metallurgical and other capital goods factories from the western zones. These reparations in kind would help rebuild the Soviet Union as well as guarantee Germany's postwar emasculation. Indeed, throughout the Crimean deliberations Roosevelt did not contest the amount of reparations with Stalin; the ambiguity of the final agreement represented an American-Soviet attempt to accommodate British objections.[26]

In the months between Yalta and Potsdam, however, American priorities changed significantly. In February, Roosevelt still sought Soviet cooperation to guarantee Germany's defeat and to perpetuate the wartime coalition into the postwar era. By July, Truman sought to revive Germany's coal production as a means to resurrect Western Europe and to contain the forces of revolution, even if it meant jeopardizing Soviet-American relations. Between February and July, the war in Europe ended and American officials became fully aware of the prospects for chaos, famine, and upheaval. In April, Assistant Secretary of War John McCloy visited Germany and Western Europe. When he returned, he talked to Secretary of War Henry L. Stimson and President Truman. "He gave me a powerful picture of the tough situation that exists in Germany," wrote Stimson, "—something that is worse than anything probably that ever happened in the world. I had anticipated the chaos, but the details of it were appalling." During the following weeks, Undersecretary of State Joseph Grew as well as Acheson, Assistant Secretary of State William Clayton, and Byrnes became alarmed by portentous signs of revolutionary upheaval. On June 24, Truman wrote Churchill, "From all the reports that reach me, I believe that without immediate concentration on the production of German coal we will have turmoil and unrest in the very areas of Western Europe on which the whole stability of the continent depends." A few days later it was decided that the president would issue a directive to ensure the export of 25 million tons of coal from Germany by April 1946. This objective was to take priority over all other considerations except the health and safety of occupation troops and the redeployment of Allied forces to the Pacific.[27]

26. For the Yalta language on reparations, see Clemens, *Yalta*, pp. 304–305. For the negotiations at Yalta regarding Germany, see Clemens, *Yalta*, pp. 158–172; Messer, *End of an Alliance*, pp. 48–49; Snell, *Meaning of Yalta*, pp. 53–63; and Bruce Kuklick, *American Policy and the Division of Germany: The Clash with Russia over Reparations* (Ithaca, N.Y.: Cornell University Press, 1972), pp. 76–86.

27. For Stimson's comment, see diary entry, April 19, 1945, Stimson Diaries. For McCloy's report to the president, see Memorandum, April 26, 1945, HST, PSF, box 178. For State Department

These considerations decisively shaped American attitudes at Potsdam and impelled American officials to distance themselves from the position taken by Roosevelt at Yalta. Byrnes sidestepped proposals for four-power control of the Ruhr industries, rejected the $20 billion reparation figure, argued that the Soviets should take reparations from their own zone in Germany, and proposed a settlement that safeguarded the potential resources of the Ruhr, Saar, and Rhine for Western European recovery. Molotov and Vyshinsky went to see Joseph Davies, whom Truman had invited to Potsdam as one of his closest advisers, and expressed disbelief at the overt violation of the meaning and spirit of the Yalta compromises. Neither Davies nor Byrnes nor Clayton really disputed Soviet claims. From the perspective of the State Department, however, new circumstances dictated new priorities and a reinterpretation of Yalta. It was now evident that Germany could not pay $20 billion without risking economic chaos and revolution throughout Western Europe and without imposing a permanent drain on American financial resources. Nor could the Soviets be allowed to use their claim for reparations as a means to gain leverage over economic developments in Germany's industrial heartland. So a new formula had to be devised that entitled the Kremlin to reparations primarily from their own zone in eastern Germany rather than "from the national wealth of Germany," as stipulated in the Yalta accord. Transfers from the western zones to the Soviet Union were made contingent on a number of variables that the Kremlin had little means of controlling.[28]

Stalin grudgingly accepted these conditions in return for Truman's equally grudging acquiescence to the Kremlin's position on the western border of Poland. Unlike the Soviet concession on reparations, which represented Soviet acquiescence to American backtracking both on the amount and the sources of reparations, the American acceptance of the Oder-Neisse line did not constitute any capitulation to a new Soviet demand or to a reversal of the Yalta language. Indeed, the Crimean accord "recognize[d] that Poland must receive substantial accessions of territory in the North and West." The question at Potsdam was where to draw the new lines. Although Truman did not like the Soviet position, he could not claim that the Soviets were repudiating a previous commitment. On the other hand, Soviet feelings about the reversal of the American position on reparations would remain a sore point because that issue was so integrally related to Soviet reconstruction needs and to So-

apprehensions, see, for example, *FRUS, Potsdam*, Vol. 1, pp. 524–525, 623. For Truman's letter to Churchill, see ibid., p. 612. For the directive to Eisenhower, see ibid., Vol. 2, pp. 1028–1030.

28. For developments at Potsdam regarding Germany, see *FRUS, Potsdam*, Vol. 1, pp. 440–443, 491–492, 520–523, 587–588, 596; ibid., Vol. 2, pp. 141–142, 183–184, 297–298, 428–431, 472–475, 481–483, 486–493, 512–522; diary entry, July 28, 1945, Davies Papers, box 19; Frederick J. Dobney, ed., *Selected Papers of Will Clayton* (Baltimore: Johns Hopkins University Press, 1971), pp. 136–139.

viet fears of a revitalized Germany. A year later, taking advantage of a very rare moment when Molotov seemed cordial and communicative, Byrnes inquired, "What is really in your hearts and minds on the subject of Germany?" Nothing more than had been asked at Yalta, Molotov responded: ten billion dollars in reparations and four-power control of the Ruhr.[29]

Apprehension that revolutionary forces in Western Europe might bring Soviet influence to the Atlantic and Mediterranean impelled American officials to repudiate the Yalta agreements on Germany just as fear that democratic forces might bring Western influence and unfriendly governments to the Danube impelled the Kremlin to ignore the principles in the Yalta Declaration on Liberated Europe. And both sides perceived that the actions of the other constituted threats to national security interests. The Americans saw Soviet domination of Eastern Europe as a means to abet Soviet recovery, set back rehabilitation in Western Europe, and lay the groundwork for revolutionary advances in Western Europe and the Mediterranean, thereby enhancing the Kremlin's long-term economic potential and strategic capabilities to wage war against the United States, should it choose to do so in the future. In turn, the Kremlin suspected that the Anglo-Americans might be trying to absorb Germany's industrial heartland into an anti-Bolshevik coalition.[30]

The East Asian provisions of the Yalta agreements also generated recriminations and ill will on both sides. During the Crimean meeting, Roosevelt secretly negotiated a Far Eastern protocol with Stalin. Almost no one but Harriman was privy to the details of the Stalin-Roosevelt discussions. Roosevelt wanted a Soviet pledge to go to war against Japan shortly after Germany's capitulation. Stalin agreed, provided that the United States recognized the status quo in Outer Mongolia, Soviet annexation of the Kuriles and southern Sakhalin, a Soviet naval base at Port Arthur, and preeminent Soviet interests in the port of Dairen and on the Manchurian railroads. Roosevelt worried about making a deal behind Chiang Kai-shek's back. He agreed to Stalin's conditions, however, provided the Kremlin recognized Chiang, offered no support to the Chinese communists, and accepted Chinese national sovereignty over Manchuria. Stalin concurred. Significantly, Harriman warned Roosevelt that he was giving away too much and that the Soviets could easily interpret

29. For the Byrnes-Molotov exchange, see Yergin, *Shattered Peace*, p. 232. For the Yalta language on Poland's western border, see Clemens, *Yalta*, p. 306.

30. For an analysis of the overall American approach to national security, see Melvyn P. Leffler, "The American Conception of National Security and the Beginnings of the Cold War," *American Historical Review*, Vol. 89 (April 1984), pp. 346–381. For Soviet suspicions of a Western European bloc, see, for example, *FRUS, Potsdam*, Vol. 1, pp. 256–264, 450; and ibid., *1946*, Vol. 2, pp. 63–64. Fear of a revived Germany was a constant theme of Molotov's. See V. M. Molotov, *Problems of Foreign Policy: Speeches and Statements April 1945–November 1948* (Moscow: Foreign Languages Publishing House, 1949), pp. 55–68.

the language to mean Soviet domination of Manchuria. But the president felt that he was getting much of what he wanted if he could secure Stalin's support for Chiang, if he could tie down Japanese armies in China with Soviet forces, if he could devote American attention to the occupation and control of the Japanese mainland, and if he could secure formal Soviet recognition of Chinese sovereignty over Manchuria.[31]

As soon as Roosevelt died, Harriman pressed for a reevaluation of the Yalta protocol on the Far East. Although few officials knew exactly what it contained, there was widespread disaffection with the prospect of Soviet gains in East Asia. During May and June, the highest level officials in the War and State departments continually discussed options for constraining Soviet gains in East Asia, including repudiation or renegotiation of the Yalta provisions. Stimson, Marshall, and U.S. Army officials cautioned against repudiation because they realized Soviet armies would be able to march into Manchuria and do as they pleased unless restrained by some accord. Abrogating Yalta would not contain the Kremlin in Northeast Asia; indeed, outright repudiation might alienate Soviet leaders and whet their appetite. Instead, Harriman and the State Department sought to define the language Roosevelt accepted at Yalta in ways that would promote American self-interest and that would circumscribe postwar Soviet influence in Northeast Asia.[32]

In this respect, the successful testing of the atomic bomb on July 16 exerted an important influence on American policy. During the spring of 1945, top military officials gradually revised their view on the need for Soviet intervention in the Pacific War.[33] Prior to the Trinity test, however, Truman sought Soviet participation. He travelled to Potsdam with this objective among his foremost concerns.[34] But once the president received a comprehensive account of the atomic test's huge success, his attitudes changed. He checked with Stimson and Marshall on the need for Soviet participation in the war against Japan. Reassured again that intervention was not a military necessity, Truman immediately sent a telegram to Chiang Kai-shek, encouraging him to pursue further negotiations with the Soviet Union until the Chinese secured an interpretation of the Yalta accords acceptable to them and compatible with

31. Harriman and Abel, *Special Envoy*, pp. 396–401; Clemens, *Yalta*, pp. 247–255; Snell, *Meaning of Yalta*, pp. 127–166; and Dallek, *Roosevelt*, pp. 485–519.

32. Harriman and Abel, *Special Envoy*, pp. 461–462, 482–483; diary entries, May 13–16, 29, 1945, June 6, 19, 26–30, 1945, Stimson Papers; Memoranda, May and June 1945, George A. Lincoln Papers (United States Military Academy, West Point, New York), War Department Files; *FRUS*, 1945, Vol. 7, pp. 868–953; and ibid., Vol. 6, pp. 577–580.

33. Grace Preston Hayes, *The History of the Joint Chiefs of Staff in World War II: The War against Japan* (Annapolis, Md.: Naval Institute Press, 1982), pp. 720–721; and Ronald Spector, *Eagle against the Sun: The American War with Japan* (New York: Free Press, 1985), p. 553.

34. Ferrell, *Off the Record*, p. 53; Robert H. Ferrell, ed., *Dear Bess: The Letters from Harry to Bess Truman* (New York: Norton, 1983), p. 519; and Rose, *Dubious Victory*, pp. 276–277.

American interests.[35] Since the Soviets had stated that they would not go to war until the Chinese accepted the substance of the Yalta agreements, Truman and Byrnes now hoped that a stalemate in the Chinese-Soviet talks would delay Soviet intervention and would allow the atomic bomb to end the Far Eastern war before the Soviets could consolidate their Yalta gains. Byrnes "determined to outmaneuver Stalin on China," noted the secretary of state's closest aide. "Hopes Soong [the Chinese foreign minister] will stand firm and then Russians will not go in war [sic]. Then he feels Japan will surrender before Russia goes to war and this will save China."[36]

While Leahy thought this strategy was naive, Truman and Byrnes were intent on bringing the war to a rapid conclusion and containing Soviet power in East Asia. Much to the chagrin of Stalin and Molotov, the American and British governments issued the Potsdam ultimatum to the Japanese without consulting Soviet officials.[37] Moreover, when high level Soviet-Chinese talks resumed in Moscow after the Potsdam Conference, Ambassador Harriman again urged Soong to contest Soviet privileges at Dairen and Soviet controls over the Manchurian railroads. Although the Yalta accords called for the restoration of Soviet rights in Manchuria as they had existed prior to the 1904 Russo-Japanese War, Harriman made a tenacious effort to define the "preeminent interests" of the Kremlin in as narrow a way as possible. Stalin was willing to accept numerous concessions, yet remonstrated that Harriman appeared to be seeking to reverse the meaning of the Crimean accords, especially as they related to Soviet security rights around Dairen. At the very least Harriman's actions contravened the American obligation, as specified in the Yalta accords, to "take measures in order to obtain [Chiang Kai-shek's]

35. Diary entries, July 21–24, 1945, Stimson Papers; Truman to Patrick Hurley, July 23, 1945, James F. Byrnes Papers (Clemson, South Carolina), File 569 (2); *FRUS, Potsdam*, Vol. 2, pp. 1223–1241.

36. Walter Brown log, July 20, 1945, Byrnes Papers; Millis, *Forrestal Diaries*, p. 78; and Harriman and Abel, *Special Envoy*, p. 492.

37. Diary entries, July 26, 28, 1945, Leahy Diaries; Brown log, July 27, 1945, Byrnes Papers; diary entry, July 27, 1945, Davies Papers, box 19; *FRUS, Potsdam*, Vol. 2, pp. 449–450. Gar Alperovitz's thesis that the bomb was used primarily to contain Soviet power generated great controversy when *Atomic Diplomacy: Hiroshima and Potsdam* was published in 1966. See, for example, Thomas T. Hammond, "'Atomic Diplomacy' Revisited," *Orbis*, Vol. 19 (Winter 1976), pp. 1403–1428. While Alperovitz overstated his argument, many subsequent studies have underscored the complex relationships between the use of the atomic bomb, the termination of the war, and the containment of Soviet power. See, for example, Sherwin, *A World Destroyed*, pp. 160–238; Barton Bernstein, "Roosevelt, Truman, and the Atomic Bomb, 1941–1945: A Reinterpretation," *Political Science Quarterly*, Vol. 90 (Spring 1975), pp. 23–69; Messer, *End of an Alliance*, pp. 71–92, 95–117; Greg Herken, *The Winning Weapon: The Atomic Bomb in the Cold War*, 2945–2950 (New York: Random House, 1980), pp. 3–94; and Mark Paul, "Diplomacy Delayed: The Atomic Bomb and the Division of Korea, 1945," in Bruce Cumings, ed., *Child of Conflict: The Korean-American Relationship, 1943–1953* (Seattle: University of Washington Press, 1983), pp. 67–91.

concurrence" with the provisions on Outer Mongolia and the Manchurian ports and railroads.[38]

In fact, Truman and his closest advisers often acted as if the United States had never entered into any secret agreement on the Far East. At the first cabinet meeting after he returned from Potsdam and after the atomic bombing of Hiroshima and Nagasaki, Truman denied the existence of any agreement relating to Manchuria.[39] At almost the same time, the president sent a message to Stalin asking for American base rights in the Kuriles. The Soviet dictator replied with a stinging rebuff, causing Truman much embarrassment and prompting him to redefine his request. Notwithstanding this development, Secretary of State Byrnes still refused to acknowledge the concessions made at Yalta, and Undersecretary of State Acheson publicly intimated in January 1946 that the Kremlin had no right to the Kuriles. In response, the Kremlin released a statement quoting the exact language of the secret protocol signed at Yalta. The equivocation of American officials was partly due to Truman's ignorance of the terms of Yalta and partly due to Byrnes's fear of facing a domestic political debate over the Yalta provisions. But whatever their motives, American circumlocution could not have but triggered doubts in the Kremlin about American willingness to adhere to the Yalta language that called upon "the Heads of the three Great Powers [to ensure] . . . that these claims of the Soviet Union shall be unquestionably fulfilled after Japan has been defeated."[40]

Soviet actions in East Asia, of course, did not always encourage American confidence. Much to the disappointment of the Truman administration, the Soviets dismantled and carried off Japanese factories in Manchuria. On several occasions, Soviet commanders relinquished Japanese arms to Chinese communist partisans and allowed them to consolidate their hold in several localities. Furthermore, Soviet troops remained in Manchuria several weeks beyond the February 1946 deadline for their withdrawal, and Chinese communist propaganda often resembled that emanating from the Kremlin. The difficulty was in reconciling the Soviet pledge to respect Chinese sovereignty over Manchuria with the Yalta language that also recognized the Soviets' "preeminent interests" on the two key Manchurian railroads and in the port of Dairen. Yet Russian officers often collaborated with Chiang's forces, a fact that was dramatically underscored when Chiang repeatedly requested that Stalin

38. *FRUS*, 1945, Vol. 7, pp. 938–973, especially pp. 962–963; ibid., *Potsdam*, Vol. 2, pp. 1243–1247; and Harriman and Abel, *Special Envoy*, pp. 493–501. Also see Tang Tsou, *America's Failure in China, 1941–1950* (Chicago: University of Chicago Press, 1963), pp. 270–287; and Herbert Feis, *The China Tangle* (New York: Norton, 1965), pp. 328–351. For the Yalta language, see Clemens, *Yalta*, p. 310.

39. Blum, *Price of Vision*, p. 474.

40. For the Kuriles, see *FRUS*, 1945, Vol. 6, pp. 670, 687–688, 692. Also see Messer, *End of an Alliance*, pp. 119–125, 145–158, 169–170. For the Yalta language, see Clemens, *Yalta*, p. 310.

delay Russian troop withdrawals. In so doing, the Soviets completed their Yalta commitments "to render assistance to China with its armed forces for the purpose of liberating China from the Japanese yoke." The Kremlin certainly wished to enhance its influence in China, as did the United States, but according to Walter Robertson, the American chargé in China, there was no proof of collusion between Chinese communist and Soviet forces in early 1946. In fact, General George Marshall, who spent most of that year in China seeking to mediate the internal strife, held the nationalists, rather than the communists, more responsible for the persistence of civil conflict and for the initial breakdown of his peacemaking efforts.[41]

## Recriminations over Other Agreements

Neither America's own lackluster commitment to Yalta nor the ambiguity and tentativeness of Soviet actions caused Truman to reassess his initial conviction that the Soviets were violating their agreements. If any doubts persisted, the Soviet failure to withdraw Russian armies from northern Iran by March 2, 1946, appeared irrefutable proof of the Kremlin's nefarious intentions. No one could question the clarity of the 1942 agreement between the Soviet Union, Great Britain, and Iran that called for the evacuation of British and Russian troops from Iran six months after the end of hostilities. At the Potsdam, London, and Moscow conferences, Byrnes inquired whether the Kremlin would adhere to its commitment to withdraw. When Stalin and Molotov equivocated and talked of Soviet strategic concerns in the Caucasus, American officials sneered at the implication that Soviet interests could be endangered in an area where there was no formidable adversary, present or potential. When Soviet troops did not depart in February and when Soviet leaders entered into negotiations with the Iranian government over prospective concessions in northern Iran, American officials were infuriated. In dramatic moves underscoring the rift in the grand alliance, the United States prodded Iran to bring charges against the Kremlin before the United Nations; Byrnes made a tough public speech; and George Kennan presented a formal diplomatic note to the Kremlin calling for an explanation of the Soviets' failure to adhere to agreements.[42]

41. *FRUS*, 1946, Vol. 9, pp. 447–450. For Marshall's views, see ibid., *1947*, Vol. 2, p. 341. Also see Tsou, *America's Failure in China*, pp. 324–421; and Akira Iriye, *The Cold War in Asia: A Historical Introduction* (Englewood Cliffs, N.J.: Prentice-Hall, 1974), pp. 98–147.

42. The Iranian crisis plays a pivotal role in all the accounts of the Cold War. The best representation of the traditional interpretation is Bruce Kuniholm, *The Origins of the Cold War in the Near East: Great Power Conflict and Diplomacy in Iran, Turkey, and Greece* (Princeton, N.J.: Princeton University Press, 1980). For the interesting and revealing discussions of Iran at the Moscow Conference in December 1945, see *FRUS*, 1945, Vol. 2, pp. 629–631, 686–687, 774–780,

The public sanctimoniousness of the American position nicely concealed the considerations that were prompting American officials in Washington to make some of the same decisions that their counterparts were making in Moscow. In January and February 1946, American policymakers faced the fact that their own wartime agreements with many countries, including Portugal, Iceland, Ecuador, Denmark, and Panama, called for the evacuation of American troops from bases established during the war against the Axis. Several of these governments were pressing for American withdrawal and resented any infringement on their sovereignty now that the wartime emergency was over. American officials fretted as they contemplated the prospect of withdrawing from critical bases in the Azores, Iceland, and Greenland (and from not-so-critical ones in Galápagos and the environs surrounding the canal zone in Panama). In April, the Joint Chiefs of Staff (JCS) resolved that "there are military considerations which make inadvisable the withdrawal of U.S. forces from overseas bases on the territory of foreign nations in every instance in strict accordance with the time limitation provision of the existing agreement with the foreign government concerned." State Department officials concurred in this viewpoint.[43]

Secretary of State Byrnes, Secretary of the Navy Forrestal, and Secretary of War Robert P. Patterson often discussed this issue at their meetings. They were embarrassed by the prospect that American actions in areas of strategic importance to the United States might contradict the high moral tone taken by the American government over the Soviet presence in Iran. Since Galápagos was not so essential, Byrnes, Patterson, and Forrestal agreed to withdraw, provided it was understood that if trouble arose, American troops would be reinserted with or without an agreement. As for the Azores and Iceland, temporary agreements were quickly negotiated that paid obeisance to Portuguese and Icelandic sovereignty and that nicely camouflaged the retention of many American base privileges, sometimes with the use of military personnel dressing in civilian garb.[44] Yet when the Kremlin worked out a deal with Iran that

---

795–797, 805–806. For the formal diplomatic protest in March 1946, see ibid., 1946, Vol. 7, pp. 340–342. For the text of the 1942 agreement, see J.C. Hurewitz, *Diplomacy in the Near and Middle East*, 2 vols. (Princeton, N.J.: Princeton University Press, 1956), Vol. 2, p. 232.

43. For an analysis of the considerations bearing on the withdrawal, see Joint Planning Staff (JPS) 784, "Withdrawal of U.S. Forces from Bases on the Territory of Foreign Nations," February 13, 1946, NA, RG 218, Records of the Joint Chiefs of Staff (JCS), CCS 360 (12-9-42), Sec. 15; for the quotation, see JCS 1648, March 24, 1946, ibid. The State-War-Navy Coordinating Committee (SWNCC) supported this position on April 18, 1946. In July the State Department reiterated the advisability of negotiating new agreements prior to withdrawal, even if this meant violating existing accords. See *FRUS*, 1946, Vol. 1, pp. 1181–1182.

44. For the discussions of the Secretaries of State, War, and Navy, see the Minutes of the Meetings of the Committee of Three, April 2, 17, 1946, June 26, 1946, July 10, 1946, December 18,

provided for an oil concession to the Kremlin in return for the evacuation of Soviet troops, American officials ridiculed it. They pushed for the total excision of Soviet influence lest Soviet leaders use the concession as a cloak for furthering Soviet military goals or for retaining Soviet troops disguised as civilians.[45]

The ironic parallels, of course, went unnoticed by American officials. While American actions and contraventions of agreements were ennobled by national self-interest and the strategic imperative of defense in depth, American officials would not attribute similar motives to the Kremlin. Although the considerations prompting both the retention and then the belated withdrawal of Russian troops from Iran still remain obscure, one suspects that Soviet military planners were eager to capitalize upon the presence of Soviet troops in Iran to safeguard their strategic interests, especially to help protect their petroleum fields and refining industry. They certainly must have known, as did American planners, that in 1940 the British and French contemplated bombing Soviet oil fields in the Caucasus in order to deny petroleum to the Nazis. Soviet planners, having observed the functioning of the Persian Corridor during World War II, must also have been wary of its future use in wartime if it should be controlled by an adversary. If they were not, they would have been remiss because the initial (and tentative) plans of the United States for waging war against the Soviet Union envisioned, among other things, an air assault from the south (from bases at Cairo-Suez). These war plans also denoted a route through the Balkans or through Iran as one of the few likely avenues for a land invasion of the Soviet Union, should it ever become necessary.[46] If such ideas, however preposterous they may now seem, turned up in American war plans, it is not too improbable that Soviet leaders

---

1946, NA, RG 107, Records of the Secretary of War, Robert P. Patterson, Safe File, box 3; Patterson to Byrnes, June 12, 1946, ibid., box 4; Patterson to Byrnes, June 19, 1946, ibid., General Decimal File, box 10; Patterson to Acheson, December 7, 1946, ibid., box 9. For the negotiations with Portugal over the Azores, see *FRUS*, 1946, Vol. 5, pp. 962–1022.

45. *FRUS*, 1946, Vol. 7, pp. 405–567; and Kuniholm, *Cold War in the Near East*, pp. 326–350, 383–399.

46. For Anglo–French plans in 1940, see Memorandum of Information by Thomas B. Inglis, January 21, 1946, James Forrestal Papers (Princeton, New Jersey), box 24; Ernest Llewellyn Woodward, British Foreign *Policy in the Second World War*, 5 vols. (London: Her Majesty's Stationery Office, 1970–76), Vol. 1, pp. 103–105. For the Persian Corridor in wartime, see T. H. Vail Motter, *The United States Army in World War II: The Middle East Theater: The Persian Corridor and Aid to Russia* (Washington, D.C.: Department of the Army, 1952). For American war plans, see JPS 789, "Concept of Operations for Pincher," March 1946, RG 218, CCS 381 USSR (3-2-46), Sec. 1; "Air Plan for Makefast," [Autumn 1946], NA, RG 165, Records of the War Department General and Special Staffs, American-British Conversations (ABC) 381 USSR (March 2, 1946), Sec. 3; "Presentation to the President," January 14, 1947, Forrest P. Sherman Papers (Naval Historical Center, Washington, D.C.), box 2.

may also have been worrying about these contingencies, especially as they would have impinged on Soviet vital interests.

Just as the Iranian crisis was ebbing in May 1946 and the Soviets were completing their belated troop withdrawal, General Lucius Clay formally and unilaterally suspended delivery of reparations from the American occupation zone in Germany. The Soviets protested but to no avail. Clay's action was in response to the failure of the four occupation powers to agree on the economic unification and administration of Germany, as provided for in the Potsdam agreement. Indeed, a few months after Clay's decision, Clifford and Elsey cited the Soviet Union's actions in Germany as one of the litany of items demonstrating Soviet perfidy and untrustworthiness. Yet Clay himself did not blame the Soviet Union for the impasse in Germany. Nor did his superiors in Washington. In June 1946, Secretary of War Patterson and Assistant Secretary Howard C. Petersen, the officials responsible for the implementation of occupation policy, wrote the president that however much the Soviets might benefit from economic unrest and chaos in the Western zones of Germany (and in Western Europe), it was the French, not the Soviets, who were the source of the problem and who were most egregiously disregarding the Potsdam accords.[47]

The Potsdam agreements were imprecise and provided ample opportunity for self-serving interpretations. Two of the most knowledgeable historians dealing with occupation policy refrain from assigning any special responsibility to the Kremlin for the breakdown of allied unity in Germany. The policies of both the United States and the USSR were beleaguered with contradictory impulses; each government tried desperately to define Potsdam in ways that promoted its own interest. By the summer of 1946, for example, the United States had determined that the reconstruction needs of Germany and Western Europe meant that no reparations from current production could go to the Soviet Union. Since Potsdam did not explicitly mandate such transfers, State Department officials argued that the Kremlin was not entitled to them (even though they had been explicitly mentioned in the Yalta agreements). Most foreign governments, including the British, did not share the American view. Yet the Americans were reluctant to modify their position—not because the

---

47. For background on the suspension of reparations, see John Gimbel, *The Origins of the Marshall Plan* (Stanford, Calif.: Stanford University Press, 1976), pp. 53–140; and John H. Backer, *Winds of History: The German Years of Lucius DuBignon Clay* (New York: Van Nostrand Reinhold, 1983), pp. 121–124. For the emphasis on France as the most flagrant violator of the Potsdam agreement, see Jean Edward Smith, ed., *The Papers of General Lucius D. Clay, Germany 1945–1949*, 2 vols. (Bloomington: Indiana University Press, 1974), Vol. 1, pp. 243–244; and Patterson to Truman, June 11, 1946, HSTP, PSF, box 157. Also see *FRUS*, 1946, Vol. 2, pp. 486–488. Although the French had not been invited to Berlin and had not signed the Potsdam accords, American officials expected the French to comply with the terms of the agreements.

legal case was unassailable—but because they were much more concerned with the "first charge" and economic unification principles, also incorporated in the Potsdam provisions.[48]

The "first charge" principle meant that reparations should not be paid until German exports were sufficient to finance German imports (thereby reducing U.S. occupation costs and abetting economic reconstruction in Western Europe). Yet the "first charge" principle was of little importance to the Kremlin, whose representatives continually insisted that the Western powers should comply with the reparations obligations spelled out at Yalta and Potsdam. Their argument was well founded because section 19 of the Potsdam agreement on economic principles explicitly exempted the transfer of equipment and products from the western zones to the Soviet Union from the application of the "first charge" principle. Notwithstanding the legitimacy of their position, Soviet leaders' contempt for the "first charge" principle and their tacit support of French opposition to the economic unification of Germany provoked Byrnes in mid-1946 to threaten a reconsideration of Poland's western border.[49] Since the boundary had been the key Soviet achievement at Potsdam and the trade-off for Soviet acceptance of Byrnes's reparation formula, the American threat must have prompted Soviet officials to wonder who indeed was adhering to agreements.

## Assessments of Compliance

The record of adherence to agreements at the onset of the Cold War is not a simple one to assess. Truman and his advisers correctly emphasized substantial shortcomings in the Soviet performance. Soviet leaders violated the Declaration on Liberated Europe in the Balkans and never carried out their pledge to hold free elections in Poland. They meddled in the internal affairs of Iran and were slow to withdraw from that nation. They interpreted "preeminent interests" in Manchuria broadly. They placed more emphasis on the extraction of reparation payments than on the economic unification of Germany. Notwithstanding these facts, the indictment of Soviet compliance written by Clifford and Elsey and articulated by Truman grossly simplified reality. The Soviet understanding of the Yalta provision on the Polish Provisional Government, the Soviet view of the Yalta and Potsdam provisions on Germany, and Soviet

48. Gimbel, *Marshall Plan*, pp. 57–175; and John Backer, *The Decision to Divide Germany: American Foreign Policy in Transition* (Durham, N.C.: Duke University Press, 1978), especially pp. 159–164. Also see *FRUS*, 1941, Vol. 2, p. 110.

49. Gimbel, *Marshall Plan*, pp. 112–126; Patricia Dawson Ward, *The Threat of Peace: James F. Byrnes and the Council of Foreign Ministers, 1945–1946* (Kent, Ohio: Kent State University Press, 1979), pp. 139–141; and Lukas, *Bitter Legacy*, pp. 65–67. For the relevant Potsdam provisions, see Senate, Foreign Relations, *Decade of American Policy*, p. 39.

expectations in Manchuria were not inconsistent with reasonable interpretations of those agreements. And prior to the proclamation of the Truman Doctrine and the announcement of the Marshall Plan, the Kremlin's actions in Eastern Europe did not consistently contravene Yalta's democratic principles. However much American officials remonstrated about Soviet perfidy in Poland, Rumania, and Bulgaria, they acknowledged that free elections initially occurred in Hungary and Czechoslovakia and that acceptable governments were established in Austria and Finland.[50]

By citing Soviet violations, however, American officials excused their own departure from wartime accords and rationalized their adoption of unilateral measures to safeguard American national security interests. But these American initiatives were not simply responses to Soviet transgressions; for the most part Soviet violations did not trigger and cannot be said to have legitimated America's own record of noncompliance. Most Soviet actions in Eastern Europe during the winter and spring of 1945, for example, were legally permissible under the armistice agreements and were compatible with a host of Anglo-Soviet understandings.[51] However reprehensible was the imposition of a new government on Rumania, the Soviets were acting within their rights. Since the war against Germany was still under way, since Rumania was governed by the armistice agreement of September 12, 1944, since the Soviet High Command was authorized to act on behalf of the Allied powers, and since the Declaration on Liberated Europe did not supplant the armistice accord, the Soviets were not behaving illegally. Likewise, the Soviet position on the composition of the Polish Provisional Government, the issue that more than any other at the time engendered acrimony, was well within the bounds of any reasonable interpretation of the meaning of the Yalta compromises.

The officials who encouraged Truman to talk tough to Molotov in April 1945 were not motivated by legal niceties. Harriman, Leahy, and Forrestal were frightened by the great vacuums of power that were emerging as a result of the defeat of Germany and Japan. They recognized that the Kremlin would be in a position to fill those vacuums. Although they did not seek a rupture in the great wartime coalition, they were convinced that Soviet power had to be limited. If it were not, and if Soviet leaders proved to have unlimited ambitions, they might use their predominance in Central and Eastern Europe to project their influence into Western Europe, the eastern Mediterranean, and the Middle East. Prudence, therefore, dictated a policy of containment. The

50. For the free elections in Finland, Hungary, and Czechoslovakia, see *FRUS*, 1945, Vol. 4, pp. 609–611, 904; ibid., *1946*, Vol. 6, pp. 197–204. For satisfaction with the situation in Austria, see ibid., *1945*, Vol. 3, pp. 623–626, 664–665, 687–688, 693–696. Also see Harriman and Abel, *Special Envoy*, pp. 405–406, 510–511.

51. Boll, *Cold War in the Balkans*, pp. 46–51; Resis, "Churchill-Stalin Percentages Agreement"; and Kimball, "Naked Reverse Right."

Yalta agreements provided a convenient lever to try to pry open Eastern Europe and to resist Soviet predominance, a predominance that temporarily (and regrettably) had been accepted in the armistice agreements (and, for the British, in the percentages deal) because of wartime exigencies.[52]

But by April 1945, the European war was in its concluding weeks, and American officials were reassessing the need for Soviet intervention in the Far Eastern struggle. The factors that had demanded compromise and concession at Yalta were no longer so compelling. Prodded by General John R. Deane, the head of the United States Military Mission in Moscow, the JCS formally reevaluated American dependence on Soviet assistance and concluded that however desirable Soviet military aid might be, American foreign policy should not be governed by this consideration. On the very day that Truman lectured Molotov on Soviet compliance, Admiral Leahy wrote in his diary, "It was the consensus of opinion . . . that the time has arrived to take a strong American attitude toward the Soviets, and that no particular harm can now be done to our war prospects even if Russia should slow down or even stop its war effort in Europe and in Asia." At the same time, Undersecretary of State Joseph Grew and other high level foreign service officers repeatedly emphasized that the Soviet Union was incomparably weaker than the United States. If Washington asserted itself and acted with determination, the Soviets would retreat and perhaps even accept a "genuinely" representative government in Poland. This way of thinking prompted Truman's bellicose approach to Molotov on April 23.[53]

A curious mixture of fear and power, not legal considerations, impelled American policymakers to disengage from their own commitments at Yalta. With the war ending in Europe, officials in the White House, the State Department, and the War Department looked at the prospects for postwar stability and were appalled by what they saw. The magnitude of economic dislocation and sociopolitical turmoil was frightening. "There is a situation in the world," Assistant Secretary of State Dean Acheson told the Senate Committee on Banking and Currency in July 1945, "which threatens the very foundations, the whole fabric of world organization which we have known in our lifetime

52. For Harriman's views, see, for example, Harriman and Abel, *Special Envoy*, pp. 441–454; Memorandum of Conversation, by Bohlen, April 20, 1945, RG 59, Bohlen Papers, box 4; *FRUS*, 1945, Vol. 5, pp. 231–234, 839–846. For Leahy's views, see, for example, ibid., *Yalta*, p. 107; diary entries, April 20, 23, 1945, Leahy Diaries; also see Millis, *Forrestal Diaries*, pp. 39–41; Joseph Grew to Truman, May 1, 1945, *FRUS*, 1945, Vol. 4, pp. 202–203; Mark Ethridge, "Summary Report," December 7, 1945, ibid., Vol. 5, p. 637; John D. Hickerson to Byrnes, December 10, 1945, ibid., Vol. 4, pp. 407–408.

53. JCS 1313, "Revision of Policy with Relation to Russia," April 16, 1945, RG 218, CCS 092 USSR (3-27-45), Sect. 1; diary entries, April 17, 23, 24, 1945, Leahy Diaries; John R. Deane, *The Strange Alliance: The Story of Our Efforts at Wartime Co-operation with Russia* (New York: Viking, 1947), pp. 255–304; *FRUS*, 1945, Vol. 5, pp. 839–846, 231–258.

and which our fathers and grandfathers knew." In liberated Europe, "You find that the railway systems have ceased to operate; that power systems have ceased to operate; the financial systems are destroyed. Ownership of property is in terrific confusion. Management of property is in confusion. Systems of law have to be changed." Not since the eighth century, when the Moslems split the world in two, had conditions been so portentous. Now again, the situation was "one of unparalleled seriousness, in which the whole fabric of social life might go to pieces unless the most energetic steps are taken on all fronts."[54]

Acheson never mentioned the Soviet Union in his testimony; it was not to blame for the conditions he described. But Soviet leaders *might* exploit these conditions to enhance their power. Hence, action had to be taken to cope with these circumstances. While Acheson pleaded for Senate ratification of the Bretton Woods agreements, his colleagues struggled to safeguard German coal, to boost German productivity, and to circumscribe the availability of reparations from the western zones, even if this meant a reversal of some of the understandings reached at Yalta. Likewise, State Department officials remonstrated over Soviet controls in Poland and Hungary not simply because the Yalta provisions on self-determination were being violated but because Polish and Hungarian natural resources, if left open to the West, could aid European recovery.[55]

If fear of revolutionary turmoil inspired an autonomous reevaluation of American interests and of American commitments under the Yalta agreements, the atomic bomb stimulated an autonomous reconsideration of American military and diplomatic capabilities. No one was more enamored of the bomb as a diplomatic lever than was Secretary of State Byrnes. From the day in early May that Stimson first briefed the secretary-designate on the Manhattan Project, Byrnes could not resist thinking that the bomb would be his trump card. On the one hand, it might precipitate a quick Japanese capitulation, thereby preempting Soviet intervention in Manchuria and obviating the need to make good on the concessions accorded Stalin in Yalta's secret protocol on the Far East. On the other hand, Byrnes also felt that "our possessing and demonstrating the bomb would make Russia more manageable in Europe." Just how this would occur, Byrnes never made clear, but American possession of the bomb certainly boosted his (and Truman's) initial determination to seek the revision of the reparation provisions of the Yalta agreement, to extricate the United States from the Far Eastern protocol of the Crimean

54. U.S. Senate, Committee on Foreign Relations, *Bretton Woods Agreements* (Washington, 1945), pp. 19–21, 48–49; diary entry, April 19, 1945, Stimson Papers; and Rosenman to Roosevelt, March 14, 1945, Byrnes Papers, 73 (1).

55. For American concern with Polish coal and Hungarian resources, see, for example, *FRUS*, 1945, Vol. 5, pp. 374–376, 702–704, 883–925.

accords, and to elicit Soviet compliance with the American interpretation of the application of the Declaration on Liberated Europe to Bulgaria and Rumania. In his diary, Davies noted that Byrnes felt the "bomb had given us great power, and that in the last analysis, it would control."[56]

Roosevelt's death catapulted Byrnes to the forefront of American diplomacy. Since Truman depended on him for a correct interpretation of Yalta, Byrnes's mistaken understanding of the provisions regarding Poland and the Declaration on Liberated Europe initially contributed to the president's erroneous impression that the Soviets were violating the meaning of Yalta.[57] But by the time of the Potsdam Conference in July 1945, Truman and Byrnes certainly grasped the fundamentals, if not all the details, of Yalta's provisions on Germany and the Far East. Their efforts, then, to safeguard the open door in Manchuria and to limit reparations from the western zones of Germany did not stem from ignorance of the Crimean decisions but from their estimation of American needs and capabilities. They were responding not to Soviet transgressions, but to the real and prospective growth of Soviet power. By seeking to backtrack on concessions granted at Yalta, however, they stimulated legitimate queries from Soviet leaders about their own compliance record.

In fact, after the capitulation of Germany, American officials assessed the risks and benefits of compliance and concluded that they had little to gain from adherence to many wartime agreements. On the one hand, compliance might allay Soviet suspicions, temper Soviet ambitions, and encourage Soviet officials to define their self-interest in terms of an interdependent relationship with the United States. On the other hand, compliance might lock the United States into a straitjacket while the Kremlin consolidated its power in Eastern Europe and Manchuria, capitalized upon economic chaos and political ferment in Western Europe, and exploited anticolonial sentiments in Asia. Given the risks, American officials chose to define compliance in ways that sought to circumscribe Soviet power in Eastern Europe, maximize American flexibility in western Germany, and buttress Chinese Nationalist interests in China. This orientation meant that, from the onset of the postwar era, American officials were interpreting the wartime accords in ways that placed a higher priority on containing Soviet power and projecting American influence than on perpetuating the wartime alliance.

The Soviets, too, had to weigh the benefits of compliance. On the one hand, compliance might moderate American suspicions, elicit American

56. For the quotations, see Sherwin, *A World Destroyed*, p. 202; and diary entries, July 29, 1945, Davies Papers. Also see Brown log, July 20, 1945, Byrnes Papers; diary entries, May 2, 3, 8, 1945, June 6, 1945, July 21, 23, 24, 30, 1945, August 12–September 4, 1945, Stimson Papers; and Messer, *End of an Alliance*, pp. 71–117.

57. Messer, *End of an Alliance*, pp. 39–70.

loans, and reap large reparation payments from the western zones in Germany; on the other hand, compliance might lead to the establishment of hostile governments on the Soviet periphery, risk the incorporation of a revived Germany into a British (or Anglo-American) bloc, and assign the Kremlin and Eastern Europe to a position of financial and economic dependency. Given these parameters, Soviet officials chose to define compliance in ways that maximized their authority in Eastern Europe, circumscribed Western power in eastern Germany, and enhanced the Kremlin's flexibility in China. These decisions meant that Soviet officials preferred to place higher priority on unilateral safeguards of their security than on preserving a cooperative approach to postwar reconstruction.

As both Moscow and Washington were prone to see the costs of compliance greatly outweighing the benefits, they began to take tentative steps to jettison or reinterpret key provisions of wartime accords. Each such step magnified the suspicions of the potential adversary and encouraged reciprocal actions. Before long, wartime cooperation was forgotten, the Cold War was under way, and a new arms race was imminent. Neither side was innocent of responsibility; each side felt vulnerable, maneuvered to take advantage of opportunities, and manipulated or violated the compromises, loopholes, and ambiguities of wartime agreements.

## Lessons for Contemporary U.S. Policy

It is worth remembering the past when contemplating the future. The Weinberger/Perle thesis, like the Clifford/Elsey report, offers a beguilingly simple approach to the conduct of American diplomacy with the Kremlin. Briefly stated, their thesis is that Soviet violations of agreements constitute a threat to national security; hence the United States should free itself from constraints and take unilateral action to safeguard its vital interests. Before accepting this view, its premises and conclusion deserve careful scrutiny. The history of compliance at the onset of the Cold War can be instructive.

Although charges of Soviet malfeasance in the fulfillment of their international obligations ring true because of the noxious nature of their internal regime, these allegations should be investigated carefully. The Kremlin's pattern of compliance with wartime agreements in the immediate aftermath of World War II appears no better or worse than the American record. American disillusionment was great because American leaders misled the American public about the real meaning of wartime agreements. American policymakers hesitated to discuss their concessions; hence Soviet officials and the American public possessed contrasting expectations about what constituted acceptable behavior. Deception created neither understanding at home nor trust abroad.

Allegations of Soviet violations, therefore, need to be checked against the negotiating history of the agreements in question. The records of the Yalta Conference make clear, for example, that the Soviet expectation for Lublin predominance in the Polish Provisional Government was a reasonable interpretation of the Crimean agreement. Likewise, the Soviet belief that the United States conceded a sphere of influence in Eastern Europe was a reasonable inference for the Kremlin to draw from Roosevelt's acquiescence to the deletion of enforcement provisions from the Declaration on Liberated Europe. Stalin never concealed his view that free elections and self-determination had to be reconciled with his determination to have friendly governments on his borders.

The temptation to make unqualified allegations of Soviet duplicity should be resisted because unsubstantiated charges can distract attention from more fundamental threats to national security. In 1945 and 1946, socioeconomic strife and revolutionary nationalist ferment constituted a much graver danger to the core interests of the United States than did Soviet violations of wartime agreements, numerous though they were. Alleged Soviet violations of the Yalta accords in Manchuria, for example, hardly accounted for the real problems in Northeast Asia. Likewise, Soviet infractions of the Yalta and Potsdam provisions on liberated Europe and Germany hardly constituted the source of Europe's travail in the aftermath of depression, war, and Nazi domination. But policymakers in the Truman Administration, including Clifford and Elsey, felt they could evade ambiguities, clarify options, and mobilize domestic support most effectively by dwelling on Soviet behavior rather than on indigenous unrest. The result was to confuse cause and effect: Americans were educated to view Soviet transgressions as the cause of postwar turmoil and as the principal threat to American national security rather than to see the Kremlin as the primary beneficiary of socioeconomic unrest and revolutionary nationalist upheaval.

The result was that Americans never really grasped the reasons for and the extent of their own government's disengagement from the wartime agreements. The United States backslid on its own commitments and moved toward a policy of unilateralism because American officials believed that the capitulation of Germany and Japan and the spread of postwar unrest jeopardized the entire balance of power on the Eurasian land mass. From the time Truman took office, which nearly coincided with the end of the European war, his advisers sought to extricate the United States from many wartime commitments in order to buttress democratic capitalism in Europe and to contain communism and revolutionary nationalism in Northeast Asia and elsewhere around the world. Finally, in the spring of 1947, claiming that the Soviets had not abided by a "single" agreement, Truman insisted that he had to resort to "other methods" and embarked on a policy of unrestrained competition.[58] Unilateralism produced benefits, but one should not minimize the costs. The total clampdown on Eastern Europe followed, rather than preceded, the Truman Doctrine and the Marshall Plan; the blockade of Berlin followed, rather than preceded, the decisions to suspend reparations, boost the level of German industry, and carry out the currency reforms in the western zones. In other words, unrestrained competition helped expedite the recovery of Western Europe and Japan, but it also contributed to the division of Europe, the American conflicts in Korea and Vietnam, and the dissipation of trillions of dollars on the arms race.

Yet Weinberger and Perle, like their predecessors in the Truman Administration, still wish to use allegations of Soviet noncompliance as a smoke screen to legitimate the lifting of restraints on American actions and to justify a policy of unilateralism. The advantages and disadvantages of a policy of unrestrained competition merit discussion. But the proponents of unilateralism commit a disservice and engage in historical distortion when they unqualifiably charge Soviet treachery in the implementation of agreements and when they exploit Americans' self-image of wounded innocence. The experiences of the early Cold War reveal that wartime agreements were violated not by the Soviets alone but by all the signatories and not necessarily because of evil intent but because of apprehension and expediency. Moreover, the greatest threats to American security emanated not from Soviet actions but from exogenous factors. Such knowledge should not cause despair. Notwithstanding the tarnished record of compliance in the past, there is still hope for the future if officials in Moscow and Washington can resist the temptations of unilateral advantage and if they can remain vigilant in the enforcement of their own behavior as well as that of their adversary.

58. *Public Papers of the Presidents of the United States: Harry S. Truman, 1947* (Washington, D.C., 1963), p. 239.

# 7

# Victory

THE "STATE," THE "WEST,"
AND THE COLD WAR


I wrote this essay because I was struck by the flawed extrapolations that were circulating about why the United States and the "West" won the Cold War. After the disintegration of the Soviet Union and the collapse of communism in the early 1990s, it became commonplace to say victory was the inevitable consequence of the superiority of free markets over a command economy regulated by the state. Although both systems had been facing formidable challenges when Ronald Reagan took office in 1981, the new president had no doubt that the key to resurrecting democratic capitalism was to constrict the role of government. In his inaugural address, he declared, "Government is not the solution to our problem; government is the problem." (See Inaugural Address, January 20, 1981, http://www.presidency.ucsb.edu/ws/?pid=43130.)

This seemed profoundly ahistorical. At the end of World War II, policymakers, diplomats, and intelligence analysts recognized that peoples around the globe were yearning for a better future and pondering alternative ways of life. After thirty years of war, depression, genocide, and forced migration, people wanted personal security as well as national security; people wanted to overcome hunger, improve their standard of living, provide educational opportunity for their children, and insure some dignity in their old age. They wanted hope, and they were deeply skeptical of the capacity of liberal capitalism to offer peace, security, stability, order, and opportunity. "They have suffered so much," declared Assistant Secretary of State Dean Acheson in 1945,

I am extraordinarily indebted to Stephen Macekura for his research and insights on this chapter.

"that they will demand that this whole business of state control and state interference shall be pushed further and further." (See Acheson testimony, March 8, 1945, U.S. Senate, Committee on Banking and Currency, *Bretton Woods Agreements Act*, 79th Cong., 1st sess. [Washington D.C.: Government Printing Office, 1945], I:35.)

The challenge for democratic leaders throughout the world was to thwart the appeal of communism and co-opt revolutionary nationalist movements. To do so, they had to reinvent the role of government—not to supplant markets, but to make markets work more effectively and equitably. Nobody grasped the challenges ahead better than President Franklin D. Roosevelt. In his State of the Union message in January 1944, he emphasized that "individual freedom cannot exist without economic security and independence," and he proceeded to spell out an economic bill of rights. (State of the Union Message to Congress, January 11, 1944, http://www.fdrlibrary.marist.edu /archives/address_text.html.) Elsewhere around the world, anticommunist leaders of many different varieties in Britain, France, Italy, western Germany, Scandinavia, and Japan reconceived the role of government in order to stabilize the business cycle, nurture economic growth, stimulate innovation, enhance living standards, provide educational opportunity, and insure minimum health and old age benefits. As I outlined in this essay, even in the 1980s, Reagan did not reduce government expenditures as a percentage of GDP, nor did he lower the percentage of GDP spent on Social Security and Medicare.

The West "won" the Cold War because statesmen made systems of democratic capitalism and social democracy work effectively. They avoided intracapitalist conflict, won the support of their own peoples, and created a culture of consumption that engendered the envy of peoples everywhere. In this contest over rival systems of political economy, the role of government was not the problem; it was part of the solution. But it had to be calibrated carefully.

This essay was published in Geir Lundestad, ed., *International Relations since the End of the Cold War: New and Old Dimensions* (Oxford: Oxford University Press, 2013), 80–99.

——

In our ongoing debates about the role of government in contemporary economic and social life, we are tempted to draw lessons from the Cold War. Taking office in 1989, George H. W. Bush declared, "We know what works. Freedom works. We know what's right: freedom is right. We know how to secure a more just and prosperous life for man on earth: through free markets, free elections, and the exercise of free will—unhampered by the state." A little more than a decade later, in the turbulent aftermath of the 9/11 attacks, and in the midst of launching a war on terror, his son, George W. Bush, proclaimed,

"The great struggles of the twentieth century between liberty and totalitarian-ism ended with a decisive victory for the forces of freedom—and a single sustainable model for national success: freedom, democracy, and free enterprise."[1]

These extrapolations are profoundly mistaken. It is wrong to celebrate the triumph of capitalism over communism in the Cold War as a simple victory of free markets and free men over totalitarian government and intrusive plan-ning. As we reexamine the virtues of free markets and private enterprise, we must not forget the role of the "state"—the importance of governmental ca-pacity—in creating the conditions for victory in the Cold War. In the "West," broadly defined, governmental policies modulated and stabilized the business cycle, nurtured economic growth, provided minimum social provision, stim-ulated innovation, empowered civil society, enhanced living standards, and made consumption the benchmark of modern civilization. The state comple-mented markets, structured markets, liberated markets, and helped allay the hardships caused by markets.

It is easy to forget what an achievement this was. After two world wars, a great depression, and mass extermination, liberal capitalism was in disrepute. The magic of the market was not part of people's vocabulary after the despair of the depression and the misery of war. In 1944, in *The Road to Serfdom*, Friedrich von Hayek lamented, "If we take the people whose views influence developments, they are now in the democracies all socialists. Scarcely any-body doubts that we must move toward socialism." A year later, A.J.P. Taylor, the renowned British historian, asserted, "Nobody in Europe believes in the American way of life—that is, in private enterprise." And even a decade later, Walter Lippmann wrote in *The Public Philosophy*, "We are living in a time of massive popular counterrevolution against liberal democracy. It is a reaction to the failure of the West to cope with the miseries and anxieties of the twen-tieth century."[2]

U.S. officials were well aware that depression, war, holocaust, and mass expulsions created unprecedented challenges to democratic capitalism. In April 1945, Assistant Secretary of War John McCloy went to Europe and re-ported to his boss, Henry Stimson, that "there is a complete economic, so-cial and political collapse going on in Central Europe, the extent of which is

1. George H. W. Bush, January 20, 1989, http://www.presidency.ucsb.edu/ws/index .php?pid=16610#axzzlTHP3zpET; George W. Bush, Introduction to the National Security Strat-egy Statement, September 17, 2002, http://georgewbush-whitehouse.archives.gov/nsc /nss/2002/ nssintro.html.

2. Quoted in Mark Mazower, *Dark Continent: Europe's Twentieth Century* (New York: Vin-tage, 1998), 203; A.J.P. Taylor, "The European Revolution," *Listener*, 34 (November 22, 1945), 576. Also see Tony Judt, *Ill Fares the Land* (New York; Penguin, 2010), 55; Walter Lippmann, *Essays in the Public Philosophy* (Boston, Mass.: Little, Brown, 1955), 63.

unparalleled in history." Stimson, in turn, informed President Harry S. Truman that "pestilence and famine" would afflict Europe during the next winter and that they were likely to be followed by "political revolution and communist infiltration."[3]

Everywhere in Europe, communist membership was soaring, the role of the state was mounting, experiments with "nationalization" were spreading, and the enchantment with "planning" was growing. The war, if not the depression, had accustomed people to new roles for the government: if the state had mobilized to kill and destroy, why could it not be administered for the furtherance of justice, the promotion of equality, and the nurturing of individual opportunity? In France, Italy, and Finland, the Communist Party vote, by 1946, was 20 percent or more; in Belgium, Denmark, Norway, Holland, and Sweden, it was close to 10 percent.[4] Elsewhere around the globe, revolutionary nationalist movements were forming. They clamored for independence and sought transformative changes in political economy, national identity, and race relations. Planned economies, many revolutionary nationalist leaders believed, might propel their emerging nations into modernity and might earn their people the dignity they merited in the international arena.[5]

President Franklin D. Roosevelt, governing in a country spared of wartime devastation but scarred by years of depression and rife with fears of looming unemployment, grasped the challenges ahead. He understood that the American "state" had to act boldly at home so that the United States could exert leadership abroad. In his State of the Union message of January 1944, he harked back to the themes of the Atlantic Charter and emphasized, "Individual freedom cannot exist without economic security and independence. . . . People who are hungry, people who are out of a job are the stuff of which dictatorships are made." He then set forth an economic bill of rights: the right to a useful and remunerative job; the right to earn enough for adequate food, clothing, and recreation; the rights of farmers to sell at a fair price and business people to compete on fair terms; the right to decent housing; the right to medical care; the right to a good education; the right to be protected and

3. Quoted in Melvyn P. Leffler, *A Preponderance of Power: National Security, the Truman Administration, and the Cold War* (Stanford, Calif.: Stanford University Press, 1993), 35–6, 63–4.

4. Donald Sassoon, *One Hundred Years of Socialism: The West European Left in the Twentieth Century* (London: I. B. Tauris, 1996), 117–66; Adam Westoby, *Communism since World War II* (New York: St. Martin's Press, 1981), 14–15; Jytte Klausen, *War and Welfare: Europe and the United States, 1945 to the Present* (New York: St. Martin's Press, 1998), 1–18; Stephen Padgett and William E. Paterson, *A History of Social Democracy* (London: Longman, 1991), 12–34.

5. David Priestland, *The Red Flag: A History of Communism* (New York: Grove Press, 2009), xxiv; Robert Service, *Comrades: A History of World Communism* (Cambridge, Mass.: Harvard University Press, 2007), 280–2; Jeffry A. Frieden, *Global Capitalism: Its Fall and Rise in the Twentieth Century* (New York: W. W. Norton, 2006), 271–7, 301–38; Archie Brown, *The Rise and Fall of Communism* (New York: Harper Collins, 2009), 313–67.

to escape the fears of old age, sickness, disability, and unemployment. "All of these rights," Roosevelt concluded, "spell security."[6]

To underscore the importance of this mission to reshape America, he repeated these rights in his last State of the Union message a year later. A liberal international economy, he explained, required a strong state at home. "An enduring peace," he admonished, "cannot be achieved without a strong America—strong in the social and economic sense as well as in the military sense. . . . The Federal Government must see to it that these rights become realities—with the help of States, municipalities, business, labor, and agriculture." He then mapped out how government must buttress private sector efforts to sustain purchasing power, stimulate business, insure liquidity, boost productivity, develop the nation's abundant natural resources, enhance aviation and transportation, and expand social security, health, and education programs.[7]

Roosevelt was not naive about the difficulties that lay ahead. The war, he knew, would bequeath fundamental problems for the world economy and the national economy. He, therefore, supported the work of his Treasury and State department subordinates to create the Bretton Woods institutions of the World Bank and the International Monetary Fund as well as the United Nations. The preamble of the UN charter, in fact, captured the aspirations and yearnings of peoples everywhere to eliminate the scourge of war and to promote social and economic progress "in larger freedom." In Article 55 of the UN charter, the signatories specifically obligated themselves to promote "higher standards of living, full employment, and conditions of economic and social progress and development."[8] Three years later, in the UN Declaration of Human Rights, these universal standards were reiterated: "Everyone . . . has the right to social security"; "Everyone has the right to work"; "Everyone has the right to a standard of living adequate for the health and well-being of himself and his family, including food, clothing, housing, and medical care and necessary social services, and the right to security in the event of unemployment, sickness, disability, widowhood, [and] old age."[9]

These commitments were the legacy of the Great Depression and the Second World War. These commitments were the legacy of nineteenth-century industrialization and of the turmoil wrought by business fluctuations in free

6. Franklin D. Roosevelt, State of the Union Message to Congress, January 11, 1944, http://www.presidency.ucsb.edu/ws/index.php?pid=16518#axzzlLISzVaUA.

7. Franklin D. Roosevelt, State of the Union Message to Congress, January 6, 1945, http://www.presidency.ucsb.edu/ws/index.php?pid=16595#axzzlLISzVaUA.

8. For the charter of the United Nations, see http://www.un.org/en/documents/charter/index.shtml.

9. "The Universal Declaration of Human Rights," http://www.un.org/en/documents/udhr/ index.shtml.

market economies. These commitments were the promises of democratic statesmen to their citizenry for enduring the hardships and misery of two world wars and a great depression.

Yet, in the literature on the international relations and political economy of the Cold War, these commitments receive scant attention. There is much stress on how the United States helped to forge new multinational organizations like the World Bank and the IMF, formulated new initiatives like the Truman Doctrine and the Marshall Plan, practiced containment, embraced the politics of productivity, and struggled tenaciously to curtail the enlargement of the state, to open markets, to combat autarky, and to thwart the drive to nationalization.[10] These themes deserve the importance that has been given to them. As we have illuminated these matters, however, we have tended to minimize how, amidst all these efforts, the role of the state grew. The success of the West inhered in its ability to marry the state with the market, to reconcile the rights of social citizenship with the dynamics of the marketplace, to insure minimal social provision while nurturing private incentives, to socialize key elements of risk-taking (in housing, insurance, and banking) while spurring private entrepreneurship and technological innovation, and to mitigate class conflict while nurturing income equality and championing consumer sovereignty.[11] Indeed, the Bretton Woods institutions themselves had been organized to reconcile the liberalization of trade and the maintenance of currency stability with the empowerment of national governments to exercise autonomy over their own economic fortunes and social policies. "The role of the state," writes John Ruggie in a seminal article, was to "safeguard the self-regulating market."[12]

10. For a small sampling of the literature, see Lloyd C. Gardner, *Economic Aspects of New Deal Diplomacy* (Madison, Wis.: University of Wisconsin Press, 1964); Gabriel Kolko, *Politics of War: The World and United States Foreign Policy, 1943–45* (New York: Random House, 1968); Gabriel Kolko and Joyce Kolko, *The Limits of Power: The World and United States Foreign Policy, 1945–1954* (New York: Harper and Row, 1972); Fred L. Block, *The Origins of International Economic Disorder: A Study of United States International Monetary Policy from World War II to the Present* (Berkeley, Calif.: University of California Press, 1977); Thomas G. Paterson, *Soviet-American Confrontation: Postwar Reconstruction and the Origins of the Cold War* (Baltimore, Md.: Johns Hopkins University Press, 1973); Michael J. Hogan, *The Marshall Plan: America, Britain, and the Reconstruction of Western Europe, 1947–1952* (New York: Cambridge University Press, 1987); Charles S. Maier, "The Politics of Productivity," reprinted in Charles S. Maier, *In Search of Stability: Explorations in Historical Political Economy* (Cambridge: Cambridge University Press, 1987), 121–52.

11. The ideas expressed here are derived from my reading, among other works, the insightful and provocative books by Victoria de Grazia, *Irresistible Empire: America's Advance through 20th Century Europe* (Cambridge, Mass.: Harvard University Press, 2005); Elizabeth Borgwardt, *A New Deal for the World: America's Vision for Human Rights* (Cambridge, Mass.: Harvard University Press, 2005).

12. John Gerard Ruggie, "International Regimes, Transactions, and Change: Embedded

In our preoccupations, for example, with U.S. efforts to attach conditions to a postwar loan to Britain and to hem in its imperial preference system, we lose sight of the remarkable creation of the British welfare state. Americans frowned on British nationalization of key industries (civil aviation, telecommunications, coal, iron, steel, railways, gas, electricity, and the Bank of England), but the Labour government went ahead nonetheless, passing the Family Allowance Act of 1945 (introducing cash payments to all poor families with children under the age of 15), the National Insurance Act of 1946 (providing sickness benefits to persons unable to work), the National Health Service Act (instituting universal free health care financed by general taxation), and the National Assistance Act of 1948 (abolishing the old Poor Law and establishing the National Assistance Board to help indigent persons based on subsistence and housing costs). Social services as a percentage of gross national product (GNP) rose from 11.3 percent in 1938 to 23.2 percent in 1970; total public expenditures rose from 30 percent of GNP in 1938 to 47.1 percent in 1970.[13]

In France, the communist quest for power was thwarted, partially as a result of U.S. aid, but French governments nationalized key industries and instituted massive reforms in social spending and welfare support. Postwar French governments, writes Philip Nord, "made a pledge" to the nation: "The state would undertake to make a better France for every citizen," and for the most part the French government did so by insuring citizens "against the perils of sickness and old age" and also by providing generous family allowances.[14]

In Italy, with considerable U.S. assistance to the government of Alcide de Gasperi, the communists were also thwarted in the closely contested elections of 1948, and thereafter they never garnered the power they yearned for. But successive Italian postwar governments embraced the principles of minimal

Liberalism in the Postwar Economic Order," *International Organization*, 36:2 (Spring 1982), 379–415, quotation on 386; Ivan Berend, *An Economic History of Twentieth Century Europe: Economic Regimes from Laissez-Faire to Globalization* (Cambridge: Cambridge University Press, 2006), especially 232–4; Anne-Marie Burley, "Regulating the World: Multilateralism, International Law, and the Projection of the New Deal Regulatory State," in John Gerrard Ruggie (ed.), *Multilateralism Matters: The Theory and Praxis of an Institutional Form* (New York: Columbia University Press, 1993), 125–56; Frieden, *Global Capitalism*, 253–300.

13. Mazower, *Dark Continent*, 300; for British laws, see Pete Alcock, *Social Policy in Britain: Themes and Issues* (London: MacMillan Press, 1996), 22; Sassoon, *One Hundred Years of Socialism*, 138–43; Richard Perry, "United Kingdom," in Peter Flora (ed.), *Growth to Limits: The West European Welfare States since World War II*, volume 2 (Berlin: Walter de Gruyter, 1986), 155–240; Arthur Gould, *Capitalist Welfare Systems: A Comparison of Japan, Britain, and Sweden* (London: Longman, 1993), 115ff.; William Hitchcock, *The Struggle for Europe: The Turbulent History of a Divided Continent, 1945 to the Present* (New York: Anchor Books, 2003), 40–56.

14. Philip Nord, *France's New Deal* (Princeton, N.J.: Princeton University Press, 2010), 382–3; also see Hitchcock, *The Struggle for Europe*, 75; Berend, *Economic History of Twentieth Century Europe*, 234.

social provision, welfare assistance, health insurance, and regional development. From 1950 to 1980, public expenditures as a percentage of gross domestic product (GDP) increased from about 25 percent of GDP to about 45 percent; social expenditures rose from about 13 percent of GDP to about 27 percent.[15]

In West Germany, Ludwig Erhard, the economics minister, repudiated the Nazi legacy of statism and embraced the free market. To boost individual standards of living, he championed growth, competition, low taxes, monetary stability, and foreign trade, but he could not disregard the clamor for social protection. Erhard and Chancellor Konrad Adenauer updated and expanded the already elaborate pension systems and accident and health insurance laws that went back to the late nineteenth century. By 1953, 20 percent of the West German population received some kind of state assistance, and, by 1955, perhaps as many as 50 percent of all German households received government largesse. The annual real growth rate of social expenditures from 1951 to 1966 was 8.4 percent annually.[16]

In Japan, U.S. occupation authorities worked with Japanese interest groups, not simply to defeat the Left and thwart the radicalization of unions, but also to revamp and modernize the health insurance laws that dated back to the 1920s. Overall, benefits were low, but by the early 1970s "Japan had a social security system which covered virtually the whole population."[17]

U.S. politicians may have sneered at the growth of welfare systems abroad, condemned the nationalization of industries, feared the epidemic of planning, worried about the growth of a garrison state, and excoriated "reds" at home. But the American state grew, instituted new monetary and fiscal practices, assumed huge responsibilities for promoting the health and welfare of the American people, and taxed Americans at unprecedentedly high peacetime levels.[18] In other words, Roosevelt's aspirations for postwar America were

15. Maurizio Ferrera, "Italy," in Flora, *Growth to Limits*, volume 2, 388–499, percentages on 393–6.

16. Ferrera, "Italy," 250–96; Jens Alber, "Germany," in Flora, *Growth to Limits*, volume 2, 4–154, especially 96–114; A. J. Nicholls, *Freedom with Responsibility: The Social Market Economy in Germany, 1918–1963* (Oxford: Clarendon, 1994), 350; Tony Judt, *Postwar: A History of Europe since 1945* (New York: Penguin, 2005), 372; James C. Van Hook, *Rebuilding Germany: The Creation of the Social Market Economy, 1945–1957* (Cambridge: Cambridge University Press, 2004), 1–3; Claus Offe, "The German Welfare State: Principles, Performance, Prospects," in Beverly Crawford and Sarah Elise Wiliarty (eds.), *The Postwar Transformation of Germany: Democracy, Prosperity, and Nationhood* (Ann Arbor, Mich.: University of Michigan Press, 1999), 202–24.

17. Kojun Furakawa, *Social Welfare in Japan: Principles and Applications* (Melbourne, Australia: Trans Pacific Press, 2008), 34–5, 53; for quotation, see Gould, *Capitalist Welfare Systems*, 36, 44; Stephen J. Anderson, *Welfare Policy and Politics in Japan: Beyond the Developmental State* (Chicago: University of Chicago Press, 1998), 43–55.

18. Alan Brinkley, *The End of Reform: New Deal Liberalism in Recession and War* (New York:

slowly realized despite the conservative reaction that culminated in a Republican takeover of Congress in 1946, the end of wartime controls, the dilution of the Full Employment Act of 1946, and the passage of the Taft-Hartley labor law in 1947. For example, for 16 million veterans, the GI Bill of 1944 provided unemployment benefits, as well as tuition and subsistence allowances for education and training, and loans for farms, homes, and businesses. A total of 5.4 million veterans made use of the unemployment benefits; 7.8 million veterans availed themselves of the education benefits. Between 1945 and 1966, 20 percent of all single-family residences were financed by GI bills.[19] In addition, in 1950, social security was extended to an additional 10 million persons; in 1954, the Agricultural Act brought 3.6 million farm operators and 2.1 million farm workers into the social security system; and, in 1956, disability insurance was added to old age and survivors' insurance. Overall, between 1945 and 1960, the number of people receiving Old Age, Survivors, and Disability Insurance increased from 3.1 to 14.8 million. Poverty in the United States fell dramatically, from 51 percent of the American people in 1935–36, to 30 percent in 1950, to 20 percent in 1960, and to 17 percent in 1965.

By that time, Lyndon B. Johnson's Great Society programs—Medicare, Medicaid, aid to education, etc.—were reshaping the social welfare landscape in America, meaning, among other things, that social welfare expenditures jumped from 7.7 percent of GNP in 1960 to 10.5 percent in 1965 and to 16 percent in 1974.[20]

The remarkable growth of safety nets, minimal social provision, and welfare assistance was rendered possible by unprecedented economic growth in the West. States embraced new forms of fiscal and monetary policies, helped mobilize capital and socialize risk, organized cartels, nurtured various forms of planning schemes, and sustained purchasing power in bad times. In short, governments modulated the business cycle, buttressed markets, slowly

---

Vintage Books, 1995); Frieden, *Global Capitalism*, 297–300. For background, also see Aaron Friedberg, *In the Shadow of the Garrison State: America's Anti-Statism and its Cold War Grand Strategy* (Princeton, N.J.: Princeton University Press, 2000); Michael J. Hogan, *A Cross of Iron: Harry S. Truman and the Origins of the National Security State, 1945–1954* (New York: Cambridge University Press, 1998).

19. Christopher Loss, "'The Most Wonderful Thing Has Happened to Me in the Army': Psychology, Citizenship, and American Higher Education in World War II," *The Journal of American History*, 92 (December 2005), 887–8; Kathleen J. Frydl, *The GI Bill* (New York: Cambridge University Press, 2009), 2; Michael J. Bennett, *When Dreams Come True: The GI Bill and the Making of Modern America* (Washington, D.C.: Brassey's, 1996), 287; Lizabeth Cohen, *A Consumers' Republic: The Politics of Mass Consumption in Postwar America* (New York: Vintage, 2003), 141.

20. James T. Patterson, *America's Struggle against Poverty, 1900–1994* (Cambridge, Mass.: Harvard University Press, 1994), especially 79, 85–6, 164–5; Gareth Davies, *From Opportunity to Entitlement: The Transformation and Decline of Great Society Liberalism* (Lawrence, Kan.: University Press of Kansas, 1996).

embraced liberalized trade, and boosted standards of living. In Western Europe, between 1950 and 1970, GDP grew at 5.5 percent per year and 4.4 percent per capita; depending on the country, annual per capita income soared between 250 and 400 percent.[21]

The public sector contributed to growth. "From 1950 to 1973 the average industrial country's public sector rose from 27 to 43 percent of GDP. Social transfers, the core of social security and insurance systems, went from an average of 7 to 15 percent of GDP."[22] Different countries pursued different paths, but the commitment of states to modernization, full employment, minimal social provision, educational opportunity, and higher standards of living was universal. Throughout noncommunist Europe in the 1950s and 1960s, the most advanced countries increased educational expenditures by almost 15 percent a year—and eliminated gender discrimination in many levels of schooling.[23]

Even in the United States, the role of the state grew. The government nurtured growth and spawned technological innovation while building safety nets. GDP in the United States grew by about 3.5 percent per annum in the 1950s and 4.2 percent a year in the 1960s. During these years, U.S. government spending as a percentage of GDP increased from 17.1 percent in 1948 to 29.5 percent in 1970. And the growth of the public sector was not primarily a matter of military Keynesianism. In fact, defense spending as a percentage of GDP dropped from a Korean War level of 14 percent in 1952 to 8.5 percent of GDP in 1970, while government expenditures on payments to individuals increased from 3.1 percent of GDP in 1952 to 6.4 percent in 1970.[24]

During these years, moreover, New Deal banking legislation was refashioned, guaranteeing deposits, authorizing the Federal Reserve Banks to supplement private banking reserves (by redefining what counted as collateral for

21. Wilfried Loth, "The Cold War and the Social and Economic History of the Twentieth Century," in Melvyn P. Leffler and Odd Arne Westad (eds.), *Cambridge History of the Cold War: Crises and Detente* (Cambridge, Mass.: Cambridge University Press, 2010), 2: 512; Berend, *Economic History of Twentieth Century Europe*, 257; Barry Eichengreen, *The European Economy since 1945: Coordinated Capitalism and Beyond* (Princeton, N.J.: Princeton University Press, 2007), 15–130.

22. Frieden, *Global Capitalism*, 297.

23. Hitchcock, *The Struggle for Europe*, 140, also 137–8; Eichengreen, *European Economy since 1945*, 86–130; Eric Hobsbawm, *Age of Extremes: The Short Twentieth Century, 1914–1991* (London: Abacus, 1995), 263–74; Berend, *Economic History of Twentieth Century Europe*, 236–7.

24. Richard N. Cooper, "Economic Aspects of the Cold War, 1962–1975," in Leffler and Westad, *Cambridge History of the Cold War*, volume 2, 49; Table 15.5, "Total Government Expenditures by Major Category of Expenditure as Percentages of GDP, 1948–2010," U.S. Office of Management and Budget (OMB), Historical tables, http://www.whitehouse.gov/omb/budget/Historical.

debt), and socializing various forms of risk-taking. After the Second World War, the Veterans Administration and the Federal Housing Administration "provided government mortgage guarantees, insured private lenders against loss, helped to standardize appraisal practices, and popularized long-term mortgages." The historian David Freund calculates that between 1947 and 1958 these agencies financed almost 50 percent of new single-family homes purchased in the United States.[25]

The U.S. government also nurtured a recalibration of power relationships between labor and capital. Union membership soared after the passage of the National Labor Relations Act (1935) and during the wartime emergency. The National Labor Relations Board, the War Labor Board, and the Office of Price Administration, among other state agencies, helped bolster the power and influence of organized labor in the United States. From the 1940s through the 1960s, workers, especially organized workers, could count on the state to be a neutral, if not partial, supporter of their efforts to get a larger part of the income pie and to join the middle class.[26]

The U.S. government also played a decisive role encouraging technological innovation and catalyzing the electronics, computer, and communication revolutions that transformed the American economy and society. Government spending for research and development increased from $940 million (or 2.4 percent of total outlays) in 1949 to $16.8 billion (or 11.7 percent of total government expenditures) in 1965. In 1959, a congressional committee estimated that about 85 percent of electronics research and development in the United States was funded by the federal government, much of which went to major corporations like IBM, Burroughs, Control Data, and Sperry. At this time, the federal government was paying for about two-thirds of all computer-related research and development.[27]

The spillover impact on the civilian economy of these research endeavors was enormous. The work on electronics, transistors, computers, and com-

25. David M. P. Freund, "Marketing the Free Market: State Intervention and the Politics of Prosperity in Metropolitan America," in Kevin M. Kruse and Thomas J. Sugrue (eds.) *The New Suburban History* (Chicago: University of Chicago Press, 2006), 11–32, quotation on 16; also see David M. P. Freund, "When the State Assumes Risk: New Deal Policy, Postwar Finance, and a New Market for Debt," unpublished paper, November 2010.

26. Nelson Lichtenstein, *State of the Union: A Century of American Labor* (Princeton, N.J.: Princeton University Press, 2002).

27. Table 9.7, "Summary of Outlays for Conduct of Research and Development, 1949–2012," Office of Management and Budget (OMB), Historical tables, http://www.whitehouse.gov/omb/budget/Historical; David Reynolds, "Science, Technology, and the Cold War," in Leffler and Westad, *Cambridge History of the Cold War: Endings*, volume 3, 379, 384, 392; Susan W. Schechter, *The Effects of Military and Other Government Spending on the Computer Industry: The Early Years* (Santa Monica, Calif.: Rand, 1989), 17, available at http://www.rand.org/content/dam/rand/pubs/papers/2009/P7536.pdf.

munications—initially supported and expedited by the state—was quickly reconfigured, reengineered, and adapted by other large corporations and by much smaller competitors for the consuming public. These efforts gradually reshaped habits, leisure, entertainment, and expectations in the United States and around the globe. At first, it meant a transformation of home life, meaning the possession of indoor plumbing, stoves, refrigerators, washing machines, televisions, and cars—and later on it meant computers and cell phones. The state and the market together encouraged innovation, improved standards of living, and empowered the West to compete successfully with the East.[28]

That competition between the communist and noncommunist worlds was extremely intense during these early decades of the Cold War because it was by no means certain that the West was ahead in stimulating economic growth and boosting standards of living. Soviet officials and their comrades in Eastern Europe took the competition extremely seriously, and—although we tend to forget or ignore it—communist governments did reasonably well during the first decades of the Cold War. Economic growth in the USSR in the 1950s was about 5.2 percent per annum (compared to 3.5 percent in the USA) and 4.8 percent in the 1960s (compared to 4.2 percent in the USA). In Eastern Europe, the growth rate was 5.1 percent in the 1950s and 4.3 percent in the 1960s, compared to 4.9 and 4.8 percent in Western Europe. During these decades, life expectancy in Eastern Europe pretty much caught up with that experienced in the West, and infant mortality rates actually dropped more quickly in the East during these years. Despite housing shortages, there were remarkable improvements in social services and health care. Between 1965 and 1970, household consumption in East Germany increased by nearly 25 percent; the percentage of homes with a refrigerator rose from 6 to 56 percent, and with a television from 16 to 69 percent. "On the basis of their overall performance in the 1960s," writes Charles Maier, "serious-minded economists could still argue that central planning might serve developing countries better as a model than western capitalism."[29]

Soviet Premier Nikita Khrushchev was certain that the Soviet Union constituted such a model. At meetings with his comrades and in speeches to his

28. Reynolds, "Science, Technology, and the Cold War," 378–94; Friedberg, *In the Shadow of the Garrison State*, 334–9; Hobsbawm, *Age of Extremes*, 265 ff.; de Grazia, *Irresistible Empire*, especially 416–46.

29. For the quotation, see Charles Maier, "The Collapse of Communism: Approaches for a Future History," *History Workshop: A Journal of Socialist and Feminist Historians*, 31 (Spring 1991), 40–1; for figures regarding East Germany, see Greg Castillo, *Cold War on the Home Front: The Soft Power of Midcentury Design* (Minneapolis, Minn.: University of Minneapolis Press, 2010), 200. For some additional comparative statistics, see Cooper, "Economic Aspects of the Cold War," 49; Angus Maddison, *The World Economy: A Millennial Perspective* (Paris: Development Centre of the Organisation for Economic Co-operation and Development [OECD], 2001), 30, 349; also see, Mazower, *Dark Continent*, 277–8; Frieden, *Global Capitalism*, 337.

countrymen, he stressed that his overriding priority was to demonstrate the superiority of socialism. Communist countries, he emphasized, would demonstrate that they were superior in constructing "the living standard of the popular masses." By 1970, Khrushchev asserted, the Soviet Union would equal America's gross national production and then surpass it a decade later. Planned economies, he had no doubt, were the wave of the future.[30]

Many observers in the 1950s and 1960s feared that Khrushchev might be right. In a generation, the Soviet Union had emancipated itself from the shackles of capitalists, managed a command economy to accelerate industrialization, developed immense military capabilities, and garnered power and prestige. Its trajectory was hugely appealing to nationalist leaders in the Third World, leaders who yearned to modernize and hungered for status.[31] At a meeting of the U.S. National Security Council in January 1956, Secretary of State John Foster Dulles observed that his colleagues "had very largely failed to appreciate the impact on the underdeveloped areas of the world of the phenomenon of Russia's rapid industrialization. Its transformation from an agrarian to a modern industrialized state was an historical event of absolutely first-class importance."[32]

While both East and West enjoyed remarkable growth rates and improving standards of living in the 1950s and 1960s, and while leaders on both sides of the ideological divide sought to represent their systems as the embodiment of the future of humankind, both systems encountered serious hurdles in the 1970s.[33] In 1974 and 1975, industrial output in the West plummeted by almost 10 percent, and unemployment rates jumped to postwar highs. The Bretton Woods system disintegrated and had to be replaced through a series of improvisations. In July 1975, one year before the 200th anniversary of America's Declaration of Independence, *Time* magazine ran a cover story, "Can Capitalism Survive?"[34]

The story of the West's triumph in the Cold War is the story of the West's slow but gradual adaptation to the new challenges stemming from monetary

30. Melvyn P. Leffler, *For the Soul of Mankind: The United States, the Soviet Union, and the Cold War* (New York: Hill and Wang, 2007), 165–70; Castillo, *Cold War on the Home Front*, 157–70; Francis Spufford, *Red Plenty* (London: Faber and Faber, 2010).

31. In addition to the citations in note 5 above, see, for example, Sergey Mazov, *A Distant Front in the Cold War: The USSR in West Africa and the Congo, 1956–1964* (Washington, D.C.: Woodrow Wilson Center Press and Stanford University Press, 2010), 255.

32. Quoted in Jonathan Haslam, *Russia's Cold War: From the October Revolution to the Fall of the Wall* (New Haven, Conn.: Yale University Press, 2011), 150.

33. For the worldwide competition of systems, see Odd Ame Westad, *The Global Cold War: Third World Interventions and the Making of Our Times* (Cambridge: Cambridge University Press, 2005).

34. "Can Capitalism Survive?" *Time*, 106 ( July 14, 1978), 52–63; Frieden, *Global Capitalism*, 363–73. For growth rates, see the table in Maier, "Collapse of Communism," 48.

disarray, skyrocketing oil prices, declining productivity, wage-price spirals, soaring unemployment, skyrocketing inflation, labor strife, and political turmoil. The familiar narrative is that Western governments responded by jettisoning their Keynesian commitments, raising interest rates, deregulating their economies, privatizing state-owned enterprises, lowering taxes, and embracing more open markets, freer trade, and capital inflows and outflows. In this analysis, Jimmy Carter, Margaret Thatcher, and Ronald Reagan led the way, and Helmut Kohl and François Mitterrand soon followed. In general, we think we know that a neo-liberal turn occurred, rejecting the state and embracing a globalized future.[35]

Again, much of that narrative tells an important part of the story, but it is only a part of the story. What it omits is the continued role of the state in cushioning people from the hardships they faced, sustaining purchasing power, and modulating even more severe fluctuations in the business cycle. In the late 1970s, Zbigniew Brzezinski, President Jimmy Carter's national security adviser, lamented the erosion of European economic vitality and feared the consequences of high unemployment and soaring inflation. Extremist parties on the right and the left, he warned, "have growing public acceptance and legitimacy." He fretted over a future that seemed as portentous as the 1940s.[36] But such a future did not materialize, partly because "governments created millions of jobs and pumped billions of dollars into struggling economies." Noncommunist governments in the West increased spending as a percentage of GDP from 33 to 42 percent. They hired more workers, employing as much as 20–33 percent of the workforce by the early 1980s. They sold off public assets but used the proceeds to subsidize key industries, augment exports, and help preserve safety nets and minimal social provision.[37] In Japan, welfare spending soared in the 1970s. During the last two decades of the Cold War social security expenditures as a percentage of GDP in Japan went from 5.3 percent to 14 percent.[38] In England, Margaret Thatcher talked about reconfig-

35. David Harvey, *A Brief History of Neoliberalism* (Oxford: Oxford University Press, 2005); Daniel Yergin and Joseph Stanislaw, *The Commanding Heights: The Battle between Government and the Marketplace That is Remaking the Modem World* (New York: Simon & Schuster, 1998); Berend, *Economic History of Twentieth Century Europe*, 275–8ff.; Daniel Swarm, *The Retreat of the State: Deregulation and Privatization in the UK and US* (New York: Harvester, 1988); Robert M. Collins, *Transforming America: Politics and Culture during the Reagan Years* (New York: Columbia University Press, 2007), 29–117.

36. Leffler, *For the Soul of Mankind*, 264–5.

37. For quotation, see Frieden, *Global Capitalism*, 368. Also see Sassoon, *Hundred Years of Socialism*, 551; Judt, *Postwar*, 556–9; Berend, *Economic History of Twentieth Century Europe*, 283–4; Christos Pitelis and Thomas Clarke, *The Political Economy of Privatization* (London: Routledge, 1993), 6–8.

38. Gould, *Capitalist Welfare Systems*, 12–13; Anderson, *Welfare Policy and Politics in Japan*, 13, 17, 55, 67–75, 128–30.

uring the relationship of the state and the individual, but welfare spending as a percentage of government expenditures (about 55 percent) and welfare spending as a percentage of GDP (about 23 percent) remained virtually constant. Spending on housing plummeted, but spending on health and education did not decline significantly. The basics of the system remained intact.[39] In France, Mitterrand ceded power from the state to the market and embraced privatization, deregulation, lower public spending, and higher productivity, as well as monetary stability and European integration. His reverse course, however, did not "mean a withdrawal of state activity but a change in the patterns of state intervention." During the 1980s, social expenditures as a percentage of GDP in France actually went from 20.8 percent to 24.9 percent, dipping slightly in the late 1980s. Across the border, in West Germany, social expenditures as a percentage of GDP grew by almost 4.5 percent a year from 1970 to 1982 and contracted only minimally thereafter. In Italy, social expenditures as a percentage of GDP also increased during the 1980s from 18 percent to 20 percent.[40]

Nor did social spending drop much in the United States, and neither did the size of the public sector. Notwithstanding all the rhetoric about a Reagan revolution, total government expenditures in the United States as a percentage of GDP in 1980 were 31.3 percent; in 1990, they were 32.5 percent. Social security and Medicare spending was 5.5 percent of GDP in 1980 and 6.2 percent in 1990.[41] The Department of Health and Human Services received 11.4 percent of government outlays in 1980 and 14.0 percent in 1990.[42] Simultaneously, from the mid-1970s to the mid-1980s, the hidden welfare state in the United States expanded rapidly. Legislators amended the tax code in various ways to achieve social purposes and to help individuals (mostly in the middle class). Without acknowledging what they were doing, lawmakers were, in fact, using the state in creative new ways to expand the social net.[43]

39. Mazower, *Dark Continent*, 332–3; Perry, "United Kingdom," 228–335; Eichengreen, *European Economy since 1945*, 291; Sassoon, *Hundred Years of Socialism*, 532–3.

40. For key statistics, also see OECD, StatExtracts, "Social Expenditure—Aggregated Data" http://stats.oecd.org/Index.aspx?datasetcode=SOCX_AGG (accessed June 7, 2011). Also see Henrik Uterwedde, "Mitterrand's Economic and Social Policy in Perspective," in Mairi Maclean (ed.), *The Mitterrand Years: Legacy and Evaluation* (Houndmills: Macmillan Press, 1998), 133–50; Eichengreen, *European Economy since 1945*, 289–90; Sassoon, *Hundred Years of Socialism*, 556–71. For developments in West Germany, see Alber, "Germany," 98–9; for developments in Italy, see Ferrera, "Italy," 393–6, 460–1.

41. Table 15.5, "Total Government Expenditures by Major Category of Expenditure as Percentages of GDP, 1948–2010," OMB, Historical tables, http://www.whitehouse.gov/omb/budget/Historical.

42. Table 4.2, "Percentage Distribution of Outlays by Agency, 1962–2016," OMB, Historical tables, http://www.whitehouse.gov/omb/budget/Historical.

43. Christopher Howard, *The Hidden Welfare State: Tax Expenditures and Social Policy in*

What all this means is that while deregulation, privatization, and liberalization proceeded to unfetter markets and trade, erode the power of labor unions, and increase levels of income inequality, the role of the state in shaping monetary policy, insuring minimum safety nets, promoting technological innovation, encouraging fuel production, and nurturing consumption and economic growth, did not abate. New Federal Reserve policies were instituted by Paul Volcker. He raised interest rates to astounding levels (almost 20 percent) to thwart inflation and promote a strong dollar.[44] The Housing Act of 1968 and the Emergency Home Finance Act of 1970 created the Federal Home Loan Mortgage Corporation and encouraged the development of mortgage-backed securities.[45] In June 1980, Congress also created the Energy Security Corporation. It encouraged the production of oil shale, alcohol fuels, and geothermal and solar energy.[46] And after protracted study and legislative logrolling, Congress passed the Omnibus Trade and Competitiveness Act of 1988. It institutionalized new forms of private-public collaboration and allocated new powers to the executive branch to negotiate trade agreements and expand commerce. The law called upon the government for new investments in technology, education, and training, investments that were deemed essential to shape a "comprehensive competitiveness or growth strategy."[47]

The strong dollar and the deregulation of financial markets in the United States accelerated world trade in the 1980s and boosted American imports, thereby lifting free world economies everywhere. West European governments, meanwhile, negotiated the "Single European Act of 1987," further buttressing market forces and igniting increases in productivity.[48] As they increased their monetary collaboration, they also increased their collective support for research and development and fashioned a more comprehensive collective social vision. They enlarged their Social Action Program (SAP) and scripted basic guidelines for full employment, better living and working con-

the United States (Princeton, N.J.: Princeton University Press, 1997), 177; Jacob S. Hacker, The Divided Welfare State (New York: Cambridge University Press, 2002), 147–63.

44. Giovanni Arrighi, "The world economy and the Cold War, 1970–1990," in Leffler and Westad, Cambridge History of the Cold War: Endings, volume 3, 23–45.

45. Louis Hyman, "American Debt, Global Capital: The Policy Origins of Securitization," in Niall Ferguson, Charles S. Maier, Erez Manela, and Daniel J. Sargent (eds.), The Shock of the Global: The 1970s in Perspective (Cambridge, Mass.: Harvard University Press, 2010), 133–42.

46. Judith Stein, Pivotal Decade: How the United States Traded Factories for Finance in the Seventies (New Haven, Conn.: Yale University Press, 2010), 218.

47. Kent H. Hughes, Building the Next American Century: The Past and Future of American Economic Competitiveness (Washington, D.C.: Woodrow Wilson Center Press, 2005), 172–204ff.

48. Loukas Tsoukalis, The New European Economy Revisited (Oxford: Oxford University Press, 1997), chapter 5; Eichengreen, The European Economy since 1945, 282–93, 335–56.

ditions, and increased participation of labor and management in the economic and social decisions of the European Community (EC) itself.[49]

In other words, while European governments were integrating their economies as never before and embracing free markets, they reconfirmed their commitment to social provision, safety nets, research, training, education, and higher standards of living. The 1989 Social Charter underscored the EC's commitments to maximum working hours, minimum working age, a right to join unions, gender equality, and assistance to people with disabilities—even though only small amounts were earmarked for these purposes.[50] But throughout the European Union (EU), social protection as a percentage of GDP reached a peak in 1993, amounting to 28.7 percent of GDP.[51]

Through deregulation, liberalization, integration, social welfare, and minimal social provision the West staggered through the 1980s, seeking to reinvent itself by reconciling the state and the market without provoking social revolution. Compensatory social spending by governments helped preserve consumption even as unemployment increased in Europe and inequality began to grow in America. In other words, safety nets, unemployment insurance, and retraining initiatives helped preserve individual opportunity and standards of living, even as liberalized world trade increased competition from low-wage producers in Asia, undercut domestic wage levels in the West, and threw millions of people out of work.[52]

Overall, there were few radical backlashes and only modest social turmoil in the West in the 1980s. Responding in their divergent ways, parliaments

49. For support for research and development, see Berend, *Economic History of Twentieth Century Europe*, 285–6; for a summary of the European Social Fund, see European Commission, *European Social Fund: 50 Years Investing in People* (Luxembourg: Office of Official Publications of the European Commission, 2007), http://ec.europa.eu/employment_social/esf/docs/50th _anniversary_book_en.pdf (accessed June 8, 2011); for background on the social policy of the European Community, also See Michael Shank, "Introductory Article: The Social Policies of the European Communities," in Paul J. G. Kapteyn (ed.), *The Social Policies of the European Communities* (Leyden: Europa Instituut of the University of Leyden, 1977), 4–6; Glenda G. Rosenthal, "Education and Training Policy," in Leon Hurwitz and Christian Lequesne (eds.), *The State of the European Community: Policies, Institutions, and Debates in the Transition Year* (Boulder, Colo.: Lynne Rienner Publications, 1991), 273–83; Pedro Corono-Viron, "Social Protection," in Hurwitz and Lequesne, *State of the European Community*, 229–42; Robin Gaster, "Research and Technology Policy," in Hurwitz and Lequesne, *State of the European Community*, 243–58.

50. John W. Young, "Western Europe and the End of the Cold War," in Leffler and Westad, *Cambridge History of the Cold War: Endings*, volume 3, 302–3.

51. Alexandra Petrasova, "Social Protection in the European Union," Eurostat Statistics in Focus 46/2008, http://epp.eurostat.ec.europa.eu/cache/ITY_OFFPUB/KS-SF-08–046/EN /KS-SF-08–046-EN.PDF (accessed June 7, 2011).

52. Charles S. Maier, "'Malaise': The Crisis of Capitalism in the 1970s," in Ferguson et al., *Shock of the Global*, 44–8; Collins, *Transforming America*, 100–15; also see Eichengreen, *European Economy since 1945*, 252–93; and Frieden, *Global Capitalism*, 356–434.

illuminated the capacity of democratic polities not only to muddle through but also to experiment, innovate, improvise, and recalibrate the proper balance between the market and the state. Notwithstanding the tougher economic circumstances in Western Europe, communism lost the appeal it once had; Eurocommunism floundered in France and Italy; and Spain, Portugal, and Greece rid themselves of their neo-fascist pasts and opted for social democracy and market economies. In fact, European workers increasingly embraced lifestyles that emulated and then began to surpass their American counterparts. They jettisoned their self-identity in terms of their relationship to the means of production and embraced a new sense of self based on their status as consumers. Easy access to credit empowered them even in hard times. Women, teenagers, and men were tantalized by household gadgets that eased their lives, by images of glamour and sexuality that whet their deepest appetites, and by symbols of power and wealth that eroded class distinctions. "By the 1980s Europe's old left," comments Victoria de Grazia, "did not have a consumer leg to stand on."[53]

Images of abundance were conveyed across Europe to the East and to the Soviet Union. Through museum exhibitions and radio broadcasting, U.S. (and other Western) officials tried to illuminate the false promises of communism and convey the superiority of democratic polities where diverse peoples could speak freely, express their individual creativity, vote for whom they wanted, and feel secure in their ownership of private property. For U.S. leaders in particular, a key component of their system's strength was its capacity to deliver a superior standard of living, the universally accepted benchmark of a successful system of political economy.[54] U.S. propagandists and broadcasters, therefore, touted the superiority of what they called "people's capitalism." They appropriated communist discourse and highlighted "how the American economy allowed individuals to flourish as citizens and consumers." Capitalism, they insisted, did not exploit workers as producers; it empowered them as consumers. Capitalism bred dignity among workers, dignity that was exemplified through personal buying power, household appliances, cosmetics, leisure, travel, and entertainment.[55]

53. De Grazia, *Irresistible Empire*, 416–73, quotation on 465; Olivier Zunz, "Introduction," in Olivier Zunz, Leonard Schoppa, and Nobuhiro Hiwatari (eds.), *Social Contracts Under Stress: The Middle Classes of America, Europe, and Japan at the Turn of the Century* (New York: Russell Sage Foundation, 2002), 2–3; Sassoon, *Hundred Years of Socialism*, 193; also see Emily Rosenberg, "Consumer Capitalism and the End of the Cold War," in Leffler and Westad, *Cambridge History of the Cold War: Endings*, volume 3, 489–512; Cohen, *Consumers' Republic*.

54. David C. Engerman notes how measurements of GNP and standards of living became the "key yardstick of the Cold War—and the twentieth century." Engerman, "American Knowledge and Global Power," *Diplomatic History*, 31 (September 2007), 615–16.

55. Laura Belmonte, *Selling the American Way: US Propaganda and the Cold War* (Philadelphia, Pa.: University of Pennsylvania Press, 2008), especially 95–135, quotation on 134; also see

After 1975, these messages from the West increasingly resonated in the East. During the first decades of the Cold War, growth rates in the USSR compared favorably to those in the United States (starting, of course, from a much lower base), those in Eastern Europe compared nicely to those in Western Europe, and those in East Germany to those in West Germany. But economic growth rates in communist Europe fell in the 1970s and 1980s. As a percentage of Western European per capita GDP, Eastern Europe declined from 49 percent in 1973 to 37 percent in 1989. Infant mortality rates and life expectancy statistics in Eastern Europe also suffered in comparison to what was happening in the West.[56]

Basically, communist regimes were unable to make the adjustments to new economic circumstances that their counterparts in the West were making, however jarringly. After 1968, Eastern Europe retreated from economic reform, failed to adjust to the oil shocks of the 1970s, and became increasingly dependent on loans from the West. Communist leaders in Eastern Europe could not institute a functioning price system that provided incentives to innovate, could not boost productivity, and could not satisfy consumer demand at home or compete successfully in international markets. Meanwhile, more travel, increased tourism, better communication, and the influx of films and television programs into the East highlighted the discrepancies to more and more people. The state without the market just did not work. Consumer goods, acknowledged the Ministry of State Security in East Germany in 1989, had become "the basic criterion for the assessment of the attractiveness of socialism in comparison to capitalism."[57]

Nowhere was this more true than in the Soviet Union. Soviet leaders from Khrushchev to Gorbachev never stopped believing and saying that the goal of communism or advanced socialism was to improve the living conditions of

Castillo, *Cold War on the Home Front*, 115–30; A. Ross Johnson and R. Eugene Parta, *Cold War Broadcasting: Impact on the Soviet Union and Eastern Europe* (Budapest: Central European University Press, 2010); Tomas Tolvaisas, "Cold War 'Bridge Building': US Exchange Exhibits and Their Reception in the Soviet Union, 1959–1967," *Journal of Cold War Studies*, 12 (Fall 2010), 3–31.

56. For GDP statistics, see the table in Cooper, "Economic Aspects of the Cold War," 49; for per capita GDP statistics, see Ivan T. Berend, *From the Soviet Bloc to the European Union: The Economic and Social Transformation of Central and Eastern Europe since 1973* (Cambridge: Cambridge University Press, 2009), 34–5; for infant mortality rates, see B. R. Mitchell, *International Historical Statistics: Europe 1750–1993*, 4th edition (London: Macmillan Reference, 1998), 125–6; for life expectancy rates, see United Nations: Demographic Yearbook, Historical Supplement, Table 9a, "Expectations of Life at Specified Ages for Each Sex, 1948–1997," http://unstats.un.org/unsd/demographic/products/dyb/dybhist.htm.

57. For quotation, see Castillo, *Cold War on the Home Front*, 201; Berend, *From the Soviet Bloc to the European Union*, 6–38; Eichengreen, *European Economy since 1945*, 142–6, 296–303; Stephen Kotkin, "The Kiss of Debt," in Ferguson et al., *Shock of the Global*, 80–93; Maier, "Collapse of Communism," 34–59; Loth, "Cold War and the Social and Economic History of the Twentieth Century," 502–23; Reynolds, "Science, Technology, and the Cold War," 378–99.

individuals and families. In November 1961, the party declared that improvements in social welfare—health, education, housing, nutrition, childcare, old age pensions—were the overriding goals of the regime. Soviet leaders promised their people full employment, higher and more equal wages, and improving standards of living. But they were unable to fulfill expectations. After the Kremlin crushed the reform movement in Czechoslovakia in 1968, Soviet economists who had been pondering ways to reconcile planning with the market were squelched. And when Gorbachev tried to revitalize their thinking and catalyze reforms in the command economy, he made things much worse. Per capita spending on social services actually began declining in the 1970s and, after 1981, fell absolutely for overall consumption, health, and education.[58]

Peoples in Eastern Europe and the USSR grew demoralized. So did their elites. Not only were they failing to catch up to the United States and Western Europe, but equally distressing was their growing knowledge that they were now trailing the modernizing economies of East and Southeast Asia. "From its inception," writes Stephen Kotkin, "the Soviet Union had claimed to be an experiment in socialism, a superior alternative to capitalism, for the entire world. If socialism was not superior to capitalism, its existence could not be justified." Not only was it not superior, it was now indisputably being crushed.[59]

But it was not being crushed simply by the superiority of a free market system. It was crushed by reformed forms of capitalism, by social democracy, and by social market economies in which governments played critically important roles in providing safety nets, insuring minimal social provision, spurring research and innovation, and dispensing compensatory income in hard times. Communism, in other words, was defeated by people in democratic polities who expected their governments to structure, support, regulate, liberalize, and ameliorate market forces. This required judgment, fine-tuning, and continual recalibrations of the role of the state and the role of the market. Different governments in the West proceeded in many different ways. But they all recognized that states and markets were co-dependent. Governments recognized that states and markets had to work collaboratively to improve

---

58. Linda J. Cook, *The Soviet Social Contract and Why it Failed: Welfare Policy and Workers' Politics from Brezhnev to Yeltsin* (Cambridge, Mass.: Harvard University Press, 1993), especially 1–8, 50–2; for living standards as the Soviet benchmark, see Stephen Kotkin, *Steeltown, USSR: Soviet Society in the Gorbachev Era* (Berkeley, Calif.: University of California Press, 1991), 260; for illuminating insights into living standards and expectations, see Alex Berelowitch, "The 1970s: Reply to a Discussion," *Russian Politics and Law*, 42 (May–June 2004), especially 25–32.

59. For the quotation, see Stephen Kotkin, *Armageddon Averted: The Soviet Collapse, 1970–2000* (New York: Oxford University Press, 2001), 19; also see Kotkin, *Steeltown*, 142; Kotkin, "Kiss of Debt," 86–9.

living conditions, to preserve the peace, and to insure that depression, war, and impoverishment would not be the lot of humankind, as had been the case during the first half of the twentieth century. Taking office at a harrowing time in the Cold War and in a dismal economic climate, Ronald Reagan declared that governments were not the solution; they were the problem. But any fair-minded assessment of Western policies during the Cold War would affirm that the "state" was an indispensable part of the solution, an indispensable key to victory in the Cold War.

Thinking that free markets alone won the Cold War is fraught with ominous consequences. Since the Soviet Union collapsed, and since communism as a serious competitor to capitalism has withered, some commentators, think tanks, political leaders, and government officials have proceeded ever more vigorously to attack entitlements and safety nets, dismantle or weaken regulatory agencies, deride the value of the state, and erode its powers to collect revenue. Some initiatives of this sort no doubt contributed to the revitalization of the West in the 1980s. And, surely, generous welfare benefits and safety nets in a globalized economy bloated the budgets of Western governments, saddled them with onerous debt burdens, increased costs of production, and weakened the capacity of their entrepreneurs to compete in international markets. But injudicious extrapolations over the last 15–20 years have been ominously consequential—contributing to the economic and social debacle in post-Soviet Russia in the early 1990s and accelerating the disarray and strife in Iraq after the toppling of Saddam Hussein's tyranny in 2003–7, as well as leading to the financial meltdown and housing debacle of 2008–10 in the United States and parts of the EU.[60]

Extrapolating the wrong lessons from the history of the Cold War is more than bad history; extrapolating the wrong lessons is diminishing the capacity of the West to act internationally and to prosper domestically. When Bill Clinton famously stated, "It's the economy, stupid," he might have added that it is

60. For application of free market ideology to post-Soviet Russia, see, for example, Peter Reddaway and Dmitri Glinksy, *The Tragedy of Russia's Reforms: Market Bolshevism against Democracy* (Washington, D.C.: U.S. Institute of Peace Press, 2001); Stefan Hedlund, *Russia's Market Economy: A Bad Case of Predatory Capitalism* (London: University College of London Press, 1999); Stephen F. Cohen, *Failed Crusade: America and the Tragedy of Post-Communist Russia* (New York: Norton, 2000). For Iraq, see David D. Phillips, *Losing Iraq: Inside the Postwar Reconstruction Fiasco* (New York: Westview Press, 2005), 147; Rajiv Chandrasekaran, *Imperial Life in the Emerald City: Inside Iraq's Green Zone* (New York: Knopf, 2005); Thomas E. Ricks, *Fiasco: The American Military Adventure in Iraq* (New York: Penguin, 2006), 165, 171. For deregulation, free market thinking, and the financial meltdown in the United States, see Financial Crisis Inquiry Commission, *The Financial Crisis: Inquiry Report* (New York: Public Affairs, 2011), xv–xviii; Joseph E. Stiglitz, *Freefall: America, Free Markets, and the Sinking of the Global Economy* (New York: Norton, 2010); Richard A. Posner, *A Failure of Capitalism: The Crisis of '08 and the Descent into Depression* (Cambridge, Mass.: Harvard University Press, 2009).

the state and the market, neither alone, that nurture a thriving economy. Getting the right balance between the state and the market, forgetting neither, is what is indispensable for meeting people's yearnings for a decent standard of living and for sustaining effective foreign policies abroad. Creating that balance, recalibrating it, and sustaining it were among the great accomplishments of the West during the Cold War, the success of which could not have been predicted in 1945, and one that we forget at our peril today.

# 8

# Dreams of Freedom, Temptations of Power

As the twentieth anniversary of the fall of the Berlin Wall approached in 2009, the historian Jeffrey Engel asked me to contribute an essay to a volume he was editing on how leaders in major strategic centers around the globe—Western Europe, Russia, China, and the United States—understood the dramatic end of the Cold War. I was then in transition from completing my book on agency, structure, and contingency in the long Cold War and returning to work on the meaning and implications of the attacks on 9/11. I embraced the opportunity to examine the policies of the 1990s, of the twelve-year interlude between 11/9/1989 and 9/11/2001.

I was impressed by the different lessons learned. I was struck by how experience, circumstance, values, and memory shaped the divergent understandings of the fall of the Berlin Wall in different capitals around the world. In the United States, however, Republican and Democratic administrations alike imbibed the same lessons: the United States won the Cold War because of its superior values, its power, its allies, and its determination. Therefore, the United States had to remain involved in the world, preserve its military hegemony (albeit at lower levels of spending), and steadfastly promote democracy and free markets. Notwithstanding the absence of any real threat, Washington officials reminded themselves and their countrymen that the American

I am indebted to Seth Center, Andrew Ferguson, and James Wilson for their research assistance, most especially to Seth for his thoughtful advice and illuminating suggestions. This chapter also benefited greatly from dialogue with Jim Sheehan, Chen Jian, William Taubman, Svetlana Savranskaya, Frank Gavin, Jeffrey Engel, and Susan Ferber as well as from a colloquium with my colleagues and graduate students at the Miller Center of the University of Virginia.

people must not be complacent. They must reject isolationism, remain vigilant, and recognize that grave peril inhered in uncertainty itself.

Yet U.S. policymakers wrestled with how and when to use America's superior military power. When Saddam Hussein invaded Kuwait in 1990, President George H. W. Bush and his advisers decided to resist wanton aggression and reinforce the rule of law. They assembled a great coalition of allies committed to the principle of respecting the territorial integrity and national sovereignty of independent states. But after driving Iraqi troops out of Kuwait, they and their Democratic successors faced more difficult decisions.

U.S. policymakers anguished over the employment of military power as Yugoslavia disintegrated, famine and civil war engulfed Somalia, and Haiti imploded. They wanted to nurture an international environment conducive to American values and American interests, but they did not want to become the world's policeman; nor did they want to use American military force for humanitarian purposes or for the promotion of human rights. Although they preached the benefits of enhancing and enlarging the democratic peace, they wrestled thoughtfully with figuring out the utility of force when U.S. security was not threatened and its values appeared triumphant.

The attack on 9/11 shattered any penchant for restraint. Fear trumped prudence. U.S. territory had been violated, American lives lost, and its values assailed. Now the United States could unleash its immense power to destroy terrorists and their state sponsors. Success was assured, thought President George W. Bush, because peoples everywhere yearned for freedom. "The toppling of Saddam Hussein's statue in Baghdad," he exclaimed, "will be recorded alongside the fall of the Berlin Wall as one of the great moments in the history of liberty." (Bush's speech at Fort Hood, April 12, 2005, http://www.presidency.ucsb.edu/ws/index.php?pid=62995&st=&st1=Engel, 159.) For the president and his advisers, memories of the Cold War resonated deeply.

While studying the Cold War, I had learned how memory and values as well as fear and power shaped the behavior of human agents. Throughout that struggle, the divergent lessons of World War II pulsated through policymaking circles in Moscow and Washington. Now, in the aftermath of 9/11, governments around the world drew upon the lessons they had learned from their divergent national experiences as those experiences had become embedded in their respective national memories. For policymakers in Washington, memories of the Cold War and dreams of human freedom tempted the use of excessive power with tragic consequences. Memory, culture, and values played a key role in shaping the evolution of U.S. national security policy.

This essay appeared in Jeffrey A. Engel, ed., *The Fall of the Berlin Wall: The Revolutionary Legacy of 1989* (New York: Oxford University Press, 2009), 132–169.

———

Many of us live with indelible images of the Cold War: mushroom clouds over Hiroshima and Nagasaki, symbolizing the end of a hot war and the beginning of another cold one; airplanes circling over Berlin in the summer of 1948, dropping supplies to the beleaguered people of that city; a barbed-wire fence appearing along the fault lines of that city in August 1961; Soviet ships dropping anchor and then turning around as they approached the blockade line during the harrowing days of the Cuban missile crisis in October 1962; helicopters taking off from the roof of a Saigon apartment in April 1975, packed with fleeing Vietnamese; American flags ablaze in the street of Tehran during the demonstrations that eventually overthrew the shah; Ronald Reagan standing before the Brandenburg Gate in Berlin in June 1987 calling upon Soviet leaders to "tear down this wall"; a lone student standing before tanks in Tiananmen Square, defying the power of the Chinese communist regime; and, remarkably, throngs of East Germans traversing the Berlin Wall and dancing on its ramparts during the thrilling days of November 9–10, 1989.

For Americans, these images invoke the trajectory of the Cold War: power, determination, crisis, defeat, humiliation, resurgence, and, finally, triumph. And Berlin, as evidenced by the frequency of its appearance in the landmark events of the Cold War, remains at the center of the story. It symbolized, in turn, resolve, tension, crisis, courage, resilience, and victory. For Americans, it meant the conquest of freedom over tyranny, the liberation of a people, the redemptive role of the United States of America. It confirmed the utility of power, the correctness of containment, the universal appeal of freedom, the triumph of good over evil. It foreshadowed the temptation to use power anew, when great threat appeared, in order to defeat a new devil and to fulfill God's intention for all men to be free.

People elsewhere interpreted the toppling of the Berlin Wall very differently. For many people in Western Europe, the meaning of the events of 1989–90 confirmed the rectitude of the trajectory they had taken since 1945: the embrace of integration, the salience of multilateral institutions, the political primacy of economic issues, and the rejection of force as the arbiter of differences among European states.[1] For leaders in Beijing, the crumbling of the wall and the turmoil in Eastern Europe meant that they had to reactivate the economic reform agenda they had previously embarked upon and deflect the

1. See James J. Sheehan, "The Transformation of Europe and the End of the Cold War," in Jeffrey A. Engel, ed., *The Fall of the Berlin Wall: The Revolutionary Legacy of 1989* (New York: Oxford University Press, 2009), 36-68; also see, for example, Frederic Bozo, "France, German Unification and European Integration," in *Europe and the End of the Cold War: A Reappraisal*, edited by Frederic Bozo et al. (London: Routledge, 2008), 148-61.

impulses for political change that had been the undoing of communist oligarchs in Eastern Europe.[2] For many Russians, the demise of the wall, the unification of Germany inside the North Atlantic Treaty Organization (NATO), and the dissolution of the Warsaw Pact demonstrated the consequences of what they regarded as naive and pusillanimous leadership.[3]

But when the wall came down, for many Americans, it did more than confirm their sense of righteous mission. Vindicating their Cold War policies, it intensified their determination to shape the evolving international system in ways that would comport with U.S. values and interests. Presidents George H. W. Bush and Bill Clinton began speaking of a "democratic peace"—a new world order dominated by democratic nations, whose norms and values encouraged the free flow of goods and capital and militated against the use of force to settle disputes among one another. But they also knew that nurturing democratic institutions and building peaceful norms would be a long and arduous process. In the interim, they tried to capitalize upon the opportunities afforded by the crumbling of the Berlin Wall. They wanted to solidify the preeminent position of the United States in the global arena, encourage orderly and liberal reform, and design a new military strategy to meet the challenges of the post–Cold War era. Yet they remained wary about employing force for humanitarian purposes or for regime change. Like Woodrow Wilson, they understood that there is a difference between making the world safe for democracy and making the entire world democratic.[4]

The self-imposed constraints disappeared after the sudden and cruel attack on the United States by al Qaeda terrorists on September 11, 2001. For President George W. Bush and his advisers, the end of the Cold War and the toppling of the Berlin Wall had conveyed dramatic lessons. Invoking memories of the recent past and inspired by recollections of Cold War triumphs, Bush proclaimed that hereafter November 9—the day the wall was breached— would be "World Freedom Day." "Like the fall of the Berlin Wall and the defeat of totalitarianism in Central and Eastern Europe," Bush said, "freedom will triumph in this war against terrorism."[5] Seventeen months later, in April 2003, when American troops marched into Baghdad and when jubilant Iraqis

2. See Chen Jian, "Tiananmen and the Fall of the Berlin Wall: China's Path toward 1989 and Beyond," in Engel, *The Fall of the Berlin Wall*, 96–131.

3. See, for example, the account of Gorbachev in Vladislav M. Zubok, *A Failed Empire: The Soviet Union in the Cold War from Stalin to Gorbachev* (Chapel Hill, N.C.: University of North Carolina Press, 2007), 303–35.

4. For this distinction, see the incisive analysis by David Kennedy, "Two Concepts of Sovereignty," in *To Lead the World: American Strategy After the Bush Doctrine*, edited by Melvyn P. Leffler and Jeffrey W. Legro (New York: Oxford University Press, 2008), 165–74.

5. George W. Bush, "Proclamation 7499—World Freedom Day, 2001," November 9, 2001, http://www.presidency.ucsb.edu/ws/index.php?pid=61796 (accessed May 16, 2009).

pulled down the statue of Saddam Hussein and slammed their shoes against the deposed dictator's stone face, U.S. Secretary of Defense Donald Rumsfeld exclaimed, "Watching them . . . one cannot help but think of the fall of the Berlin Wall and the collapse of the Iron Curtain."[6]

This chapter will show how the discourse about the events of 1989 and the dismantling of the Berlin Wall assumed distinctive meanings and shaped distinctive policies in the United States. U.S. officials harnessed the past to mold the collective memory of Americans and used the rhetorical trope of freedom to mobilize support for their policies.[7] America's new foes, policymakers explained, were totalitarians akin to past adversaries. They, too, would be defeated, however protracted the conflict might be. Many people had once thought the Berlin Wall would last forever, but it was no more. Freedom would triumph over nihilism, much as it had vanquished fascism and communism because freedom—in George W. Bush's words—was "the design of our Maker, and the longing of every soul."[8] However, Americans would also learn, rather sorrowfully, that their peculiar mix of military power and ideological zealotry could have portentous consequences, facts well understood by George H. W. Bush and by Bill Clinton in the turbulent and unpredictable circumstances that initially followed the toppling of the Berlin Wall.

## The Berlin Wall and the End of the Cold War

No modern American president was more ideological than Ronald Reagan. He condemned communists for their beliefs in "treachery, deceit, destruction, & bloodshed."[9] They "are the focus of evil in the modern world," he declared in one of his most famous speeches as president.[10] The regime that these communists had built in the Soviet Union was powerful militarily but

6. "DOD [Department of Defense] News Briefing–Secretary Rumsfeld and Gen. Myers," April 9, 2003, http://www.defenselink.mil/transcripts/trariscript.aspx?transcriptid=2339 (accessed May 17, 2009).

7. For the use of "keywords" in American history, see Daniel T. Rodgers, *Contested Truths: Keywords in American History* (New York: Basic Books, 1987), esp. 3–16, 212–17.

8. Bush, "Remarks to the Democracy and Security Conference in Prague," June 5, 2007, http://www.presidency.ucsb.edu/ws/index.php?pid=75306&st=&sti= (accessed May 17, 2009); Bush, "Speech to the OECD [Organisation for Economic Co-operation and Development]," June 13, 2008, http://www.oecd.org/document/50/0,3343,en_2649_201185_40835506_1_1_1_1,00 .html (accessed May 16, 2009).

9. Kiron K. Skinner, Annelise Anderson, and Martin Anderson, eds., *Reagan in His Own Hand* (New York: Simon and Schuster, 2001), 15.

10. Ronald Reagan, "Remarks at the Annual Convention of the National Association of Evangelicals [March 8, 1983]," in *Public Papers of the Presidents: Ronald Reagan* (Washington, D.C.: Government Printing Office, 1984), 743 [hereafter, citations of the Reagan volumes of *Public Papers of the Presidents* are abbreviated *RR* (year), page].

economically incapacitated and spiritually impoverished. It would founder, he said, because it ran "against the tide of history by denying freedom and human dignity to its citizens."[11] In contrast, America would be forever young, renewing itself and remaining a beacon for all humankind. America, he said, was not just a country; it was an idea—"the love of freedom."[12] We Americans were "one people under God, dedicated to the dream of freedom that He has placed in the human heart, called upon now to pass that dream on to a waiting and hopeful world."[13]

In 1987, Reagan traveled to Berlin to commemorate the city's 750th anniversary. One of his speech writers, Peter Robinson, had gone to the city in advance, chatted with Berliners, and concluded that they longed to rid themselves of the wall that divided them. He drafted a speech for the president in which he would challenge Mikhail Gorbachev, the chairman of the Communist Party of the Soviet Union, to tear down the wall. Neither the State Department nor the National Security Council wanted Reagan to make such a pitch; he might antagonize or provoke the Soviet leader, who was seemingly embarked on promising reforms at home and calling for more openness and restructuring inside his country.[14] But Reagan wanted to speak of freedom. On June 12, 1987, with the chancellor of West Germany and the mayor of West Berlin at his side, he remarked, "Behind me stands a wall that encircles the free sectors of this city, part of a vast system of barriers that divides the entire continent of Europe." He went on, "As long as this scar of a wall is permitted to stand, it is not the German question alone that remains open, but the question of freedom for all mankind." And then, five paragraphs later, came the challenge: "General Secretary Gorbachev, if you seek peace, if you seek prosperity for the Soviet Union and Eastern Europe, if you seek liberalization: Come here to this gate! Mr. Gorbachev, open this gate! Mr. Gorbachev, tear down this wall!"[15]

Gorbachev was not impressed.[16] Nor was the Western media at the time. Despite the iconic place this speech has taken in our memory of the Cold War

11. Reagan, "Address to Members of British Parliament [June 8, 1982]," *RR* (1982), 745.

12. Quoted in Paul Kengor, *God and Ronald Reagan* (New York: HarperCollins, 2004), 94–96.

13. Reagan, "Second Inaugural Address [January 21, 1985]," *RR* (1985), 58; also see Hugh Heclo, "Ronald Reagan and American Public Philosophy," in *The Reagan Presidency: Pragmatic Conservatism and Its Legacies,* edited by W. Elliot Brownlee and Hugh Davis Graham (Lawrence, Kan.: University Press of Kansas, 2003), 17–39.

14. Peter Robinson, "Tear Down This Wall," *Reader's Digest,* http://www.rd.com/content/printContent.do?contentId=28515&KeepThis=true&TB_iframe=true&height=500&width=790&modal=true (accessed May 16, 2009).

15. Reagan, "Remarks on East-West Relations at the Brandenburg Gate [June 12, 1987]," *RR* (1987), 635.

16. Anatoly S. Chernyaev Diary, June 15, 1987, translated by Anna Melyakova and Svetlana

and despite the fact that it received attention on the nightly television news shows, press coverage in newspapers and magazines was rather muted and, to some extent, overshadowed by the president's lackluster performance at an economic summit meeting the week before in Venice. None of the major newsweeklies—*Time*, *Newsweek*, and *U.S. News and World Report*—focused much attention on the speech; to the extent that they covered it, they did not think that the American president was tarnishing the growing luster of the young Soviet leader in the East-West propaganda wars. *The Wall Street Journal* contained an opinion piece by Philip Revzin on June 17 arguing that Gorbachev was "outplaying the West." *The New York Times* put Reagan's speech on page 3 and made passing mention of it in an editorial calling for more reform inside the Soviet Union. *The Washington Post* did highlight it on page 1 but did not offer any editorial comment. Reagan's popularity did go up measurably in the week after the speech, perhaps because of the television coverage, but the speech itself lacked staying power, because German unification was simply not on anyone's policy agenda in June 1987.[17]

Yet two and a half years later, the wall did come down. No one in the United States anticipated this development at the time, notwithstanding the signing of a treaty outlawing intermediate-range nuclear missiles in December 1987, notwithstanding Reagan's immensely successful trip to Moscow in late May 1988, notwithstanding the dramatic parliamentary changes taking place in Poland and Hungary during the summer of 1989, and notwithstanding the tumultuous demonstrations occurring on the streets of Leipzig and other East German cities in the early autumn. The ruling Communist Party (SED) in East Germany did not intend to open the gates; confusion was rampant; the regime's public spokesperson, Günter Schabowski, did not grasp the import of his statements when he answered queries at a press conference and stated that people did not have to leave the German Democratic Republic through other countries (as they had been doing, in record numbers). Yes, he said, they could "go through the border." Yes, they had freedom

Savranskaya. Manuscript on file at the National Security Archive, George Washington University, Washington, D.C., http://www.gwu.edu/~nsarchiv/NSAEBB/NSAEBB220/index.htm.

17. George J. Church, "Back to the Wall: Reagan Rallies with a Strong Speech," *Time*, June 22, 1987, 18; Russell Watson et al., "Waiting for Gorbachev," *Newsweek*, June 22, 1987, 18; William L. Chaze, "Once Again, the President's Age is at Issue," *U.S. News & World Report*, June 22, 1987, 20; Gerald M. Boyd, "Raze Berlin Wall, Reagan Urges Soviet," *The New York Times*, June 13, 1987, 3; Helen Thomas, "Reagan to Call for Berlin Wall's End," *The Washington Post*, June 12, 1987, A1; Lou Cannon, "Reagan Challenges Soviets to Dismantle Berlin Wall, *The Washington Post*, June 12, 1987, A1; and Philip Revzin, "Gorbachev Plays All the Right Cards against Allies," June 17, 1987, *Wall Street Journal*, 22. I am indebted to two research assistants, Andrew Ferguson and James G. Wilson, for their research in newspapers and newsweeklies. Also see Philip Zelikow and Condoleezza Rice, *Germany Unified and Europe Transformed: A Study in Statecraft* (Cambridge, Mass.: Harvard University Press, 1997), 20.

to travel. Television newscasters quickly reported that the borders had been opened. They created the reality as crowds gathered in front of several key crossings, and the guards, facing chaos and not having instructions, opened the gates. East Germans started flocking across the wall and then pulled parts of it down.[18]

Standing in front of the gate, the NBC anchorman Tom Brokaw conveyed the news to Americans: "This is a historic night. . . . The East German Government has just declared that East German citizens will be able to cross the wall . . . without restrictions."[19] The news media in the United States reacted jubilantly. *Newsweek* declared that all "vestiges of the totalitarian past seemed gone." On November 12, *The New York Times* editorialized, "Crowds of young Germans danced on top of the hated Berlin wall Thursday night. They danced for joy, they danced for history. They danced because the tragic cycle of catastrophes that first convulsed Europe 75 years ago, embracing two world wars, a holocaust and cold war, seems at long last to be nearing an end."[20]

The president of the United States did not dance with joy. George H. W. Bush said he "welcomed" the decision of East German leaders to open the borders. When reporters noted that he did not seem elated, he said he was "not an emotional kind of guy." He was pleased, but wanted to remain prudent.[21] When West German Chancellor Helmut Kohl called him to summarize the dramatic events taking place, Bush said that he wanted "to avoid hot rhetoric that by mistake might cause a problem."[22] Although Bush was chastised by his domestic foes for his restraint, he deemed such criticism to be ridiculous. "Some have wanted me to go jump up on top of the Berlin Wall," he told foreign journalists. "Well, I never heard such a stupid idea. I mean what good would it do for an American president to be posturing while Germans were

18. Hans-Hermann Hertle, "The Fall of the Wall: The Unintended Self-Dissolution of East Germany's Ruling Regime," [Cold Wax International History Project] *Bulletin* 12/13 (Fall/Winter 2001): 134–37.

19. Ibid., 137.

20. Michael Meyer et al., "The Wall Comes Down: Is It Possible?" *Newsweek*, November 20, 1989, 24; "The End of the War to End Wars," *The New York Times*, November 11, 1989, 26; also see, for example, George J. Church, "Freedom! The Wall Crumbles Overnight, Berliners Embrace in Disbelieving Joy, and a Stunned World Ponders the Consequences," *Time*, November 20, 1989, 24ff.

21. "Remarks and a Question-and-Answer Session with Reporters [November 9, 1989]," *Public Papers of the Presidents: George Herbert Walker Bush* (Washington, D.C.: Government Printing Office, 1989), 1488–90 [hereafter, citations of the Bush volumes of *Public Papers of the Presidents* are abbreviated *GHWB* (year), page].

22. Memorandum of Telephone Conversation, November 10, 1989, box 3, End of Cold War Collection, National Security Archive, Washington D.C. Manuscript on file at the National Security Archive, George Washington University, Washington, D.C., http://www.gwu.edu/~nsarchiv/NSAEBB/NSAEBB220/index.htm.

flowing back and forth by the millions? It makes no sense at all. We are conducting ourselves in a prudent way."[23]

Prudence, of course, had been the watchword of Bush and his advisers since they had entered office in January 1989. Rather than quickly building upon the warm relations that Reagan and Gorbachev had cultivated with one another, the new president had decided to "pause" and reevaluate the significance of the changes taking place in the Soviet Union. In his inaugural address, Bush noted that the totalitarian era might be passing, but caution was imperative. Three weeks after taking office, he told Congress, "The fundamental facts remain that the Soviets retain a very powerful military machine in the service of objectives which are still too often in conflict with ours. So, let us take the new openness seriously, but let's also be realistic. And let's also be strong."[24]

The president and his key assistants—National Security Adviser General Brent Scowcroft, Secretary of State James A. Baker, Secretary of Defense Dick Cheney, Chairman of the Joint Chiefs of Staff General Colin Powell, and Deputy National Security Adviser Robert Gates—did not trust Gorbachev. "I was suspicious of Gorbachev's motives and skeptical of his prospects," recalled Scowcroft. He continued, "I believed that Gorbachev's goal was to restore dynamism to a socialist political and economic system and revitalize the Soviet Union domestically and internationally to compete with the West."[25] Cheney agreed: "We must guard against gambling our nation's security on what may be a temporary aberration in the behavior of our foremost adversary."[26] Thoroughgoing change in the Soviet Union was not likely to take place, thought Gates.[27] Consummate pragmatists who believed in the art of realpolitik, the men who gathered around George H. W. Bush believed it was too soon to say the Cold War was over.

In May 1989, however, they announced that they wanted to go "beyond containment." They wanted to achieve a Europe "whole and free." They wanted to challenge Gorbachev with new initiatives in order to ascertain if he was sincere about being a reformer. If he was, they hoped to integrate the Soviet Union into an American-led world order, structured along liberal and capitalist lines. They hoped to push Soviet armies out of Eastern Europe or, at least, dilute the power of the Warsaw Pact in the middle of Europe. The

23. Bush, "Interview with Foreign Journalists [November 21, 1989]," *GHWB* (1989), 1588.

24. "Inaugural Address [January 20, 1989]," *GHWB* (1989), 1; "Address Before a Joint Session of Congress [February 9, 1989]," *GHWB* (1989), 79.

25. George Bush and Brent Scowcroft, *A World Transformed* (New York: Vintage Books, 1998), 13.

26. "Remarks at the Swearing-in Ceremony [March 21, 1989]," *GHWB* (1989), 277.

27. Robert M. Gates, *From the Shadows: The Ultimate Insider's Story of Five Presidents and How They Won the Cold War* (New York: Touchstone, 1997), 474.

initial goal, said Scowcroft, was "to lift the Kremlin's military boot from the necks of the East Europeans."[28]

Bush and his advisers were amazed when, during the late spring and summer of 1989, Gorbachev allowed the communists to be ousted from power in Warsaw and to be challenged in Budapest. They were equally astonished by Gorbachev's willingness to make disproportionately large troop cuts in Europe.[29] When hundreds of thousands of East German citizens marched down the streets of their major cities calling for openness and political change, when the longstanding ruler of the nation—Erich Honecker—was removed from office, and when his successors allowed the wall to be breached, however unintentionally, U.S. officials could hardly believe their good fortune. "With the fall of the Wall, suddenly anything was possible," thought Scowcroft.[30]

Nonetheless, Bush did not want to overreach. He was mightily affected by the turmoil in China and by the Chinese crackdown on dissidents in Tiananmen Square in June 1989. He vividly recalled the dashed hopes of reformers in Hungary in 1956 and Czechs in 1968. When Bush visited Poland and Hungary in July 1989, he heralded the democratic reforms taking place, but in measured words. He did not want to encourage violence. He did not want to "poke a stick in the eye of Mr. Gorbachev." The United States, he stressed, should "not over-promise, ought not to overexhort for others to be like us." He was extremely conscious, recalled Gates, that "if violence was avoided, reform would inexorably proceed."[31]

Four months later, as Berliners flocked across the border during the middle of November without signs of a Soviet crackdown, Bush was even more careful. He was delighted by the trajectory of events, but he did not want Gorbachev to think that he was fomenting disorder; he did not want the Kremlin to assume that the demonstrations in East Germany and throughout

28. Bush and Scowcroft, *World Transformed*, 44; James A. Baker III, with Thomas M. De-Frank, *The Politics of Diplomacy: Revolution, War and Peace, 1989–1992* (New York: G. P. Putnam's Sons, 1995), 93–94.

29. For background, see Melvyn P. Leffler, *For the Soul of Mankind: The United States, the Soviet Union, and the Cold War* (New York: Hill and Wang, 2007), 423–27; and Tim Naftali, *George H. W. Bush* (New York: Times Books, 2007), 1–100. For an example of the astonishment, see Cheney, "Interview with Reporters," October 30, 1989, Public Statements of Richard B. Cheney, Secretary of Defense, George Herbert Walker Bush Presidential Library (Texas A&M University) [hereafter, the Richard B. Cheney public statements collection in the Bush Presidential Library will be abbreviated RBC-BPL].

30. Bush and Scowcroft, *World Transformed*, 151.

31. "Interview with Members of the White House Press Corps [ July 13, 1989]," *GHWB* (1989); 951–53; "Interview with Hungarian Journalists [ July 6, 1989]," *GHWB* (1989), 914; "President's News Conference [ July 6, 1989]," *GHWB* (1989), 899, 900; "The President's News Conference in Paris [ July 16, 1989]," *GHWB* (1989), 973; and Gates, *From the Shadows*, 466.

Eastern Europe were an "American project." He did not want to invite a "crackdown" that "could result in bloodshed." He knew he was being criticized for not doing enough. He believed, however, that "things were coming our way, so why do we have to jump up and down, risk those things turning around and going in the wrong direction." He could live with the fact that "he was not seen as a visionary, but I hope I'm seen as steady and prudent and able."[32]

On Thanksgiving Day 1989, President Bush addressed the nation and summarized his reactions to the remarkable events that were transpiring. For forty years, he said, Berlin had been "the test of Western resolve" and the symbol of the "contest between the free and the unfree." The West German foreign minister had given him a piece of the Berlin Wall, and he intended to keep it on his desk, "a reminder of the power of freedom to bring down the walls between people." Noting that he would be meeting with Gorbachev in about ten days, he again stressed that "a time of historic change is no time for recklessness." He hoped Gorbachev would permit the processes of reform in Eastern Europe to continue, and he was willing to offer support toward that objective. "Our goal is to see this historic tide of freedom broadened, deepened, and sustained."[33]

His advisers celebrated freedom's forward march, but they also remained wary. "The year 1989," Secretary of Defense Cheney told the Budget Committee of the House of Representatives, "may be one of those years, like few others in history—that is a watershed—that separates everything that went before from everything that comes after." But he and General Powell cautioned against substantial cuts in the defense budget. Gorbachev's future, they said, was uncertain; reforms were reversible. The Soviet Union, notwithstanding all the changes taking place, remained "a military superpower." Only when the "profound" changes in the Soviet system were "firmly rooted in democratic institutions—and that is certainly not the case at present," Powell said—could the United States make "deep, irrevocable changes to the foundations" of its own military strength.[34] "Simple common sense," Cheney admonished, "tells us that we should not abandon defense on the weight of one year's good news." Dangers would emerge quickly if the United States retrenched and permitted vacuums to develop in different parts of the globe.[35] It was essential,

32. George Bush, *All the Best, George Bush: My Life in Letters and Other Writings* (New York: Scribner, 1999), 446, 451; Bush and Scowcroft, *World Transformed*, 148–49.

33. Bush, "Thanksgiving Address to the Nation [November 22, 1989]," *GHWB* (1989), 1581–84.

34. Cheney and Powell, testimony and statements, February 7, 1990, House Committee on the Budget, *Administration's Defense Budget*, 101st Cong., 2nd sess. (Washington, D.C.: Government Printing Office, 1990), quotations on 5, 12, 114.

35. Cheney, "Remarks Prepared for Delivery at the National Newspaper Association,"

Undersecretary of Defense for Policy Paul Wolfowitz told the Senate Armed Services Committee, "to retain a prudent hedge against uncertainties." While some budget cutting made sense, dangers lurked in a world of "dizzy" change.[36]

On January 23, 1990, William Webster, the director of Central Intelligence, presented a comprehensive review of looming threats to the members of the Senate Armed Services Committee. He was especially worried about the Middle East and the Persian Gulf. "Western dependence on Persian Gulf oil will rise dramatically," he warned. At the same time, transnational terrorists were in the region, and they were developing capabilities "to operate in many parts of the world." For the moment, they were less active in Iraq, Libya, and Syria, but looming large in Iran. Some of these countries that supported terrorists were also developing ballistic missiles. "This is a particularly alarming prospect because many of them are also in the advanced stages of developing nuclear, chemical and biological warheads that could turn ballistic missiles into weapons of mass destruction. As a result, regional problems that have been of lesser policy importance to the United States could become significantly more urgent." Summing up, Webster noted that there was reason to rejoice over developments in Eastern Europe, where the conventional military threat had declined, but "the dangers inherent in rapid and unpredictable global change require that we remain firm and vigilant in our commitment to our national interests."[37]

In the wake of the collapse of the Berlin Wall, U.S. officials wanted to nurture the democratic revolutions taking place in Eastern Europe and design a new architecture for a Europe, whole and free, that would be appealing to the new noncommunist governments emerging in Poland, Hungary, and elsewhere.[38] But no matter of diplomacy and security was more important to the president and his advisers than German unification. Webster said it starkly: "The central question is the future of Germany."[39] And Bush, Scowcroft, and Baker knew precisely what they wanted: a united Germany inside NATO. For forty years NATO had been an institutional mechanism to absorb German

---

March 16, 1990, RBC-BPL; Cheney, "Remarks Prepared for Delivery at the United Jewish Appeal National Young Leadership Conference," March 13, 1990, RBC-BPL.

36. Paul D. Wolfowitz, statement, December 12, 1989, Senate Committee on Armed Services, *Threat Assessment; Military Strategy; and Operational Requirements*, 101st Cong., 2nd sess. (Washington, D.C.: Government Printing Office, 1989), 5–10, 32.

37. William H. Webster, statement, January 23, 1990, Senate Committee on Armed Services, *Threat Assessment; Military Strategy; and Operational Requirements*, 101st Cong., 2nd sess. (Washington, D.C.: Government Printing Office, 1989), 57–61 (quotations on 60 and 61).

38. See, for example, James Baker, "A New Europe, A New Atlanticism: Architecture for a New Era," *Vital Speeches of the Day*, 56 (January 15, 1990), 195–99.

39. Webster, statement, January 23, 1990, Senate, Armed Services, *Threat Assessment*, 58.

power into a peaceful Western Europe. NATO had helped allay French anxieties and reconcile Franco-German differences. It had deterred the expansionist aspirations of Soviet Russia and projected American power and influence into the heart of Europe. From the perspective of Washington, NATO had been the key to postwar stability and order and to the Pax Americana that had made liberal democracy and consumer capitalism so attractive to the peoples of Eastern Europe. Once Germany was united, NATO would be even more vital for these purposes than ever before.[40]

But President Bush and his advisers also recognized the import of what they were doing: a united Germany inside NATO had ominous ramifications for the Soviet Union. "It would be fatal," acknowledged Scowcroft, "to post-war Soviet military strategy. . . . East Germany was the prize of World War II. . . . Losing it, and accepting that loss, would mean [the Kremlin] acknowledging the end of Soviet power in Eastern Europe and the complete erosion of Moscow's security buffer of satellite states, the very core of its security planning."[41]

Gorbachev and Foreign Minister Eduard Shevardnadze recognized that East Germans wanted unification. In elections in March 1990, the citizens of East Germany went to the polls and expressed their sentiments clearly. Candidates supporting retention of an East German state won less than 20 percent of the popular vote.[42] Soviet leaders understood they could not thwart the impulse toward unification without totally undercutting their professed commitment to democratic reform and self-determination. But they were not at all ready to accept the incorporation of a united Germany inside NATO.[43] No foreign policy matter had more resonance in the Soviet Union than this one. Germany was Soviet Russia's traditional enemy. Almost all Soviet citizens of Gorbachev's and Shevardnadze's generation remembered the anguish of the Great Patriotic War. "The past must never be repeated," Shevardnadze exclaimed. "The Soviet people have not forgotten and will never forget history's lessons."[44] These feelings, Secretary Baker recognized, were not feigned. He had the "overriding impression that Gorbachev was feeling squeezed. . . . Germany was over-loading his circuits. I had believed that Shevardnadze was

40. Baker, "A New Europe, A New Atlanticism."

41. Bush and Scowcroft, *World Transformed*, 186; Leffler, *For the Soul of Mankind*, 439–48.

42. Konrad Jarausch, *The Rush to German Unity* (New York: Oxford University Press, 1994), 115–17.

43. Leffler, *For the Soul of Mankind*, 439–46; Zelikow and Rice, *Germany Unified and Europe Transformed*; Mary Elise Sarotte, *1989 and the Architecture of Order: The Competition to Lead the Post–Cold War World* (Princeton, N.J.: Princeton University Press, 2009).

44. Shevardnadze, speech, November 17, 1989, Foreign Broadcasting Information Service (FBIS), November 20, 1989, 46.

more emotional and less logical on Germany than his boss, but . . . both of them were having trouble squaring the circle."[45]

Baker tried to allay the anxieties of Soviet leaders. He told them that if they would allow the German people to determine their own future and select whatever alliances they wanted, the United States and its allies would provide incentives and reassurances to the Soviet Union. Among other things, they would limit NATO forces in Europe; restate that Germany would never be allowed to possess or produce nuclear, biological, or chemical weapons; pledge that NATO forces would not be stationed on the territory of the former East Germany during a transition period; reorient the Western alliance toward a more political focus; reaffirm the integrity of the Polish-German border; and nurture increased economic ties between the new Germany and the Soviet Union. "Germany would not be untethered in the center of Europe, thus creating a dangerous instability," Baker promised Shevardnadze.[46]

When Gorbachev and Shevardnadze visited Washington at the end of May for another summit meeting, Bush pressed the issue of German unification. Did not Gorbachev agree that people could determine their own future? Did he not agree that the Helsinki Accords permitted nations to choose whatever alliance they preferred? Should not a united Germany have the right to make its own choices? Grudgingly, and to the astonishment of his advisers, Gorbachev shrugged his shoulders and nodded agreement. "The dismay in the Soviet team was palpable," wrote Bush. "It was an unbelievable scene." Gorbachev quickly tried to retreat and started talking about a long transition period.[47]

Bush, Baker, and Scowcroft did not sew up the matter at the Washington summit. The president labored unsuccessfully to gain Gorbachev's unequivocal assent. "Germany can be trusted," he told Gorbachev. "For fifty years there has been democracy in Germany. This should not be ignored."[48] A democratic Germany, Bush was trying to reassure Gorbachev, would be a peaceful Germany. The reunited Germany, moreover, would be embedded in NATO and other supranational institutions like the European Community and the Conference on Security and Cooperation in Europe. These institutions would circumscribe the exercise of a united Germany's autonomous power.

But still more work needed to be done to allay Gorbachev's anxieties and win his support, and much of it was accomplished by the extraordinary ef-

45. Baker, *Politics of Diplomacy*, 252.

46. For a cogent summary, see Hannes Adomeit, "Gorbachev's Consent to United Germany's Membership of NATO," in *Europe and the End of the Cold War: A Reappraisal*, edited by Frédéric Bozo et al. (London: Routledge, 2008), 112; Baker, *Politics of Diplomacy*, 244–54 (quotation on 245).

47. Bush and Scowcroft, *World Transformed*, 281–83.

48. Mikhail Gorbachev, *Memoirs*, 533; Bush and Scowcroft, *World Transformed*, 281–82.

forts of the West German chancellor, Helmut Kohl. He was willing to offer huge amounts of money (about 12 billion deutsche marks) to assist Gorbachev's reform efforts, promise that Germany would never develop weapons of mass destruction, and recognize (yet again) the prevailing German-Polish border in exchange for the Kremlin's assent to the incorporation of a united Germany inside NATO. Kohl and Bush collaborated with other members of NATO to recast the alliance along more political and defensive lines. For three or four years, they agreed, NATO's activities would be restricted to the territory of the former West Germany, permitting Soviet troops to withdraw gradually from the eastern part of the country.[49] When Gorbachev finally agreed to a deal in talks that stretched through the summer of 1990, it marked a tremendous strategic victory for the West. "For me," commented Scowcroft, "the Cold War ended when the Soviets accepted a united Germany in NATO."[50]

## Shaping the Post–Cold War World

Bush and his advisers were amazed and gratified by the march of events. On their watch—without the expenditure of any American blood or much money—Europe was being transformed and Germany reunited.[51] The United States was beginning to stand alone as the world's preeminent power, perhaps weakened economically relative to its allies in Western Europe and Japan, but still the linchpin of a burgeoning democratic capitalist world order. On October 2, 1990, President Bush heralded the unification of Germany and the advance of freedom: "Today the Wall lies in ruins, and our eyes open on a new world of hope."[52] But expectations could be dashed if complacency set in. The president and his advisers were worried that their successes would reignite the isolationist impulses of the American people.[53] They feared that Congress would decimate the defense budget. "We must understand," Cheney warned, "that there are threats outside those posed by the Soviet Union. . . . It is absolutely vital that we retain sufficient military force to sustain our worldwide commitments." Aside from defending American lives and territory, he emphasized, U.S. military capabilities had to be able to

49. Sarotte, *1989 and the Architecture of Order*, especially chapters 3–5; Adomeit, "Gorbachev's Consent to United Germany's Membership of NATO," 113–15.

50. Bush and Scowcroft, *World Transformed*, 299.

51. For the standard account by two officials, see Zelikow and Rice, *Germany Unified and Europe Transformed*.

52. Bush, "Address to the German People on the Reunification of Germany [October 2, 1990]," *GHWB* (1990), 1348.

53. For a traditional account of isolationism in American history, see Selig Adler, *The Isolationist Impulse: Its Twentieth Century Reaction* (New York: Abelard-Schuman, 1957).

nurture "an environment in which freedom and democracy and market economics can flourish."[54]

As his advisers began to identify new challenges and threats, Bush outlined the contours of the nation's post–Cold War defense posture in a talk in Aspen, Colorado, on August 2, 1990. Although the arc of freedom was widening and forces could be reduced by as much as 25 percent over the next few years, peril remained. The United States, Bush said, had to guard its "enduring interests." Forces would be shaped and sized to meet regional contingencies. They would be configured "to respond to threats in whatever corner of the globe they may occur. . . . Terrorism, hostagetaking, renegade regimes and unpredictable rulers, new sources of instability—all require a strong and engaged America." The task was clear: "to shape our defense capabilities to these changing strategic circumstances."[55] With Soviet power in retreat, all regions of the world needed to be made secure for the onward rush of democratic capitalism.

As Bush spoke, Saddam Hussein's Iraqi armies marched into Kuwait. This unexpected aggression was precisely what administration officials worried about. "Unprovoked aggression," Secretary of State Baker told the Senate Committee on Foreign Relations, "is a political test. . . . The Iraqi invasion of Kuwait is one of the defining moments of a new era. It is an era full of promise, but it is also one that is replete with new challenges." The international community, Baker said, had to decide whether it had "the collective will" to thwart aggression. What most obviously was at stake, according to the secretary of state, was access to the energy resources of the Persian Gulf. The crisis emanated from "a dictator who, acting alone and unchallenged, could strangle the global economic order, determining by fiat, if you will, whether we all enter our recession [*sic*] or whether even we enter the darkness of a depression."[56] Secretary of Defense Cheney said much the same to the Senate Armed Services Committee: Saddam Hussein was seeking a "choke-hold on the world's economy." If he succeeded, he "would be in a position to blackmail any nation which chose not to do his bidding."[57]

54. Cheney, "Commencement Address at Graduation Ceremonies of the National Wax College," June 13, 1990, RBC-BPL; Cheney, "Address to the Tenth Anniversary Celebration of the World Affairs Council," June 8, 1990, RBC-BPL.

55. "Remarks at the Aspen Institute Symposium [August 2, 1990]," *GHWB* (1990), 1089–93.

56. Statement by Baker, September 5, 1990, Senate Committee on Foreign Relations, *U.S. Policy in the Persian Gulf*, 101st Cong., 2nd sess. (Washington, D.C.: Government Printing Office, 1990), 8–11; for background, also see Hal Brands, *From Berlin to Baghdad: America's Search for Purpose in the Post–Cold War World* (Lexington, Ky.: University Press of Kentucky, 2008), 1–73.

57. Cheney, statement, September 11, 1990, Senate Committee on Armed Services, *Crisis in the Persian Gulf: U.S. Policy Options and Implications*, 101st Cong., 2nd sess. (Washington, D.C.: Government Printing Office, 1990), 643–44.

Baker and Cheney clarified U.S. goals. "Our strategy," said Baker, "is to lead a global alliance . . . to isolate Iraq politically, economically, and militarily." This meant putting together an international coalition, including the Soviet Union and the Arab states of the Middle East as well as NATO allies. The coalition required Iraq to pull its troops out of Kuwait and restore its legitimate government. "Security and stability" had to return to the region.[58]

President Bush and his advisers were not seeking to spread freedom and democracy in the Persian Gulf through the use of force. They sought stability and access to petroleum. They also wanted to uphold a basic principle: territorial aggression (in a vital region) would not be tolerated. When French President François Mitterrand talked about repulsing Iraqi troops, not restoring the "legitimate" government of the al-Sabah family in Kuwait, Bush was upset. "I did not think we should impose democracy on the Kuwaitis," he recollected.[59] Nor for all their distaste for Saddam Hussein's brutality—in his diary Bush recounted how, in Kuwait, Saddam's troops were shooting citizens in their cars, ransacking their homes, and stealing their food—did the administration seek to remove the evil dictator from power.[60] Talking to reporters in mid-April 1991, Cheney bluntly stated, "We are not going to Baghdad. Our military objectives [do] not include changing the Iraqi government." The United States would not get into the business of governing Iraq; this, said Cheney, is

a quagmire we don't want to be involved in. I can't think of any way to make myself any clearer. . . . There isn't any way the President or those of us in the Administration would send American military forces into Iraq to take over the responsibility for governing that country. . . . It is not a military objective of the United States to go to Baghdad or to topple this government, or to get rid of Saddam Hussein.[61]

In the midst of the Persian Gulf crisis, President Bush began talking about "a new world order." Addressing a joint session of Congress on September 11, 1990, to explain American goals in Kuwait, he said:

Out of these troubled times . . . a new world order can emerge: a new era—freer from the threat of terror, stronger in the pursuit of justice, and more secure in the quest for peace. An era in which the nations of the world, East and West, North and South, can prosper and live in harmony. A hundred generations have searched for this elusive path to peace, while a thousand

58. Baker, statement, *U.S. Policy in the Persian Gulf*, 10, 11; Cheney, statement, *Crisis in the Persian Gulf*, 644.

59. Bush and Scowcroft, *World Transformed*, 376.

60. Ibid., 374.

61. Cheney, "Interview with Editors and Reporters," April 16, 1991, RBC-BPL.

wars raged across the span of human endeavor. Today that new world is struggling to be born, a world quite different than the one we've known. A world where the rule of law supplants the rule of the jungle. A world in which nations recognize the shared responsibility for freedom and justice. A world where the strong respect the rights of the weak.[62]

These were inspiring words, but it was not easy to discern exactly what would constitute this "new world order." In June 1991, Bush's aides summarized the contrasting ways in which the president had used the concept: sometimes emphasizing new forms of collaboration with the Soviet Union, sometimes focusing on stopping aggression and implementing collective security, sometimes highlighting the role of the United Nations and multilateral forms of collaboration.[63] While extolling the virtues of freedom, Bush reiterated in his State of the Union message in January 1991 that military force was being used in the Persian Gulf War to achieve other purposes: to deter aggression, restore "legitimate" government in Kuwait, preserve access to the region's oil, and insure stability. "We seek a Persian Gulf," Bush declared, "where conflict is no longer the rule, where the strong are neither tempted nor able to intimidate the weak."[64]

During the run-up to the war in the Persian Gulf, Bush sought out Gorbachev's assistance, and he heralded the collaboration of the United States and the Soviet Union as a key element of the "new world order." But Gorbachev's position inside his country eroded as Boris Yeltsin gathered strength in the newly created Republic of Russia and as conservative elements in Gorbachev's Kremlin plotted an unsuccessful coup to remove him. Amidst the political turmoil in Moscow, U.S. officials had to determine whom they should support and to what extent they should champion the "center"—Gorbachev's base—as opposed to the newly emerging and rather autonomous republics led by Yeltsin's Russia. Although Bush still felt a strong bond with Gorbachev after the coup to topple the Soviet leader failed, geopolitical and strategic calculations in Washington trumped personal, political, and economic concerns. Cheney clearly wanted to use American influence to strengthen the republics at the expense of the center. Powell, too, favored the "dissolution of the old Soviet

62. Bush, "Address Before a Joint Session of the Congress [September 11, 1990]," *GHWB* (1990), 1219.

63. Dan Jahn to John Snow, June 26, 1991, Speech File, George Herbert Walker Bush Presidential Library (Texas A&M University); for assessments of the "New World Order," also see Brands, *Berlin to Baghdad*, 74–100; Derek Chollet and James Goldgeier, *America between the Wars From 11/9 to 9/11* (New York: Public Affairs, 2008), 6–41; Zbigniew Brzezinski, *Second Chance: Three Presidents and the Crisis of American Superpower* (New York: Basic Books, 2007), 45–82.

64. Bush, "Address on the State of the Union [January 29, 1991]," *GHWB* (1991), 78.

Union." Baker was not so inclined, but Scowcroft acknowledged that "our primary security interest would be best served by the breakup [of the Soviet Union], thus fractionating [*sic*] the military threat we faced." Bush eventually agreed: the "best arrangement would be diffusion, with many different states, none of which would have the awesome power of the Soviet Union."[65]

These policy preferences were of rather little consequence in the unfolding of events—Yeltsin outmaneuvered Gorbachev and the Soviet Union disintegrated. "It was a rare great moment in history," commented Scowcroft:

> The final collapse of Soviet power and the dissolution of its empire brought to a close the greatest transformation of the international environment since World War I and concluded nearly eight decades of upheaval and conflict. . . . We were suddenly in a unique position, without experience, without precedent, and standing alone at the height of power. It was, it is, an unparalleled situation in history, one which presents us with the rarest opportunity to shape the world.[66]

In this new environment, Bush and Cheney announced major changes in the nation's nuclear posture and significant cuts in the military budget. They grounded America's strategic bomber force for the first time since the 1950s and took 45 percent of its ICBM force off alert. They agreed to reduce the number of strategic and tactical nuclear warheads from about 21,000 to 8,000. Feeling enormous congressional and public pressure, Cheney cut over $250 billion out of the long-range five-year defense budget, abolished more than 85,000 civilian jobs in the Department of Defense, terminated over 100 different weapons systems, and planned to close about 300 bases worldwide. In real terms, he explained, the defense budget would be reduced 4 percent annually through fiscal year 1997.[67]

Notwithstanding these cuts, the aim of the Bush administration was to consolidate and perpetuate American geopolitical and strategic preponderance. Since the fall of the Berlin Wall, Secretary Cheney and General Powell told legislators, they had been thinking about reshaping strategy, reconfiguring forces, and making appropriate budget cuts. The strategy, said Cheney, "is

65. Bush and Scowcroft, *World Transformed*, 541–43; Cheney, "Interview with Jim Lehrer," January 17, 1992, RBC-BPL. Although Bush agreed, his affection and admiration for Gorbachev were clear. See Bush, *All the Best*, 532–33, 542–43.

66. Bush and Scowcroft, *World Transformed*, 564.

67. Powell and Cheney, testimony, March 24, 1992, House Committee on Foreign Affairs, *The Future of U.S. Foreign Policy in the Post–Cold War Era*, 102nd Cong., 2nd sess. (Washington, D.C.: Government Printing Office, 1992), 354–61, 297–98, 331; Cheney, "Interview with *San Diego Union*," November 12, 1991, RBC-BPL; Cheney, "Interview with Judy Woodruff," October 1, 1991, RBC-BPL.

designed to shape the future, to shape the course of events, and to change the course of history." Threats, he conceded, were now "remote," so remote "they are difficult to discern."[68] But in a more complicated world the United States had to prepare forces that could deal with uncertainty, anywhere. "I cannot tell," Powell said to members of the House Foreign Affairs Committee, "where the next . . . Saddam Hussein will appear to threaten stability in the world, but you can be certain that somewhere it will happen. It may be in the Middle East, in Europe, in East Asia, or in Latin America—wherever it occurs, we must be prepared to respond. The key to preparedness is building forces flexible enough to react to the unknown."[69]

Cheney and Powell warned Congress that it "would be a mistake of historic proportions" to cut too much or to retrench too far from Europe and Asia. The mistakes of the 1920s and 1930s must not be repeated. The United States had to lead the world, had to preserve its position of preeminence. "We are the world's sole remaining superpower," said Powell. There were no challengers, and none should be allowed. "This is a position we should not abandon," he declared. Facing a "turning point in world history," occasioned by the crumbling of the Berlin Wall, the demise of communism, the breakup of the Soviet Union, and the defeat of Saddam Hussein, Cheney emphasized that forces must be configured in new ways to preserve American leadership. We must work "to create a world in which free societies such as our own can thrive."[70]

The new strategy was designed to deal with regional contingencies, not a great war in the heart of Europe as had been the case during the Cold War. The "core goals of the regional defense strategy," Cheney told Congress, "are to protect American interests and to promote a more stable and democratic world." With little warning, threats could arise in Europe, East Asia, Southwest Asia, and Latin America. "We want to ensure that nondemocratic powers will not dominate regions of the world critical to us or come to pose a serious global challenge. To accomplish these goals, we must preserve U.S. leadership, maintain leading-edge military capabilities, and enhance collective security among democratic nations." The defense secretary outlined the four key elements of the strategy: strategic deterrence and defense; forward presence of U.S. military forces overseas; crisis response; and capacity to reconstitute additional capabilities quickly, should circumstances so dictate. The key ingredient, Cheney explained, was to have flexible forces, deployed in

68. Cheney, testimony, *Future of U.S. Foreign Policy*, 291, 304; also see Cheney, "Remarks to the U.S. Naval Academy," October 8, 1991, RBC-BPL.

69. Powell, testimony, *Future of U.S. Foreign Policy*, 369–70.

70. Ibid., 425, 367; Cheney, "Remarks to the World Affairs Council of Northern California," February 12, 1992, RBC-BPL.

forward positions to "to help provide stability in critical regions of the world and to enable us to act quickly to meet crises that affect our security."[71]

In March 1992, *The New York Times* published excerpts from the Defense Policy Guidance (DPG) that Cheney's subordinates in the Pentagon had been drafting for more than six months. The news story ignited controversy. The *Times* reported that the United States was seeking to prevent the reemergence of any rival superpower in Western Europe, Asia, or the territories of the former Soviet Union. Why it stirred such emotions then (and since) is hard to fathom, because Cheney had been saying much of this publicly for many months. The new regional defense strategy was quite clear: its dominant rationale was "to prevent any hostile power from dominating a region whose resources would, under consolidated control, be sufficient to generate global power."[72] This type of thinking extrapolated previous Cold War strategy to the new era: from the late 1940s to the late 1980s, the overriding strategic goal was to prevent the Soviet Union from gaining control of the preponderant resources of Eurasia, either directly or indirectly.[73] Now, the objective was to prevent any aspiring regional hegemon from dominating any area deemed vital to U.S. security interests. According to Bush's defense strategists, mechanisms needed to be designed to deter "potential competitors from even aspiring to a larger regional or global role." Further, the new strategy required the United States to develop the capabilities to "address sources of regional conflict and instability." This meant promoting respect for international law, limiting international violence, and encouraging "the spread of democratic forms of government and open economic systems."[74]

In the February 18 draft of the DPG, defense officials acknowledged that the United States should not "become the world's policeman by assuming responsibility for righting every wrong." The objective was to design forces that could be employed selectively to address those wrongs that threatened its interests or those of its allies as well as those threats that "could seriously unsettle international relations." Cheney's subordinates clearly identified the

71. Cheney, testimony, *Future of U.S. Foreign Policy*, 320–21; Cheney, "Remarks to the World Affairs Council of Northern California," February 12, 1992, RBC-BPL.

72. Dick Cheney, Defense Strategy for the 1990s: The Regional Defense Strategy, 1–3, in "The Nuclear Vault—The Making of the Cheney Regional Defense Strategy, 1991–1992," National Security Archive, Washington, D.C., http://www.gwu.edu/~nsarchiv/nukevault/ebb245/doc15.pdf (accessed May 17, 2009).

73. Melvyn P. Leffler, *A Preponderance of Power: National Security, the Truman Administration, and the Cold War* (Stanford, Calif.: Stanford University Press, 1992).

74. Chollet and Goldgeier, *America between the Wars*, 44–45; successive drafts of the Defense Policy Guidance, from which I am quoting, may be found in "The Nuclear Vault—The Making of the Cheney Regional Defense Strategy, 1991–1992," http://www.gwu.edu/~nsarchiv/nukevault/ebb245/index.htm.

"interests" they had in mind: "access to vital raw materials, primarily Persian Gulf oil; proliferation of weapons of mass destruction and ballistic missiles; threats to US citizens from terrorism or regional or local conflict; and threats to US society from narcotics trafficking."[75]

In short, the crumbling of the Berlin Wall and the dissolution of Soviet power meant that the United States had to consolidate and preserve its hegemonic position in the global arena, deter and dissuade challengers from arising, and "maintain a world environment where societies with shared values can flourish."[76] The aim was not to use force to promote democracy within particular nations or to deploy force for humanitarian ends or for the protection of human rights. Capabilities were designed for the purpose of nurturing an international environment conducive to American values and U.S. interests. "The concept that we have to work out every problem, everywhere in the world, is crazy," Bush cryptically wrote during the outbreak of civil war in Yugoslavia.[77]

The controversy aroused by the leaked DPG forced defense officials to revise and redraft, but the final product, signed by Secretary Cheney, put the administration's imprimatur on the new regional strategy. "Together with our democratic allies, we must preclude hostile nondemocratic powers from dominating regions critical to our interests and otherwise work to build an international environment conducive to our values." But if collective efforts were not likely to work, the United States had to have the capabilities and the will to act alone "to protect our critical interests." The challenge was "to preserve the extraordinary environment" that had emerged—"an environment within which the values of freedom that we and our principal allies hold dear can flourish. We can secure and extend the remarkable democratic 'zone of peace' . . . , preclude threats, and guard our national interests."[78]

While defense officials were configuring a strategy to preserve "a new world order," shaped by the United States and conducive to its interests and values, President Bush launched his campaign for reelection. The economy was contracting, and he faced challengers within his own party as well as independent candidates seeking the support of traditional Republican voters. Bush now sought to claim credit for the new environment and to mold the nation's collective memory. "Think of it," he declared in his maiden speech as candidate Bush:

75. "Defense Policy Guidance, FY 1994–1992," February 18, 1992, 2, http://www.gwu.edu /~nsarchiv/nukevault/ebb245/index.htm.

76. Ibid., 8.

77. Bush, *All the Best*, 527.

78. Cheney, *Defense Strategy for the 1990s: The Regional Defense Strategy*, January 1993, 1, 27, http://www.gwu.edu/~nsarchiv/nukevault/ebb245/index.htm (accessed May 17, 2009).

The Berlin Wall came tumbling down. And last year, the Soviet Union collapsed. Imperial communism became a four-letter word D-E-A-D, dead. And today, because we stood firm, because we did the right things, America stands alone the undisputed leader of the world. We put an end to the decades of cold war and reaped a springtime harvest of peace. The American people should be proud of what together we have achieved. Now, together, we can transform the arsenal of democracy into the engine of growth.[79]

Candidate Bush now wanted Americans to take pride in their unique victory and to give him credit for it. Addressing the American Society of Newspaper Editors, he urged them to look around and take note of the extraordinary developments that had occurred. The Berlin Wall was down, communism had been vanquished, and Saddam's armies had been repulsed. Dispense with the gloom, he urged audiences, and bask in the glory that "we brought about the fall of the Iron Curtain" and "the death of imperial communism" without enduring the "cataclysm" of a third world war.[80]

The Republican Party tried to make the most of it. At its convention in August 1992, it adopted the following platform:

> The Fall of the Berlin Wall symbolizes an epochal change in the way people live. . . .
>
> We Republicans saw clearly the dangers of collectivism: not only the military threat, but the deeper threat to the souls of people bound in dependence. . . .
>
> Building on the legacy of Ronald Reagan, George Bush saw the chance to sweep away decadent Communism. . . . He took the free world beyond containment, led the way to aiding democracy in Eastern Europe, and punched holes through the rusting Iron Curtain. We all remember the joy we felt when we saw the people of Berlin dancing on top of the crumbling Wall that had symbolized four decades of Communist oppression. . . .
>
> George Bush made it happen. . . .
>
> Yet now that we have won the Cold War, we must also win the peace. We must not repeat the mistake of the past by throwing away victory through complacency.[81]

At the Republican convention in August 1992, Ronald Reagan appeared for his last major political speech, putting his imprimatur on candidate Bush.

79. Bush, "Remarks Announcing the Bush-Quayle Candidacies for Reelection [February 12, 1992]," *GHWB* (1992), 233–34.

80. Bush, "Remarks at the Ohio Freedom Day Celebration [May 21, 1992]," *GHWB* (1992), 512–14.

81. "Republican party Platform of 1992," August 17, 1992, The American Presidency Project, http://www.presidency.ucsb.edu/ws/index.php?pid=78545.

It was vintage Reagan, celebrating America for being "forever young," with its "best days yet to come." Nor was he bashful about taking credit for recent events: "We stood tall and proclaimed that communism was destined for the ash heap of history." The sky would not fall, Reagan said, if an American president spoke the truth. "The only thing that would fall was the Berlin Wall." Americans should not forget that they were "the moral force that defeated communism"; they thwarted those who "would put the human soul itself into bondage."[82]

Notwithstanding Reagan's imprimatur, Bush could not overcome the economic woes and the deep divisions among conservatives. In a close election in which the independent candidate Ross Perot got almost 19 percent of the popular vote, Bush was defeated by Democratic nominee Bill Clinton. Many conservatives who ordinarily might have supported a Republican candidate wanted the United States to retrench after decades of onerous defense expenditures and dangerous commitments overseas. On December 15, 1992, at Texas A&M University, where he would build his library, Bush delivered a legacy address, seeking to shape how Americans would think about the past and plan for the future. "The Soviet Union did not simply lose the cold war," he stressed, "the western democracies won it," and U.S. leadership had been crucial. The American people now had to muster the will to win the democratic peace. "The advance of democratic ideals reflects a hard-nosed sense of our own, of *American* self-interest. For certain truths have, indeed, now become evident: Governments responsive to the will of the people are not likely to commit aggression. They are not likely to sponsor terrorism or to threaten humanity with weapons of mass destruction. Likewise, the spread of free markets . . . will sustain the expansion of American prosperity. In short, by helping others, we help ourselves."

Bush summarized the astounding achievements of the last four years: "The Berlin Wall demolished and Germany united; Russia democratic; whole classes of nuclear weapons eliminated, the rest vastly reduced." He took great pride in forming the great coalition to thwart and reverse Saddam Hussein's aggression in Kuwait, and he trumpeted the progress that had been made in Arab-Israeli peace negotiations. But he warned: the "abandonment of the worldwide democratic revolution could be disastrous for American security. . . . The new world could, in time, be as menacing as the old. And let me be blunt: A retreat from American leadership . . . would be a mistake for which future generations, indeed our own children, would pay dearly."[83]

82. Reagan, "Address to the Republican National Convention," August 17, 1992, http://en.wikisource.org/wiki/Ronald_Reagan's_Speech_to_the_1992_GOP_Convention.

83. Bush, "Remarks at Texas A&M University [December 15, 1992]," *GHWB* (1992), 2189–94.

Bush perhaps thought people might misconstrue his message. Before leaving office, he gave another thoughtful, reflective speech at West Point on January 5, 1993. The end of the Cold War was a great blessing; a new world order, a democratic peace, beckoned. To bring it about, he reiterated once again, the United States had to lead. But then he admonished that the United States should not become the world policeman; it should not "exhaust itself" in pursuit of a democratic peace. It should "not respond to each and every outrage of violence. The fact that America can act does not mean that it must." In other words, ideals should not undercut interests, he emphasized.

Force, Bush emphasized, must be used carefully and selectively. There were no rigid guidelines. There was no substitute for the exercise of judgment. "In the complex new world we are entering, there can be no single or simple set of fixed rules for using force. Inevitably, the question of military intervention requires judgment. Each and every case is unique." Even if an interest was vital, Bush explained, it did not mean that employing force was the best means of achieving it; and, paradoxically, he pointed out, sometimes using force might make sense to achieve a goal less than vital.

Whereas there were no fixed rules and judgment was the key, he did offer some guidelines: "Using military force makes sense as a policy where the stakes warrant, where and when force can be effective, where no other policies are likely to prove effective, where its application can be limited in scope and time, and where the potential benefits justify the potential costs and sacrifice." He also explained that, whereas it was desirable to employ force as part of a coalition, "sometimes a great power has to act alone." Clearly, the outgoing president was agonizing over decisions he had just made to send limited troops for a humanitarian mission to Somalia while hesitating to deploy troops to the former Yugoslavia, where regional strife and civil conflict beleaguered the former communist country. "But in every case involving the use of force," he concluded, "it will be essential to have a clear and achievable mission, a realistic plan for accomplishing the mission, and criteria to be realistic for withdrawing U.S. forces once the mission is complete."[84]

## Prudence and the Democratic Peace

Three weeks later, a new man from the opposing party took the presidential oath. People expected vast changes. Bill Clinton had assailed Bush during the campaign for his restraint, for his realpolitik, and for his refusal to support freedom in China and to protect human rights and human lives in the Balkans and in Haiti. But after taking office, Clinton's rhetoric and actions resembled

84. Bush, "Remarks at the United States Military Academy [January 5, 1993]," *GHWB* (1992–93), 2228–33.

those of Bush: there was the same euphoria, the same determination to pre-serve America's preponderant power in the global arena, the same regional strategy, and the same ambivalence over the use of force.[85]

In his inaugural address, Clinton said the American people needed to em-brace change and overcome drift. He then sounded much like his predeces-sor: "Today, a generation raised in the shadow of the Cold War assumes new responsibilities in a world warmed by the sunshine of freedom, but threat-ened still by ancient hatreds and new plagues." Suggesting that Bush had lacked vision and determination, Clinton stressed that he would tackle the new challenges that now appeared on the horizon. "The world," he empha-sized, "was more free but less stable. . . . When our vital interests are chal-lenged, or the will and conscience of the international community is defied, we will act—with peaceful diplomacy whenever possible, with force when necessary," as in the Persian Gulf and Somalia. But he then replicated the language of his former Republican foe and went on to say: "But our greatest strength is the power of our ideas, which are still new in many lands. Across the world, we see them embraced—and we rejoice. Our hopes, our hearts, our hands, are with those on every continent who are building democracy and freedom. Their cause is America's cause." The United States, he stressed, had to engage the world, avoid a return to isolationism, and enlarge the dem-ocratic peace.[86]

In Clinton's vision and memory, the collapse of the Berlin Wall also had a special place. "If the Soviet empire was a prison," he said, "then Berlin was the place where everyone could see the bars and look behind them. On one side of the wall lived a free people, shaping their destiny in the image of their dreams. On the other lived a people who desperately wanted to be free, that had found themselves trapped beyond a wall of deadly uniformity and daily indignities, in an empire that, indeed, could exist only behind a wall." What brought the wall down, Clinton opined, was courage, vision, determination, persistence, power, conviction, and, most of all, U.S. leadership. "America's resolve and American ideals so clearly articulated by Ronald Reagan helped to bring the wall down."[87]

85. For background, see David Halberstam, *War in a Time of Peace: Bush, Clinton, and the Generals* (New York: Simon and Schuster, 2001), 1–194.

86. Bill Clinton, "First Inaugural Address [January 21, 1993]," *Public Papers of the Presidents: William Jefferson Clinton* (Washington, D.C.: Government Printing Office, 1993), 1–3 [hereafter, citations of the Clinton volumes of *Public Papers of the Presidents* are abbreviated *WJC* (year), page]. Also see the White House, "A National Security Strategy of Engagement and Enlargement" (Washington, D.C.: The White House, 1996).

87. Clinton, "Remarks at Georgetown University [November 8, 1999]," *WJC* (1999), 2009; Clinton, "Remarks at the Dedication of the Ronald Reagan Building and International Trade Center [May 5, 1998]," *WJC* (1998), 690–92.

According to Clinton, the crumbling of the wall and the embrace of free-dom in Berlin ignited a wave of democratic revolutions. "More people live in freedom today," he exclaimed at the end of his administration, "than at any other time in history." The march of events, moreover, began in the divided city of Berlin in November 1989. "The fall of the Berlin Wall a decade ago," Clinton declared in July 1999, "finally enabled us to pursue democratic reform in Central and Eastern Europe and to lay the firm foundations of freedom, peace, and prosperity."[88]

These beliefs did not simply inform President Clinton's rhetoric, they shaped the central contours of his foreign policy. The crumbling of the wall, in other words, not only demonstrated the rectitude of past American policies but also served as a reminder of how things would turn out in the future if policy was conceived wisely. Clinton and his advisers defined their strategy as one of "engagement and enlargement." They sought to enlarge the democratic peace by incorporating Eastern European nations into NATO, establishing a "partnership" with democratic Russia, and expanding open trade through the adoption of the North American Free Trade Act and the embrace of the World Trade Organization. They wanted to repulse isolationist impulses, harness the forces of globalization, and embrace new technologies to advance American interests. "Underpinning our international leadership," Clinton's national security advisers explained, was "the power of our democratic ideals":

> In designing our strategy, we recognize that the spread of democracy supports American values and enhances both our security and prosperity. Democratic governments are more likely to cooperate with each other against common threats, encourage free trade, and promote sustainable economic development. They are less likely to wage war or abuse the rights of their people. Hence, the trend toward democracy and free markets throughout the world advances American interests. The United States will support this trend by remaining actively engaged in the world. This is the strategy to take us into the next century.[89]

The fall of the Berlin Wall shaped Clinton's military strategy, much as it had molded the planning of Bush and Secretary of Defense Cheney. In the first "bottom-up" strategic review conducted by Clinton's Pentagon, the thinking

88. Clinton, "Proclamation 7386—Human Rights Day, Bill of Rights Day, and Human Rights Week, 2000," December 9, 2000, http://www.presidency.ucsb.edu/ws/index.php?pid=62339; Clinton, "Proclamation 7209—Captive Nations Week, 1999," July 16, 1999, http://www.presidency.ucsb.edu/ws/index.php?pid=57894&st=proclamation+7209&str=.

89. White House, *A National Security Strategy for a New Century*, October 1998 (Washington, D.C.: The White House, 1998), 2 (for quotation), 5, 6, 33, 41, 47, 50, 54; for Clinton's own summary of his policies, see Clinton, "Remarks on Receiving the International Charlemagne Prize in Aachen, Germany [June 2, 2000]," *WJC* (2000–2001), 1064–68.

was remarkably similar to the final version of the Bush administration's Defense Policy Guidance. It began: "The Cold War is behind us. The Soviet Union is no longer the threat that drove our defense decision-making for four and a half decades. . . . In 1989, the fall of the Berlin Wall and the collapse of communism throughout Eastern Europe precipitated a strategic shift away from containment of the Soviet empire." The new strategy was focused on engaging the international community, enlarging democratic alliances, and expanding world trade. There was no longer any great immediate danger, but there were looming threats—the same ones identified by the earlier Bush administration: proliferating weapons of mass destruction, regional strife, backsliding in the former Soviet Union, and a faltering American economy. To meet these threats, "our primary task, then, as a nation is to strengthen our society and economy for the demanding competitive environment of the twenty-first century, while at the same time avoiding the risks of precipitous reductions in defense capabilities and the overseas capabilities they support." Specifically, to meet these dangers the United States needed to engage in counterproliferation and cooperative threat reduction activities, but the heart of the military strategy was based on a strategy designed to promote regional stability.[90]

Clinton's military strategists, like Bush's, believed that the United States had to have the capabilities to fight two regional wars simultaneously. Such capabilities provided "a hedge against the possibility that a future adversary might one day confront us with a larger-than-expected threat."[91] During the 1990s, the concept was refined, but its core principles did not alter from Cheney and Powell's articulation in 1991–92. "As a global power with worldwide interests," stated Clinton's strategists in the 1997 Quadrennial Defense Review:

> it is imperative that the United States now and for the foreseeable future be able to deter and defeat large-scale, cross-border aggression in two distant theaters in overlapping time frames, preferably in concert with regional allies. Maintaining this core capability is central to credibly deterring opportunism—that is, to avoiding a situation in which an aggressor in one region might be tempted to take advantage when U.S. forces are heavily committed elsewhere—and to ensuring that the United States has sufficient military capabilities to deter or defeat aggression by an adversary that is larger, or under circumstances that are more difficult, than expected. We can never know with certainty when or where the next major theater will occur, who our next adversary will be. . . . A force sized and equipped

90. Secretary of Defense, *National Security in the Post–Cold War Era*, October 1993, quotations on 1, 3, http://www.fas.org/man/docs/bur/partor.htm (accessed May 17, 2009).
91. Ibid., 3–4.

for deterring and defeating aggression in more than one theater ensures the United States will maintain the flexibility to cope with the unpredictable and the unexpected. Such a capability is the sine qua non of a super-power and is essential to the credibility of our overall national security strategy.[92]

The overriding motif was that the United States had to preserve its position of preponderance against all potential competitors and challengers. "As we move into the next century," Clinton's strategists emphasized, "it is imperative that the United States maintain its military superiority in the face of evolving, as well as discontinuous, threats and challenges. Without such superiority, our ability to exert global leadership and to create international conditions conducive to the achievement of our national goals would be in doubt." And in order to preserve this leadership, the military had to embrace new technologies, modernize its business practices and intelligence capabilities, and enhance the forward positioning of U.S. troops and capabilities overseas. Prudent steps needed to be taken "today" to "respond more effectively to unlikely, but significant, future threats, such as the emergence of a regional great power or a 'wild card' scenario. Such steps provide a hedge against the possibility that unanticipated threats will emerge."[93]

The goal, as President Clinton stated in his second inaugural address, was for the United States to stand alone "as the world's indispensable nation."[94] He supported the goal of "full spectrum dominance," as his military chiefs called it, because it afforded the United States the ability to act in concert with others if it could, but to act alone if it must.[95] Clinton, like Bush, never tired of emphasizing that the United States had to lead the world. And to lead required courage, vision, determination, and, when necessary, the will to act alone. "We must always be prepared to act alone," said his national security team in 1998.[96]

Furthermore, as the perception of threat multiplied and as the reality and frequency of terrorist actions grew, Clinton's doctrine embraced the concept of possible preemption (or prevention) as well as unilateralism. In Presidential Decision Directive 39, Clinton endorsed preventative action as well as deterrence in the fight against terrorism.[97] "As long as terrorists continue to

92. Secretary of Defense, *Quadrennial Defense Review*, May 1997, 6, http://www.fas.org /man/docs/qdr/ (accessed May 17, 2009).

93. Ibid., 7–11 (quotations on 7, 9).

94. Clinton, "Inaugural Address [January 20, 1997]," *WJC* (1997), 43–46.

95. "To act alone," see White House, *National Security Strategy of Engagement and Enlargement*, ii; for "full spectrum" dominance, see Secretary of Defense, *Quadrennial Defense Review*, 8.

96. White House, *National Security Strategy for a New Century*, 2.

97. Presidential Decision Directive 39, "U.S. Policy on Counterterrorism," June 21, 1995, http://www.fes.org/irp/offdocs/pdd39.htm (accessed May 17, 2009).

target American citizens," his strategists wrote, "we reserve the right to act in self-defense by striking their bases and those who sponsor, assist, or actively support them."[98]

For Clinton, as for Bush, the military capabilities of the United States had to be used selectively. The reconfiguration of world power in America's favor after the demise of the Berlin Wall and the breakup of the Soviet Union meant that the United States had unprecedented strength. But Clinton's national security advisers acknowledged that force had to be used carefully. "Our strategy is tempered by recognition that there are limits to America's involvement in the world. We must be selective in the use of our capabilities."[99] Accordingly, Clinton did not challenge China's repressive political policies or use force to avert genocide in Rwanda or to sustain a humanitarian mission in Somalia. Late in his second administration, he did employ force against Serbia, retaliated against an alleged terrorist factory in Sudan, and readied to take action against Osama bin Laden in Afghanistan.[100] In these instances, Clinton's advisers felt that "our interests and values were affected to a sufficient degree to warrant U.S. military intervention."[101]

But, in general, Clinton and his advisers believed they could be patient, much as U.S. Cold Warriors had demonstrated patience and resolve—leading eventually to the crumbling of the wall. Freedom would come to oppressed peoples everywhere, much as it had cracked the wall and lured East Germans into the West. "I believe," said Clinton, "that the impulses of society and the nature of the economic change will work together, along with the availability of information from the outside world, to increase the sphere of liberty over time. I don't think there is any way that anyone who disagrees with that in China can hold back that [sic], just as eventually the Berlin Wall fell. I just think it's inevitable."[102]

## Existential Threats and the Use of Force

Clinton's hesitation to act in Iraq to overthrow Saddam Hussein, however, evoked increasing ridicule from neoconservative foes and other opponents.

98. White House, *A National Security Strategy for a Global Age* (Washington, D.C.: The White House, 2000), 11–15 (quotation on 14).

99. White House, *National Security Strategy of Engagement and Enlargement*, ii; White House, *National Security Strategy for a New Century*, 2.

100. White House, *National Security Strategy for a Global Age*, 3–4; for background, also see Warren I. Cohen, *America's Failing Empire: U.S. Foreign Relations since the Cold War* (Maiden, Mass.: Blackwell Publishing, 2005), 56–122; Chollet and Goldgeier, *America between the Wars*; Halberstam, *War in a Time of Peace*; Brands, *Berlin to Baghdad*.

101. White House, *National Security Strategy for a Global Age*, 3.

102. "The President's Press Conference [January 28, 1997]," *WJC* (1997), 84.

In January 1998, Donald Rumsfeld, Paul Wolfowitz, Richard Armitage, and Robert Zoellick (among others) signed a letter calling upon Clinton "to act decisively" to remove "Saddam's regime from power," employing a "full complement of diplomatic, political, and military efforts." Their rationale said nothing of Saddam's brutality and repression, but focused on his alleged development of weapons of mass destruction and their "destabilizing effect on the entire Middle East."[103] Their sponsor, the Project for the New American Century, followed this up with a more comprehensive strategic study, completed in September 2000. Written by Donald Kagan, Gary Schmitt, and Thomas Donnelly, it harkened back to Cheney's Defense Policy Guidance in 1992, but its findings also strikingly resembled those that had shaped the Clinton national security strategy. "At present the United States faces no global rival. America's grand strategy," they wrote, "should aim to preserve and extend this advantageous position as far into the future as possible." Their gripe with Clinton was that he had not been doing enough (even though the United States was spending more on defense than all the rest of the countries in the world combined). The "core missions" they delineated were almost precisely the ones enumerated in Clinton's defense documents: defend the American homeland; fight and decisively win multiple, simultaneous major theater wars; perform the "constabulary" duties associated with shaping the security environment in critical regions; and transform U.S. forces to exploit the "revolution in military affairs."[104]

What they really sought to do was not to reconfigure strategy, but to highlight the greater scale of forces required to implement it. They pontificated briefly about expanding the "zones of democratic peace," but their focus was on deterring the rise of great-power competitors, defending key regions around the globe, developing ballistic missile defenses, and preserving "American preeminence." The key to preeminence was in not allowing aspiring regional hegemons to acquire weapons of mass destruction lest they use such capabilities "to deter U.S. military action" and thereby gain the potential to blackmail the United States.[105]

In their campaign to win the presidency in 2000, the Republicans accused Democrats of weakness. The Republican platform stated: "The administration

103. The Project for the New American Century (PNAC) Clinton Letter, January 26, 1998, http://www.newamericancentury.org/iraqclintonletter.htm.

104. A Report of the Project for the New American Century, *Rebuilding America's Defenses: Strategy, Forces and Resources For a New Century*, September 2000, http://www.newamerican century.org/RebuildingAmericasDefenses.pdf, i, iv (accessed May 17, 2009); for relative military expenditures, see William E. Odom and Robert Dujairic, *America's Inadvertent Empire* (New Haven, Conn.: Yale University Press, 2004), 64–96; Andrew Bacevich, *American Empire: The Realities and Consequences of U.S. Diplomacy* (Cambridge, Mass: Harvard University Press, 2004).

105. Project for the New American Century, *Rebuilding America's Defenses*, 2, 6, 13.

has run America's defenses down over the decade through inadequate resources, promiscuous commitments, and the absence of a forward looking military strategy."[106] George W. Bush, the Republican nominee for president, chose foreign policy advisers, like Condoleezza Rice, renowned for their commitment to realpolitik. Rice condemned the Clinton administration for eroding the nation's military strength and employing U.S. military forces for humanitarian purposes and nation-building.[107] When asked during a presidential debate whether he "had formed any guiding principles for exercising [America's] enormous power," Bush responded, "I have. I have. First question is what's in the best interests of the United States? What's in the best interests of our people? When it comes to foreign policy that will be my guiding question. Is it in our nation's interests?"[108]

But the trope of freedom was too tempting for the Republican candidate. He was deeply conflicted about the respective roles of interests and of values in the formation of policy. The United States, he insisted, had to have more power, but it had to use it humbly. It had to have greater capabilities, but they must not be used, Bush said, "for what's called nation-building."[109] In his inaugural address, he said that the United States must "build our defenses beyond challenge, lest weakness invite challenge." But despite these references to power and interests, the theme of freedom was the defining feature of his inaugural address: "Through much of the last century, America's faith in freedom and democracy was a rock in a raging sea. Now it is a seed in the wind, taking root in many nations. Our democratic faith is more than the creed of our country, it is the inborn hope of our humanity, an ideal we carry but do not own, a trust we bear and pass along. And even after nearly 225 years, we have a long way yet to travel."[110]

To reconcile his concern for power and his embrace of freedom, Bush concocted the notion, rarely defined or explained, "of a balance of power in favor of freedom." America, Bush emphasized, "remains engaged in the world by history and by choice, shaping a balance of power that favors freedom. We will defend our allies and our interests. We will show purpose without arro-

---

106. Republican Party Platform of 2000, July 31, 2000, http://www.presidency.ucsb.edu/ws /index.php?pid=25849 (accessed May 17, 2009).

107. Condoleezza Rice, "Campaign 2000—Promoting the National Interest," *Foreign Affairs*, 79 (January–February 2000): 1–8.

108. "Presidential Debate in Winston-Salem, North Carolina," October 11, 2000, http://www .debates.org/pages/trans2000b.html (accessed May 17, 2009).

109. Ibid.

110. Bush, "Inaugural Address [January 20, 2001]," *Public Papers of the Presidents: George Walker Bush* (Washington, D.C.: Government Printing Office, 2001), 1–3 [hereafter, citations of the George W. Bush volumes of *Public Papers of the Presidents* are abbreviated *GWB* (year), page].

gance. We will meet aggression and bad faith with resolve and strength. And to all nations, we will speak for the values that gave our nation birth."[111]

Freedom dominated the new president's discourse—although it did not shape his foreign policy—during his first nine months in office. In speech after foreign policy speech, George W. Bush talked about freedom. Addressing Congress about the administration's goals, he said that he would promote "a distinctly American internationalism. We will work with our allies and friends to be a force for good and a champion of freedom. We will work for free markets, free trade, and freedom from oppression." On March 4, 2001, while championing missile defense, he exclaimed, "America, by nature, stands for freedom." On May 1, at the National Defense University, he noted the vastly different world that had evolved in recent years. "The Wall is gone," and the international landscape had been transformed. On May 3, to the American Jewish Committee, he voiced alarm about freedom of religion in the world: that freedom must be protected—"the first freedom of the human soul." On May 25, at the Naval Academy, he stressed "that no one can be neutral between right and wrong, tyranny and freedom." And, in Poland, on June 15, he heralded the spread of freedom: "Today, a new generation makes a new commitment. . . . The Iron Curtain is no more. Now we plan and build a house of freedom, whose doors are open to all of Europe's peoples and whose windows look out to global challenges beyond." And, on July 17, at the World Bank, he offered his own interpretation of globalization: "What some call globalization is, in fact, the triumph of human liberty stretching across national borders."[112]

Freedom, however, was beleaguered by rogue states and terrorist organizations. Bush warned that they might acquire weapons of mass destruction and blackmail the United States. "Unlike the cold war," he noted,

> today's most urgent threat stems not from thousands of ballistic missiles in Soviet hands but from a small number of missiles in the hands of these states, states for whom terror and blackmail are a way of life. . . . Like Saddam Hussein, some of today's tyrants are gripped by an implacable hatred of the United States of America. They hate our friends. They hate our values.

111. Ibid.
112. Bush, "Address Before a Joint Session of Congress [February 27, 2001]," *GWB* (2001), 145; Bush, "Remarks at the Christening Ceremony for the U.S.S. Ronald Reagan at Newport News, Virginia [March 4, 2001]," *GWB* (2001), 190; Bush, "Remarks at the National Defense University [May 1, 2001]," *GWB* (2001), 471; Bush, "Remarks to the American Jewish Committee [May 3, 2001]," *GWB* (2001), 487–88; Bush, "Commencement Address at the United States Naval Academy [May 25, 2001]," *GWB* (2001), 579; Bush, "Address at Warsaw University [June 15, 2001]," *GWB* (2001), 681; and Bush, "Remarks at the World Bank," July 17, 2001, http://www.presidency.ucsb.edu/ws/index.php?pid=73621 (accessed May 17, 2009).

They hate democracy and freedom and individual liberty. . . . In such a world cold war deterrence is not enough.[113]

The United States, according to President Bush, needed to use its power "for a broad strategy" of counterproliferation. "We need new concepts of deterrence," he explained, "that rely on both offensive and defensive forces." He wanted the United States to move beyond the constraints of the 1972 Anti-Ballistic Missile Treaty, harness technology for new forms of defense, and reconfigure (and downsize) the composition of nuclear forces to meet the new threats of a post–Cold War world. The overriding task was to thwart the spread of weapons of mass destruction. Should adversaries acquire these weapons, Bush reiterated, they would blackmail the United States and deter it from "forward thinking about fighting terrorism." The president asked Congress for an increase of $39 billion over the original 2001 military request submitted by the previous administration—the largest expansion in military spending since the Reagan buildup in the early 1980s.[114] The discourse about freedom and its universal appeal—reinforced by recollections of the wall's coming down—buttressed the administration's case to augment U.S. military capabilities to meet the challenges of a new era.

But alongside the plans to augment U.S. power, Bush's focus during these first nine months in office was also on the role of trade in the promotion of liberty. Open trade, he emphasized, was one of his top priorities. "Open trade fuels the engines of economic growth. . . . It applies the power of the market to the needs of the poor. It spurs the processes of economic and legal reform. . . . And open trade reinforces the habits of liberty that sustain democracy over the long term." And, again, on May 29, he reiterated that open trade "is a force for freedom in China, a force for stability in Asia, and a force for prosperity in the United States."[115]

This eclectic and ill-defined amalgam of freedom, power, interests, and openness came to an end on September 11, 2001. On that day, the looming threat materialized with dramatic suddenness: not long before, it had seemed distant and inchoate; now it was ferocious and omnipresent. Administration

113. Bush, "Remarks at the National Defense University [May 1, 2001]," *GWB* (2001), 471–72.

114. Ibid.; Bush, "The President's News Conference [June 12, 2001]," *GWB* (2001), 640–41; Bush, "The President's News Conference [June 15, 2001]," *GWB* (2001), 672; Bush, "Remarks at the Veterans of Foreign Wars Convention," August 20, 2001, http://www.presidency.ucsb.edu/ws/index.php?pid=63225&st=remarks+at+the+veterans+of+foreign+wars+convention&str (accessed May 17, 2009).

115. Bush, "Remarks to the Organization of American States [April 17, 2001]," *GWB* (2001), 408–409; Bush, "Remarks to the Los Angeles World Affairs Council [May 29, 2001]," *GWB* (2001), 593–98.

officials felt that war had been declared on the United States. Danger lurked everywhere, reinforced by the anonymous delivery of letters containing anthrax in the immediate aftermath of the attack on the Twin Towers and the Pentagon. The events of 9/11, said Condoleezza Rice, "crystallized our vulnerability." "After 9/11," she went on, "there is no longer any doubt that today America faces an existential threat to our security—a threat as great as any we faced during the Civil War, World War II, or the Cold War."[116]

Facing peril, the Bush administration unleashed America's awesome military power, first against the Taliban in Afghanistan and then against Saddam Hussein in Iraq. Its rationale was straightforward: "The greater the threat, the greater is the risk of inaction." Peril justified the preemptive and unilateral use of America's military force. Peril meant that the United States had to shock and overwhelm the adversary. But the president and his advisers emphasized that the mission was larger than defense of country: "We fight, as we always fight," they stressed, "for a just peace—a peace that favors liberty."[117]

The tropes of the Cold War and the memories of Berlin were vivid. When Iraqi forces were crushed and American troops entered Baghdad, the president rejoiced. America's mission had been accomplished; its commitment to liberty vindicated. Iraqis—like Germans, and like all human beings—yearned to be free.[118] "The toppling of Saddam Hussein's statue in Baghdad," he later explained, "will be recorded alongside the fall of the Berlin Wall as one of the great moments in the history of liberty."[119] Most Americans shared this viewpoint. They believed that the crumbling of the wall had been an important, perhaps even one of the most decisive, moments in the twentieth century.[120]

Tragedy and peril transformed the quest for a democratic peace into a national security imperative that justified the use of force and the exercise of America's unparalleled power. Advancing America's ideals, Bush proclaimed in his second inaugural address, had "become the urgent requirement of our nation's security and the calling of our time." It was now the policy of the United States, he declared, "to seek and support the growth of democratic

116. Condoleezza Rice, "A Balance of Power that Favors Freedom," October 1, 2002, http://www.manhattan-institute.org/html/wl2002.htm (accessed May 17, 2009).

117. The administration's clearest statement of strategy was "The National Security Strategy of the United States of America," September 17, 2002 (Washington, D.C.: The White House, 2002)].

118. Bush, "Remarks from the USS Abraham Lincoln," May 1, 2003, http://www.presidency.ucsb.edu/ws/index.php?pid=68675&st=&str= (accessed May 17, 2009).

119. Bush, "Remarks at Fort Hood," April 12, 2005, http://www.presidency.ucsb.edu/ws/index.php?pid=62995&st=&str= (accessed May 17, 2009).

120. Gallup Poll, November 1999, Roper Center for Public Opinion Research, University of Connecticut.

movements and institutions in every nation and culture, with the ultimate goal of ending tyranny in our world."[121] Tolerating tyranny, he explained, had been a strategic as well as moral failure. "Pursuing stability at the expense of liberty does not lead to peace—it leads to September the 11th, 2001."[122] Although the quest for freedom was fraught with difficulty, and the liberation of Iraq had become a nightmare, the challenge could not be avoided. During the long Cold War, he recollected, people also had despaired, but courage and persistence had paid off. "When Harry Truman promised American support for free peoples resisting Soviet aggression," Bush told the American people on the fifth anniversary of the September 11 attacks, Truman "could not have foreseen the rise of the Berlin Wall, but he would not have been surprised to see it brought down. Throughout our history," Bush continued, "America has seen liberty challenged, and every time, we have seen liberty triumph with sacrifice and determination." In other words, the battle of ideas could not be forsaken. Freedom now prevailed across the European continent, and one day it would "ring out across the world." Like President Clinton before him, Bush loved to remind audiences that "more people now live in freedom than ever before."[123]

Except that they didn't. Freedom House, an organization with no wish to embarrass George W. Bush, reported in 2007 and 2008 that worrisome trends had set in: "The year 2007 was marked by a notable setback for global freedom," it reported. It was the first time in fifteen years that freedom had registered setbacks in two consecutive years. In 2007, thirty-eight countries showed evidence of declines in freedom, while only ten displayed a positive trajectory. In the Middle East, in particular, the region that George W. Bush so desperately wanted to transform, the signs were especially portentous: declines were evident in Egypt, Syria, Lebanon, and the Palestinian Authority. Many of these countries had been moving in a positive direction, but that no longer was the case.[124]

121. Bush, "Second Inaugural Address," January 20, 2005, http://www.presidency.ucsb.edu/ws/index.php?pid=58745&st=&str= (accessed May 17, 2009).

122. Bush, "Remarks to the Democracy and Security Conference in Prague," June 5, 2007, http://www.presidency.ucsb.edu/ws/index.php?pid=75306&st=&str= (accessed May 17, 2009).

123. Bush, "Address to the Nation on the War on Terror," September 11, 2006, http://www.presidency.ucsb.edu/ws/index.php?pid=73962&st=&str= (accessed May 17, 2009); Bush, "Speech to the OECD," June 13, 2008, http://www.presidency.ucsh.edu/ws/index.php?pid=77488&st=&str= (accessed May 17, 2009); Bush, "Remarks to the Democracy and Security Conference in Prague," June 5, 2007, http://www.presidency.ucsb.edu/ws/index.php?pid=75306&st=&str= (accessed May 17, 2009).

124. Arch Puddington, "Findings of Freedom in the World 2008—Freedom in Retreat: Is the Tide Turning?" http://www.freedomhouse.org/template.cfm?page=130&year=2008 (accessed May 17, 2009); also see Arch Puddington, "Freedom in the World 2007: Freedom Stagnation

Freedom was faltering for many reasons, but one of the most conspicuous was the fallout of 9/11. America's use of force had tarnished America's reputation and undercut its capacity to be a force for democratic change.[125]

## Power, Mission, and Threat Perception

Power and a sense of mission can be intoxicating as well as uplifting. George H. W. Bush and Bill Clinton rejoiced in the crumbling of the Berlin Wall. They believed it confirmed America as the world's one indispensable nation. They sought to rebuff isolationist impulses, solidify U.S. preponderance, and enhance the nation's capabilities to intervene in regions far from America's shores. Yet they also recognized that force had to be used soberly, prudently, and judiciously. Freedom did not come easily—certainly not through the barrel of a gun or even by simply depositing a ballot in an election box. Freedom required tolerance, openness, and the rule of law.[126] Their actions and inactions—for good and for bad—illuminated how complicated such matters were.

George W. Bush embraced many of the same ideas of his predecessors and wanted to employ and augment the capabilities they had nurtured to effectuate a more open world conducive to U.S. interests and values and amenable to U.S. power. He wanted to build missile defenses and deter potential foes. He wanted to promote U.S. interests and spread U.S. ideals, ideals that in his view had universal appeal and a divine imprimatur. He hoped to do all these things without acting arrogantly and counterproductively. But once the United States was attacked and its vulnerabilities exposed, the temptation to use its unmatched capabilities was irresistible.[127]

Threat and peril transformed rhetorical tropes into an action agenda. After all, policymakers in Washington had been planning for regional wars for almost a decade and now had justification and incentive to put planning to practice. Declaring a righteous mission, President George W. Bush set out to defeat evil and end tyranny, confident that the story of the Cold War and the crumbling of the Berlin Wall vindicated America's past efforts and portended ever more glory, more freedom, and more power in the future.

---

Amid Pushback against Democracy," http://www.freedomhouse.org/template.cfm?page=363&year=2007 (accessed May 17, 2009).

125. See, for example, Peter W. Galbraith, *Unintended Consequences: How War in Iraq Strengthened America's Enemies* (New York: Simon and Schuster, 2008).

126. See, for example, George H. W. Bush's highly criticized but quite thoughtful "chicken Kiev" speech in the Ukraine, August 1, 1991, *GHWB* (1991), 1005–8.

127. For an elaboration of my views on this matter, see Melvyn P. Leffler, "9/11 and American Foreign Policy," *Diplomatic History*, 29 (June 2005): 395–413.

No matter how desperate the situation appeared in Baghdad during the awful days of 2004–07, the president and his advisers could recall the bleakest days of the Cold War—the blockade of Berlin in 1948 and the face-off of Soviet and American tanks at checkpoint Charlie in 1961—and then recall the unanticipated joys of victory on November 9, 1989. For them, the mystic chords of memory ran deep and long. Freedom would prevail—even in the Middle East—if the United States demonstrated its resolve and applied its power. Were not those the best-informed lessons of the long twilight struggle with communism? Or were they illusory dreams emanating from rhetorical tropes and manufactured memories that associated the end of the Cold War with Berliners traversing the wall—dancing for joy, dancing for history?[128]

128. This evokes the language of the editorial "The End of the War to End Wars," *The New York Times*, November 11, 1989, 26.

# 9

# 9/11 and American Foreign Policy

When the George W. Bush administration declared a global war on terror and issued its National Security Strategy Statement in September 2002, many commentators and scholars concluded that a radical transformation in American national security strategy was under way. They focused on U.S. readiness to take unilateral action, preserve military hegemony against all rivals, and take "anticipatory" or preventative actions against looming threats.

I did not think that this interpretation was correct. I believed such analyses confused tactics and goals. In my view the National Security Strategy Statement of 2002 restated traditional goals of U.S. foreign policy: a desire to preserve a stable and open international order based on the free movement of goods, capital, and people. It stipulated that the aim of U.S. policy was "to ignite a new era of global economic growth through free markets and free trade." It reiterated the longstanding Cold War policy of seeking "a balance of power in favor of freedom," meaning preserving America's preponderant power. Like many predecessor administrations, President Bush wanted to promote democracy, freedom, and human dignity, and he reiterated America's desire to "expand the circle of development by opening societies and building the infrastructure of democracy." The basic goals of U.S. national security policy had not changed. (See "The National Security Strategy Statement of the United

I want to express my appreciation to the Stanford University Institute for International Studies for inviting me to deliver the Robert Wesson Lecture in May 2004. The ideas in this article were formulated for that occasion. I am also grateful to Bill Burr for his comments and insights.

States of America," September 2002, *http://www.state.gov/documents/organi-zation/63562.pdf*.)

What had shifted was the calculation of threat and the means to achieve goals. In the article below I emphasized that 9/11 dramatically altered the threat perception of U.S. policymakers. "The greater the threat," said the strategy statement, "the greater the risk of inaction." In this new threat environment, policymakers declared that the old tactics of deterrence and containment could not work. Although the employment of preemptive or preventative action was not entirely new in the U.S. diplomatic experience, the emphasis accorded to it was much more pronounced. Threat perception altered tactics, not goals. To justify the new tactics, President Bush raised the rhetorical trope of democracy promotion to a new level of importance, and this was even more true after weapons of mass destruction were not located in Iraq. For me, 9/11 raised interesting and complicated questions about the relationships between interests, values, threat perception, and the employment of power. In this article I tried to grapple with those relationships.

In my ongoing research about the response to 9/11, what stood out was the level of fear about another prospective attack. Some of the apprehension related to worries that Democrats might capitalize politically if another attack occurred, but much of the fear was more profound. Officials felt a sense of responsibility to protect American lives, property, sovereignty, and honor. They worried that another attack might arouse demands for monitoring domestic subversives, protecting borders, and regulating the economy that could amount to a reconfiguration of American values and institutions. "The president knew," Secretary of Defense Donald Rumsfeld wrote in his memoir, "that a series of 9/11- type attacks—in conjunction with biological toxins or suitcase nuclear weapons, or other nightmare combinations—could drastically alter the free and open nature of our society." (Donald Rumsfeld, *Known and Unknown: A Memoir* [New York: Sentinel, 2011], 356, 361–62.)

Concerns of this sort reminded me of some of the apprehensions that resided in the minds of U.S. officials when faced with Axis domination of Eurasia in 1940 and 1941 and Soviet/communist advances during the early years of the Cold War. These fears might have been excessive, but they were sincerely felt by officials at the time, and they illuminated the ongoing relationships between national security and core American values. (See my article "The Foreign Policies of the George W. Bush Administration: Memoirs, History, Legacy," *Diplomatic History* 37 [April 2013]: 190–216.)

This article appeared in *Diplomatic History*, 29 ( June 2005): 395–413.

———

There is enormous controversy about the foreign policy of the administration of George W. Bush in the aftermath of 9/11.[1] Both supporters and critics make the case for revolutionary change. These claims serve the interests of both sides of the controversy. Supporters want to argue that policymakers are bold, creative, and imaginative in response to what they allege are unprecedented threats. Critics want to claim that the administration is adventurous, provocative, and imprudent.

My argument is that there is more continuity than change in the policies of the Bush administration. Bush's rhetoric and actions have deep roots in the history of American foreign policy. Understanding these roots is important because they help to illuminate the different trajectories that inhere in the American diplomatic experience. The possession of immense power and the belief in a universal mission have the potential to produce great good and great harm. Given this dynamic mix of power and ideals, there is no substitute for the exercise of good judgment.

While stressing continuities, there has also been important change. Change, however, does not constitute a revolution. The change I see constitutes a recalibration in the complicated interaction between the assessment of threat, the calculation of interest, the enunciation of values, and the mobilization of power. In the history of U.S. foreign policy, threats, interests, ideals, and power always have had a dynamic and changing relationship with one another. At times of heightened threat perception, the assertion of values mounts and subsumes careful calculation of interests. Values and ideals are asserted to help evoke public support for the mobilization of power; power, then, tempts the government to overreach far beyond what careful calculations of interest might dictate. The genius of American foreign policy is the capacity to recalibrate the relationships between these variables; the

---

1. For criticism, see, for example, James Mann, *Rise of the Vulcans: The History of Bush's War Cabinet* (New York, 2004); Ivo H. Daalder and James M. Lindsay, *America Unbound: The Bush Revolution in Foreign Policy* (Washington, D.C., 2003); John Newhouse, *Imperial America: The Bush Assault on the World Order* (New York, 2003); for praise, see, for example, Rowan Scarborough, *Rumsfeld's War: The Untold Story of America's Anti-Terrorist Commander* (Washington, D.C., 2004); for understanding, see Robert Kagan, *Paradise and Power: America and Europe in the New World Order* (London, 2003); David Frum and Richard Perle, *An End to Evil: How to Win the War on Terror* (New York, 2003); for a sympathetic portrait, Bob Woodward, *Bush at War* (New York, 2002); for a subsequent, less sympathetic portrait of the administration's policymaking, Bob Woodward, *Plan of Attack* (New York, 2004); for reflective, insightful evaluations placing Bush policy in historical perspective, see especially Niall Ferguson, *Colossus: The Price of America's Empire* (New York, 2004); John Lewis Gaddis, *Surprise, Security, and the American Experience* (Cambridge, Mass., 2004); Andrew Bacevich, *American Empire: The Realities and Consequences of U.S. Diplomacy* (Cambridge, Mass., 2003).

nightmare of American foreign policy is that the relationships forever remain unstable, subject, as they should be, to changing perceptions of threat.

Let me begin by explaining why post-9/11 American foreign policy is not revolutionary. The principal guide to Bush national security policy is his September 2002 strategy statement. All of the administration's subsequent documents have been written to conform with it.

What does the National Security Strategy Statement advocate? Its critics tend to focus on preemption, unilateralism, and military hegemony. These features merit the attention they have received, and I will get to them in a moment, but one should not overlook the fact that Bush national security strategy focuses on much more than preemption, unilateralism, and hegemony. The Bush strategy statement first affirms very traditional objectives: "political and economic freedom; peaceful relations with other states, and respect for human dignity." In fact, its overriding goal is to promote an international order that favors freedom. The United States, says the Bush National Security Strategy Statement, "must defend liberty and justice because these principles are right and true for all people."[2]

The path toward this overriding goal is spelled out in the subsections of the national strategy paper. The United States must "champion aspirations for human dignity"; "strengthen alliances to defeat global terrorism"; "work with others to defuse regional conflicts"; "prevent our enemies from threatening us, our allies, and our friends, with weapons of mass destruction"; "ignite a new era of global economic growth through free markets and free trade"; "expand the circle of development by opening societies and building the infrastructure of democracy"; "develop agendas for cooperative action with other main centers of global power"; and "transform America's national security institutions to meet the challenges and opportunities of the twenty-first century."[3]

If you read this agenda alone, you could not make a claim that there was anything revolutionary about Bush foreign policy. Think of the Open Door Notes of 1899 and 1900, the Fourteen Points, Wilsonian rhetoric during World War I, the Atlantic Charter, the Truman Doctrine. More recently, you might compare the Bush national security agenda to the last mission statement of the Clinton administration's Department of State, the aim of which was to "create a more secure, prosperous and democratic world for the benefit of the American people." To achieve this task, the Clinton people laid out their own agenda: first, "secure peace; deter aggression; prevent, and defuse, and manage crises; halt the proliferation of weapons of mass destruction; and advance

2. "The National Security Strategy of the United States of America," September 2002, p. 3, available at http://www.whitehouse.gov/nsc/nss.html [hereafter cited as "Bush National Security Strategy"].

3. Ibid.

arms control and disarmament"; second, "expand exports, open markets, assist American business, foster economic growth, and promote sustainable development"; third, "protect American citizens abroad and safeguard the borders of the United States"; fourth, "combat international terrorism, crime, and narcotics trafficking"; fifth, "support the establishment and consolidation of democracies, and uphold human rights"; sixth, "provide humanitarian assistance to victims of crisis and disaster"; and seventh, "improve the global environment, stabilize world population growth, and protect human health."[4]

The generalizations are remarkably similar, the continuities compelling, notwithstanding different emphases on arms control and the environment. But, of course, the devil is in the details. What appears "revolutionary" in Bush's national strategy is the alleged dismissal of deterrence, alliance formation, multilateralism, and containment in favor of a strategy of preemption, prevention, unilateralism, and hegemony. Deterrence, insists the Bush strategy statement, will not suffice against rogue states and terrorists. Terrorists seek to target innocent people; they seek martyrdom; and their "most potent protection is statelessness." Hence the need "to adapt the concept of imminent threat to the capabilities and objectives of today's adversaries"; hence the need for preemptive, one might even call it preventative, action. "The greater the threat," asserts the strategy statement, "the greater is the risk of inaction—and the more compelling is the case for taking anticipatory action to defend ourselves, even if uncertainty remains as to the time and place of the enemy's attack."[5]

Much has been made of this statement. Preemption, along with a willingness to act unilaterally and maintain military preponderance, constitutes the case for a transformative foreign policy. The Bush national security team, writes James Mann, "set down an entirely new set of ideas and principles. They were deliberately choosing to create a new conception of American foreign policy, just as the Truman administration had constructed a new framework of ideas and institutions at the beginning of the cold war."[6] In addition to the preemption doctrine, Mann emphasizes the Bush team's determination to build and configure forces "strong enough to dissuade potential adversaries from . . . surpassing, or equaling, the power of the United States."[7]

But none of this is really revolutionary. Preemptive military action is not new. When Theodore Roosevelt justified intervention in the Caribbean and Central America, it was explicitly a preemptive form of intervention, indeed "protective imperialism," as Samuel Flagg Bemis called it many years ago. The

4. "A National Security Strategy for a Global Age," December 2000, available at http://www.au.af.mil/au/awc/awcgate/nss/nss_dec2000_contents.htm.

5. "Bush National Security Strategy," 10–11.

6. Mann, *Rise of the Vulcans*, 329–30; see also Daalder and Lindsay, *America Unbound*, 199.

7. Mann, *Rise of the Vulcans*, 20.

point was to use military force to intervene, establish order, and preclude European powers from having any excuse for inserting their forces on America's periphery. Actually, when you think about it, it was more than preemption; the use of force was explicitly preventative because there was no imminent threat to American security.[8]

In 1941, Theodore's distant cousin, Franklin, also justified preemptive, or one might even say preventative, use of force. After the USS *Greer*, an American destroyer, was attacked by Nazi submarines, President Roosevelt distorted the circumstances surrounding the incident and announced, "This is the time for prevention of attack." Thereafter, German and Italian vessels traversing the North Atlantic would do so "at their own peril." In a fireside chat, Roosevelt explained his thinking to his countrymen: "When you see a rattlesnake poised to strike, you do not wait until he has struck before you crush him." Hitler, of course, was not about to declare war on the United States, but Roosevelt saw a looming threat and decided to take preventative action. "The time for active defense," he declared, "is now."[9]

Nor were preemptive, preventative, and unilateralist strategies and tactics abandoned during the Cold War. Of course, they were not always the strategy of choice, but they were always options, just as they remain today. The Bush strategy states: "The United States will not use force in all cases to prevent emerging threats, nor should nations use preemption as a pretext for aggression."[10] Condoleezza Rice and Colin Powell have stated many times that preemption is not a favored policy.[11] They have not acted preemptively or unilaterally (thus far) against Iran or North Korea. The new mission statement of the Department of State says, "We will strive to strengthen traditional alliances . . . , but when necessary, we will act alone to face the challenges, provide assistance, and seize the opportunities of this era. . . . The history of American foreign policy suggests that we will increase our chances of success abroad by exerting principled leadership while seeking to work with others to achieve our goals."[12]

8. Samuel Flagg Bemis, *The Latin American Policy of the United States: An Historical Interpretation* (New York, 1943), 110, 151–67; in a recent account, Frank Ninkovich calls it "preemptive imperialism." See Frank Ninkovich, *The United States and Imperialism* (Malden, Mass., 2001), 91.

9. Samuel I. Rosenman, ed., *The Public Papers and Addresses of Franklin D. Roosevelt, 1941* (New York, 1950), 384–92.

10. "Bush National Security Strategy," 11.

11. Condoleezza Rice, "A Balance of Power that Favors Freedom," Wriston Lecture at the Manhattan Institute for Policy Research, October 1, 2002, available at http://www.manhattan-institute.org/html/wl2002.htm; testimony by Secretary of State Colin L. Powell, U.S. Senate Committee on Foreign Relations, February 6, 2003, p. 43. Available from: LexisNexis Congressional (online service). Bethesda, Md.: Congressional Information Service.

12. U.S. Department of State and U.S. Agency for International Development (USAID),

This language accords with the thinking of the officials who waged the Cold War. Although many writers want to believe that the Cold War signified the heyday of multilateralism, collaboration, and deterrence, this should not blind us to the presence of unilateralist and preventative options whenever it was deemed advantageous to choose them. The wise men of the Truman administration worked brilliantly to forge alliances, but they never foreswore the right to act unilaterally. President Dwight D. Eisenhower and Secretary of State John Foster Dulles recognized this fact. They sought solidarity with allies. In fact, they wrote guidelines into their national security strategy for the maintenance of alliance cohesion. But they also emphasized that the United States should "act independently of its major allies when the advantage of achieving U.S. objectives by such action clearly outweighs the danger of lasting damage to its alliances. In this connection, consideration should be given to the likelihood that the initiation of action by the United States prior to allied acceptance may bring about subsequent allied support. Allied reluctance to act should not inhibit the United States from taking action, including the use of nuclear weapons, to prevent Communist territorial gains when such action is clearly necessary to U.S. security."[13]

In fact, during the Eisenhower years, although there was a conscious rejection of preventative war against the Soviet Union, there was always the explicit readiness to adopt bold, unilateralist, even preventative options elsewhere should it seem necessary and desirable to do so. This was particularly the case when the Eisenhower administration pondered the strategic principles for dealing with "local Communist aggression," which included civil wars and indigenous strife. While prudently rejecting intervention in Indochina in 1954, Eisenhower and Dulles nonetheless insisted that the United States had to preserve the flexibility and capability to defeat local aggression, hopefully without initiating general war. The United States, they resolved, "must be determined to take, unilaterally if necessary, whatever additional action its security requires, even to the extent of general war, and the Communists must be convinced of this determination."[14]

Eisenhower and Dulles did not want to become locked in another land war in Asia, but they explicitly reserved the option of preventative military action against Communist China. They stated in one of their national security documents that it was the policy of the United States to "reduce the power of Communist China in Asia even at the risk of, but without deliberately provoking,

---

Security, Democracy, Prosperity: Strategic Plan, Fiscal Years 2004–2009 (Washington, D.C., 2003), USAID Publications 11084, p. 1.

13. Department of State, *Foreign Relations of the United States, 1952–1954* (Washington, D.C., 1984), 2:721 [hereafter cited as *FRUS*].

14. Ibid., 718.

war."[15] In other words, in response to local contingencies, the United States might choose to employ force in the wider region. But this remained an option, not a foregone conclusion. Eisenhower agreed with Dulles when the secretary of state insisted at a National Security Council meeting that "he did not wish to see the United States become involved in a major war where world public opinion would be wholly against the United States, because that, he said, was the kind of war you lose."[16]

Preventative war against the Soviet Union was dismissed because it was deemed impractical and suicidal. At a National Security Council meeting shortly before he died, President John F. Kennedy asked "whether even if we attacked the USSR first, the loss to the U.S. would be unacceptable to political leaders." "Even if we preempt," said General Leon Johnson, "surviving Soviet capability is sufficient to produce an unacceptable loss in the United States."[17] Probing further, Kennedy inquired, "What about pre-empt today with the Soviets in a low state of alert." This time Secretary of Defense Robert McNamara replied. "In the many studies I have had done for me," McNamara told Kennedy, "I have not found a situation in which a pre-empt during a low-alert condition would be advantageous. Under no circumstances have I been able to get US casualties under 30-million. . . . They can destroy us with a few weapons and we can do the same to them. Therefore, pre-empt is not advantageous for either side."[18]

But this did not mean that preemptive or preventative military actions were foresworn. It simply meant that Kennedy would not use them against the Soviet homeland. At the very same time that he was confirming that preventative war against Soviet Russia was suicidal, President Kennedy and his top advisers pondered preventative military action against the emerging Chinese nuclear threat. Kennedy "felt this was probably the most serious problem facing the world today." We should be prepared, he thought, "to take some form of action unless they agreed to desist from further efforts in this field."[19] Kennedy wanted to ascertain the Kremlin's views about "limiting or preventing Chinese nuclear development." Specifically, the president wanted to find out whether Khrushchev might "take Soviet action or . . . accept US action aimed in this direction."[20]

15. Ibid., 12:772.

16. Ibid., 12:753.

17. Ibid., 1961–1963, 8:499–500.

18. Ibid., 506.

19. Ibid., 22:339; see the illuminating article by William Burr and Jeffrey T. Richelson, "Whether to 'Strangle the Baby in the Cradle': The United States and the Chinese Nuclear Program, 1960–1964," *International Security* 25 (Winter 2000/2001): 54–99.

20. *FRUS*, 1961–1963, 7:801.

After Kennedy's death, intelligence analysts and East Asian experts convinced President Lyndon B. Johnson and McGeorge Bundy, his national security adviser, that China's acquisition of nuclear capabilities would not endanger vital U.S. interests.[21] Consequently, they did not employ preventative force directly against China or the Soviet Union, but the Kennedy and Johnson administrations did adopt unilateralist, preventative measures in relation to other perceived threats. The most conspicuous case, of course, was the deployment of force to blockade Cuba in October 1962.[22] But Johnson's decisions to send troops to the Dominican Republic and to deploy combat forces to Indochina were preventative in nature, although we often do not think of them in that way. But we should, if we wish to place Bush national security strategy in proper historical perspective. Certainly, in thinking about Cuba, the Dominican Republic, and Indochina, Kennedy's and Johnson's best and brightest advisers embraced the notion that the United States should be prepared to take preventative initiatives to counter a looming threat. The Bundys, Secretary of State Dean Rusk, and McNamara would not have disputed the language of the Bush national strategy statement: "The greater the threat, the greater the risk of inaction—and the more compelling the case for taking anticipatory action to defend ourselves, even if uncertainty remains as to the time and place of the enemy's attack."[23]

When they perceived threats, especially in the Third World, U.S. officials during the Cold War did not refrain from acting unilaterally. Against French and British advice, they moved ahead with their Vietnam venture, more or less unilaterally.[24] Their thinking was preventative: they had to prevent dominos from falling. They knew they were acting according to the dictates of their own assumptions. At a particularly excruciating moment, President Johnson exclaimed to Bundy, "What in the hell am I ordering our kids to Indochina? What in the hell is Vietnam worth to me? What is Laos worth to me? . . . We've got a treaty but hell, everybody else has got a treaty out there, and they're not

21. Burr and Richelson, "Whether to 'Strangle the Baby in the Cradle,'" 73–91.

22. The Kennedy tapes reveal that all the discussion was about what form of preventative action the United States should take. The discussions were not about whether to take preventative action. The issue was how to get the missiles out of Cuba without provoking a nuclear war; the need for some sort of preventative military action was assumed by all the decision-makers. See Ernest R. May and Philip D. Zelikow, *The Kennedy Tapes: Inside the White House during the Cuban Missile Crisis* (Cambridge, Mass., 1997).

23. "Bush National Security Strategy," 11.

24. Fredrik Logevall, *Choosing War: The Last Chance for Peace and the Escalation of War in Vietnam* (Berkeley, Calif., 1999), 2–3, 84, 123–33, 222–28, 278–80, 373. The British tempered their criticism, but refused to assist the United States militarily. "We can't kick our creditors in the balls," said Prime Minister Harold Wilson. See the review article, John W. Young, "Britain and LBJ's War, 1964–1968," *Cold War History* 2 (April 2002): 63–92. The quotation is on p. 88.

doing a thing." But then, significantly, Johnson added: "Of course, if you start running from the communists, they may just chase you right into your own kitchen."[25]

And one should remember that, although Johnson and his advisers were subsequently excoriated for exercising poor judgment in estimating the nature of the threat and in deploying force, it was not the unilateralism that bothered opponents. Long before Vietnam was a controversial issue tearing the nation apart, George Kennan wrote Walt Rostow: "Insofar as problems of security are concerned . . . , I am skeptical of the utility of collective and multilateral arrangements, in many instances. I suspect we lose more, by such arrangements, in the way of promptness and flexibility of action and privacy of decision than we gain in the way of added military and political resources."[26]

Nor would the Cold Warriors who advised Presidents Truman, Eisenhower, Kennedy, and Johnson have objected to the Bush administration's determination to maintain military superiority. Cold Warriors knew that deterrence might fail, or that its principles did not apply well to unrest and insurgencies in the Third World. They, too, wanted to build forces to ensure that no adversary could impose its will on the United States. The United States, they agreed, must never allow itself to be "blackmailed," to use a favorite term of the Bush people. No enemy, or potential enemy, should be allowed to acquire comparable power. Paul Nitze, the most representative Cold Warrior from Truman to Reagan, wrote in 1950 that the state of world affairs was fluid. "One side will gain and the other will decline as a factor in world affairs. It must be our objective to be the one which gains. . . . [T]he United States and the Soviet Union are engaged in a struggle for preponderant power. . . . [T]o seek less than preponderant power would be to opt for defeat. Preponderant power must be the objective of U.S. policy."[27] Nitze's successors in the Eisenhower administration embraced this idea. In their strategy paper, they acknowledged that the "nuclear balance [was] unlikely to create a permanent stalemate in the arms race. Therefore a sustained effort must be made to invent and develop capabilities which will provide decisive preponderance to U.S. power."[28]

Cold Warriors did not seek preponderant power because they contemplated a preemptive or preventative attack on the Soviet Union. As indicated, they knew that such an idea was suicidal. Preponderant power was a means to support a risk-taking, often unilateralist diplomacy, aimed at maximizing situations of strength. Containment, Paul Nitze emphasized, was not a defensive, reactive strategy. Containment, he stressed, was coercive diplomacy. Govern-

25. *FRUS*, 1964–1968, 27:135.
26. Ibid., 1961–1963, 8:291.
27. Ibid., 1952–1954, 2:64.
28. Ibid., 657.

ments needed strength to cast shadows and buttress their diplomacy. Government ments needed strength to dominate the escalatory process in crisis situations.[29] Even after the Soviets achieved nuclear parity, for example, Nixon and Kissinger still worked tenaciously to readjust war planning and to alter the Strategic Integrated Operations Plan (SIOP) in order to develop "politically meaningful threats."[30] Not many Cold Warriors would find it surprising for Bush's advisers to write in their strategy paper that it was the aim of the United States to prevent adversaries "from surpassing, or equaling, the power of the United States." This principle is as traditional as apple pie.

Nor did policy or strategic attitudes change much after the Cold War. When the elder Bush departed from office, Clinton and his advisers did not reverse course. In fact, America's military superiority grew. By the late 1990s, the United States was spending more money on arms than practically all the rest of the world combined.[31] This was not just accidental; it was explicit policy formulation. In their last strategy paper, "A National Security Strategy for a Global Age," Clinton's advisers made it clear that their "ability to respond to the full spectrum of threats requires that we have the best-trained, best-equipped, most effective armed forces in the world."[32] Forces needed to be mobile and agile. To deploy them effectively, American technology had to be the best. In fact, the vision statement prepared by the Joint Chiefs of Staff was breathtaking in its ambitions: "The overall goal . . . is the creation of a force that is dominant across the full spectrum of military operations—persuasive in peace, decisive in war, preeminent in any form of conflict."[33]

Ostensibly, these military capabilities were for deterrence, but deterrence was entwined with compulsion. "Efforts to deter an adversary," according to the Clinton team, "be it an aggressor nation, terrorist group or criminal organization—can become the leading edge of crisis response. In this sense, deterrence straddles the line between shaping the international environment and responding to crises."[34] The joint chiefs made the same point. The United States would continue to face threats to its global interests and responsibilities. In this environment "the strategic concepts of decisive force, power

29. I develop this argument at considerable length in *A Preponderance of Power: National Security, the Truman Administration, and the Cold War* (Stanford, Calif., 1992), 18–19, 208–19, 262–63, 354–63, 396–410, 438–50, 488–92, 502–10.

30. William Burr, "The 'Horror Strategy' and the Nixon Administration's Search for Limited Nuclear Options, 1969–1972," *Journal of Cold War Studies*, 7 (Summer 2005): 34–78.

31. Bacevich, *American Empire*, 125–27; see also William E. Odom and Robert Dujarric, *America's Inadvertent Empire* (New Haven, Conn., 2004), 64–96.

32. "A National Security Strategy for a Global Age," Part 2, p. 11.

33. Combined Joint Chiefs of Staff [JCS], *Joint Vision 2020: America's Military: Preparing for Tomorrow*, 1. The performance of the U.S. military establishment, of course, did not always match its ambition. See Bacevich, *American Empire*, 133–40.

34. "A National Security Strategy for a Global Age," Part 2, p. 11.

projection, overseas presence, and strategic agility [would] continue to govern" the nation's efforts in peace as well as in war.[35]

In public speeches and congressional testimony, Secretary of State Madeleine Albright talked eloquently about cooperating with our allies, but the strategy of the Clinton administration preserved the right to act unilaterally and to strike preemptively. The United States, Clinton's national security advisers stated, had vital interests—those "directly connected to the survival, safety, and vitality of our nation." These included the physical security of the American homeland and the territories of our allies, the physical safety of American citizens at home and abroad, the protection of our infrastructure, including energy, banking, finance, transportation, and water systems, and the protection against the proliferation of weapons of mass destruction. "We will do what we must," said the Clinton national security team, "to defend these [vital] interests. This may involve the use of military force, including unilateral action, where deemed necessary or appropriate."[36]

In fact, Clinton already had approved the option of preemptive action. In June 1995, he signed Presidential Decision Directive 39 (PDD) regarding counterterrorism. Much of it is still classified, but the redacted version is suggestive. "It is the policy of the United States," it begins, "to deter, defeat, and respond vigorously to all terrorist attacks on our territory and against our citizens, or facilities, whether they occur domestically, in international waters or airspace or on foreign territory. The United States regards all such terrorism as a potential threat to national security as well as a criminal act and will apply all appropriate means to combat it. In doing so, the U.S. shall pursue vigorously efforts to deter and preempt, apprehend and prosecute, or assist other governments to prosecute, individuals who perpetrate or plan to perpetrate such attacks." The PDD went on to say that the United States would seek to identify groups or states "that sponsor or support such terrorists, isolate them and extract a heavy price for their actions." Much of the document is still classified, but it does not take much imagination to see that the administration contemplated covert and overt military action, sometimes to prevent and sometimes to preempt. Toward the end of the document, in a section on weapons of mass destruction, the PDD states: "The United States shall give the highest priority to developing effective capabilities to detect, prevent, defeat, and manage the consequences of nuclear, biological or chemical (NBC) materials or weapons use by terrorists. The acquisition of weapons of mass destruction by a terrorist group, through theft or manufacture, is unacceptable. There is no higher priority than preventing the acquisition of this capability from terrorist groups potentially opposed to the U.S."

35. JCS, *Joint Vision 2020*, 1.
36. "A National Security Strategy for a Global Age," Part 1, p. 4.

These statements are followed by a redacted page, "denied in full" for purposes of declassification.[37]

In their last strategy statement, Clinton's advisers made clear that they supported preemptive action. The threat emanating from the nexus of terrorists, rogue states, and weapons of mass destruction was indeed terrifying. "We make no concessions to terrorists," the Clinton team declared. "Whenever possible, we use law enforcement, diplomatic and economic tools to wage the fight against terrorism. But there have been, and will be, times when these tools are not enough. As long as terrorists continue to target American citizens, we reserve the right to act in self-defense by striking at their bases and those who sponsor, assist, or actively support them, as we have done over the years in different countries."[38] Samuel L. (Sandy) Berger, Clinton's national security adviser, recently testified that President Clinton was prepared to take preemptive military action if it could be determined that it would be efficacious. In 2000, "The President ordered two nuclear submarines to deploy off the coast of Pakistan for additional missile strikes, and was ready to use them at a moment's notice, had reliable intelligence materialized on bin Laden's whereabouts." Nor was the president averse to putting "boots on the ground," according to Berger. Clinton asked his military advisers to study options. But given Pakistani opposition, the absence of a useable base near Afghanistan, and the paucity of timely intelligence, "Clinton's military leadership," said Berger, "concluded that such a mission would very likely fail."[39]

The point of the foregoing is to underscore the considerable continuities in strategic thinking and policies. Seeking military preponderance is not new. Reserving the right to act unilaterally is not new. During the Cold War, policymakers adroitly and skillfully formed alliances and held them together, but never foreclosed the right to act unilaterally and often did so. Unilateralism is quintessentially American. And when the Cold War ended, temptations to act unilaterally multiplied, often infuriating allies.[40] Clinton sometimes worked assiduously to contain and co-opt unilateralist pressures, but he, too, recognized that unilateralism was not only politically expedient, but also might be strategically imperative. As the threats of terrorism, WMD proliferation, and

37. Presidential Decision Directive 39, "U.S. Policy on Counterterrorism," June 21, 1995, especially pp. 1, 3, 9, available at http://www.fas.org/irp/offdocs/pdd39.htm.

38. "A National Security Strategy for a Global Age," Part 2, p. 14.

39. Samuel Berger, "9/11 Prepared Testimony," National Commission on Terrorist Attacks upon the United States, March 24, 2004, pp. 3–4, available at http://www.msnbc.msn.com/id/4593926.

40. For recent analyses of American unilateralism as it is perceived by non-Americans, see Richard Crockatt, *America Embattled: September 11, Anti-Americanism and the Global Order* (London, 2003); David Malone and Yuen Foong Khong, *Unilateralism and U.S. Foreign Policy: International Perspectives* (Boulder, Colo., 2003).

rogue and failed states escalated through the 1990s, most members of the poli-cymaking community, rightly or wrongly, came to believe that, notwithstand-ing the desirability of alliance cohesion and even alliance expansion, the United States would find itself having to act unilaterally. Paul Wolfowitz, Don-ald Rumsfeld, and Dick Cheney were not members of the bipartisan United States Commission on National Security in the 21st Century. Appointed by Clinton, it was cochaired by Warren Rudman and Gary Hart and included Les Gelb and Lee Hamilton as well as James Schlesinger and Newt Gingrich. Among its findings, it noted: "The United States will increasingly find itself wishing to form coalitions but increasingly unable to find partners willing and able to carry out combined military operations."[41]

While there is little that is revolutionary about Bush foreign policy, change has occurred. This has to do with the balance between interests and ideals when threat perception is high. What is noteworthy about Bush foreign policy is how values and ideals have trumped interests; how great military power has shaped policy; how risk taking has overcome prudence. In a provocative little book, *Paradise and Power*, Robert Kagan argues that disparities in military capabilities shape strategic perceptions and strategic culture. "Strong pow-ers," he says, "naturally view the world differently than weaker powers. They measure risks and threats differently, they define security differently, and they have different levels of tolerance for insecurity. Those with great military power are more likely to consider force a useful tool of international relations than those who have less military power. The stronger may, in fact, rely on force more than they should."[42]

But the reliance on force is most of all a function of threat perception; 9/11 transformed threat perception. For years, intelligence analysis warned of ter-rorism. Year after year through the 1990s, with growing urgency, the directors of the CIA warned about the threats emanating from terrorism and the pro-liferation of WMD.[43] Bush, Cheney, Rumsfeld, Powell, Wolfowitz, and Rice grasped the threat but underestimated its imminence and urgency.[44] Then,

41. The United States Commission on National Security in the 21st Century, "New World Coming: American Security in the 21st Century," p. 6, September 15, 1999, available at http://govinfo.library.unt.edu/nssg/Reports/NWC.pdf.

42. Kagan, *Paradise and Power*, 27.

43. See, for example, testimony, by R. James Woolsey, January 10, 1995, Senate Select Com-mittee on Intelligence, "World Wide Threats to U.S. National Security," available at LexisNexis Congressional (online service); testimony, by George J. Tenet, February 6, 1997, Senate Com-mittee on Armed Services, "World Wide Threats to National Security," ibid.; testimony, by Tenet, February 2, 2000, Senate Select Committee on Intelligence, "Annual Assessment of Security Threats against the United States," ibid.; testimony, by Tenet, February 7, 2001, Senate Select Committee on Intelligence, "World Wide Threats to U.S. National Security," ibid.

44. This is my conclusion based on my reading of the testimony before the 9/11 Commission.

9/11 shocked them and revolutionized their sense of American vulnerability. I would go further. I would suggest that on some deep and elemental level, they felt a combination of guilt, outrage, and responsibility.

"Nine-eleven," said Condoleezza Rice, "crystallized our vulnerability." "No less than Pearl Harbor, September 11 forever changed the lives of every American and the strategic perspective of the United States." After 9/11, she said, the country faced an "existential threat" as great as any in its history, as great as the Civil War and World Wars I and II.[45]

"We've seen on September 11th," said Paul Wolfowitz, "a glimpse of how terrible the world will be when these kinds of capabilities are magnified by weapons of mass destruction." For twenty years, he continued, we lived with this hovering threat, but it was not possible to do so anymore. "What changed everything was September 11th."[46] After September 11, he stressed, "we have a visceral understanding of what terrorists can do with commercial aircraft, in a way that seemed remote and hypothetical before. We cannot afford to wait until we have a visceral understanding of what terrorists can do with weapons of mass destruction, before we act to prevent it."[47]

In another interview, Wolfowitz's boss amplified the concerns of those charged with protecting the American people. The question for the twenty-first century, Secretary of Defense Donald Rumsfeld explained, is what to do with terrorists who might possess biological weapons "that could kill hundreds of thousands of people. . . . Does one wait until they're attacked, or does one look at a . . . fact pattern and draw a conclusion?" What threshold of risk must one accept, Rumsfeld asked. Three thousand lives had been lost on September 11. Should one wait, he queried, until another attack occurred, perhaps a biological attack, with 300,000 deaths?[48]

---

See http://www.9-11commission.gov/. Also see the revealing testimony of Rumsfeld, June 21, 2001, Senate Armed Services Committee, "U.S. National Security Strategy," available at Lexis-Nexis Congressional (online service); Richard A. Clarke, *Against All Enemies: Inside America's War on Terror* (New York, 2004).

45. Rice, "A Balance of Power that Favors Freedom"; remarks by Condoleezza Rice at the International Institute for Strategic Studies, London, June 26, 2003, available at http://www.iiss.org/showdocument.php?docID=220.

46. Testimony, by Paul Wolfowitz, September 19, 2002, Senate Select Committee of Intelligence and House Permanent Select Committee on Intelligence, "Joint Inquiry Hearing on Counterterrorist Center," pp. 22, 24, 31, available at LexisNexis Congressional (online service); Paul Wolfowitz, Remarks at Conference on Iraqi Reconstruction, Georgetown University, November 4, 2003, available at http://www.defenselink.mil/speeches/2003/sp20031104-depsecdef0662.html.

47. Remarks by Paul Wolfowitz at the 38th Munich Conference, February 2, 2002, p. 3, available at http://www.dod.mil/speeches/2002/s20020202-depsecdef2.html.

48. Press Conference with Donald Rumsfeld and General Richard Myers, January 29, 2003, available at http://www.dod.mil/transcripts/2003/to1292003_to129sd.html.

Having failed to put the dots together once, threat perception impelled an offensive strategy. Rumsfeld acknowledged, "The coalition did not act in Iraq because we had discovered dramatic new evidence of Iraq's pursuit of weapons of mass murder. We acted because we saw the existing evidence in a new light, through the prism of our experience on September 11th."[49] That prism demanded boldness. "History will judge harshly," said President Bush, "those who saw this coming danger but failed to act. In the new world we have entered the only path to peace and security is the path of action."[50]

Threat perception impelled offensive strategies.[51] But it did more than that; it elevated a discourse of values and ideals. Like other times in American history when threat perception had been high, policymakers gravitated to rhetorical strategies emphasizing ideals and values. Conversely, when threat perception is low, officials tend to dwell on interests rather than ideals.

Many of the great rhetorical speeches of the last century focused on the pursuit of ideals in times of crisis.[52] These include Wilson's speeches during World War I, Roosevelt's addresses and fireside chats in 1940 and 1941, Truman's messages during the Korean War, Kennedy's evocative rhetoric during the Berlin and Cuban crises, and Reagan's rhetorical fervor after the invasion of Afghanistan and the shooting down of the Korean civilian airliner.

But when threats were low, rhetoric was more prosaic, public speeches more infrequent, and the engagement with interests more pronounced. As the Cold War ended, for example, the 1991 strategy statement of President George H. W. Bush, noted that the prevailing strategic environment was more like the 1920s than the 1940s. Then, too, "the great threat to our interests had collapsed and . . . no comparable threat was evident." Fearing that the United States might turn inward, the senior Bush, along with his national security advisers, stressed that the United States needed to adopt a strategic posture that would preserve American strength and cope with whatever threats still existed. "Such an approach," they emphasized, "begins with an understanding of our basic interests and objectives." There was little focus on ideals and values.[53]

49. Quoted in Joseph Cirincione, Jessica T. Mathews, George Perkovich, with Alex Orton, *WMD in Iraq: Evidence and Implications* (Washington, D.C., 2004), 57.

50. Bush's introductory letter to the National Security Strategy Statement, September 17, 2002, available at http://www.whitehouse.gov/news/releases/2003/02/counter_terrorism_counter_terrorism_strategy.pdf.

51. See Woodward, *Bush at War*; Woodward, *Plan of Attack*; National Security Council, "National Strategy for Combating Terrorism," February 2003, available at http://usinfstate.gov/topical/pol/terror/strategy.

52. Steven Rappoport, "The Use of Exceptionalist Rhetoric in Times of Crisis," seminar paper at the University of Virginia, 2004.

53. "National Security Strategy of the United States," August 1991, pp. 1–3ff., available at http://www.fas.org/man/docs/918015-nss.htm.

Indeed, throughout the 1990s, Clinton and his advisers sought to reconcile interests and ideals.[54] But claiming that the Democrats were steering the country in the wrong direction, Condoleezza Rice emphasized during the 2000 presidential campaign that "American foreign policy in a Republican administration should refocus the United States on the national interest and the pursuit of key priorities." "Power matters," she boldly declared, but it should not be employed for "second-order" effects such as the enhancement of humanity's well-being. The challenge was to define interests in a concrete way, and to assume that freedom, democracy, and peace would follow from the calculated pursuit of American interest.[55] The United States, said Bush in the first and most major foreign-policy speech of his campaign for the presidency, must do more than manage crises. The United States must assert its values and possess a vision, and that vision must be to sustain an enduring peace. "This is accomplished," Bush then emphasized, "by concentrating on enduring national interests."[56]

It is striking, therefore, to see the changes in the Bush administration's thinking and rhetorical strategies after 9/11! The overall goal of American policy, says the Bush strategy statement of September 2002, is to configure a balance of power favoring freedom. "Our principles," declares the strategy statement—not our interests—"will guide our government's decisions." "The national security strategy of the United States must start from these core beliefs and look outward for possibilities to expand liberty."[57]

"Moral clarity," according to the president, is essential. "Our struggle," President Bush explained to the graduating class at West Point in June 2002, "is similar to the Cold War. Now, as then, our enemies are totalitarians, holding a creed of power with no place for human dignity. Now, as then, they seek to impose a joyless conformity, to control every life and all life." Leaders, said Bush, must not shy away from "the language of right and wrong. . . . Moral truth is the same in every culture, in every time, and in every place. . . . There can be no neutrality between justice and cruelty, between the innocent and the guilty. We are in a conflict between good and evil, and America will call evil by its name. By confronting evil and lawless regimes, we do not create a problem, we reveal a problem."[58]

54. This was particularly true in their last strategy statement, "A National Security Strategy for a Global Age," December 2000, especially Part I, pp. 4–5.

55. Condoleezza Rice, "Campaign 2000—Promoting the National Interest," *Foreign Affairs*, 79 (January–February 2000): 1–8.

56. George W. Bush, "A Distinctly American Internationalism," November 19, 1999, available at http://www.mtholyoke.edu/acad/intrel/bush/wspeech/htm.

57. "Bush National Security Strategy," 4.

58. "President Delivers Graduation Speech at West Point," June 1, 2002, available at http://www.whitehouse.gov/news/releases/2002/06.

We might be tempted to think this is just rhetoric, but it is more than rhetoric. It reflects conviction, conviction inspired by the events of 9/11. Freedom, Bush told Bob Woodward, "is not America's gift to the world. Freedom is God's gift to everybody in the world. I believe that. As a matter of fact," Bush explained, "I was the person who wrote that line, or said it. I didn't write it, I just said it in a speech. And it became part of the jargon. And I believe that. And I believe we have a duty to free people. I would hope we wouldn't have to do it militarily, but we have a duty."[59]

This rhetoric is significant, all the more so because it infuses the thinking of the men who run the Pentagon. With great pride and great conviction, Rumsfeld noted that President Bush, like President Reagan, "has not shied from calling evil by its name." Nor has Bush been shy, said Rumsfeld, about "declaring his intention to defeat its latest incarnation—terrorism—just as free men and women of all political persuasions, here and abroad, defeated fascism and communism before."[60] "Like the Cold War," declared Deputy Secretary of Defense Paul Wolfowitz, "the global war on terrorism is also a war of ideas, and [it] promises, like President Kennedy said, to be a long twilight struggle."[61] According to Undersecretary of Defense Douglas Feith, championing freedom was the key to Reagan's success in winning the Cold War. "The advance of freedom," Feith went on to say, must likewise be "the calling of our time," must be "the calling of our country."[62]

Across the Potomac River, the rhetoric of idealism and the force of values also have cast their shadows. The new mission statement of the Department of State begins: "American diplomacy in the 21st century is based on fundamental beliefs: our freedom is best protected by ensuring that others are free; our prosperity depends on the prosperity of others; and our security relies on a global effort to secure the rights of all. The history of the American people is the chronicle of our effort to live up to our ideals."[63]

In February 2004, Secretary of State Powell went to Princeton University to commemorate the 100th birthday of George F. Kennan. Kennan was not present, but he would have been astounded to listen to Powell. Distorting Kennan's view of realism and misconstruing his critique of American diplomacy, Powell maintained that Kennan "has never forgotten that ideas have

59. Woodward, *Plan of Attack*, 88–89.

60. Remarks as delivered by Secretary of Defense Donald H. Rumsfeld at the Ronald Reagan Presidential Library, October 10, 2003, available at http://www.dod.mil/speeches/2003/sp20031010-secdef0582.html.

61. Remarks by Wolfowitz at Georgetown University School of Foreign Service, October 30, 2003, p. 7, ibid.

62. Douglas J. Feith, "Strategy and the Idea of Freedom," November 24, 2003, p. 2, ibid.

63. U.S. Department of State and U.S. Agency for International Development, *Strategic Plan, Fiscal Years 2004–2009*, 1.

power, nor has he ever doubted that noble ideals guide us to victory in the end." Seeking eloquence and simplicity, Powell declared, "We must acknowledge the power of ideas, and champion the nobility of democratic ideals, in our times."[64]

Some readers might feel that this focus on values and ideals is refreshing and inspiring. Some may feel that it is innocuous yet ennobling. Some may think that it is purely instrumental: to arouse public support for sacrifices and dangers they might wish to avoid. Some may be amused that scholars take it seriously.

But the rhetoric should be taken seriously. The rhetoric reflects a vast change in the public persona of the Bush administration after 9/11. It reflects a heightened level of threat perception; it signifies an evolution from assertive nationalism to democratic imperialism; it justifies and inspires the employment of unprecedented power. It is a worrisome development.[65]

The analogies to the Cold War are instructive, and I think less reassuring than Bush and his advisers think. Memory is important in decision-making. Decision-makers make use of the lessons of the past.[66] The president and his aides are enamored with the lessons of the Reagan administration. Power, they believe, harnessed to ideals vanquished evil. Reagan's "talk of democracy and good versus evil," declared Douglas Feith, "were widely criticized, even ridiculed, as unsophisticated and de-stabilizing. But it's now widely understood as having contributed importantly to the greatest strategic victory in world history: the collapse of Soviet communism and the liberation of the peoples of the Soviet Union and Eastern Europe without war."[67] President Bush embraces this view. Reagan, he declared, "is a hero in the American story. A story in which a single individual can shape history. A story in which evil is real, but courage and decency triumph."[68]

Yet if we think of the full course of the Cold War, different lessons might compete with those extrapolated from the Reagan years. The greatest successes of the Cold War—the initiatives that were most decisive in the long twilight struggle—came in its early years, prior to the Korean War. Not-

64. Colin Powell, "Remarks on the Occasion of George Kennan's Centenary Birthday," February 20, 2004, available at http://www.globalsecurity.org/wmd/library/news/usa/2004/usa-040220-usia01.htm.

65. Daalder and Lindsay, *America Unbound*; also see Clyde Prestowitz, *Rogue Nation: American Unilateralism and the Failure of Good Intentions* (New York, 2003); Newhouse, *Imperial America*.

66. See, for example, Ernest R. May, *"Lessons" of the Past: The Use and Misuse of History in American Foreign Policy* (New York, 1973); Richard E. Neustadt and Ernest R. May, *Thinking in Time: The Uses of History for Decision-Makers* (New York, 1986); Yuen Foong Khong, *Analogies at War: Korea, Munich, Dien Bien Phu, and the Vietnam Decisions of 1965* (Princeton, N.J., 1992).

67. Feith, "Strategy and the Idea of Freedom," 2.

68. Bush, "A Distinctly American Internationalism," 1.

withstanding the rhetoric of the Truman Doctrine, George Kennan, Dean Acheson, Robert Lovett, John McCloy, and their colleagues carefully calibrated interests. They focused on reconstructing and co-opting West Germany, Western Europe, and Japan. They constrained military expenditures. They assigned priority to economic reconstruction.[69]

The delicate balance between threat perception, the definition of interests, and the employment of power changed in 1950. The Soviet detonation of an atomic bomb, the fall of China, the signing of the Sino-Soviet alliance, and the outbreak of hostilities in Korea accentuated the perception of threat, institutionalized the hyperbolic language of NSC 68, and inaugurated a full-scale war on communism everywhere.[70] Eisenhower and Dulles, we now know, were more nuanced than we once thought, but their rhetoric calling on nations to take sides was a precursor of the rhetoric of the Bush years.[71] The war against communism blurred important distinctions, distorted priorities, and complicated threat perception. Defining policy in terms of good versus evil made it difficult to grasp the nature of revolutionary nationalism. Defining policy in terms of good versus evil invited overcommitments in the Third World. Moral clarity distorted and delayed the capacity of the United States to exploit the Sino-Soviet rift and embroiled the American people in a tragic war in Vietnam, a war that America's allies, such as France and Britain, warned against.[72]

69. Melvyn P. Leffler, *A Preponderance of Power*, 141–81; John Lewis Gaddis, *Strategies of Containment: A Critical Appraisal of Postwar American National Security Policy* (New York, 1982), 25–88; David Mayers, *George Kennan and the Dilemmas of US Foreign Policy* (New York, 1988), 105–88; Wilson D. Miscamble, *George F. Kennan and the Making of American Foreign Policy, 1947–1950* (Princeton, N.J., 1992).

70. Leffler, *Preponderance of Power*, 312–97; Gaddis, *Strategies of Containment*, 89–126.

71. For the nuanced view of Eisenhower and Dulles, see Richard H. Immerman and Robert R. Bowie, *Waging Peace: How Eisenhower Shaped an Enduring Cold War Strategy* (New York, 1998); David L. Snead, *The Gaither Committee, Eisenhower, and the Cold War* (Columbus, Ohio, 1999); H. W. Brands, *The Specter of Neutralism: The United States and the Emergence of the Third World, 1947–1960* (New York, 1989); but also see H. W. Brands, *The Devil We Knew: Americans and the Cold War* (New York, 1993), 31–85; Robert J. McMahon, "Eisenhower and Third World Nationalism: A Critique of the Revisionists," *Political Science Quarterly* 101 (Fall 1986): 453–73; Jeff Broadwater, *Eisenhower and the Anti-Communist Crusade* (Chapel Hill, N.C., 1992); Ira Chernus, *General Eisenhower: Ideology and Discourse* (East Lansing, Mich., 2002).

72. There is a vast literature, but see Richard J. Barnet, *Intervention and Revolution: America's Confrontation with Insurgent Movements around the World* (New York, 1968); Gordon H. Chang, *Friends and Enemies: The United States, China, and the Soviet Union, 1948–1972* (Stanford, Calif., 1990); Robert J. McMahon, *The Cold War on the Periphery: The United States, India, and Pakistan* (New York, 1994); Logevall, *Choosing War*; David Kaiser, *American Tragedy: Kennedy, Johnson, and the Origins of the Vietnam War* (Cambridge, Mass., 2000); George Herring, *America's Longest War: The United States and Vietnam, 1950–1975*, 3rd ed. (New York, 1996); Gareth Porter, *Perils of Dominance: Imbalance of Power and the Road to War in Vietnam* (Berkeley, Calif., 2005);

The quest for moral clarity can lead to an arrogance of power. The quest for moral clarity can lead to abuses of power. The quest for moral clarity can obfuscate the definition of interests. Indeed, even in the Reagan years, moral clarity and the employment of power may not have been nearly as important as the attraction of soft power, the lure of consumer capitalism, the role of NGOs, and the appeal of democratic socialism.[73]

What, then, are the appropriate lessons to be learned from the past? Heightened threat perception tempts U.S. officials to stake their policy on the universality and superiority of American values. Paradoxically, heightened threat perception tempts officials to obfuscate interests and dwell on ideals. Yet a careful calculation of interests is essential to discipline American power and temper its ethnocentrism. There is no greater and sadder irony, perhaps even tragedy, that while Bush officials assert the superiority of American values, the overweening use of American power breeds cynicism about U.S. motives and distrust of U.S. intentions. A recent survey of world public opinion by the Pew Research Center is shocking. Large majorities of people in countries such as Pakistan, Turkey, Jordan, and Morocco believe that the United States ignores their interests when making foreign-policy decisions. Large majorities believe that the United States wants to dominate the world; most suspect that the underlying motive is control of Middle East oil. So strong is the antipathy that overwhelming majorities of people in Jordan and Morocco view suicide attacks on Americans and Westerners in Iraq as justifiable. Osama bin Laden is looked upon favorably by 65 percent of Pakistanis, 55 percent of Jordanians, 45 percent of Moroccans, and 31 percent of Turks. The stature and reputation of America in the world, especially in the Islamic world and particularly after the revelations of degradation and torture of prisoners, have never been lower.[74]

The balance between ideals and interests has been dangerously skewed in favor of the former, and the result has been an ominous overassertion of American power. There has been no revolution in American foreign policy;

---

Douglas Little, *American Orientalism: The United States and the Middle East since 1945* (Chapel Hill, N.C., 2002); Walter LaFeber, *Inevitable Revolutions: The United States in Central America* (New York, 1984).

73. See, for example, Matthew Evangelista, *Unarmed Forces: The Transnational Movement to End the Cold War* (Ithaca, N.Y., 1999); Robert D. English, *Russia and the Idea of the West: Gorbachev, Intellectuals, and the End of the Cold War* (New York, 2000); Jacques Levesque, *The Enigma of 1989: The USSR and the Liberation of Eastern Europe* (Berkeley, Calif., 1997); Walter D. Connor, "Soviet Society, Public Attitudes, and the Perils of Gorbachev's Reforms," *Journal of Cold War Studies* 5 (Fall 2003): 43–80; Timothy W. Ryback, *Rock around the Bloc: A History of Rock Music in Eastern Europe and the Soviet Union* (New York, 1990).

74. The Pew Global Project Attitudes, "A Year after Iraq War: Mistrust of America in Europe Ever Higher, Muslim Anger Persists," March 16, 2004, available at http://www.people-press.org.

there has been a frightening recalibration of the relationships between ideals and interests in the face of "existential" threats. There is an imperative need to reassess this balance. Interests need to temper ideals and discipline power. This does not require a revolution in thinking; it requires the exercise of good judgment.

# 10

# Austerity and U.S. Strategy

## LESSONS OF THE PAST

The financial collapse and great economic recession of 2007–09, coupled with political gridlock in Washington and the ongoing costs of fighting in Iraq and Afghanistan, hugely exacerbated American budgetary woes. Congress imposed new constraints on military spending, arousing immense worries about the ability of the U.S. defense establishment to protect the nation's security. Many think tanks and defense analysts went to work assessing the impact of austerity on America's role in the international arena.

During the summer of 2013, the Aspen Strategy Group dedicated its summer workshop to this topic. I was asked to prepare a lecture looking at the issue from an historical perspective.

I pointed out that attention often focused on the U.S. failure to stay prepared after waging major war. Many commentators believed that after World War I and World War II, policymakers and legislators felt complacent, reined in defense spending, and left the nation vulnerable to mounting threats. Long ago, John Braeman showed that this memory of the 1920s and early 1930s was profoundly misleading. (See John Braeman, "Power and Diplomacy: The 1920s Reappraised," *The Review of Politics*, 44 [July 1982]: 342–69.) What I tried to do in my lecture was to interrogate what happened during critical

*Editor's Note*: Melvyn Leffler presented the annual Ernest R. May Memorial Lecture at the Aspen Strategy Group's (ASG) August 2013 workshop in Aspen, Colorado. The following are his remarks as written for delivery. The Ernest May Memorial Lecture is named for Ernest May, an international relations historian and Harvard John F. Kennedy School of Government professor, who passed away in 2009. ASG developed the lecture series to honor Professor May's celebrated lectures.

periods of austerity on the eve of World War II, during the Cold War, and after it was over. As I reexamined the past and tried to extrapolate some modest lessons, I found that times of austerity often impelled policymakers to think creatively and to assess and manage risks in a disciplined way. Austerity forced officials to make tough trade-offs, choose among priorities, and balance means and ends. Austerity did not necessarily harm America's role in the world; in fact, it spurred some extraordinarily creative choices, as when the Truman administration chose to reconstruct Western Europe (in 1947–49) rather than rearm, and when the Nixon administration opted for détente with the Soviet Union and rapprochement with the People's Republic of China. The worst errors in the history of modern U.S. diplomacy—the march to the Yalu River in the late summer of 1950 that provoked Chinese intervention in the Korean War, the quagmire in Vietnam, the morass in Iraq—did not stem from austerity; in fact, one might argue that those decisions stemmed from an excess of capabilities that tempted overreach.

Austere times, I argued, presented opportunities to reassess strategic concepts, think rigorously about goals, recalibrate priorities, and link means and ends. Constraints on defense spending forced policymakers to think more creatively about diplomatic solutions, sometimes catalyzing bold initiatives to reassure friends and engage adversaries. In the past, budgetary austerity also forced officials to wrestle more forthrightly with the trade-offs between priorities at home and commitments abroad, an exercise that invariably reminded all Americans that the real sources of U.S. strength in the world were the health of its domestic economy, the vitality of its people, and the resilience of its political institutions.

This essay appeared (without notes) in Nicholas Burns and Jonathon Price, eds., *The Future of American Defense* (Washington, D.C.: The Aspen Institute, 2014), 21–34.

————

It is an honor to be asked to deliver the Ernest May memorial lecture. Ernest was a great historian. He wrote thoughtfully about disparate events, from World War I to the Spanish-American War to the Monroe Doctrine to the Cold War. He wrote about the loss of China and the fall of France. Among other things, he focused on public opinion, organizational behavior, bureaucratic politics, and human agency. Few historians have approximated his breadth and depth.

Ernest emphasized that policymakers could learn important lessons from thinking about the past. By looking at key moments in the twentieth century—World War II, the origins of the Cold War, the reaction to North Korea's attack on South Korea, the decision to escalate in Vietnam in the mid-1960s—

Ernest showed that policymakers, however wise and experienced, often used history badly. In books, articles, and his famous courses at the Kennedy School, he sought, along with Dick Neustadt, to show how history could serve policymakers. He and Dick were always modest in their claims, suggesting only that history could help officials think more incisively about appropriate analogies, thereby enhancing policymaking at the margins—not transforming decision-making, just marginally improving it.

More than anything else, May and Neustadt stressed that present crises should be examined as part of a historical stream. Thinking in time, they said, would not yield clear-cut solutions to ongoing crises but would help illuminate context, options, and dilemmas. Thinking in time, they argued, would make officials realize that most challenges are not new; uncertainty is persistent; risks and imponderables are omnipresent. Therefore, they regarded "prudence" as the ultimate prize. "Thinking in time as a stream," May and Neustadt emphasized, was most important for the achievement of prudence.

So, we should begin by recognizing that making strategy in a time of austerity is not new. U.S. officials have repeatedly faced times of austerity. Today, I want to look quickly at five such times: before World War II; at the onset of the Cold War; after the armistice in Korea; during the denouement in Vietnam in the early 1970s; and after the end of the Cold War, 1990–93. I want to suggest how history—in the spirit of Ernest May—might illuminate, not answer, but provide ways of thinking about how to handle moments of austerity to craft national security strategy. This is not a new challenge.

Lest you think it is novel, you might recall the tragic death of James Forrestal, the first secretary of defense. On May 22, 1949, sometime after midnight, he sat in his room on the thirteenth floor of Bethesda Naval Hospital reading and copying passages of a brooding poem by Sophocles. Then, he rose from his chair, tied one end of his dressing gown sash to a radiator just below his window and tied the other end around his neck. He then removed the screen from the window, climbed outside, and either jumped or hung until the sash broke. Forrestal plunged to his death.

Forrestal was suffering from anxiety and paranoia. Dr. William Meninger, perhaps the nation's most renowned psychiatrist, had been summoned to Florida to assess Forrestal's condition in mid-March, just a few days after he had announced his resignation from office. Meninger met with Forrestal and concluded that he was suffering from "reactive depression," a condition he equated to battle fatigue during World War II. Menninger believed that Forrestal's dramatic decline stemmed from the strains of his last two years in office.

Contrary to what is often said about James Forrestal, these anxieties were not the product of his obsession with Soviet power and/or communist ideology. Those concerns about the communist threat did loom large and set a backdrop for his suicide. But Forrestal's depression emanated from his inability to control the raging controversies among the military services over missions, roles, and budgets; his sense of failure stemmed from his belief that he had designed recipes for military unification and for the defense establishment that were failing. More than any other official in the Truman administration, Forrestal had championed the integration of military and foreign policy; more than anyone else, he supported a national security council whose function was to reconcile military, economic, and foreign policy concerns into coherent national strategy. More than anyone else in the American government, he wanted to integrate means and ends, tactics and goals, resources and commitments. More than anyone else, he believed that the Truman administration was failing to achieve these objectives, partly because of his own protection of the organizational interests of the Navy and his insistence on a confederation of the military services rather than real unification under a powerful secretary of defense.

Truman had insisted that Forrestal design a defense budget with a $14.4 billion ceiling. His military chiefs did not think it could be done; they wanted $21.3 billion; they were willing to acquiesce to $16 billion. Forrestal called in Dwight Eisenhower, who had recently assumed the presidency of Columbia University, to mediate the inter-service fighting and forge a consensus solution. Ike failed. Truman blamed Forrestal, whom he did not like for many reasons. To shape a budget in a time of austerity, Truman named Louis Johnson, his chief fund-raiser and former assistant secretary of the Army. Forrestal was distraught. He left office, sensing he had flunked the task of making strategy in a time of austerity.

Forrestal's despair stemmed from his knowledge of history and his experience in government. After a very successful career in investment banking, Forrestal joined the Roosevelt administration in June 1940 as a White House aide. After only a couple of months, he was appointed undersecretary of the Navy by Frank Knox. Forrestal's focus was on procurement, production, base structure, and other administrative tasks. But he acutely recognized the inadequacy of military-civilian coordination in a time of mounting danger, insufficient capabilities, and scarce financial resources.

In June 1940, Germany's conquest of Western Europe and defeat of France eviscerated the relevance of the evolving Rainbow war plans. The signing of the Tripartite Pact in September 1940 confirmed the specter of a global totalitarian menace. But the United States had no strategic concept, no agreed upon war plan, and no mechanisms for coordinating military and foreign policy. The chiefs of staff of the Army and Navy, George C. Marshall and Harold E. Stark, doubted whether Britain would survive, and they were more than a little skeptical about President Roosevelt's insistence on aid to London. At the same time, they deemed Roosevelt's military deployments in the Pacific, initiation of economic sanctions toward Japan, and insistence on the open door in China to be risky and provocative. In short, goals seemed vague and unachievable; resources were constrained; means and ends were out of sync.

Austerity imposed discipline and creativity. There were insufficient forces to deal with the Japanese in the Pacific and the Germans in the Atlantic. Admiral Stark in November 1940 crafted a strategic concept that would shape U.S. foreign policy for the next half-century. Stark determined that the principal threat to U.S. security was German power. He feared the prospect that Germany would defeat Britain, assume dominance in the Atlantic, and buy time for the assimilation of the resources, industrial infrastructure, and skilled labor of all of northwestern Europe. No single power, he argued, could be permitted to dominate the continent, control the trade routes of the Atlantic, and penetrate the Western Hemisphere. Simply stated, Stark insisted that Germany was the major threat, the Atlantic had to be the country's priority, and war had to be avoided with Japan while the United States bolstered British and Canadian capabilities and prepared for eventual hostilities on the European continent itself.

The salient point here is not the discussion of the intricacies of war planning, but the boldness and comprehensiveness of the strategic concept itself. Stark surveyed four strategic options, calculated means and ends, assessed priorities, and recommended a course of action he deemed most likely to achieve broad national security goals. His views resonated not because of Stark's influence with Roosevelt but because his ideas comported with the evolving thinking inside and outside government about what the United States required to prosper economically and thrive politically with its basic democratic institutions intact. The planning of the Department of State and the more extensive war and peace studies of the Council on Foreign Relations delineated the same requisites as did Stark for a secure, prosperous, and free America. Walter Lippmann summarized these views in a widely read *Life* magazine article: The American free enterprise system could not survive, Lippmann stressed, if the workshops of Europe and Asia were in totalitarian hands. Gigantic government monopolies managed by dictators would crush private competitors, circumscribe free markets, and impel the United States to emulate the statist behavior of its adversaries.

President Roosevelt agreed. If totalitarian enemies controlled the preponderant resources and industrial infrastructure of Europe and Asia, Roosevelt said, the United States would have "to embark upon a course of action which would subject our producers, consumers, and foreign traders, and ultimately the entire nation, to the regimentation of a totalitarian system. For it is naive to imagine that we could adopt a totalitarian control of our foreign trade and at the same time escape totalitarian regimentation of our national economy."

With great fervor Roosevelt declared that the United States "could not become a lone island in a world dominated by the philosophy of force. Such an island represents to me—the nightmare of a people lodged in prison, handcuffed, hungry, and fed through the bars day to day by the contemptuous, unpitying masters of other continents." The free economic and political system of the United States could not flourish, perhaps could not survive, if the tripartite powers, perhaps along with Soviet Russia, dominated Europe and Asia.

What is important here is that in a time of austerity, when means were circumscribed, when goals far exceeded resources, Stark presented a plan, Plan Dog, as it came to be called, that established a strategic framework for thinking about America's vital interests, that defined the nature of the threat, that encompassed the preservation of values and interests, that assigned priority to the Atlantic, that underscored the need to sustain our British ally while avoiding conflict with our Pacific adversary.

Of course, Plan Dog left many aspects of strategy unresolved. How much equipment should go to allies and how much to rearm our own inadequate forces? How much effort to accommodate Japan, compromise the open door with China, retract sanctions, and avoid conflict? Roosevelt remained wary of defining goals with any precision, Secretary of State Cordell Hull remained reluctant to coordinate diplomatic and military policy, neither wished to placate Japan's ambitions in China, and public opinion remained deeply divided until December 7, 1941. But austerity had helped forge a strategic concept, an assessment of threat, an appreciation of the indissoluble links between interests and values, and a calibration of priorities.

After World War II, the basic strategic concept forged in 1940 persisted. In 1945, some of the nation's most eminent strategic thinkers—Frederick Dunn, Edward Earle, Grayson Kirk, Harold Sprout, David Rowe, and others—collaborated on a Brookings Institution study on the formulation of national security strategy. They concluded that it was essential to prevent any one power or coalition of powers from gaining control of Eurasia. "In all the world," they emphasized, "only Soviet Russia and the ex-enemy powers are capable of forming nuclei around which an anti-American coalition could form to threaten the security of the United States. The indefinite westward movement of the Soviet Union, they stated, could not be permitted "whether it occurs by formal annexation, political coup, or progressive subversion."

The Joint Chiefs of Staff (JCS) embraced this strategic thinking, as did most civilian officials. But in the domestic context of post–World War II America, most Americans were focused on demobilization and reconversion. President Truman was eager to balance the budget and stifle inflation, basic requisites, he felt, for sustaining wartime prosperity and U.S. strength. Republicans insisted on these domestic priorities. Military spending plummeted.

Gaps immediately emerged between foreign policy goals and military capabilities. The war plans of the joint chiefs postulated Soviet capabilities to overrun much of Europe, the Middle East, and northeast Asia. Meanwhile, crises in Iran, Turkey, and Greece focused attention on peripheral areas, as did the civil war in China.

In these circumstances, austerity compelled a careful assessment of threat. And what is noteworthy was the consensus among top officials that the gravest threat did not emanate from the likelihood of Soviet military aggression. The Russians, they assessed, were too weak economically to initiate military aggression. Ferdinand Eberstadt, the former director of the Army-Navy Munitions Board, wrote Forrestal, his close friend and former banking partner: "None but mad men would undertake war against us." But the threat was grave nonetheless because the Soviets might exploit the widespread hunger, social strife, and political ferment that beleaguered most of Europe and Asia. As early as May 16, 1945, Secretary of War Henry Stimson wrote Truman: "There will be pestilence and famine in Central Europe next winter. This is likely to be followed by political revolution and Communist infiltration." The next month Undersecretary of State Joseph Grew warned the president that Europe was a breeding ground for "spontaneous class hatred to be channeled by a skillful agitator."

Policymakers debated priorities, yet agreed that foreign assistance was more important than rearmament. Even Forrestal acknowledged in December 1947, "As long as we can out-produce the world, can control the seas, and can strike inland with the atomic bomb, we can assume certain risks otherwise unacceptable in an effort to restore world trade, to restore the balance of power—military power—and to eliminate some of the conditions which breed war." Forrestal went along with Dean Acheson's desire to form a subcommittee of the State-War-Navy Coordinating Committee (SWNCC) to devise a comprehensive assistance program and to determine priorities. Within SWNCC, the urgency of the situation was the chief criterion for determining priorities: Greece, Turkey, Iran, Italy, Korea, France, and Austria topped the list. The JCS crafted its own study and categorically recommended aid to Great Britain, France, and western Germany. It concluded: "The complete resurgence of German industry, particularly coal mining, is essential for the economic recovery of France—whose security is inseparable from the combined security of the United States, Canada, and Great Britain. The economic revival of Germany is therefore of primary importance from the viewpoint of United States security."

This thinking comported well with George Kennan's first Policy Planning Staff studies and with the predilections of many senior foreign service officers working on European affairs in the State Department. Obviously, this thinking set the backdrop for the making of the Marshall Plan. "The only really dangerous thing in my mind," wrote Kennan, "is the possibility that the technical skills of the Germans might be combined with the physical resources of Russia."

In brief, austerity forced planners to think hard about priorities and trade-offs—about economic reconstruction abroad ahead of domestic rearmament. Rebuilding Western Europe and co-opting former enemies, especially western Germany and Japan, were judged to be of primary importance. If such initiatives strained relations with Moscow and intensified the emerging Cold War, so be it. Kennan grasped the trade-offs and knew his priorities. He acknowledged that Soviet decisions to launch the Cominform and orchestrate the coup in Czechoslovakia were "quite logical" developments in the face of U.S. initiatives.

Soviet countermoves, of course, heightened fears of war. But measuring Soviet intentions and capabilities carefully, Secretary of State Marshall, George Kennan, and most of their colleagues in the State Department—and also in the National Military Establishment (NME)—still wagered that the Soviets would not go to war. Truman did call for universal military training and selective service and asked Congress for some prudent increases in defense expenditures, but even during the Berlin crisis of 1948, Kennan estimated that the Soviets would not go to war. General Clay, the commander of U.S. forces in Germany, concurred: They are bluffing, he wrote on June 27, and "their hand can and should be called."

These strategic choices amidst budgetary austerity for the defense establishment engendered Forrestal's mounting anxiety. Increasingly, the administration identified priorities, but did not forgo peripheral concerns: in Turkey, Greece, Italy, Palestine, and elsewhere. Forrestal's military chiefs told him that commitments far exceeded capabilities; they did. His military chiefs told him that U.S. moves and Soviet countermeasures were making war more likely; they were. Yet Truman would not budge. He insisted that the new budget not exceed $14.4 billion. Essentially, he was betting that major war would not erupt; that domestic priorities must not be compromised; that economic reconstruction abroad was more important than rearmament at home; that co-opting and reconstructing former enemies were more important than engaging the new adversary; and that Western Europe, western Germany, and Japan were more important than China.

Within a broad strategic concept, one that had emerged from the World War II experience, austerity forced tough choices. Risk had to be managed. Different men could live with different amounts of risk, dependent on where you sat in the government and what your immediate responsibilities were. Forrestal increasingly abhorred the gap between means and ends, between commitments and capabilities. Truman dismissed him.

One can argue over the quality of strategy-making in the austere years, 1946–49, but what is indisputable is that the years of scarcity ended with the

Korean War. Over the next three years, the United States, following the pre-scriptions of NSC 68, tripled its defense expenditures and more than doubled its forces. Only a tiny percentage of this vast increase actually went to wage war in Korea; most of it was used to prepare for global war with the Soviet Union.

Dwight Eisenhower made it clear both before and after his election that he did not think the build-up could be sustained. He insisted that the foundation of military strength was economic vitality, and the key to economic health was fiscal solvency. In May 1952 he wrote a close friend, "The financial solvency and economic soundness of the United States constitute the first requisite to collective security in the free world. That comes before all else." He believed that defense expenditures had to be reined in and the budget balanced.

Ike quickly ordered a comprehensive reassessment of national security strategy, perhaps the most thorough such reassessment ever undertaken. Task forces were created to argue three different approaches. Eisenhower claimed to be impressed by elements of all three and instructed that they be integrated into a new comprehensive national security policy statement.

Actually, the study produced no substantive change in the strategic concept of containment; in other words, no change in the thinking that the United States must prevent the Soviet Union from gaining control of the preponderant resources of Europe and Asia: Western Europe, West Germany, and Japan remained of greatest consequence. Yet to nurture the revival and co-option of the workshops of Europe and Asia into an American-led orbit, it was also necessary for these workshops to have markets and resources in the turbulent underdeveloped periphery now wracked with revolutionary ferment and nationalist ambitions—in Southeast Asia, the Middle East, Africa, and Latin America. "The preponderance of the world's resources," Ike wrote, "must not pass into the hands of the Soviets." The governments in those areas, Ike insisted, must "be friendly to our way of life"; they needed to believe in open trade and free enterprise. The United States had to use its superior power, so long as it lasted, to shape a world order amenable to America's domestic institutions.

The strategic concept had not changed, but Ike insisted that the United States must act with far more fiscal prudence than had the Truman administration in its last years. The so-called "new look" and the doctrines of deterrence and massive retaliation put a premium on air power and atomic weapons. Ike constrained the growth of conventional land forces and talked a lot about ratcheting down the U.S. troop commitment to NATO. He did not believe Kremlin leaders, either the new ones or even Stalin, would risk nuclear war and the destruction of the power of their regime. He believed that the United States through a variety of mechanisms could contain Soviet expansion. But he recognized that such containment was becoming infinitely more complicated by the revolution of rising expectations in the Third World, the modernizing ambitions of revolutionary nationalist leaders in Asia and Africa, and the appeal of state planning and the Soviet model of development.

Eisenhower exercised prudence and self-confidently managed risk. But as Soviet strategic capabilities mounted, as the demands of allies became more insistent, and as revolutionary nationalist ferment spread, his prudence attracted more and more criticism. The budgetary constraints he advocated could not persist when his basic strategic concept was not reexamined in view of the mounting threat from revolutionary nationalism in the Third World. As U.S. interests in the periphery grew, as claims to credibility became more widespread, the gap between means and ends widened.

In 1953–54, Ike's fiscal prudence was warranted, but his administration failed to adjust strategy over the long term for the austere budgets that he deemed desirable. Actually, those budgets were never that austere, and U.S. strategic capabilities mounted rapidly. But the gap between means and ends grew even more quickly, ineluctably leading to new expenditures, weapons, doctrines, and interventions during his last years in office and even more so during the 1960s.

During 1938–40, austerity had nurtured an enduring strategic concept; between 1946 and 1949, austerity had bred a nuanced sense of threat perception and a sophisticated calibration of priorities. But in 1953–54, the "new look" was designed primarily to manage the widening gap between goals and tactics, a management that was feasible in the hands of the able president, but which could not long endure partisan politics, organizational pressures, mounting Soviet strategic capabilities, and growing turbulence in the Third World.

During 1953–54, Ike and John Foster Dulles pretty much rejected détente as a way to bridge the gap between means and ends. Significantly, when Ike ordered the comprehensive review of national security strategy, he did not task anyone to explore the option of relaxing tensions, notwithstanding the halfhearted overtures presented by the new leaders in the Kremlin. Ike, of course, did not rule out negotiations; indeed, he showed interest in arms control and did consummate the Austrian State Treaty in 1954. But, for Ike, talking to adversaries was always less important than negotiating and solidifying alliances with existing or potential friends. Those friends, of course, pursuing their own interests, often made it more difficult to overcome the gap between ends and means during austere budgetary years.

What is so interesting about the policies pursued by Richard Nixon and Henry Kissinger during the early 1970s was that they decided to manage the gap between means and ends in an era of austerity by ratcheting down the U.S. commitment to Indochina and by engaging adversaries. Nixon and Kissinger did not change the nation's basic strategic orientation. The Soviet Union remained the key adversary, and the strategy of containment was not abandoned. Aware of mounting Soviet strategic capabilities and the paramount need to avoid nuclear conflict, they labored to leverage the Soviets to exercise self-restraint. They wanted the Kremlin to stop exploiting crises in Asia and Africa, to curtail efforts to divide America's friends, and to encourage Hanoi to negotiate.

If you read the many foreign policy statements of Nixon and Kissinger, they often brilliantly illuminated changes in the global environment. They dwelled on the evolution of multipolarity, the revitalization of our allies in Western Europe and northeast Asia, the intensification of the Sino-Soviet split, and the assertiveness of nationalist leaders in the Third World seeking a new international economic order, especially after the Yom Kippur War and the alarming growth of petroleum prices. They articulated a need to extricate the United States from Vietnam with America's honor and credibility intact. They were beleaguered by partisan acrimony at home, urban strife, racial tension, inflationary pressures, gold outflows, and financial constraints. Although they exquisitely outlined the need for a prudent pursuit of interests in an international order defined by great Soviet strategic capabilities and the omnipresent threat of nuclear war, they were tantalizingly ambiguous in their definition of U.S. interests, except the inchoate need to balance Soviet power and the obvious necessity of avoiding nuclear war.

Their challenge was to design a strategy to balance Soviet power in a demanding political, fiscal, and legislative environment. The Nixon Doctrine; the détente with the Kremlin; the opening of relations with Beijing; and the covert actions in southern Africa, Chile, and elsewhere were all efforts to bolster allies, divide adversaries, and contain Soviet power when U.S. officials were acutely aware that Congress would not allocate funds to regain strategic supremacy or support overt U.S. interventionism in critical regions. Nixon himself stated this succinctly in a memo in May 1972: "All of us who have worked on . . . [SALT] . . . know that the deal we are making is in our best interest, but for a very practical reason that the right-wing will never understand—that we simply can't get from the Congress the additional funds needed to continue the arms race with the Soviets in either the defensive or offensive missile category." In a National Security Council meeting, deflecting Defense Secretary Mel Laird's insistence that the Soviets were seeking superiority, Nixon bluntly stated: "It's imperative to get a deal. We can't build and they know it."

In an era of austerity, Nixon and Kissinger's approach to strategy was not to rethink the fundamental elements of containment, not to redefine goals or threats, but to engage adversaries and to devolve more responsibility on allies. Indeed, engaging adversaries often exacerbated relations with allies, a trade-off, however regrettable, that Nixon and Kissinger found acceptable.

Nixon and Kissinger did not close the great gap between resources and commitments, between means and ends should détente falter, as eventually it did. They improvised, rather adroitly, in an era of perceived decline, contracting resources, tumultuous politics at home, and eroding strength and credibility abroad.

After the Cold War ended, policymakers expected austerity. President George H. W. Bush, Secretary of Defense Dick Cheney and Colin Powell, the chairman of the JCS, knew the American people and the U.S. Congress demanded a peace dividend. They wanted to make necessary defense cuts—more than a million military and civilian personnel—within a coherent post–Cold War strategy. In fact, President Bush was supposed to announce that new strategy right here in Aspen on August 2, 1990, when Saddam Hussein triggered the crisis over Kuwait.

The announcement of that strategy was delayed, but work on it resumed after the end of the Persian Gulf War. Bush administration officials said they did not want to repeat the errors that had allegedly occurred after World War I and World War II. In other words, they did not want to cut as much as people expected. Acknowledging the absence of a global threat, they shifted focus and stressed regional "challenges," hence the name of the strategy itself, the "Regional Defense Strategy." Defense officials now stressed that the overriding threat was "uncertainty" or "unpredictability." In such an environment, they claimed, forces needed to be configured to exert leadership and shape the future. The U.S. defense establishment needed capabilities to preserve strategic deterrence, strengthen and enlarge alliances, establish forward presence, and project power to foster regional stability, especially in the Persian Gulf, Middle East, and northeast Asia. Capabilities also needed to be preserved so that forces could be reconstituted swiftly in order to confront a global competitor should one reemerge.

In designing the Defense Policy Guidance of 1992, two key legacies of Cold War strategic concepts persisted. Planners stipulated that the United States must "preclude any hostile power from dominating a region critical to our interests." The regions included Europe, East Asia, the Middle East/Persian Gulf, and Latin America. In so doing, planners hoped "to strengthen the barriers against the reemergence of a global threat to the interests of the United States and our allies." Cheney's aides also insisted that the United States had to have defense capabilities sufficient to create an international order conducive to America's way of life. This, too, was a strategic legacy of the battles against totalitarianism in the Second World War and the Cold War. This requirement lurked behind the emphasis on "leadership" and "shaping the future."

Cheney's strategic concept and his definition of threat—preparing for uncertainty, shaping the future, thwarting regional instability, nurturing an international environment suitable to democratic capitalism at home—guaranteed gaps between means and ends, given the constraints imposed by legislators' priorities and public sentiment. Of course, Washington had no peer competitors, and over the next few years the United States achieved so-called "full spectrum superiority." But so long as goals were so ambitious, threats so vague, and interests so ill-defined, U.S. capabilities could never suffice to meet all the regional crises and humanitarian missions that were certain to unfold. By the end of the 1990s, the United States was pretty much outspending all the rest of the world combined, but many defense experts were lambasting the Clinton administration for insufficient attention to defense matters, even though it, too, had embraced Cheney's regional defense strategy.

What then can be gleaned from this whirlwind retrospective on U.S. strategy-making in times of perceived austerity? In the spirit of Ernest May, we should seek to avoid simplistic extrapolations. Not quite two years ago, Secretary of Defense Leon Panetta warned that "after every major conflict— World War I, World War II, Korea, Vietnam, the fall of the Soviet Union," the United States hollowed out its forces and invited disaster. President Obama invoked the same theme: "We have to remember the lessons of history," he said. "We can't afford to repeat the mistakes that we have made in the past— after World War II, after Vietnam—when our military was ill-prepared for the future."

Yet austere postwar defense budgets did not endanger U.S. national security as much as other developments. Actually, after World War I, the United States did not make itself vulnerable to attack. Many historians have now shown that in the 1920s, U.S. defense policies were not imprudent given the absence of prevailing threats and the constraints on British, German, and Japanese forces until the mid-1930s. The mistake was not budgetary retrenchment after World War I but the erroneous threat perception of the late 1930s and the flawed diplomacy of neutrality and appeasement. Likewise, the constrained defense budgets of 1946–49 did not cause the Cold War nor stifle creative responses to looming threats. In the 1950s and 1960s, inadequate U.S. military forces did not catalyze the revolutionary nationalist ferment that endangered U.S. interests, nor would larger forces have allayed the perceived threat. The rancorous domestic climate and austere budget environment that beleaguered Nixon, Ford, and Carter did not cause the upheaval in Iran nor spawn Soviet intervention in Afghanistan; in fact, austerity inspired creative diplomatic adaptation, including détente with the USSR, rapprochement with China, and human rights initiatives that would reshape international relations in the 1980s. And after the Cold War ended, the demands for a peace dividend did not cause the spread of political Islam, the rise of the Taliban, or the proliferation of missile technology and weapons of mass destruction—nor did austerity prevent the Bush-Cheney-Powell team from formulating a new strategy to sustain American military hegemony.

Of course, we know that problems arose during these times of austerity, but they were rarely, or only partly, the result of austerity itself. Too often, officials clung to prevailing strategic concepts without fully reevaluating their utility, reassessing costs and benefits, reexamining threats and opportunities, or rethinking goals and tactics. It would be hard to make the case that the country's most baleful decisions since World War II—the march to the Yalu, the quagmire in Vietnam, the morass in Iraq—emanated from austere defense budgets.

What, then, are the appropriate lessons to be learned? They are modest, as Ernie May and Dick Neustadt insisted they should be. First, austerity should not breed despair. Austerity, after all, is a relative term. What does it even mean? Austerity compared to what? When the United States is outspending most of its competitors combined, is there really austerity? Austerity seems to mean that defense budgets will decline, or not grow as quickly as in the past. But in the best of times, that should inspire innovative thinking about threats, goals, and tactics within a coherent strategic concept, keeping in mind that overweening power often tempts over-commitment, just as insufficient power sometimes invites adventurism from adversaries. Designing strategy in a time of austerity should nurture an artful combination of initiatives to reassure allies and engage adversaries; it should also inspire rigorous assessments of the relative costs and prospective efficacy of the many tools of statecraft—economic, diplomatic, and cultural as well as military. Austerity should force officials to design a coherent strategic concept, calibrate threats, define goals and interests precisely, set priorities, embrace creative diplomacy, and take political risks.

In the past, periodic bouts of austerity imposed discipline and improvisation, sometimes sound and sometimes not so sound. But the constraint tended to underscore that domestic economic vitality within an open world order—not military primacy—were the ultimate sources of American national security. If World War II and the Cold War were competitions between alternative ways of life, which they were, cycles of austerity helped officials keep a focus on the main sources of U.S. primacy: the productivity of its economy; the solvency of its government; the health of its financial institutions; the education of its people; the appeal of its consumer culture; and the vitality of its political and economic system. In short, austerity can be a good thing if it imposes discipline, inspires trade-offs, and nurtures prudence—all qualities that May and Neustadt deemed of fundamental importance.

# 11

# National Security

As I was finishing my book in 1991 on the Truman administration and the origins of the Cold War, the historians Thomas Paterson and Michael J. Hogan asked me to contribute an essay on national security to a volume they were editing on new approaches to explaining the history of American foreign relations. Until then, I had not thought in any rigorous way about the overall utility of the concept of "national security." Writing that essay forced me to define the concept more carefully and more generically and to assess its value in relation to other interpretive frameworks like ideology, public opinion, corporatism, and world systems.

For me, national security had come to mean the defense of core values from external threats. Admittedly, this definition was very vague, but I emphasized that its ambiguity was a strength. As understood by U.S. officials, national security was a dynamic, changing concept, responding to the evolution of threats abroad and the definition of core values at home. Core values themselves were elusive, forcing historians and scholars of international relations to discover and analyze precisely what interests, ideals, or values policymakers most wanted to defend. Similarly, external threats existed in the eyes of beholders; different observers perceived danger in dramatically different ways. What were real threats and what were perceived threats might only be resolved in the aftermath of events, and perhaps not even then. Nonetheless, to understand the making of national security policy, the historian had to empathize with the policymakers and had to understand their perception of threat (however accurate or skewed). Historians then had to illuminate how the perception of threat abroad related to interests, values, ideals, or political objectives that policymakers were seeking to further. The intensity of the perceived threat might drastically influence the means embraced to pursue new (or old) goals. This framework integrated external and internal developments and obligated analysts to illuminate how national security itself was a constructed concept.

Friends and colleagues wondered if the concept of national security, a term that was rarely used before World War II, had much applicability to early American foreign policy. When I rewrote my essay for the third edition of *Explaining the History of American Foreign Relations* (2016), Frank Costigliola, who joined with Michael Hogan to edit the new volume, asked me to reflect on this matter and to illuminate the relationships between the concept of national security and the burgeoning numbers of books and articles dealing with grand strategy. In the essay below, I tried to fulfill those two requests.

This essay appeared in Frank Costigliola and Michael J. Hogan, eds., *Explaining the History of American Foreign Relations*, 3rd ed. (New York: Cambridge University Press, 2016), 25–41.

———

Since I wrote my initial chapter on national security more than twenty years ago, the concept's utility for studying American foreign policy has grown. Increasingly linked to the proliferating scholarship on and interest in grand strategy, the attractiveness of the national security paradigm stems from its synthetic qualities; its synthetic qualities arise from the fact that it is not a specific interpretation that focuses on a particular variable as much as a comprehensive framework that relates variables to one another and allows for diverse interpretations in particular periods and contexts.

National security policy encompasses the decisions and actions deemed imperative to protect domestic core values from external threats.[1] This definition is important because it underscores the relation of the international environment to the internal situation in the United States and accentuates the importance of people's ideas and perceptions in constructing the nature of external dangers as well as the meaning of national identity and vital interests. Like grand strategy, the national security paradigm takes cognizance of the fluidity and contingency of events at home and abroad, encourages efforts to identify goals, priorities, and trade-offs, and focuses on means, resources, and ends.[2]

1. This definition emerges from the writings of P. G. Bock and Morton Berkowitz. See, for example, Bock and Berkowitz, "The Emerging Field of National Security," *World Politics* 19 (October 1966): 122–36.

2. Lawrence Freedman, *Strategy: A History* (New York, 2013): xi, 610–11; Robert J. Art, *America's Grand Strategy and World Politics* (New York, 2009); John L. Gaddis, *Strategies of Containment: A Critical Appraisal of American National Security Policy during the Cold War* (New York, 2005); Hal Brands, *What Good is Grand Strategy: Power and Purpose in American Statecraft*

By encouraging students of American foreign policy to examine both the foreign and the domestic factors shaping policy, by obligating them to look at the structure of the international system as well as the domestic ideas and interests shaping policy, the national security approach seeks to overcome some of the great divides in the study of American diplomatic history. Heretofore, the most influential studies have stressed the moralistic or legalistic or idealistic strains in American foreign policy, or, alternatively, the quest for territorial expansion, commercial empire, and geopolitical influence.[3] Recent accounts tend to reinforce such binaries, pitting America's quest for freedom, democracy, and human rights against its drive for hegemony and empire, although sometimes these divergent interpretive frames are reconciled by discussions of "empire for liberty" or "empire of liberty."[4] Generally, realist historians believe that diplomatic behavior responds (or should respond) to the distribution of power in the international system; most revisionist and corporatist scholars, and most historians who dwell on ideas and ideology, assume that domestic economic requirements, social and cultural forces, and political constituencies are of overwhelming importance. By relating foreign threats to internal core values, the national security model encourages efforts to bridge the gaps between these divergent interpretative approaches, or, more precisely, to see that these variables must be studied in relation to one another and nuanced judgments made about how they bear on one another.

Although the national security approach acknowledges that power plays a role in the functioning of the international system and that interests shape the behavior of nations, it does not reify the salience of power or the centrality of interest in the construction of foreign policy. Barry Buzan, the eminent theorist of international relations, points out that realists who dwell on power and idealists who focus on peaceful norms and liberal institutions often have obscured the meaning of national security, defined as the protection of core values from external threats.[5] "Properly understood," Michael Lind argues,

---

*from Harry S. Truman to George W. Bush* (Ithaca, N.Y., 2014); Charles N. Edel, *Nation Builder: John Quincy Adams and the Grand Strategy of the Republic* (Cambridge, Mass., 2014).

3. George Kennan, *American Diplomacy, 1900–1950* (Chicago, 1951); William Appleman Williams, *The Tragedy of American Diplomacy* (Cleveland, Ohio, 1959).

4. Robert Kagan, *Dangerous Nation* (New York, 2006); Tony Smith, *America's Mission: The United States and the Worldwide Struggle for Democracy in the Twentieth Century* (Princeton, N.J., 1994); Michael H. Hunt, *The American Ascendancy: How the United States Gained and Wielded Global Dominance* (Chapel Hill, N.C., 2007); Walter L. Hixson, *The Myth of American Diplomacy* (New Haven, Conn., 2008); David Reynolds, *America, Empire of Liberty: A New History of the United States* (New York, 2009); Richard H. Immerman, *Empire for Liberty: A History of American Imperialism from Benjamin Franklin to Paul Wolfowitz* (Princeton, N.J., 2010); Gordon S. Wood, *Empire of Liberty: A History of the Early American Republic, 1789–1815* (New York, 2009).

5. Barry Buzan, *People, States, and Fear: The National Security Problem in International Relations* (Brighton, U.K., 1983), 4–9.

"liberal internationalism and realism are complementary, not antithetical." The national security policy of the United States, Lind emphasizes, has sought to protect "the American way of life by making the world less dangerous with a combination of liberal internationalism in the realm of norms and realism in the realm of power politics."[6]

Like approaches to grand strategy, the national security model explicitly acknowledges that U.S. national security interests are defined in terms of power, economic openness, and the promotion of U.S. ideals.[7] In other words, sophisticated approaches to national security reconceptualize the concept and take explicit cognizance of the impact of culture and identity. National security interests, argues Peter Katzenstein, "are constructed through a process of social interaction"; "security interests are defined by actors who respond to cultural factors." States are social actors operating in social environments. National security and national identity are socially constructed as a result of human agency, and external threats are measured in relation to their perceived impact on core values.[8]

National security, as Arnold Wolfers wrote many years ago, nonetheless remains an ambiguous symbol. Security is used to encompass so many goals that there is no uniform agreement on what it encompasses and hence no universal understanding of the concept. Certainly, it involves more than national survival. But just what is involved is often left vague and indeterminate.[9] Although the ambiguity presents formidable problems to policymakers and contemporary analysts, it should not handicap the work of historians. Indeed, it should explicitly encourage historians to focus attention on matters of central importance: How have policymakers assessed dangerous threats? How have they understood the configuration of power in their own neighborhood, or globally? How have they defined national interests? How have they defined the relationships between interests, the distribution of power, and core values? How have they tried (and sometimes failed) to formulate policies to ensure that their costs do not undermine the core values they are designed to foster? After all, the purpose of American national security strategy, Lind reminds us, "is to defend the American way of life by means that do not endanger the American way of life."[10]

6. Michael Lind, *The American Way of Strategy* (New York, 2006), 23, 38.

7. Christopher Layne, *The Peace of Illusions: American Grand Strategy from 1940 to the Present* (Ithaca, N.Y., 2006), 8–10.

8. Peter J. Katzenstein, ed., *The Culture of National Security: Norms and Identity in World Politics* (New York, 1996), 1–32, and, for the quotations, see p. 2; for a valuable illumination of these matters in the historiography regarding Woodrow Wilson, see Andrew M. Johnston, "The Historiography of American Intervention in the First World War," *Passport*, 45 (April 2014): 22–9.

9. Arnold Wolfers, "'National Security' as an Ambiguous Symbol," *Political Science Quarterly*, 67 (December 1952): 481–502.

10. Lind, *American Way of Strategy*, 22; for an account that stresses how the pursuit of na-

External dangers come in many varieties. The historian of U.S. foreign policy must appraise the intentions and capabilities of the nation's prospective foes. But that step is only the beginning. Views of a potential adversary, after all, are heavily influenced by perceptions of other variables such as one's own strength and cohesion, the appeal of one's own organizing ideology, the lessons of the past, the impact of technological change, and the structural patterns of the international system itself.[11] After independence in 1776, the United States lived in a dangerous neighborhood, surrounded by European adversaries—some strong, some tottering—all eager to contain or crush the infant, vulnerable, faltering young republic. Early American diplomacy evolved in an environment of perceived danger (as well as opportunity). "From the 1780s through the 1820s," writes James Lewis, "the first two generations of policymakers worked to develop policies that would function in harmony to strengthen the bonds between the states, to contain the centrifugal forces within the union, and to lessen the threats from external pressures."[12] After the Civil War, perceptions of external danger receded as the sources of internal division were resolved, a tenuous balance on the European continent persisted, Anglo-American rapprochement began, and U.S. economic strength soared. But that sense of security, which gathered even greater momentum after the defeat of the Central Powers in World War I, was eroded by the faltering of liberal capitalism during the Great Depression, the growth of totalitarianism in the late 1930s, the appeal of fascism and Nazism, and the growth of air power. After World War II, when U.S. policymakers defined the Soviet Union as an inveterate foe, they were influenced by their perception of Stalin as a ruthless, aggressive tyrant and by their inclination to associate Communist Russia with Nazi Germany.[13] But assessments of the international system were also instrumental in shaping the threat perception of American policymakers. Officials imparted dangerous connotations to developments

---

tional security has contradicted and undermined America's core values, see William O. Walker III, *National Security and Core Values in American History* (New York, 2009).

11. Kenneth N. Waltz, *Theory of International Politics* (Reading, Mass., 1979), 79–101; John J. Mearsheimer, *The Tragedy of Great Power Politics* (New York, 2001), 1–82; Ernest R. May, *"Lessons" of the Past: The Use and Misuse of History in American Foreign Policy* (New York, 1973).

12. James E. Lewis, Jr., *The American Union and the Problem of Neighborhood: The United States and the Collapse of the Spanish Empire, 1783–1829* (Chapel Hill, N.C., 1998), 10; also see Jay Sexton, *The Monroe Doctrine: Empire and Nation in Nineteenth Century America* (New York, 2011); Edel, *Nation Builder*.

13. John Lewis Gaddis, *We Now Know: Rethinking Cold War History* (New York, 1997), 24–25, 294–96; Wilson D. Miscamble, *From Roosevelt to Truman: Potsdam, Hiroshima, and the Cold War* (New York, 2007); Ralph B. Levering and Verena Botzenenhart-Viehe, "The American Perspective," in *Debating the Origins of the Cold War*, ed. Ralph B. Levering, Vladimir O. Pechatnov, et al. (Lanham, Md., 2001), 1–63; Les K. Adler and Thomas G. Paterson, "Red Fascism: The Merger of Nazi Germany and Soviet Russia in the American Image of Totalitarianism, 1930s–1950s," *American Historical Review*, 75 (April 1970): 1046–64.

within the international system, such as the proliferation of bilateral trade agreements and exchange controls, the dollar gap, the political instability within European governments, the popularity of leftist and communist parties, and the rise of revolutionary nationalist movements, especially in Asia.[14] Overall, U.S. officials have realized that the preservation of their core values at home requires them to prevent "the domination of the international system by imperial and militarist states and the disruption of the international system by anarchy" and autarky.[15]

In studying the systemic sources of foreign policy behavior, the national security approach demands that analysts distinguish between realities of external danger and the imagined perceptions of threat. This task, as simple as it sounds, is fraught with difficulty because it is often hard for contemporaries and historians alike to agree on what constitutes an actual danger or a perceived threat.[16] Fear drove much of America's early foreign policy, emphasizes Jay Sexton in his recent history of the Monroe Doctrine. "As much as Jefferson and many of his contemporaries waxed lyrical about the virtues of an expanding 'empire of liberty,' their insecurities and perception of threat were just as significant to expansion as was ideology." Yet Sexton also stresses that recognition of their legitimate security concerns should not obscure the fact that there was often a huge gap between perception and reality. "The Holy Allies were not on the verge of intervening in Spanish America when Monroe delivered his message in 1823," even if the president and his advisers thought they were.[17] Likewise, in the 1840s, Sam W. Haynes acknowledges that "although their fears were largely unfounded, proannexation Democrats viewed alleged British meddling in Texas with genuine alarm."[18] Similarly, Nancy Mitchell shows that although German imperial actions in the early 1900s engendered enormous feelings of insecurity and hostility among Americans, German poli-

14. Gabriel Kolko and Joyce Kolko, *The Limits of Power: The World and United States Foreign Policy, 1945–1954* (New York, 1972); Kevin M. Casey, *Saving International Capitalism during the Early Truman Presidency: The National Advisory Council on International Monetary and Financial Affairs* (New York, 2001); Benjamin O. Fordham, *Building the Cold War Consensus: The Political Economy of U.S. National Security Policy, 1949–1951* (Ann Arbor, Mich., 1998); Curt Cardwell, *NSC 68 and the Political Economy of the Cold War* (New York, 2011); Melvyn P. Leffler, "The American Conception of National Security and the Beginnings of the Cold War, 1945–48," *American Historical Review*, 89 (April 1984): 356–78.

15. Lind, *American Way of Strategy*, 22.

16. C. Vann Woodward presented the classic argument that U.S. foreign policy was shaped by a long era of "free security," a view that Andrew Preston embraces in his overview of the concept of "national security." See Andrew Preston, "Monsters Everywhere: A Genealogy of National Security," *Diplomatic History*, 38 (June 2014): 477–500.

17. Sexton, *Monroe Doctrine*, 32–33, 10–11.

18. Sam W. Haynes, "Anglophobia and the Annexation of Texas: The Quest for National Security," in *Manifest Destiny and Empire*, ed. Sam W. Haynes and Christopher Morris (College Station, Texas, 1997), 117.

cies were far less threatening than widely perceived. She analyzes how rhetoric, military images, and trade competition conjured up fears and shaped perceptions that were inconsistent with the realities of German behavior.[19] If
contemporaries often had trouble discerning reality, historians have found
themselves confounded by similar difficulties. For example, the very different
interpretations of American diplomacy in the 1920s and 1930s between "realists" on the one hand and "revisionists" or "corporatists" on the other hand
rest in part on assessments of the degree of threat to vital U.S. security interests in the interwar years. If there were no real threats before the middle or
late 1930s, then contemporary proponents of arms limitation treaties, arbitration agreements, and nonaggression pacts can be viewed as functional pragmatists seeking to create a viable liberal capitalist international order rather
than as naive idealists disregarding the realities of an inherently unstable and
ominous balance of power.[20]

Perceptions of events abroad, however, are themselves greatly influenced
by the ideas, ideals, and core values of the perceiver. The national security
approach demands that as much attention is focused on how the American
government determines its core values as on how it perceives external dangers. The term "core values" is used here rather than "vital interests" because
the latter implies something more material and tangible than is usually the
case for a national security imperative. The United States has rarely defined
its core values in narrowly economic or territorial terms. Core values usually
fuse material self-interest with more fundamental goals like the defense of the
state's organizing ideology, such as liberal capitalism, the protection of its
political institutions, the championing of its honor and autonomy, and the
safeguarding of its physical base or territorial integrity. "The purpose of
America is to defend a way of life rather than merely to defend property,
homes, or lives," said Dwight D. Eisenhower.[21] Those "who dismiss the idea
of 'the American way of life' and focus on 'vital interests' as the basis of U.S.
foreign policy," emphasizes Michael Lind, "are guilty of a profound philo-
sophical and political error. For there is no interest more vital in American

---

19. Nancy Mitchell, *The Danger of Dreams: German and American Imperialism in Latin
America* (Chapel Hill, N.C., 1999).

20. For reevaluations of the relative strength and efficacy of American military capabilities
and foreign policies in the 1920s and early 1930s, see John Braeman, "Power and Diplomacy: The
1920s Reappraised," *Review of Politics*, 44 ( July 1982): 342–69; also see Melvyn P. Leffler, "Political Isolationism, Economic Expansionism, or Diplomatic Realism: American Policy toward
Western Europe, 1921–1933," *Perspectives in American History* 8 (1974): 413–61; Patrick O. Cohrs,
*The Unfinished Peace After World War I: America, Britain and the Stabilization of Europe, 1919–
1932* (New York, 2006); Adam Tooze, *The Deluge: The Great War, America and the Remaking of
the Global Order, 1916–1931* (New York, 2014).

21. Quoted in Robert R. Bowie and Richard H. Immerman, *Waging Peace: How Eisenhower
Shaped an Enduring Cold War Strategy* (New York, 1998), 45.

foreign policy and no ideal more important than the preservation of the 'American way of life.' "[22]

To determine core values, historians must identify key groups, agencies, political parties, and individuals, examine their goals and ideas, and analyze how trade-offs are made. Decision-makers, interest groups, legislators, and politicians will have different internal and sometimes conflicting internal and external objectives. Core values are the goals that emerge as priorities after the trade-offs are made; core values are the objectives that merge ideological precepts and cultural symbols such as democracy, self-determination, honor, and race consciousness with concrete interests such as access to markets and raw materials; core values are the interests that are pursued (and sometimes jeopardized) notwithstanding the costs incurred; core values are the goals worth fighting for. In their work on Thomas Jefferson, Robert W. Tucker and David C. Hendrickson illuminate how he converted "questions of interest into matters of right and wrong, which then assumed a kind of independent character and became inseparably annexed to the honor and independence of the country." Likewise, in his work on Woodrow Wilson, N. Gordon Levin, Jr., beautifully describes how the president fused ideological, economic, and geopolitical considerations when faced with unrestricted German submarine warfare. Together, these factors became core values and influenced his decisions for war, for intervention, and for the assumption of political obligations abroad.[23]

Different groups may have different core values or different strategies for pursuing the same core values. Historians argue over whether Jeffersonian Republicans and Hamiltonian Federalists possessed divergent core values or whether they were mostly battling over strategies to achieve the same core values.[24] But there is no question that southern slaveholders and northern abolitionists possessed a conflicting core value that hugely shaped the foreign policy of the antebellum era. Republicans, such as Abraham Lincoln, argues Michael Holt, could not allow slavery "any chance to spread . . . [because it would] betray the legacy of the nation's Founders who dedicated the United States to freedom, not slavery."[25] The struggle between interventionists and

22. Lind, *American Way of Strategy*, 7. Of course, just what constitutes the "American way of life" is open to debate. For example, contrast Lind to William A. Williams, *Empire as a Way of Life* (New York, 1980). Frank Ninkovich links the protection of the American way of life at home to the preservation of "international society" abroad. See Frank Ninkovich, *The Global Republic* (Chicago, 2014).

23. Robert W. Tucker and David C. Hendrickson, *Empire of Liberty: The Statecraft of Thomas Jefferson* (New York, 1990), 179, 72; Levin, *Woodrow Wilson and World Politics: America's Response to War and Revolution* (New York, 1968); also see Buzan, *People, States, and Fear*, 36–72.

24. For a succinct and incisive analysis, see George Herring, *From Colony to Superpower* (New York, 2008), 64–7ff.

25. Kagan, *Dangerous Nation*, 181–264; Michael F. Holt, *The Fate of Their Country: Politi-*

isolationists on the eve of World War II illuminates how groups sharing similar core values could disagree about strategies. Interventionists believed aid to the Allies was essential to protect American liberal capitalism and the territorial integrity of the United States; isolationists believed such aid would aggrandize the powers of the chief executive and the federal government, provoke the Axis powers, and thereby endanger not only the nation's physical safety but also its political institutions and ideology—its American way of life.[26] Explaining how core values of interest groups, classes, and voluntary associations are translated into policy requires a careful investigation and a viable theory of the relationship of the state to society.[27]

The effort to show how core values emerge in the policymaking process forces the diplomatic historian to study the importance of foreign policy goals in relation to the officials' other objectives. As they seek to achieve diplomatic aims, officials (and leaders of private organizations) may encounter costs that exceed the value of the goals themselves.[28] For example, much as Republican officials in the 1920s yearned for markets abroad, they were unwilling to forgo the protection of the home market; much as they wanted international financial stability, they were reluctant to cancel the war debts or raise taxes; much as they sought good relations with the Japanese, they were unwilling to eliminate the discriminatory provisions in the immigration laws. In these cases the foreign policy benefits did not seem to outweigh the domestic costs. Hence, the diplomatic objectives, significant though they were, never became core values.[29] American history is replete with examples demonstrating a quest for territory, markets, and influence and with examples demonstrating restraint.

---

*cians, Slavery, Expansion, and the Coming of the Civil War* (New York, 2004), 125–6; William Earl Weeks, *The New Cambridge History of American Foreign Relations, I: Dimensions of the Early American Empire, 1754–1865* (New York, 2013), 210–72.

26. Justus D. Doenecke, *Storm on the Horizon: The Challenge to American Intervention, 1939–1941* (Lanham, MD, 2000); Waldo Heinrichs, *Threshold of War: Franklin D. Roosevelt and American Entry into World War II* (New York, 1988); Lynne Olson, *Those Angry Days: Roosevelt, Lindbergh, and America's Fight Over World War II* (New York, 2013).

27. One can choose from a variety of Marxist or pluralist approaches. One can see the state acting autonomously or as a captive of particular groups or classes. For some stimulating views and essays see Ralph Miliband, *The State in Capitalist Society: An Analysis of the Western System of Power* (New York, 1969); Charles E. Lindblom, *Politics and Markets: The World's Political Economic Systems* (New York, 1977); and Peter J. Katzenstein, ed. *Between Power and Plenty: Foreign Economic Policies of Advanced Industrial States* (Madison, Wis., 1978); and Charles Bright and Susan Harding, eds., *Statemaking and Social Movements: Essays in History and Theory* (Ann Arbor, Mich., 1984).

28. Robert Gilpin, *War and Change in World Politics* (New York, 1981), 50–105.

29. Melvyn P. Leffler, "1921–1932: Expansionist Impulses and Domestic Constraints," in *Economics and World Power: An Assessment of American Diplomacy since 1789*, ed. William H. Becker and Samuel F. Wells, Jr. (New York, 1984), 225–75; Cohrs, *Unfinished Peace After World War I*.

An interpretive framework for the study of American foreign relations should try to explain why the United States did not go to war over Cuba in the 1820s or 1870s, but did so in 1898; why Theodore Roosevelt sent troops to the Caribbean and Central America and why Franklin Roosevelt did not; why Wilson hesitated to intervene in Europe in 1914–16 but chose to do so in 1917; why the United States resisted the role of hegemon in the interwar years yet assumed it after World War II; why the United States eschewed political commitments and strategic obligations in one era while it welcomed them in another.

The protection and pursuit of core values requires the exercise of power. Power is the capacity to achieve intended results. Power may be an end in itself as well as a means toward an end. In the twentieth century, power (including military power) derived primarily from economic capabilities, social cohesion, and political unity. Power stemmed from the scale, vigor, and productivity of one's internal economy and its access to or control over other countries' industrial infrastructure, skilled manpower, and raw materials. Power meant the capacity to inflict harm on adversaries. Power was relative.[30]

But at the outset of the U.S. diplomatic experience, the young nation had little power, considerable disunity, and adversaries on its borders as well as Native American nations within its borders. Individual rights, private property, and open trade as well as territorial integrity and personal safety seemed imperiled by the actions of the British, French, and Spanish as well as by the divisions among the states inflected by sectional, class, and racial strife. The U.S. constitution itself was a peace pact among the states, designed to preserve harmony among themselves as well as to enhance their combined leverage against adversaries abroad.[31] "The greatest fear among American statesmen was the possibility that Old World powers would exploit internal divisions by allying with sections or factions of the union, thus fusing internal and external threats."[32] Fear of their own vulnerability meshed with their rec-

---

30. This definition of power comes from Bertrand Russell and was used by Paul Nitze's Policy Planning Staff in the Department of State in the early 1950s. See paper drafted by the Policy Planning Staff, "Basic Issues Raised by Draft NSC 'Reappraisal of US Objectives and Strategy for National Security,'" n.d. [July 1952], U.S. Department of State, *Foreign Relations of the United States, 1952–1954* (Washington, D.C., 1984) 2:61 [hereafter, *FRUS*]; Freedman, *Strategy*, 162–4; Gilpin, *War and Change*, 67–8; Paul Kennedy, *The Rise and Fall of the Great Powers: Economic Change and Military Conflict from 1500 to 2000* (New York, 1987); and Klaus Knorr, *Power and Wealth: The Political Economy of International Power* (New York, 1973).

31. David C. Hendrickson, *Peace Pact: The Lost World of the American Founding* (Lawrence, Kan., 2003); Frederick W. Marks II, *Independence on Trial: Foreign Affairs and the Making of the Constitution* (Wilmington, Del., 1986); Max L. Edling, *A Revolution in Favor of Government: Origins of the U.S. Constitution and the Making of the American State* (New York, 2003).

32. Sexton, *Monroe Doctrine*, 28; Eliga H. Gould, *Among the Powers of the Earth: The American Revolution and the Making of a New World Empire* (Cambridge, Mass., 2012).

ognition that "frequent war and constant apprehension" might produce stand-ing armies and a strong central government that could crush the very liberties the new nation had been created to preserve.[33] The core values of the young republic seemed dependent on a policy of nonentanglement, a balance of power in Europe, and a precarious union at home.

Open trade, neutral rights, and territorial consolidation and expansion became the foreign policy goals of the new nation, and they were inextricably linked to perceptions of threat abroad coupled with the possibility of disunion at home. Avarice and greed, fear and vulnerability, racism and idealism in-spired *and* constrained the drive for markets and territory, for officials were forever aware that the Union was a fragile entity needing to grow yet suscep-tible to disintegration as a result of its growth. And since the core values of the republic itself—personal security, individual freedom, representative govern-ment, private property (life, liberty, and the pursuit of happiness)—were in-extricably linked to the preservation of the Union, the configuration of power in the American neighborhood and in the Old World always was perceived as crucial to the survival of the physical security, territorial consolidation, and core values of the new nation.[34]

After the American Civil War, external danger receded and U.S. power grew. Although foreign threats were inconsequential in motivating the deci-sion for war in 1898, historians have spent prodigious energy arguing over the mix of ideals, interests, and politics that spurred President William McKinley's decisions to free Cuba from Spain, annex the Philippines, and declare an open door policy in China. The consequences of the Spanish-American War, along with developments in shipbuilding, naval technology, industry, agricultural productivity, and racial consciousness sparked a growing interest in the con-figuration of power in East Asia and Europe. Germany was increasingly per-ceived as a looming danger, a specter that became more ominous during World War I. Woodrow Wilson did not fear an imminent German victory, but he did worry about Germany's ambitions and mounting power. Should Ger-many win, Wilson worried that "we shall be forced to take such measures of defense here as would be fatal to our form of Government and American ide-als." His embrace of a "community of power," to supplant the balance of power, reflected Wilson's deep conviction that he had to reform the interna-tional system in order to project America's influence abroad—and its values—and avert "Prussianizing the country and turning it into a garrison state." In

33. Lind, *American Way of Strategy*, 49.
34. Drew R. McCoy, *The Elusive Republic: Political Economy in Jeffersonian America* (New York, 1980); Sexton, *Monroe Doctrine*; Gould, *Among the Powers of the World*; David L. Dykstra, *The Shifting Balance of Power: American-British Diplomacy in North America, 1842–48* (Lanham, Md., 1999).

other words, America's core values were seen as inextricably linked to the distribution of power in the international arena.[35]

But the perception of threat again receded after the defeat of the Central Powers. This view did not mean that Republican officials turned isolationist. On the contrary, they continued to desire to expand markets, stabilize European affairs, pursue investment opportunities, and gain control over raw materials abroad. Yet those goals did not generate strategic commitments nor become vital interests worth fighting for until changes in the configuration of power in the international system impelled American officials to redefine them as core values.[36] The Axis domination of much of Europe and Asia in 1940 and 1941, for example, endangered markets and investment opportunities.[37] But far more important, Axis aggrandizement enabled prospective adversaries of the United States to mobilize additional resources, co-opt other nations' industrial infrastructure, and secure forward bases. Nazi conquests, moreover, raised the possibility that Latin American countries, which had traditionally traded largely with the European continent, would be sucked into the Axis orbit. To deal with autarkic and regimented trade practices abroad and to protect the United States from the growing military capabilities of the adversary, American officials felt they had to mobilize, raise taxes, monitor potential subversives, and prepare to assist or perhaps even take over the export sector of the American economy. Even if the United States had not been attacked and even if the accounts of economic strangulation were exaggerated, core values were at stake. This was not because the Axis powers crushed the self-determination of other nations or jeopardized the world capitalist system, but because foreign threats of such magnitude required a reordering of the domestic political economy, portended additional restrictions on civil liberties and individual rights, and endangered the nation's physical integrity and organizing ideology. The purpose of Roosevelt's partial internationalism, writes John Harper, "was not universal salvation for its own sake but the safeguarding of democracy in the United States." He did not want the United States to become a garrison state. Roosevelt grasped that what happened abroad would affect America's way of life at home.[38]

35. Frank Ninkovich, *Modernity and Power: A History of the Domino Theory in the Twentieth Century* (Chicago, 1994), 52–6; Ross A. Kennedy, *The Will to Believe: Woodrow Wilson, World War I, and America's Strategy for Peace and Security* (Kent, Ohio, 2008).

36. Cohrs, *Unfinished Peace after World War I*; Melvyn P. Leffler, *The Elusive Quest: America's Pursuit of European Stability and French Security, 1919–1933* (Chapel Hill, N.C., 1979).

37. For this view, see Patrick J. Hearden, *Roosevelt Confronts Hitler: America's Entry into World War II* (DeKalb, Ill., 1986); Lloyd C. Gardner, *Economic Aspects of New Deal Diplomacy* (Madison, Wis., 1964).

38. John Lamberton Harper, *American Visions of Europe: Franklin D. Roosevelt, George F. Kennan, and Dean G. Acheson* (New York, 1994), 64; Ninkovich, *Modernity and Power*, 112–22;

After World War II, the Soviet presence in Eastern Europe, the vacuums of power in Western Europe and Northeast Asia, and the emergence of revolutionary nationalism in the Third World created a similar specter. American core values were perceived to be at risk. The Kremlin might have neither the intention nor the capability to wage war effectively against the United States, but prudence dictated that the United States organize and project its own power to protect its core values. If the country did not do so, if it withdrew to the Western Hemisphere, President Harry S. Truman warned that the American people would have to accept

> a much higher level of mobilization than we have today. It would require a stringent and comprehensive system of allocation and rationing in order to husband our smaller resources. It would require us to become a garrison state, and impose upon ourselves a system of centralized regimentation unlike anything we have ever known. In the end, . . . we would face the prospect of bloody battle—and on our own shores. The ultimate costs of such a policy would be incalculable. Its adoption would be a mandate for national suicide.[39]

During the Cold War years, the perception of an external threat to core values inspired U.S. officials to mobilize American power in unprecedented ways. The Marshall Plan and the North Atlantic Treaty Organization (NATO) were two excellent examples. For the first time in American history, the U.S. government appropriated billions of dollars for the rehabilitation of European economies and assumed strategic obligations to protect European countries. In the 1920s, Republican policymakers also had been cognizant of the interdependence of the economies of Europe and the United States.[40] Nevertheless, they had eschewed long-term governmental aid and security commitments. How does one account for the willingness of American officials to incur such financial sacrifices and strategic commitments after World War II but not after World War I?

According to the national security approach, the answer rests primarily in the ways American officials perceived external threats to core values. In the mid-1940s, the political and economic vulnerability of Western European

David Reynolds, *From Munich to Pearl Harbor: Roosevelt's America and the Origins of the Second World War* (Chicago, 2001); Art, *America's Grand Strategy and World Politics*, 69–110.

39. *Public Papers of the Presidents of the United States: Harry S. Truman, 1952–1953* (Washington, D.C., 1966), 189; Melvyn P. Leffler, *A Preponderance of Power: National Security, the Truman Administration and the Cold War* (Stanford, Calif., 1992), 1–24, 151–7, 495–8.

40. Leffler, *Elusive Quest*; Michael J. Hogan, *Informal Entente: The Private Structure of Cooperation in Anglo-American Economic Relations, 1918–1928* (Columbia, Mo., 1977); Frank Costigliola, *Awkward Dominion: American Political, Economic, and Cultural Relations with Europe, 1919–1933* (Ithaca, N.Y., 1984); Tooze, *Great Deluge*.

governments, the popularity of communist parties in France, Italy, and Greece, and the economic and social problems beleaguering Germany adumbrated a significant strengthening of the Soviet Union. And if this happened, Truman and his advisers believed, there would be profound repercussions in the way the U.S. government would have to structure its domestic economy and conduct its internal affairs. Because the configuration of power in the international system was profoundly different in the mid-1920s, external developments did not pose as much danger and hence did not justify the allocation of government aid and the assumption of overseas strategic obligations.

But even when the perception of threat was great, the existence of core values placed constraints on the pursuit of foreign policy goals. Aaron Friedberg insightfully shows how "the basic structure of American government institutions, the interests and relative strength of various groups (both within the government itself and in society at large), and the content of prevailing ideas or ideology" circumscribed the growth of a garrison state even during the most scary years of the Cold War. And although these fundamental ideas and institutions did not prevent widespread infringements on personal liberties and individual freedoms during the McCarthy era and did not thwart the growth of executive power and military spending, they nonetheless had a profound impact on the evolution of the Cold War. "By preventing some of the worst, most stifling excesses of statism, these countervailing tendencies made it easier for the United States to preserve its economic vitality and technological dynamism, to maintain domestic political support for a protracted strategic competition and to stay the course in that competition better than its supremely statist rival."[41]

Although occasionally criticized for its disregard of ideological and cultural concepts, the national security approach to the study of American foreign relations should be conceived as perfectly congruent with the new directions of scholarship that dwell on culture, identity, religion, and emotion.[42] Central to the national security approach is the concept of core values. National security is about the protection of core values, that is, the identification of threats and the adoption of policies to protect core values. The new studies on culture, ideology, modernization, religion, and emotion mesh seamlessly with the synthetic qualities of a national security paradigm because they help to illuminate the construction, meaning, and implications of America's core

41. Aaron L. Friedberg, *In the Shadow of the Garrison State: America's Anti-Statism and Its Cold War Grand Strategy* (Princeton, N.J., 2000), especially pp. 4–5, 60–1; Michael J. Hogan, *A Cross of Iron: Harry S. Truman and the Origins of the National Security State, 1945–1954* (New York, 1998).

42. For critiques, see William O. Walker III, "Melvyn P. Leffler, Ideology, and American Foreign Policy," *Diplomatic History*, 20 (Fall 1996): 663–73; Bruce Cumings, "Revising Postrevisionism: Or, the Poverty of Theory in Diplomatic History," ibid., 17 (Fall 1993): 563–4ff.

values. The new books on religion, for example, illuminate how religious values, organizations, and symbols inspired the Cold War struggle with communism. Religious leaders and ethnic groups did see their most basic values endangered by an atheistic system that denied the existence of God. They "saw religion," emphasizes Andrew Preston, "as a source of democracy because it protected freedom of conscience, and thus the individual's autonomy from the state. The Soviets, avowedly atheist and materialist, rejected faith completely. Both sides of the Cold War claimed to want peace, progress, and prosperity for the world. But only one side could claim God."[43]

In order to create the conditions for a free society in which individuals could pray, vote, work, and prosper, U.S. officials believed they had to contain state planning, command economies, and totalitarian regimes seeking hegemony of their own systems and ways of life. The many new books on development and modernization show how nonstate actors—social scientists, universities, philanthropic organizations, voluntary associations—embraced this struggle to prove the salience of the American way of life to revolutionary nationalist regimes in the Third World. They wanted to use "development aid, technical assistance, foreign investment, and integrated planning," Michael Latham emphasizes, "to accelerate the passage of traditional societies through a necessary yet destabilizing process in which older values, ideas, and structures gave way to the liberal, capitalist, and democratic ways of life that they recognized most clearly in the United States itself."[44] This did not mean that American nongovernmental organizations or U.S. policymakers emphasized democracy—indeed, they often supported repressive regimes[45]—but they did embrace "development" and "human rights" as part of an American mission to counter the appeal of state-led modernization according to a Soviet model. "Development," writes David Ekbladh, "is crucial to understanding how the United States confronted other ideological systems when they emerged as threats."[46]

43. Andrew W. Preston, *The Sword of the Spirit, the Shield of Faith: Religion in American War and Diplomacy* (New York, 2012), 412; also see William Inboden, *Religion and American Foreign Policy, 1945–1960: The Soul of Containment* (New York, 2008); Jonathan P. Herzog, *The Spiritual-Industrial Complex: America's Religious Battle against Communism in the Early Cold War* (New York, 2011); Colleen Doody, *Detroit's Cold War: The Origins of Postwar Conservatism* (Urbana, Ill., 2013), 76–92.

44. Michael E. Latham, *The Right Kind of Revolution: Modernization, Development, and U.S. Foreign Policy from the Cold War to the Present* (Ithaca, N.Y., 2011), 3; also see Nick Cullather, *The Hungry World: America's Cold War Battle against Poverty in Asia* (Cambridge, Mass., 2010).

45. See, for example, David Schmitz, *Thank God They're on Our Side: The United States and Right-Wing Dictatorships* (Chapel Hill, N.C., 1999); David F. Schmitz, *The United States and Right-Wing Dictatorships* (New York, 2006); Steven G. Rabe, *The Killing Zone: The United States Wages Cold War in Latin America* (New York, 2012).

46. David Ekbladh, *The Great American Mission: Modernization and the Construction of the American World Order* (Princeton, N.J., 2010), 2; for human rights, see Sarah Snyder, *Human*

The fervor with which the United States waged the Cold War can only be grasped by understanding the role of ideology in the construction of American national identity and national security policy. In his succinct and valuable volume on "manifest destiny," Anders Stephanson reminds us of the puritanical, millenarial, and religious impulses that infused America's approach to the world. Other factors might have influenced the Cold War, he writes, "but the operative framework in which they all fit is the story of American exceptionalism, with its missionary implications."[47] Stephanson's emphasis on American nationalist ideology, sometimes conflated with notions of an American century or a Wilsonian century, pulsates through the literature dealing with modern American foreign relations. "American nationalist ideology," writes John Fousek, "provided the principal underpinning for the broad public consensus that supported Cold War foreign policy."[48]

But when translated into policy, the ideological fervor was always calibrated, sometimes by calculation and sometimes by emotion, sometimes by allies and sometimes by domestic constituencies, sometimes by external danger and sometimes by ideals. In his book on World War II diplomacy and the origins of the Cold War, Frank Costigliola skillfully shows how the emotional sensibilities and personality makeups of Roosevelt and Truman affected their understanding of what could and could not be done in pursuit of America's core values and national security goals. Such accounts remind us of the importance of human agency in the construction of core values and the significance of contingency in their implementation.[49] Likewise, Michael Hogan explains how "the most important constraints on the national security state were built into the country's democratic institutions and political culture." They "channeled American policy and American state making in some directions while damming them up in others. The American people and their leaders, or at least the best of them, would go so far and no further, lest a reckless abandon destroy the very Republic they sought to protect."[50]

---

*Rights Activism and the End of the Cold War: A Transnational History of the Helsinki Network* (New York, 2011); Daniel C. Thomas, *The Helsinki Effect: International Norms, Human Rights, and the Demise of Communism* (Princeton, N.J., 2001); Barbara J. Keys, *Reclaiming American Virtue: The Human Rights Revolution of the 1970s* (Cambridge, Mass., 2014).

47. Anders Stephanson, *Manifest Destiny: American Expansion and the Empire of Right* (New York, 1995), 124.

48. John Fousek, *To Lead the Free World: American Nationalism and the Cultural Roots of the Cold War* (Chapel Hill, N.C., 2000), 2; also see, for example, Frank Ninkovich, *The Wilsonian Century: U.S. Foreign Policy since 1900* (Chicago, 1999); Smith, *America's Mission*.

49. Frank Costigliola, *Roosevelt's Lost Alliances: How Personal Politics Helped Start the Cold War* (Princeton, N.J., 2012); for agency and contingency, also see Immerman, *Empire for Liberty*, 14–15ff.

50. Hogan, *Cross of Iron*, 474–5, 482.

As the Cold War ended, Americans celebrated the triumph of their core values. From 11/9/89 to 9/11/2001—from the demise of the Berlin Wall to the attacks on the Pentagon and the World Trade Center—the United States's physical safety seemed assured and its organizing ideology appeared ascendant. Nonetheless, Saddam Hussein's aggression against Kuwait precipitated the orchestration of an American-led grand coalition to restore the status quo ante. George H. W. Bush believed that a core value was at risk—the territorial integrity and national sovereignty of a small nation in a critically important oil-producing region of the world; a law-abiding international community had to act with the collective use of force. Power, interest, and principle reinforced one another and impelled intervention. After the Persian Gulf War, the president's advisers laid out a national security strategy that comported with the long history of American foreign policy: with the Cold War over, the United States and its allies now had "an unprecedented opportunity to preserve with greater ease a security environment within which our democratic ideals can prosper." Although Bush remained deeply ambivalent about the use of American military power in a post–Cold War environment devoid of threats, he and his advisers planned for "uncertainty" and sought "to shape the future"—a future world order that would be based on America's core values: self-determination, personal freedom, open trade, free enterprise, and private marketplaces. Bill Clinton embraced this same agenda with his strategy of enlargement and engagement, but his foreign policy, like his predecessor's, seemed erratic and episodic.[51] The national security paradigm actually explains this floundering: without any perceived danger to core values, foreign policy was of secondary or tertiary importance to the American people, to legislators, and even to policymakers.

The terrorist attacks on 9/11 shattered this complacency. Fear inspired action. Power enabled action. Hubris justified action. "The great struggles of the twentieth century between liberty and totalitarianism," began George W. Bush's 2002 National Security Strategy Statement, "ended with a decisive victory for the forces of freedom" and demonstrated "a single sustainable model

51. The generalizations in this paragraph are based on: Hal Brands, *From Berlin to Baghdad: America's Search for Purpose in the Post–Cold War World* (Lexington, Ky., 2008); Derek Chollet and James Goldgeier, *America between the Wars: From 11/9 to 9/11* (New York, 2008); Melvyn P. Leffler, "Dreams of Freedom: Temptations of Power," in *The Fall of the Berlin Wall: The Revolutionary Legacy of 1989*, ed. Jeffrey A. Engel (New York, 2009), 132–69; Eric S. Edelman, "The Strange Career of the 1992 Defense Planning Guidance," in *In Uncertain Times: American Foreign Policy after the Berlin Wall and 9/11*, ed. Melvyn P. Leffler and Jeffrey Legro (Ithaca, N.Y., 2011), 63–77. The quotations are from the last iteration of the "Defense Planning Guidance." See Secretary of Defense Dick Cheney, *Defense Strategy for the 1990s: The Regional Defense Strategy* (Washington, D.C., 1993), pp. 2ff., available at www.informationclearinghouse.info/pdf/naarpr _Defense.pdf (accessed February 20, 2014).

for national success: freedom, democracy, and free enterprise."[52] Officials, legislators, politicians, and pundits could argue over what constituted a real danger and how the war on terror should be conducted, but almost everyone concurred that another terrorist attack had to be prevented. The terrorists, stressed Bush, "kill not merely to end lives," they sought to extinguish a "way of life."[53] Bush's advisers feared that terrorism had the capacity to undo the trust on which democratic governance and liberal society were postulated. "Beyond the cost in lives and property," emphasized Undersecretary of Defense Douglas Feith, "the 9/11 attack—*or rather our reaction to it* [my emphasis]—could have far-reaching consequences, especially if it were followed by more such attacks. To protect ourselves physically, we might have to change fundamentally the way we live, sacrificing our society's openness for hoped for safety."[54]

Such motives might evoke skepticism, scorn, or worse. After all, the Bush administration reacted with policies that disregarded international law and individual freedom. For many critics, the national security strategy of the George W. Bush administration actually crushed the very core values that the strategy was supposedly designed to protect.[55]

This paradox actually reminds us of the enduring challenge that has inhered in the national security policies of the United States since its founding. External dangers—sometimes real, sometimes illusory—conjure up perceptions of threat. Officials and observers believe that configurations of power are evolving, or vacuums of power are developing, that will necessitate painful adjustments domestically should they not be thwarted. The founding fathers thought this way when they worried about encirclement and violations of America's neutral trade; they feared that they might need to build standing armies or crush internal dissent. Wilson thought this way when he worried about the growth of German power, and so did Franklin Roosevelt. Events abroad could mean endangering core values at home, imperiling the American way of life. Yet, thwarting the trajectory of those developments required actions that also endangered core values. Finding the right balance was (and is) daunting.

52. "The National Security Strategy," September 2002, http://georgewbushwhitehouse .archives.gov/nsc/nss/2002/ (accessed February 22, 2014).

53. "Address to a Joint Session of Congress," September 20, 2001, http://georgewbush -whitehouse.archives.gov/news/releases/2001/09/20010920-8.html (accessed February 22, 2014).

54. Douglas J. Feith, *War and Decision: Inside the Pentagon at the Dawn of the War on Terrorism* (New York, 2008), 68–9.

55. See, for example, Jane Mayer, *The Dark Side: The Inside Story of How the War on Terror Turned into a War on American Ideals* (New York, 2008); Lind, *American Way of Strategy*, 125–259; Walker, *National Security and Core Values*, 259–92.

National security policy invites wise statecraft. Sometimes we have had it; sometime we have not. As a democratic polity, we possess the ability to debate and correct mistakes; hence the growing interest in grand strategy. It forces us to ponder the meaning of vital interests and core values, the identification of priorities, and the ways to balance means and ends. The challenges are formidable for policymakers—and for historians. The national security paradigm forces us to think more carefully about threats, interests, goals, priorities, and values. We must do so. Our core values are at stake.

# INDEX

Kellogg-Briand Pact, 4, 11, 53, 103, 104–8, 111
Kennan, George F., 209, 309–10; European reconstruction stressed by, 300; "long telegram" of, 144, 149, 170; multilateralism criticized by, 290; Powell's misrepresentation of, 298–99; Soviet attack doubted by, 167, 310
Kennedy, John F., 21, 288, 290, 296, 298
Kent, Fred, 33
Kerr, Archibald Clark, 195, 196
Keynesianism, 230, 234
Kharkov, Ukraine, 172
Khrushchev, Nikita, 21, 232–33, 239–40, 288
King, Martin Luther, Jr., 3
Kirk, Grayson, 308
Kissinger, Henry, 119, 291, 312–14
Knox, Frank, 306
Kohl, Helmut, 234, 250, 257
Kolko, Gabriel, 14, 47
Korea, 140, 156, 161, 309
Korean War, 24, 181, 220, 230, 296, 300, 304–5, 310–11
Korman, Gerd, 2
Kotkin, Stephen, 240
Kuniholm, Bruce Robellet, 17, 119, 169
Kuriles, 205, 208
Kuwait, 244, 258–60, 266, 333

labor unions, 228, 236, 237
LaFeber, Walter, 2, 3–4, 28
Laird, Melvin, 313
Lamont, Thomas, 35, 62
Laqueur, Walter, 19
Latham, Michael, 331
Latin America, 201, 262; anti-Americanism in, 3; nationalism in, 311; as prospective market, 85, 131; strategic importance of, 95–96, 122, 129, 130–31, 314, 328
Laval, Pierre, 109
League of Nations, 10, 102; sanctions urged by, 108, 110, 112; successes of, 91; U.S. rejection of, 4, 12, 55, 77, 102
Leahy, William D., 126, 133, 193, 196, 207, 214, 215
Lebanon, 278
Legro, Jeff, 25–26
lend-lease, 200
Lenroot, Irvine, 101
Lensen, George A., 191
lessons of the past, 23–24, 118–19, 241–42, 243–45, 279–80, 301, 303–16, 321
Levin, N. Gordon, Jr., 324
Lewis, James, 321
Libya, 152, 254

life expectancy, 231, 239
Lincoln, Abraham, 324
Lincoln, George A., 146, 173; anti-Soviet provocations feared by, 133; Soviet expansionism feared by, 132, 149–50; Soviet intentions viewed by, 136, 139, 142, 167
Lind, Michael, 319–20, 323–24
Lippmann, Walter, 107, 307
liquidity, 64, 69, 225
Logan, James, 99
London Conference of Foreign Ministers (1945), 200, 209
London Economic Conference (1933), 112
London Naval Conference (1930), 108
Lovett, Robert, 137, 138–39, 150, 155, 156–57, 179, 300

MacArthur, Douglas, 140
MacDonald, Ramsay, 109
Macedonia, 199
Maier, Charles, 12, 232
Malenkov, Georgiĭ, 21
Manchuria, 13, 217; Chinese claims on, 205–6, 208; Japanese designs on, 115; Soviet designs on, 143, 149, 161, 205–6, 207–8, 213–14, 216, 219; Soviet withdrawal from, 146, 208
Manhattan Project, 216
Manila, 128
Mann, James, 285
Mark, Eduard, 165, 201
Marshall, George C., 129–30, 153, 159, 193, 209, 306–7; base strategy reviewed by, 123–24; Chinese civil war viewed by, 209; Cold War rhetoric eschewed by, 147; defense spending caps backed by, 156–57; Soviet attack doubted by, 310; Soviet expansionism feared by, 132, 155; Yalta repudiation opposed by, 206
Marshall Plan, 117, 150, 153, 161, 214, 220, 226, 309, 329
Marxism-Leninism, 145, 188, 189
May, Ernest, 11, 23, 304–5, 315, 316
McCarthy, Joseph, 191, 330
McCloy, John, 126, 129, 134, 141, 203, 223–24, 300
McCormick, Tom, 28
McGhee, George C., 182, 183
McKellar, Kenneth, 38
McKinley, William, 327
McMahon, Bob, 24
McNamara, Robert S., 288, 289
McNary, Charles, 84
Medicaid, 229
Medicare, 229, 235

## A NOTE ON THE TYPE

This book has been composed in Adobe Text and Gotham. Adobe Text, designed by Robert Slimbach for Adobe, bridges the gap between fifteenth- and sixteenth-century calligraphic and eighteenth-century Modern styles. Gotham, inspired by New York street signs, was designed by Tobias Frere-Jones for Hoefler & Co.